COGNITIVE ETHOLOGY

COMPARATIVE COGNITION
AND NEUROSCIENCE

Thomas G. Bever, David S. Olton,
and Herbert L. Roitblat, Senior Editors

COGNITIVE ETHOLOGY
THE MINDS OF OTHER ANIMALS

Essays in Honor of
Donald R. Griffin

EDITED BY
CAROLYN A. RISTAU
The Rockefeller University

LEA LAWRENCE ERLBAUM ASSOCIATES, PUBLISHERS
1991 Hillsdale, New Jersey   Hove and London

Lawrence Erlbaum Associates, Inc., Publishers
365 Broadway
Hillsdale, New Jersey 07642

Help in the preparation of indexes for this volume was provided by Christopher Marler.

Library of Congress Cataloging-in-Publication Data

Cognitive ethology: the minds of other animals: essays in honor of
 Donald R. Griffin / edited by Carolyn A. Ristau.
   p. cm. — (Comparative cognition and neuroscience)
   Includes bibliographical references and index.
   ISBN 0-8058-0251-7 (case). — ISBN 0-8058-0252-5 (pbk.)
   1. Cognition in animals. 2. Animal behavior. I. Griffin, Donald
Redfield. 1915–   . II. Ristau, Carolyn A. III. Series.
QL785.C52 1990
591.51 – dc20   90-3864
                                                                        CIP

Printed in the United States of America
10 9 8 7 6 5 4 3 2 1

CONTENTS

PREFACE

This book is dedicated to Donald R. Griffin. He has been a teacher, a colleague, and a most perceptive friend to those of us who have had the very fortunate opportunity of working with him. His creativity and infectious enthusiasm coupled with his wary critical faculties, have made him a formidable scientist.

He is the scientist who demonstrated that bats navigate, even find minute prey, by very high pitched sound waves (sonar) — a seemingly mysterious sense, insensible to humans that Don Griffin investigated with diligence, intuition, and new technology. He likewise probed bird navigation through heavy cloud conditions in which the normal visual cues that might guide the birds are not available. By using tracking radar, he determined that migrating birds, although they usually attempt to avoid flying blind, can nevertheless orient correctly in clouds. The sensory basis for this ability still remains in large part an unsolved mystery.

It should not, therefore, be considered out of character for him to have explored and inspired others to explore yet another realm, out of the ken of the usual — animal cognition and mental experience. He created the field of cognitive ethology, an exploration of the mental experiences of animals, particularly as they behave in their natural environment in the course of their normal lives. The field had its beginnings in areas such as comparative psychology, classical ethology, laboratory experimental psychology, and philosophy of science.

So we present this set of papers in his honor. The collection does not pretend to be a broad sample of the researchers studying animal cognition. It is instead, in part, contributions from scientists who have been associated with or simply influenced by him. But it is fitting to his character that this collection is not the usual Festschrift. It is a lively array of views, some quite disparate from each other and some especially selected to present approaches at variance from his by scientists not associated with him. The papers derive from a symposium in animal cognition at the Animal Behavior Society (ABS) meetings in Williamstown, Massachusetts in June 1987. It was an extremely lively session with long periods given to interchange between the audience, discussants and presenters of papers.

The mere scheduling of such a symposium was interesting and important. In prior years, the Animal Behavior Society meetings, though presenting many areas of research in animal behavior, rarely covered the area of animal cognition. This symposium was a day-long event. The following year brought yet more presentations dealing with both animal cognition and issues in communication not often tackled by researchers. As a consequence of the ABS meeting, at the International Ethological Conference in Wisconsin during the summer of 1987 a special lunch session in animal cognition was convened to continue spirited discussion.

The contributions have, to the editor's delight, further developed from the presentations at the symposium as the participants continued to wrestle with the issues. The papers are indeed representative of a burgeoning new field and can each be appreciated in a different light. Recognizing that in new areas of research, there is unlikely to be much theoretical structure to guide the way, some urge investigation into unexplored areas, posing new questions of animals, and allowing for the possibilities that animals may have abilities to experience, communicate, reason, and plan beyond those usually scribed to them in a "black box" or "stimulus-response" interpretation. Donald Griffin moves strongly in that direction. However, he and all the other contributors to this volume urge caution in our interpretations. Part of the exploration involves using data that have often been disregarded and/or are unavailable in published form; different researchers may not have gathered them in systematic and similar ways. The reporting of events that only happened once or a few times is a most important example of this, as noted in this volume by both Jolly and Ristau. Alison Jolly cites unique instances of deception and planning collected by researchers such as de Waal studying chimpanzees.

Researchers are also encouraged to look to existing theories and push them as far as possible. Yoerg and Kamil, for example, enjoin cognitive ethologists to utilize the concepts from human cognitive psychology.

New endeavors are underway in the use of what are generally known as folk psychological terms such as *want* and *belief*. In response to these approaches, some urge us to worry about the possible pitfalls that might emerge with their use by researchers in other disciplines. George Michel, for example, discusses difficulties with the folk psychological approach as it has been used in developmental psychology.

Yet another response is to stand firm and retain and continue to use the terms that seemed to suffice in the past and not get lost in mentalism. None of the contributors have quite this view, although others in biology, psychology, and ethology certainly do.

Some, noting the need for conceptual clarification in theory, have contributed to this development. Colin Beer has traced the historical and conceptual evolution of philosophical ideas central to cognitive ethology; the philosopher Jonathan Bennett has further developed the belief-desire-behavior approach of folk psychology to include an emphasis on the context and environment.

Finally, a number of researchers have concentrated on reporting new empirical research findings from laboratory and field work involving animal communication, cognition, and mental states. They also note possible limitations.

In one way or another, each contributor usually emphasizes the need for empirical data. However, each researcher also points out that the others may not be sufficiently concerned about the limitations of their results and the appropriate interpretations to be drawn.

I have probably expressed the concerns and points of view of the authors more mildly than the authors themselves would have. Yet they are all reasonable concerns and contributions. Let us continue the dialogue, remain open-minded, and allow and encourage a diversity of approaches to cognitive ethology.

So we welcome you, the reader, to this most unusual Festschrift. It is not a collection of chapters that praises all of Donald Griffin's ideas, but rather in the true, intellectual, critical, and scientific spirit, this volume presents ideas and experiments that have been stimulated and provoked by Donald Griffin's work. We hope it will stand as a fine tribute to him.

1. ?	14. Anne Rawson	25. Alvin Novick
2. Donald Kennedy	15. Doty Dunning	26. Roderick Suthers
3. Janet Williams	16. Kenneth Rawson	27. Peter Marler
4. Roy Horst	17. Alison Jolly	28. Peter Tyack
5. Jocelyn Crane Griffin	18. Timothy C. Williams	29. Carl Hopkins
6. Donald R. Griffin	18a. ?	30. Doug Quine
7. Robert Seyfarth	19. John Teal	3l. ?
8. Carolyn Ristau	20. Christopher Clark	32. Jeremy Hatch
9. Irene Pepperberg	21. Charles Walcott	33. Haven Wiley
10. Colin Beer	22. George Michel	34. W. John Smith
11. Anne Marie Smith	22a. Dorothy Cheney	
12. Kenneth Able	23. Alan Kamil	
13. Ronald Larkin	24. Jack W. Bradbury	

REMINISCENCES

We planned a surprise celebratory dinner for Don Griffin (DRG) in Williamstown after the Animal Cognition symposium and before the next day's more general symposium in his honor. Several people gathered the names of all the persons we could recall who were students or close associates of Don Griffin. In particular, Ron Larkin, now of the Illinois State Natural History Survey, worked with me, but Timothy and Janet Williams of Swarthmore College helped as did Roger Payne. As I remember, Roger both initially suggested and helped persuade Donald Kennedy, a former student of DRG's and now President of Stanford, to be the Master of Ceremonies for the evening (a great choice!). Don Kennedy's advice: Keep the talks about Don Griffin short, funny, and not too sentimental.

So we were in cahoots—Cheryl Szabo, Don Griffin's secretary; Jocelyn Crane Griffin, his wife; and myself, his research associate. That year Don had already "retired" from Rockefeller University (would that some of us in our prime could get done what he does in his "retirement"), and I was teaching 90 miles away at Vassar College. Don's secretary, whose services I was always permitted to use, had secret files on her word-processing disk with addresses of the dinner guests, menu choices, and so forth. My daughter and her best friend were pressed into service addressing mounds of envelopes in 11-year-old scrawls. Sometimes in the midst of deciding between a banquet menu with Breast of Chicken Divan or Veal Cutlet Cazadora on it I thought of the papers I should be writing, but realized in a sense that all this was far more important. His ever efficient, now retired secretary of 17 years, Roseanne Kelly, was the first to respond, though unfortunately unable to go the long distance and attend.

Don said it *was* a surprise, although he did wonder about a sudden influx of letters wishing him well from old friends (those unable to attend the celebration). During the evening of the event, one incident did suddenly rouse his suspicions. Instead of leaving for the restaurant Jocelyn had arranged for their dinner, he suggested another, which encountered somewhat overheated resistance from Jocelyn — a most peculiar reaction by his wife, he thought. When Don Kennedy arrived at the dinner, having flown in that afternoon from meetings with congressional members in Washington D.C., Don Griffin *was* surprised — he had to sit down for that one. All were placing bets as to arrival of Roger Payne, of humpback whale song fame. He did arrive, having flown in from England and the International Whale meetings, slightly detouring to Williamstown, Massachusetts on his way to Russia.

So we told stories on Don Griffin, all remembering him fondly and recalling with some trepidation those pencil marks and questions that covered the sheets of our manuscripts that he had reviewed for us. The evening *did* produce funny stories. I relate several, adapted from those after-dinner "speeches."

In the late 1960s and early 1970s, many young colleagues were swept up in DRG's project to learn whether birds could maintain oriented flight inside or between clouds, without any visual reference. They wanted to discover the answer by playing with a new toy — a 1-ton, military surplus tracking radar. At that time the operation was based at the Institute for Research in Animal Behavior at the New York Zoological Park in the Bronx. The radar unit and associated paraphernalia were towed on several trailers into nearby rural areas to gather data and then return back to the Bronx Zoo afterward. (DRG called these "forays" or "sorties" more out of natural vigor than because of the heritage of the radar.) Zoo vehicles with the famous ram's head emblem towed two heavy trailers in convoy, while DRG's small green Rambler station wagon usually towed the third trailer. It was a special Griffin-designed mobile hanger for large helium-filled kite balloons, with a huge (Griffin would say "great") volume resting on a lightweight structure and minuscule wheels. On one such trip the graduate student driving the middle vehicle noticed a somewhat bewildered coin-taker at a toll booth leaning out to get a better look at the radar being hauled behind the frontmost zoo vehicle. The temptation was irresistible. The student pulled up in another zoo vehicle and aswered the man's questioning look by pointing back to Griffin towing the bulky balloon trailer, announcing, "he's got the hippopotamus," then driving away. Opportunities for that kind of fun kept DRG's sorties populated with volunteers.[1]

---

[1]This anecdote is written by Ronald Larkin (Illinois State Natural History Survey), previously a graduate student and then a postdoctural fellow with Donald Griffin.

Those who know him will attest that Don Griffin is a "gadget man." José Torre Bueno, now in San Diego, California, was a graduate student during those times of bird migration studies with the old surplus army radar unit. His wife Susie was helping on the project, wrapping endless quantities of foam balls in aluminum foil ("Susie balls"). These, when attached to huge red helium filled balloons, were used with the radar to determine wind velocity for comparison with the migrating birds' speed.

José remembered one of the more lighthearted occasions of equipment malfunction in the lab. Don was soon due to be checking a recalcitrant piece of gadgetry. "Hmm . . ." noted Beverly Greenspan, another graduate student compatriot, "The black insulation covered BNC cables don't look all that different from licorice strings . . . do they?" So José and Beverly gleefully exchanged a licorice connected cable for a more ordinary one on the equipment. Then they left for lunch in the cafeteria where Don was going to meet them after working in the lab. He arrived to join them at lunch. They waited expectantly. No comments. They rushed back to the lab. The licorice connectors were now neatly labelled "bad cable." Again DRG had the last laugh (A more recent accounting suggests maybe he didn't that time. As DRG recalls the incident, he's not sure he ever realized why it was a bad cable.)

Don Griffin also manages to have the requisite calm and aplomb when the occasion demands. Don was once demonstrating his bat echolocation experiments to distinguished foreign visitors (Marie-Claire and René-Guy Busnel). Part of the visit took place in the backyard of Kenneth Roeder, who was doing electrophysiological studies of moth's hearing, particularly their response to bat vocalizations. Griffin had with him a slingshot, which he used to throw pebbles into the air a couple of meters in front of a bat, so as to elicit insect pursuit maneuvers. So Griffin took careful aim and shot off a pebble. And . . . to the surprise of all, it hit the bat's flight membrane. The Busnels were much impressed by this cowboy American field biologist, who hit a bat at first try from 10 or 15 meters. As DRG notes, he made excuses so as not to have to use the slingshot again. What the humans didn't realize at the time was that bats actively reach out with their wing membranes to catch insects (and flying pebbles).[2]

There was the occasion of live bats on TV, WGBH-TV then being a fledgling one-room studio in Boston. As Charlie Walcott (Cornell University) reports it, Don Griffin, at that time a Harvard Professor, was asked to demonstrate the echolocation ability of bats. He arrived with mounds of

---

[2]This episode is described in more detail in Griffin, D.R. (1980) The Early History of Research in Echolocation, Busnel, R.G., & J.F. Fish (Eds.), *Animal Sonar Systems*. New York and London: Plenum Press, p. 5–6.

equipment and live bats which were released and, on live TV, flew as they ought around obstacles. But they didn't fly back to their cages and were resolute about not being caught. So the evening news came on next as scheduled and the newscaster Louie Lines reported the world's events surrounded by bats on the wing.

Roger Payne too had tales of bats and equipment. One hot July night he and DRG were loading an incredible amount of equipment for a bat sonar experiment onto a truck, feeling most sweaty, but quite pleased with their efforts and their gadgetry. The botanist William "Cap" Weston was walking by and was called over by them for his comments. Weston looked for a long time and then is reported to have said "I am reminded of the ancient recipe for Welsh hare. First catch ye hare." It did indeed take the next three weeks to find a place to get the proper bats and setting for their research. But all *was* finally successful as it so often turns out to be with DRG.

Success typically results from much preparedness for diverse contingencies. Don's wife Jocelyn Crane Griffin recalled a trip to Italy with Jim Simmons (Brown University) to study bats. None of them spoke Italian, so the task of translating fell to Jocelyn, dictionary in hand, a set of sentences to be used during various emergencies. She particularly remembered contingency plans for use in the case of a farmer becoming irate as he approached his house and saw a long ladder leaning against it with a strange man halfway up the steps. The man on the ladder was to say in Italian, "Oh sir, I have not come to elope with your daughter. I just want to look at your bats."

But there were also occasions when Don Griffin was not adequately prepared. Jocelyn retold Don's recollection of a summer day in Cape Cod when he was a teenager. He had taken out his own sailboat and was teaching a younger boy how to sail, but weather conditions were not ideal. A strong squall blew up with rain, lightning, and much wind. A neighbor saw him as he was sailing in and shouted, "Call your mother; she'll be so worried." Don replied, "No she won't, she doesn't know I'm out. She knows I have too much sense to be sailing in this sort of weather."

Don always managed to be in the right place at the right time. Robert Seyfarth (University of Pennsylvania) noted the time Don Griffin stopped by on his travels to visit him and his wife Dorothy Cheney (University of Pennsylvania) at their vervet monkey site in Kenya. They all had the extremely rare opportunity to have an excellent vantage point to observe simultaneously five lionesses engaged in a finely coordinated cooperative hunt. That observation (of what seemed to be planned by the lionesses according to Don) has since been described in his book *Animal Thinking* and in the New York Times. Immediately afterwards, recalls Robert, Don leapt out of the car and said "This is it! They've got to be aware of what's going on!" Robert, not quite so oblivious to other possible eating habits of the lionesses yelled, "Get back to the car!" Presumably he did.

I recalled his most apt and genteelly presented advice, often what one *needed* to hear, if not what one *wanted*. It was during my first field season studying piping plovers on a barrier island off the coast of Virginia. I used an inflatable boat which I navigated through the marshes each day, loaded high with all the necessary and possibly necessary equipment for the day. Once as I was leaving the island to avoid an approaching storm, the tide was turning, the boat was full, the wind was rising and the overladen boat took on salt water. But all was safe in the watertight containers . . . except one container turned out not to be. So the video recorder was no longer functioning. Don Griffin, hearing of the event from me, said he'd send on some informational material for me about boating. He'd already piled me high with manuals on the intricacies of battery functioning, and scientific treatises on coastal ecology and flora and fauna, so I expected another technical manual. Instead, the "manual" arriving along with my new assistant, Laura Payne (daughter of Katy and Roger), was Michener's *Chesapeake*. Underlined was a section in which a headstrong, adventurous lady, mother of several children, ignoring advice from those around her about the vicissitudes and fury of the Chesapeake Bay weather, went off in her boat. She was later found dead in the storm-wrecked boat, long brown hair streaming, children now orphaned. Lesson understood—I didn't even go out in the slight drizzle the next day, much to Laura's frustration. (And my children are still not orphaned.)

Many of us recalled frequent conversations over lunch with Don Griffin and remembered his enthusiastic interest in so many topics. Roger Payne, for instance, recalled his first meeting with DRG. "It matters a great deal to me what a person is like," noted Roger. And here in DRG was a person totally interested in what he was doing: Roger volunteered to work for him. Gordon Burghardt recalled his year at Rockefeller shortly after DRG's first book in cognitive ethology, *The Question of Animal Awareness* (1976). Gordon had come to work with both Don and Carl Pfaffmann. At the time Gordon was studying multitudinous aspects of the behavior and olfactory capacity of snakes with a special interest in his two-headed snake. Gordon recalls Don's immersion in all kinds of research literature and papers from a far-flung cadre of correspondents and Don's continuing interest in animal awareness, thinking, communication, and consciousness. All the while Don maintained his research with students on bird migration, infrasound and bee dancing. For Gordon this year was fundamental in his continuing interest in the cognitive revolution in ethology and psychology.

A constantly recurring theme among those who had worked with Don Griffin, expressed spontaneously over and over, was the respect each of us held for him and the respect he held for us; he encouraged our own individual interests and concerns. To each of us, Don Griffin was a gentleman. And each of us recognized it was a special privilege to have been associated with him. Using Roger Payne's words for us all, our "affection and admiration for Don is quite immoderate."

Compiled by Carolyn A. Ristau

PART I:
THEORETICAL
PERSPECTIVES

1 PROGRESS TOWARD A COGNITIVE ETHOLOGY

Donald R. Griffin
The Rockefeller University
Princeton University

ABSTRACT

The investigation of animal cognition and mental experience is beginning to reveal that animals guide their behavior by surprisingly complex thinking. The versatile adaptability of some animals in the face of unpredictable challenges suggests simple conscious thinking about alternative actions and their probable results. When animals communicate with each other, their communicative signals may provide objective data about their thoughts. Although this "window" on animal thoughts may not be ideally transparent, it can help us to escape from the lingering inhibitions of behaviorism that have impeded research into animal minds. Simple conscious thinking may be an efficient and economical mode of operation by which the central nervous systems enable animals to cope with the multiple problems of finding food, avoiding predators, finding mates, and raising young. If so, it may be most advantageous for animals with small brains.

Cognition and conscious thinking by nonhuman animals present a variety of exciting and significant research challenges for scientists concerned with animal behavior. The extent to which animals think about what they are doing and about the behavioral choices they make is a highly significant attribute that must be understood before we can fully appreciate what it is like to be a certain type of animal. We don't yet know much about this subject, and until quite recently we have been reluctant even to think about it, let alone study it. This is changing, however, and the number of papers devoted to cognitive ethology at the 1987 meeting of the Animal Behavior Society reflected this rekindling of interest. Animal cognition is now a

3

recognized scientific subject, and several books and symposia have recently been devoted to this topic (e.g., Griffin, 1984; Roitblat, 1987; Roitblat, Bever, & Terrace, 1984; Walker, 1983).

Many students of animal behavior are concerned not only with what animals do, but also with the cognitive processes within their central nervous systems that interact with sensory information to produce the observed behavior. Nevertheless, many of us still hesitate to consider the possibility that some animal cognition may also entail conscious awareness on the animal's part. Contemporary behavioral scientists tend to limit their investigations of animal cognition to patterns of information processing within the central nervous systems of the animals they study and ignore the possibility that subjective mental experiences may occur and may influence behavior. This reluctance to consider subjective mental experiences, so clearly expressed by Yoerg and Kamil in this volume, may result, in part, from unrecognized vestiges of behaviorism that inhibit inquiry—even when we believe we have recovered from the negative dogmatism of strict behaviorism. We tend to find the notion of conscious awareness disturbing and struggle to find ways of analyzing animal behavior without allowing what seem like subversive notions of subjectivity to get a foot in the door. But Radner and Radner (1989) have recently explained how insubstantial a philosophical basis underlies this widespread antipathy to animal consciousness among behavioral scientists. Cognitive ethology should certainly include, but not be limited to, information processing in animal brains.

DEFINITIONS

One reason for avoiding the question of animal consciousness is a feeling that it is too vague a subject for scientific investigation because we lack objective criteria by which to judge whether an animal is conscious. Although we all know in a rough and general way the sorts of things that are meant by thinking and consciousness, these meanings are multiple; they do not refer to homogeneous categories. Given the variety of phenomena and processes that the word *thinking* calls to mind, it seems premature to expect a unitary definition as a prerequisite for scientific investigation. Because we remain almost totally ignorant of the neurophysiological basis of either conscious or unconscious thinking, we cannot define thinking in as concrete terms as molecular geneticists employ when defining genes in terms of DNA. Other widely used terms, such as *learning, motivation,* or *metabolism* are also resistant to rigorous definition; but this has fortunately not prevented effective scientific analysis of the phenomena described by these terms. It is therefore neither necessary nor advisable to become so bogged down in quibbles about definitions that the investigation of animal cognition and consciousness is neglected altogether.

I suggest that we cope with the difficulty of formulating wholly satisfactory definitions by employing the same basic procedure that has proved fruitful with many other complex and challenging scientific problems. This is to start with some of the least complicated cases, and then, if we can make progress toward understanding them, move on to the more complex and difficult examples. One promising approach of this general type is to inquire whether animals may experience relatively simple thoughts about things that are important to them. When faced with a threatening predator, does an animal think something roughly like: "If that beast gets me, it will hurt?" Or does a hungry animal think about what a particular food will taste like?

This approach suggests the following preliminary working definition of elementary animal consciousness: An animal may be considered to experience a simple level of consciousness if it subjectively thinks about objects and events. Thinking about something in this sense means attending to the animal's internal mental images or representations of objects and events. These may represent current situations confronting the animal, memories, or anticipations of future situations. Such thinking often leads to comparisons between two or more representations and to choices and decisions about behavior that the animal believes is likely to attain desired results or avoid unpleasant ones. It is important to recognize that this working definition leaves open the possibility of more complex sorts of consciousness; it focuses on processes and phenomena that are basic to conscious thinking and which we can hope to identify by gathering objective evidence bearing on their occurrence and nature by employing procedures outlined below. This definition does, however, assume the presence of both internal representations or mental images about which the animal thinks and also of simple beliefs and desires about what it likes and dislikes.

This definition does not include two other attributes that are sometimes proposed as necessary features of consciousness: self-awareness and thinking about the process of thinking itself. Because an animal's own body is a very prominent feature of its situation and contributes enormously to its sensory input, it seems likely that if an animal thinks consciously about anything, it must sometimes think about parts of its own body. But many who tend to deny consciousness to nonhuman animals require for true self-consciousness the capacity to experience such thoughts as: "It is I who see that predator or smell that delicious food." Or they may claim that animals know but are incapable of knowing that they know. In an attempt to keep a preliminary investigation of animal consciousness as manageable as possible, I suggest leaving aside the question whether nonhuman animals are capable of this sort of propositional self-awareness or of thinking about their own thoughts as well as other more complicated forms of conscious thinking. If and when cognitive ethologists learn how to determine the presence or absence of the simpler sorts of conscious thinking defined above, later stages of investigation can include these and other more complex levels of consciousness.

CRITICAL STANDARDS

Our traditional inhibitions that have discouraged the study of animal minds can be relaxed without lowering critical scientific standards. Indeed, the danger of jumping prematurely to definite convictions is so great that it is desirable to increase scientific caution rather than relax it. There are two pitfalls to be guarded against. The first has been to ignore the problem of animal thoughts and feelings because such phenomena are considered beyond the reach of scientific investigation. That was an easy way out a few years ago, but the progress in identifying cognitive processes in a wide variety of animals has forced a retreat to a second line of defense. This line of defense recognizes the existence and significance of animal cognition but denies that we can tell whether it is ever accompanied by conscious thinking.

The second pitfall is to leap enthusiastically to firm conclusions and to advocate positions that cannot be convincingly supported by the available evidence. Scientists ordinarily make strong and positive assertions only when the supporting evidence is convincing. But when questions of animal mentality arise, we have an unfortunate tendency to do just the opposite; the vigor of assertions tends to be inversely, rather than directly, proportional to the quality of the evidence available. Thus, we sometimes hear vehement arguments that a nonhuman animal cannot possibly have certain kinds of mental experiences. Meanwhile, others are equally certain that some particular beast must want, wish, or believe something related to its current or impending behavior. As critical scientists we must first recognize the extent of our ignorance as a prerequisite for reducing it.

PREMATURE PERFECTIONISM

In many areas of science, we cannot aspire to entirely satisfactory logically watertight evidence when a subject is first studied. But when questions of possible conscious thinking by animals are raised, we tend to demand perfection prematurely. We often conclude a priori that it is not worthwhile to study this sort of phenomenon because we are convinced that we cannot hope to prove anything with absolute certainity. But why are we so much more demanding of perfection in this area than in other scientific areas? It is helpful to contrast these attitudes with the enthusiastic investigation of the adaptive significance of behavior and how it appears to contribute to inclusive fitness. Underlying this active area of research is an unmentioned implicit assumption that in the remote past the ancestors of living animals reproduced more effectively because they behaved in certain ways. Yet the behavior of extinct animals cannot be studied directly, and we are limited to inferences based on contemporary behavior under current conditions. Such inferences are reasonable and fruitful, but in this popular area of investigation we refrain from demanding the sort of rigorous proof that many scientists require as prerequisite for studying animal consciousness.

EPIPHENOMENALISM

Many scientists find reasons for believing that conscious thinking, even in our own species, has no effect on behavior. This view is known as *epiphenomenalism,* defined by Edwards and Pap (1973) as the belief that "mental states are caused by brain processes, but do not in turn exert any causal influence" (p. 177). This is a very strong claim that one process — conscious thinking — never, under any circumstances, has even the slightest effect on another process — overt behavior. Absolute proof of such a global negative statement is notoriously difficult to obtain, and this one is so counterintuitive that strong evidence would be required to render it convincing. Indeed, it is not accepted by many philosophers. Yet adherence to epiphenomenalism is often taken by scientists as evidence of commendable rigor when, in fact, it may be little more than an excuse for neglecting or ignoring an important scientific problem.

Some biologists tend to feel that it does not matter for questions of evolutionary adaptiveness whether a given behavior pattern is executed with or without conscious awareness on the animal's part. But insofar as an animal can think consciously about its situation and the results of its own behavior, and can make simple rational choices about its problems and prospects, this ability is clearly an advantageous phenotypic trait. Therefore, insofar as conscious thinking occurs, neglecting it will result in an incomplete and inaccurate understanding of the species in question.

IMPLICATIONS OF ASSUMING HUMAN MENTAL UNIQUENESS

It is conceivable that conscious thinking is a uniquely human accomplishment, wholly lacking in all other species. Even if this rather extreme view is correct, it raises an important scientific question: What is different about human brains that permits them to give rise to consciousness, while the central nervous systems of all other species lack this capacity despite the similarity if not identity of all known basic properties of neurons and synapses? Thus the existence or nature of animal consciousness is a central question of major scientific importance. If it occurs only in our species, or perhaps is shared only by our closest relatives, neuroethologists must look for those properties that allow some central nervous systems, but not others, to produce conscious thinking. Conversely, if conscious thinking is more widespread among nonhuman animals, it is scientifically significant to learn its extent and limits and, in particular, how the content of animal consciousness differs between species or according to the circumstances in which animals find themselves.

COGNITIVE CREATIVITY

The ability to think about the probable results of alternative actions and to choose the one most likely to achieve a desired result is especially valuable when animals face unpredictable problems in carrying out important activities such as obtaining food, avoiding predators or other hazards, seeking mates, or raising young. The traditional view of animal behavior has emphasized prior determination of responses either genetically, through learning, or by some interactive combination of the two. But a fundamental limitation of prescribed responses is that to be effective, the prescriptions must provide for most or all contingencies the animal is likely to encounter. The real world in which animals live under natural conditions is characterized by complex variability. Few if any of the important details lend themselves to simple descriptions or simple rules that can prescribe the most effective way of coping with complicated contingencies. The most appropriate responses vary according to innumerable factors, and the necessary instructions would become astronomically voluminous if they adequately covered the contingencies an animal is likely to encounter.

If, on the other hand, an animal can think about what it wants and how desired objectives can be achieved, many relevant factors can be taken into account and modestly rational decisions can lead to appropriate actions. Even quite simple conscious thinking can be creative in the limited sense that it adaptively integrates a variety of information from current perceptions, memories, and anticipations of probable events—including the anticipated results of the animal's own actions. Of course such thinking, human or animal, is unlikely to achieve perfection. Mistakes will be made, but if they are not fatal, they can often be corrected by learning what does and does not achieve what the animal wants.

SPECIES SOLIPSISM

Skeptical philosophers can argue eloquently that no one can ever prove, with logical rigor, that another person is conscious. We can only make inferences (some would say merely guesses) about the existence or content of another person's thoughts. If a solipsist claims that he is the only conscious organism in the universe, and that all evidence of consciousness in others is inconclusive, we cannot refute his arguments in any rigorously logical fashion. But only in specialized philosophical discussions are such arguments taken seriously. We all go through life assuming that other people do have conscious thoughts, plans, beliefs, intentions, and the like. Indeed it is difficult to imagine how human societies (or perhaps any society) could function effectively if their members acted as consistent solipsists. Of course the difficulties of inferring what animals may be thinking are much greater than with our conspecifics, and many scientists continue to feel that it is not worth the bother of trying. But the extensive and significant discoveries that have resulted from investigations of animal behavior suggest increasingly that these inhibitions may be outdated impediments to research. Species solipsism may be as impractical and arcane an intellectual exercise as its more familiar philosophical counterpart when applied to other people.

DISPARAGEMENT OF "FOLK PSYCHOLOGY"

Three eloquent philosophers (among others) recently advanced another argument that may tend to discourage consideration of animal consciousness. Stich (1983), P. S. Churchland (1986), and Dennett (1987) have argued with varying degrees of vigor that what they disparage as folk psychology relies on inappropriate and misguided concepts. Churchland defines folk psychology as "commonsense psychology—the psychological lore in virtue of which we explain behavior as the outcome of beliefs, desires, perceptions, expectations, goals, sensations, and so forth. . . . the preeminent elements in folk psychological explanations of behavior include the concepts of *belief* and *desire*" (p. 299). Churchland and Stich assert that these terms are as obsolete and misleading as witchcraft or a flat earth, and they anticipate that a complete understanding of brain function will eventually lead to new concepts so superior that they will replace familiar notions such as wishing or fearing that something will happen, expecting some result of a certain kind of behavior, or intending to accomplish a goal. But neither Stich nor Churchland tells us just what the new and superior concepts will be.

Because beliefs and desires are key components of conscious thinking, consigning them to a trash heap labelled folk psychology tends to discourage ethologists from inquiring whether nonhuman animals are conscious. The principal objection of these philosophers is that folk psychology does not provide a philosophically adequate explanation of human behavior. They seem to expect that a proper theory will neatly account for all human, and perhaps also animal, actions and mental experiences. This surely is a large order, and scientists accustomed to struggling with incompletely understood phenomena will be more easily reconciled to explanations that lack the apparent completeness and tidy finality of nineteenth century deterministic physics. An argument that carries great weight with Churchland is that our concepts of belief and desire have not changed appreciably since the time of the Greek philosophers. Since our basic concepts about physics, chemistry and astronomy have been revolutionized by modern science, she asks why not psychology?

Dennett, on the other hand, recognizes that "if we discard folk psychology as a theory, we would have to replace it with another theory, which, while it did violence to many ordinary intuitions, would explain the predictive power of the residual folk craft" (p. 47). In other words, the concepts of folk psychology are as indispensable in the ordinary day-to-day interactions between people and animals as is folk physics in practical matters of dealing with physical objects, machinery, and the like without worrying about quantum mechanics of the Heisenberg uncertainty principle. An example from obsolete folk astronomy is relevant. Thanks to the Copernican revolution, we now know why the sun appears to sink below the horizon and rise again in the east next morning. We no longer imagine god-driven chariots conveying the sun across the sky or carrying it back eastward below ground, but that understanding has not abolished the concepts of sunset and sunrise, which remain useful for many purposes. Churchland likens folk psychology to Ptolemaic astronomy as an argument for rejecting the former in the confident expectation that neurophysiology will someday discover a true and beautiful analog of Copernican astronomy. But she overlooks a major difference: Copernicus and Galileo rejected Ptolemaic astronomy only because they had in hand a clearly superior replacement.

These arguments for abandoning folk psychology have not convinced a number of philosophers and neuroscientists. Double (1985), Millikan (1984), Marras (1987), Russow (1987), and Sanford (1986) find the major philosophical arguments advanced by Stich to be unconvincing; they doubt that concepts such as belief and desire have outlived their usefulness. And the neuroscientist Stent (1987) is far from persuaded that beliefs and desires will cease to be meaningful and useful concepts in the forseeable future. Millikan (1986) points out that the concepts of folk psychology such as belief and desire are real and significant attributes of human minds, at least, and that they should be treated as realities to be explained rather than as profound explanatory theories.

Furthermore, the arguments advanced by Stich and Churchland *confuse explanation with abolition.* A pertinent example is the concept of heredity, surely as ancient and basic a notion as belief and desire. Thanks to the magnificent discoveries of molecular genetics, we now understand the basis of heredity, at least in broad outline. But the phenomenon of inheritance has not vanished into obsolescence or oblivion. It may well be that the neurophysiological basis of beliefs and desires, will eventually be understood in the same way that heredity has been largely explained in terms of DNA and RNA, and that will be an equally important triumph of science. But this hoped-for future understanding will not abolish the phenomena thus explained any more than molecular genetics has done away with the concept of heredity.

In terms of cognitive ethology, an explanation of the neural basis of beliefs and desires, if and when it is achieved, will greatly facilitate identification of whatever beliefs and desires may occur in nonhuman central nervous systems. But in the forseeable meantime, there is no reason to take the disparagement of folk psychology as an excuse for abandoning the attempt to understand whatever beliefs and desires may be experienced by nonhuman animals. Indeed it may not be unreasonable to suspect that the disparagement of folk psychology is itself a sort of excuse for turning away from difficult but fundamental problems of cognitive science.

CRITERIA OF ANIMAL AWARENESS

What sort of evidence can we hope to gather that can support or weaken the inference of simple conscious thinking in other species? One general criterion that we tend to employ is enterprising versatility of behavior. When the animal does something that seems appropriate but its behavior is not a stereotyped pattern, we feel more inclined to infer some conscious thinking. Many suggestive examples are discussed by Walker (1983), Roitblat, Bever, and Terrace, (1984), Griffin (1984), and Mitchell and Thompson (1986).

An especially pertinent case is the use of bait to attract fish. Although not an entirely new discovery, this type of innovative behavior has recently been studied in revealing detail by Higuchi (1986, 1987). The heron picks up a small object, drops it in the water, and waits for small fishes to approach the bait. When this happens the heron often manages to catch a fish by the customary stabbing motion achieved by a rapid extension of the neck. Bait fishing has been observed in only a tiny fraction of green-backed herons, but the herons that engage in this activity do it repeatedly. Yet it has not spread among the population. This sort of fishing with bait was reported many years ago; in fact it was illustrated clearly in a *National Geographic* article (Sisson, 1974). (I must confess that when reviewing this subject [Griffin, 1984] I overlooked this reference constrained by the typical scientist's conceit that serious data will not be found in popular magazines.) Higuchi has observed that green-backed herons show individual differences in their techniques of bait fishing. Some throw the bait out a meter or so from where they are standing and then, when fish come up around it, they fly to the bait and seize a fish. Sometimes the bait is edible material like pieces of bread dropped by children, but in other cases herons use inedible bits of vegetation. Some herons modify the bait, for example, by breaking a twig to get a piece of appropriate size. These individual differences suggest that there is no fixed genetic basis for bait-fishing behavior. Is it reasonable to suppose that a heron develops this kind of behavior and uses it successfully without thinking about what it is doing and looking ahead for at least a short time to what it hopes to achieve?

We can probably all think of other examples where an animal does something that we find it rather difficult to imagine doing without some conscious thinking. Several pertinent cases are described in a recent symposium volume dealing with deceptive behavior (Mitchell & Thompson, 1986). Particularly impressive examples are the deceptive use of alarm calls by certain birds (Munn, 1986) and the observations of social deception in baboons reported by Byrne and Whiten (1985) and Whiten and Bryne (1988). An even better example is the description by de Waal (1986) of the way in which a subordinate male chimpanzee conceals his erect penis when trying to approach a female without attracting the notice of the dominant male who is almost certain to attack if he sees what is going on.

But this sort of inference can always be disputed; inclusive behaviorists are likely to argue that the animal may be carrying out the observed versatile behavior without any conscious thinking. After all, an enormous majority of the processing of information and adaptive changes in behavior that are regulated by our central nervous systems occur without any conscious thinking. Consciousness accompanies only a small but important part of our own behavior. And of course other organs also do a great deal of activity regulating. Kidneys, for example, respond to levels of substances in the blood by reabsorbing or secreting them at different rates to regulate the chemical composition of our body fluids. So, it is often argued that just because an animal's behavior is efficient and adaptive, this is not convincing evidence that the animal is consciously aware of what it is doing.

COMMUNICATION AS EVIDENCE OF THINKING

One avenue of escape from this difficulty is to make use of procedures similar to those we employ with our conspecifics. Although we cannot rigorously prove that they experience thoughts or precisely what the contents of their thoughts may be, we do nevertheless manage to make useful and reasonably reliable inferences about the thoughts and feelings of our human companions. We do so primarily on the basis of their communicative behavior. They often exhibit revealing forms of nonverbal communication, and they sometimes tell us what they are thinking about. Their communication of thoughts is never totally complete or perfectly precise, and only a very small fraction of what their central nervous systems are doing is revealed by their communicative behavior. But certainly that subset of the total activity of their brains is important to them and to us.

Many kinds of animal communication convey to other animals information that affects the recipient's behavior. Signals are often exchanged reciprocally with two or more animals alternating in the roles of sender and receiver or playing both roles at once as in two-way threat displays. But do animals also communicate to others any thoughts and feelings that they may experience? If so, their communicative signals provide cognitive ethologists with objective data about the content of animal thoughts. Recognition that such data are valid evidence of animal thinking could go a long way toward eliminating one of the principal objections that has been advanced against the inference of conscious thinking on the part of nonhuman animals—namely the alleged impossibility of independently verifying or falsifying such inferences. Of course it remains only a hypothesis that some animal communication serves to convey conscious thoughts or feelings. But such hypotheses often serve as fruitful entering wedges to begin the long and complex process of explaining phenomena that would otherwise remain opaque and unapproachable. The assertion that no communicating animal ever thinks consciously about the information it is conveying to others amounts to another global negative as difficult to prove as solipsism or epiphenomenalism. Only quite recently have a few cognitive ethologists begun to ask to what extent communicative behavior might be a source of objective data about any conscious thoughts that animals may experience, and it will take some time to determine whether this approach will prove as fruitful as I expect.

Ethologists are not yet accustomed to think about animal communication in this way. Instead, communication has been considered just one more kind of behavior to be studied with the hope of understanding (a) how it arose, (b) how it increases inclusive fitness, and (c) the degree to which it has been genetically influenced or determined by the experience of the individual. Communicative signals are generally viewed as a direct result of internal physiological conditions. If an animal's stomach contractions produce sounds that affect the behavior of other animals, this does not mean that it is thinking consciously about food. The cries of anguish from a seriously wounded animal presumably do not result from any conscious attempt to communicate. We have tended to consider that all animal communication falls into this "groans of pain" or GOP category (Griffin, 1985, p. 620). One significant criterion for distinguishing between involuntary GOP communication and intentional communication is the effect of an audience. If the signals are emitted regardless of the presence or absence of potential recipients, intentional communication seems unlikely. Important examples that give every evidence of audience effects are described and analyzed in the chapters by Marler and by Cheney and Seyfarth in this volume.

It is possible that all animal communication is involuntary in the sense that much human nonverbal communication is not readily brought under voluntary control. Of course we are usually aware of the emotions that lead to involuntary nonverbal signals such as blushing, but we cannot ordinarily exert conscious control over these emotional states or the signals that accompany them. Thus it seems best to distinguish the question of voluntary control from the question of whether an animal is consciously aware of its mental states and of the signals by which it may communicate them to others. An aggressive animal might be quite aware of its anger and of the growls by which it threatens a rival even though it had no voluntary control over the onset of the aggressive impulse. In other cases an animal might consciously think about communicating in order to achieve some desired result. For example, one of the birds studied by Munn (1986) might give an alarm call in the complete absence of danger with the conscious intention of causing another bird to break off the pursuit of an insect it was about to capture.

Animal communication has often turned out to be much more complicated and adapted to the animal's needs and situation in more subtle and versatile ways than formerly believed. Semantic information may be conveyed as in the well known case of the three different alarm calls used by vervet monkeys to report the approach of three different categories of predators (Seyfarth, Cheney, & Marler, 1980). The GOP view of animal communication leads to increasing complications when one considers the degree to which many animals exchange communicative signals that serve to coordinate their cooperative interactions. At the very least, we must recognize that the internal physiological state that is supposed to generate the communicative behavior must be strongly influenced by signals received from others—often in reciprocal exchanges. We are thus forced to ascribe more and more complex properties to these internal physiological states, and this necessary enrichment makes these states more and more like conscious thinking.

For example, it once seemed that the calls given by juvenile rhesus macaques during agonistic interactions, that is, squabbles or preliminaries to fights, were a continuously graded series that varied only in intensity and conveyed only the state of arousal of the calling monkey. But the recent work of Gouzoules, Gouzoules, and Marler (1984) has shown that the screams of juveniles convey information about the social status of the antagonist as well as the degree of arousal of the caller. This does not, of course, prove rigorously (though it does suggest) that the monkeys are really thinking about such things as "That guy is a relative" or "His mother is a dominant," but it does require that our concept of the internal state leading to the communicative signals must include such information in addition to levels of anger, fear, or general arousal.

Thus the communicative signals employed by many animals may well provide objective data that reveal part of what they are consciously thinking and subjectively feeling as I have discussed elsewhere (Griffin, 1984). Acceptance of this view does not constitute rigorous proof of animal consciousness, but it does offer a promising window through which cognitive ethologists can tentatively infer what animals may be thinking and feeling. Thus the hypothesis that vervet monkeys think about three classes of dangerous predators is strengthened by the experiments of Seyfarth, Cheney, and Marler (1980), but it is not conclusively confirmed. With sufficient imagination and ingenuity, cognitive ethologists can probably devise testable predictions based on such hypotheses. For example, if alarm calls are intentional warnings to companions, they should not be given if no companions are present.

Finally, there is a tendency to feel with Walker (1983) and many others that if there is any sort of conscious thinking in nonhuman animals, it is more likely to be found (or perhaps only to be found) in our closest relatives. But as far as we know, the central nervous system of multicellular animals all operate by means of the same basic processes regardless of the species or even the phylum in which they are found. Because we know that at least one species does indulge in conscious thinking, and take it for granted that conscious and unconscious thinking result from the activities of the central nervous system, we have no solid basis for excluding a priori the possibility that conscious thinking takes place in any animal with a reasonably well-organized central nervous system. In fact, as I have suggested elsewhere (Griffin, 1984), conscious thinking may be an efficient way to use the central nervous system for solving the more complex and challenging problems faced by any animal. If so, such economy may be more important in animals with a small central nervous system than it is to us and the Cetaceans. The symbolic communication used by honeybees to inform their sisters about the direction, distance, and desirability of various things suggests that even social insects may experience and communicate simple thoughts. We know too little about this whole area to reject even such an unfamiliar notion as this.

For all the reasons previously outlined above and many more that are discussed in appropriate detail by Walker (1983), Griffin (1984) and Roitblat (1987), cognitive ethology is in a very exciting state of ferment and development. It has certainly come a long way since I reviewed its prospects 10 years ago (Griffin, 1978). Furthermore, cognitive ethology has significant ramifications, because (as discussed by Beer and Bennett in this volume) whatever cognitive ethologists can learn about the existence and nature of conscious and unconscious thinking in nonhuman animals contributes significantly to the fundamental philosophical problem of other minds.

REFERENCES

Byrne, R. W., & Whiten, A. (1985). Tactical deception of familiar individuals in baboons (*Papio ursinus*). *Animal Behaviour, 33*, 669–673.
Churchland, P. S. (1986). *Neurophilosophy, toward a unified science of the mind-brain.* Cambridge, MA: MIT Press.
Dennett, D. C. (1987). *The intentional stance.* Cambridge, MA: M.I.T. Press.
Double, R. (1985). The case against the case against belief. *Mind, 94*, 420–430.
Edwards, P., & Pap, A. (1973). *A modern introduction to philosophy, readings from classical and contemporary sources* (3rd ed.). New York: MacMillan.
Gouzoules, S., Gouzoules, H., & Marler, P. (1984). Rhesus monkey (*Macaca mulatta*) screams: Representational signalling in the recruitment of agonistic aid. *Animal Behavior, 32*, 182–193.
Griffin, D. R. (1978). Prospects for a cognitive ethology. *Behavioral and Brain Sciences, 1,* 527–538. (see also commentaries ibid. 1:555–629 and 3:615–623).
Griffin, D. R. (1984). *Animal thinking.* Cambridge, MA: Harvard University Press.
Griffin, D. R. (1985). Animal consciousness. *Neuroscience & Biobehavioral Reviews, 9,* 615–622.
Higuchi, H. (1986). Bait-fishing by the green-backed heron *Ardeola striata* in Japan. *Ibis, 128,* 285–290.
Higuchi, H. (1987). Cast master. *Natural History, 96*(8), 40–43.
Marras, A. (1987). Stephen Stich's from folk psychology to cognitive science: The case against belief. *Philosophy of Science, 54*, 115–127.
Millikan, R. G. (1984). *Language, thought, and other biological categories: New foundations for realism.* Cambridge, MA: M.I.T Press.
Millikan, R. G. (1986). Thoughts without laws: Cognitive science without content. *Philosical Review, 95*, 47–80.
Mitchell, R. W. & Thompson, N. S. (Eds.). (1986). *Deception, perspectives on human and nonhuman deceit.* Albany, NY: State University of New York Press.
Munn, C. A. (1986). The deceptive use of alarm calls by sentinel species in mixed-species flocks of neotropical birds. In (R. W. Mitchell & N. S. Thompson (Eds.), *Deception, perspectives on human and nonhuman deceit* Albany, NY: State University of New York Press.

Radner, D. & Radner, M. (1989) *Animal consciousness*. Buffalo, N.Y.: Prometheus Books.

Roitblat, H. L. (1987). *Introduction to comparative cognition*. New York: Freeman.

Roitblat, H. L., Bever, T. G., & Terrace, H. S. (Eds.). (1984). *Animal cognition*. Hillsdale, NJ: Lawrence Erlbaum Associates.

Russow, L. M. (1987). Stich on the foundations of cognitive psychology. *Synthese, 70,* 401–413.

Sanford, D. H. (1986). [Review of *From folk psychology to cognitive science: The case against belief*]. *Philosophy and Phenomenological Research, 47,* 149–154.

Seyfarth, R. M., Cheney, D. L., & Marler, P. (1980). Vervet monkey alarm calls: Semantic communication in a free-ranging primate. *Animal Behaviour 28,* 1070–1094.

Sisson, R. F. (1974). Aha! It really works! *National Geographic 145,* 142–147.

Stent, G. S. (1987). The mind-body problem. *Science, 236,* 990–992.

Stich, S. P. 1983. From folk psychology to cognitive science, the case against belief. Cambridge, MA: MIT Press.

de Waal, F. (1986). Deception in the natural communication of chimpanzees. In R. W. Mitchell & N. S. Thompson (Eds.), *Deception, perspectives on human and nonhuman deceit*. Albany, NY: State University of New York Press.

Walker, S. (1983). *Animal thought*. London: Routledge & Kegan Paul.

Whiten, A., & Byrne, R. W. (1988). Tactical deception in primates. *Behavioral and Brain Sciences, 11,* 233–273.

2 FROM FOLK PSYCHOLOGY TO COGNITIVE ETHOLOGY

Colin G. Beer
Rutgers University

ABSTRACT

Cognitive ethology assumes a kind of commonsense theory of mind, which has been described as folk psychology. This essay discusses philosophical versions of this theory as they pertain to cognitive ethology and arguments against them such as Stephen Stich's case against belief and the eliminative materialism of Patricia and Paul Churchland. It also comments on the work of Ruth Millikan who has used a biological notion of function in defense of a naturalistic theory of mind, which retains intentionality and the propositional attitudes of folk psychology. The case argued is that the philosophical issues about the nature of mind sampled here have a profound bearing on the prospects for cognitive ethology.

INTRODUCTION

People often attribute consciousness and a wide range of mental states to animals. Many would say that it is only common sense to do so. However, this common sense view raises a number of questions of sorts that cause students of animal behavior to have mental cramps when they try to come seriously to grips with animal mentality. These questions include the following: How do we and can we know about mental states in animals? To what extent does absence of human-style language restrict the possibility of animal intentionality? To what extent are animal mental states like or unlike human mental phenomena? To what extent does confusion about the nature of human intentionality lead to confusion about the possibility of animal intentionality?

Clearly these are philosophical questions. I have little idea how a philosopher might deal with them, but I doubt that he or she would send us away thinking that we had been given any final answers. As a rule, philosophers seem to be more interested in showing you how you can be wrong than how you can be right. In any case, I shall not try to deal with the questions head on. However, the philosophical concerns to which they are related are central to the concerns of cognitive ethology and so warrant consideration in this symposium. Consequently, I have chosen to try to play the philosopher even though I lack the competence to give more than an ethologist's impressions of some of the issues. I shall conduct a sort of Cook's tour of recent views in the philosophy of mind, which I think bear on the background from which we, ethologists and nonethologists alike, approach animal mind.

FOLK PSYCHOLOGY

As I suggested at the start, common sense and personal experience provide the basis for belief in animal minds. This, surely, is where we all start. We each of us employ and take for granted an everyday sort of psychology, which is assumed in our dealings with one another and often with animals. It consists of our ascribing mental states such as belief and desire to people and animals and drawing inferences on the basis of how such states are related to one another, to stimulation received, and to behavior performed. For example, the simple action of a driver pressing the gas pedal when a traffic light changes from red to green can be explained in terms of the interconnection of stimulation, mental states, and action: The light changing to green leads the driver to believe that the light has changed to green; this together with an understanding of the traffic code means to the driver that he may proceed: Conformity to custom, the desire to move on, and, the belief that stepping on the gas pedal will make the car move result in stepping on the gas pedal. All of this and the additional details that could be added is so commonplace that spelling it out seems silly. Indeed, the driver would no doubt be unmindful of most of the belief-desire underpinnings of his action unless suitably questioned. "Common sense psychology works so well it disappears" (Fodor, 1987, p. 3).

Although, we take such explanation for granted most of the time or assume it to be so self-evident that it can be left unquestioned except in abnormal cases, it has been represented as relying on a theory—a theory of mind which, for all its ubiquity, is subject to assessment like any other theory (Sellars, 1956). This theory has been described as folk psychology.

Its soundness has been challenged in ways that have implications for our ideas about animal intentionality since these ideas are predicated on folk psychology to an extent that I think goes unrecognized. However, before turning to the criticisms of folk psychology I need to make two additional points about why folk psychology might be thought to stand on ground apart from and more solid than that of theories such as one finds in science. The first point has to do with the concept of intentionality; the second with the incorrigibility claimed for sensory experience.

Intentionality, as used by philosophers of mind, has a much broader meaning than the notion of acting with intent, which we usually assume when we encounter the word (see Boden, 1972; Chisholm, 1967; Dennett, 1969; Millikan, 1984; Searle, 1983). For the philosophers, intentionality encompasses believing, desiring, wishing, knowing, guessing, forgetting, and intending—all of the idioms for "propositional attitudes". What they all have in common is that they are attitudes about or towards or of something; they make reference to a content, and that is what constitutes intentionality: An attitude directed towards a content, which Brentano (1874) called the "intentional object." Thus, believing is always believing that something is the case. You cannot just believe in the way that you can just sleep. Likewise, desire is always desire for something, knowledge is knowledge of or about something, and so on. Intentional terms have some logical characteristics which, with some exceptions, differentiate them from comparable terms applying to physical entities. For example, there is no doubt that Hamlet intended to kill the man behind the arras, but it does not follow from this that he intended to kill Polonius. In contrast, from the fact that the man behind the arras was Polonius, it does follow that the man behind the arras was Ophelia's father (Boden, 1972). In the first case, the logic is said to be "intensional" and "referentially opaque"—if terms having the same reference are substituted for one another, there is no guarantee that truth will be preserved. In the second case, the logic is said to be "extensional" and "referentially transparent"—coreferring terms can be substituted for one another without affecting the truth of the statement. Another of the intentional attributes is lack of existential commitment; an intentional state does not imply the existence of that to which it refers. For example, if I say that I wish I had a friend I do not assume the existence of any particular friend.

When Brentano (1874) introduced this concept of intentionality, he said it was the mark of the mental and that "No physical phenomenon manifests anything similar" (Vol. 1, p. 144). The logical peculiarities of intentional idioms have been taken by some philosophers to support such sui generis status for the realm of intentionality, implying that its principles are neither reducible to those of a physical science, nor to be assessed by the criteria applying to the theories of a physical science.

The incorrigibility of sensory experience is a much older argument for the unquestionable nature of mentality compared with the fallibility of a scientific understanding of physical nature. By the incorrigibility of sensory experience I mean the alleged impossibility of a person calling into question his or her present sensations in their phenomenal immediacy. That you experience a sensation that you call a sensation of red, or suffer a pain that you describe as excruciating cannot be doubted by you, even though you could be mistaken in thinking that the redness betokened an apple where there was only a blob of paint or that the pain was in your toe when the leg had been amputated. The immediacy and indubitability of such "simple ideas" or "raw feels" or "qualia," as they are variously called, have been repeatedly invoked as the certain ground of knowledge and understanding ever since John Locke launched empricism on its way. For example, Bertrand Russell (1912) distinguished knowledge by acquaintance from knowledge by description and argued that the latter is ultimately based on the former. Likewise, Stephan Korner (1959), in his book *Conceptual Thinking,* grounded concepts on what he called their "ostensive bases" (p. 7ff). Earlier, Ernst Mach (1914) took the position that all the concepts of science must ultimately come down to definition in terms of elementary sensation, and thus to some extent anticipated the operationism of Bridgeman and the verificationism of the logical positivists. Such attempts to get down to basics provoked J.L. Austin (1962) to comment: "The pursuit of the incorrigible is one of the most venerable bugbears in the history of philosophy" (p. 104).

Appeal to the intrinsic character of sensory experience has also been made to argue against the possibility of reducing the mental to the physical and hence for an autonomous psychology of mental states. A recent example, which gives little encouragement to the quest for animal awareness, is Thomas Nagel's paper "What is it like to be a bat?" (1974). In his paper Nagel argues that our inability to experience sonar echoes as a bat does puts the bat's phenomenology forever beyond our ken regardless of the advances neuroscience might make. Likewise, neuroscience will never truly comprehend what it is like to have a sensation, for that requires having the sensation. (For a critique of Nagel's argument see Churchland, 1985.)

My mention of operational definition a moment ago may have put you in mind of behaviorism. Behaviorism, of course, dismissed folk psychology as unscientific — a resort to ghostly entities having no more substance than the alchemists' belief that matter is ensouled by nonmaterial spirits. Behaviorism came in both psychological and philosophical forms. The psychological versions combined methodological reform with empiricist and associationistic doctrine: All the concepts admissible in the science of psychology were to be defined in terms of observable behavior—experimental manipulations and measurement procedures—and the results of investigation accounted for in terms of environmental contingencies and reinforcement histories. Philosophical behaviorism had its roots in logical positivism and the later philosophy of Wittgenstein (1958). The classic statement is Gilbert Ryle's book *The Concept of Mind* (1949). Ryle undertook an analysis of mentalistic language and claimed to find that it is full of "category mistakes" (p. 16ff). For example, to think that words such as belief and desire refer to inner states of being is comparable to asking for the telephone number of the average taxpayer. Instead, according to Ryle, such words should be understood as referring to dispositions to act in certain ways. Thus, my belief that Williams College is in Massachusetts is equivalent to a set of predictions about what I should do in certain circumstances. For example, (a) I should answer Massachusetts if asked which state Williams College is in; (b) I should drive north east from where I live in New Jersey if I wanted to get to Williams College; and (c) I should look up Massachusetts in the encyclopedia if I needed to find out something about Williams College. From this point of view you would no more expect to find beliefs and desires dotted about in someone's head than you would expect to find solubility if you took apart a lump of sugar. So all the mystery about the relationship between minds and bodies evaporates as mind is revealed as no thing and mental ascriptions turn out to be about behavior. This dodge also means that there is no longer a problem about ascribing beliefs and desires to animals, for such ascription can be just as predictive of animal behavior as of human behavior.

After dominating psychology for about 50 years, especially in America, behavioristic psychology, at least in its radical form, is on the wane. Both conceptually and methodologically it proved to be ill-equipped to deal with cognitive phenomena such as perception, memory, and thinking, interest in which was boosted by, among other developments, the rise of computer science with its prospect of artificial intelligence. The reign of philosophical behaviorism was shorter and more localized. Its analysis of meaning as behavioral disposition has turned out to be less thorough than was originally thought. For one thing, the number of predictions that can be generated from attribution of a mental state is endless, so the "cash value" of such attribution is left undetermined. More serious is the point that the predictions usually invoke other cognitive conditions the behavioral cashing of which would entail still further cognitive reference and so on ad infinitum. Thus my reply to the question about the state in which Williams College is located assumes that I know about the institution of statehood and my driving north east is predicated on my desire to get to Williams College, and so on.

In place of operational definition as the means of determining the meanings of terms, many scientists and philosophers have resorted to a network conception of meaning. According to this view the terms of a science or theory get their meaning from the place they occupy within the system of laws and other terms constituting the framework of the science or theory. Thus, the concept of electron is tied up with notions of energy, atomic structure, Heisenberg's uncertainty principle, and so on. Rather than a single autonomous explicit definition governing the term, its meaning is given implicitly by its connections with other terms and how it enters into the laws and generalizations of subatomic physics. Similarly, it is argued that the terms we use in talking about mental life are informed by the network of theory that is folk psychology. It is this commonsense yet immensely rich structure of laws and generalizations that gives sense to words like pain, belief, and desire rather than the subjective qualities of experience or introspection, which, for all their immediacy and indubitability, are private to each mind and therefore unavailable as a means of establishing the semantic agreement necessary for communication.

It may have occurred to you that this conception of psychological terms may raise difficulties about their application to animals in which much of the network assumed in the human case is lacking. For example, if a cat chases a mouse into a hole and waits expectantly beside the hole, perhaps reaching into the hole with a paw from time to time, we might be inclined to say that the cat believed that there was a mouse in the hole. But would that be accurate? Our concept of a mouse is tied to our concepts of mammal, animal, living, warm-blooded and so on, none of which is likely to be understood by the cat. So what is the thing we call a mouse to it? A related point was made by Quine in his book *Word and Object* (1960). He described a scenario in which a linguist in a strange land encounters a native who utters "gavagai" at the appearance of what the linguist recognizes as a rabbit. Does gavagai mean what *rabbit* means in English? Quine argues that with no words in common and only gestures like pointing to go on, there is no way for the question to be settled. The linguist might determine the "stimulus meaning" (p. 32) — what circumstances lead the native to say gavagai — but the meaning of the term to the native would remain indeterminate. David Premack (1986) has recently used gavagai for the title of a book, subtitled "the future history of the animal language controversy." He thinks that there are nonverbal means of testing for synonymy that can get beyond Quine's "indeterminacy of radical translation" (p. 27). However, Premack ends his book with the reflection that infatuation with language may have drawn attention away from characteristics that might make for more fruitful cognitive comparison between humans and animals. If so, most current philosophical theories of mind may be ill-equipped for such comparison for they are imbued with linguistic preoccupation.

FUNCTIONALISM

Among current philosophical theories of mind those conforming to what is described as *functionalism* probably have the largest following. Functionalism, in this context, is an approach that considers each mental event to be a brain event, that is, there is token-to-token identity between mental events and brain events, but denies that there can be one-to-one mapping of kinds of mental events to kinds of brain events, that is, no type-to-type identity. There are several arguments for this including the thought experiment of constructing a brain with chemistry different from the human kind and finding that the two kinds of brain can harbor the same beliefs and desires just as the same arithmetical operations can be executed in a mechanical and an electronic computer, and the same computer program can be run on a variety of kinds of hardware. This conception of functional equivalence in material diversity underlies those artificial intelligence projects that aspire not only to simulate human mentality but also to duplicate it. Some cognitive scientists have gone so far as to claim that the mind is a program functionally equivalent to a program in a computer. This is a view that John Searle (1980) believes he has demolished with his Chinese room argument. Searle envisions a man ignorant of Chinese who is placed in a room with a bin full of Chinese characters and a list of instructions telling him which characters to draw from the bin in response to ones delivered to him from outside. The man becomes so adept at selecting the right answers to the questions presented to him in accordance with his instructions that, from outside, his performance cannot be distinguished from that of a Chinese-speaking person. Does the man in the room understand Chinese? Or the system consisting of the man in the room? According to the Turing test, two systems with indistinguishable input-output relations are essentially the same, so the man in the room and the Chinaman must be on a par. But Searle says that this is nonsense. The man in the room is simply shuffling squiggly shapes without a clue about what they mean. Likewise, a program in a computer has syntax only; it lacks the semantics of intentionality and the "aboutness" that is the mark of mentality. (For responses to this argument, see the issue of *The Behavioral and Brain Sciences* [1980] in which it first appeared; Douglas Hofstadter's commentary on it in Hofstadter & Dennett [1981]; Cummins [1983].)

According to functionalism, mental states do not reduce to brain states; consequently, development of a theory of mind is an autonomous endeavour in no danger of being preempted by developments in neuroscience. The resulting theories come in several forms. Among the more popular are representational theories of the mind according to which beliefs, desires, and the other propositional attitudes consist of relations to mental representations, perhaps sentences in the head, the contents of which have semantic significance. For example, my belief that Williams College is in Massachusetts consists in my having a mental token of "Williams College is in Massachusetts" in a belief store. Some versions of such theories hold that propositional attitudes relate causally to one another by virtue of their semantic contents. So my belief that Williams College is in Massachusetts and my desire to get to Williams College resulted in my driving north east from my house in New Jersey. The theory attempts to develop generalizations that capture such content-determined relationships for all cognitive beings. The theory that John Searle offers in his book on *Intentionality* (1983) has features in common with this sort of representational theory. He holds that an intentional state is a mental attitude towards a content representing some state of affairs that could or might exist, the existence or realization of which would be the condition of satisfaction of the intentional state—it would make a belief true and fulfill a desire. Thus, my belief that Williams College is in Massachusetts is satisfied, that is, made true by its being the case that Williams College is in Massachusetts.

Another version of a representational theory of mind argues that the causal relations among propositional attitudes are due to the formal or syntactic properties of the mental representations rather than their symbolic or semantic properties. This version views mental operations in the same light as information processing in a computer, that is, as consisting of symbol manipulation dictated by purely formal or syntactic rules. Such a computational theory assumes that the syntax somehow corresponds or correlates with the semantics although even its strongest supporters admit that it has yet to be shown just how a "syntactic engine" can also work as a "semantic engine" (Dennett, 1981, p. 156)—how, in other words, the symbols manipulated are linked to a world they represent. In any case, theories of this sort aspire to join folk psychology to the powerful resources of computational formalism and thus chart the territory through which the bottom-up approaches of brain science will have to pass if they are to make useful contact with intentionality.

One of the most eloquent spokesmen for a representational theory of mind is Jerry Fodor (1975). (Dennett [1986] has described M.I.T. as the Vatican of High Church Computationalism and Fodor as its "theologian in residence," (p. 63) but Fodor has since moved his mission to New York). He has gone so far as to say that this sort of theory is "the only kind of psychological theory we've got" (p. 27). Fodor's view is that intentional states are attitudes towards mental sentences that have semantic content. This links up with the remark I made earlier that most current philosophies of mind have linguistic features. One is prompted to ask what language the mental sentences are expressed in. If it is the language the thinker happens to speak, does it follow that prelinguistic children and animals are devoid of thought and mentality? Fodor's answer was to postulate what he called a "language of thought," (p. 33) which is universal to cognitive beings and into and out of which the sentences of spoken language are translated or mapped if such language is possessed. According to this view children are "linguaformal" from the outset and hence even before they learn to speak; presumably the same applies to cognitively endowed animals that never acquire surface language. The idea has echoes of Chomsky's postulation of a universal grammar determining the deep structure of linguistic ability (the M.I.T. connection again?). In any case, Fodor takes the position that such a medium is required to render folk psychology in a form that elevates it to cognitive science (For critiques of Fodor's language of thought theory, see Churchland [1978]; Churchland [1986]; Dennett [1978].)

There are philosophers who disagree with Fodor. For example, Stephen Stich, in his book *From Folk Psychology to Cognitive Science–The Case Against Belief* (1983), finds that the folk psychological notion of belief does indeed involve a relationship to semantic content, but that such a notion cannot be fitted into a coherent and comprehensive cognitive theory. He argues that the notion of content employed by representative theories of mind is too vague for the precision required and yet excludes minds for which no clear conception of content can be formed, such as prelinguistic children, victims of brain damage, and animals. Consequently, cognitive generalizations that would include the full range of cognitive beings appear to be beyond the range of this approach. In the place of representational theories of mind Stich argues for a purely syntactic theory of mind. Briefly put this is to the effect that cognitive states correspond to syntactic entities in such a way that causal relations between cognitive states and causal links to stimuli and behavior conform to the syntactic properties and relations of the syntactic entities to which the cognitive states are mapped. In other words, we have the formalized computational part of the second sort of representational theory I sketched, except that the states whose causal relations are mirrored in the computation, are without semantic or representational significance. The conclusion seems to be that the mind is, afterall, equivalent to a computer program, which merely manipulates symbols, the interpretation of which has to be supplied from elsewhere. For John Searle, you might recall, this disqualifies such a theory from serious consideration because a program, however ingenious, cannot really understand anything in the way that a mind does if all it can do is shuffle symbols according to rules; unless it has a place for intentionality, no such system can constitute a mind. Stich's retort is to say so much the worse for intentionality and the folk psychological theory of mind. He concludes that "folk concepts have no part to play in an empirical science aimed at explaining the mental processes underlying behavior" (p. 110). He does not, however, see folk psychology being replaced in the foreseeable future as the commonsense way of accounting for thought and action. Afterall, we still find it convenient to revert to ancient folk astronomy when we talk of the sun's rising in the east, and quantum mechanics and relativity theory have yet to make inroads to the practical reasoning of people at large. Despite the old adage, science is really much more than organized common sense (think how unintuitive we find a concept such as antimatter), and so the possibility that cognitive science might have to abandon folk psychology is not without precedent.

However, folk psychology has been called into question from another standpoint as well, and this time the suggestion is that it might be due to be dumped even by commonsense. Patricia Churchland (1982, 1986) and Paul Churchland (1979, 1981, 1985) have drawn attention to the fact that folk psychology has remained virtually unchanged since the time of Aristotle, and in this respect contrasts with other fields such as folk astronomy, folk physics, and folk medicine (see also Churchland & Churchland [1981]). This longevity might be thought of as a result of the unlikely possibility that in the singular case of folk psychology people got it essentially right the first time. But, as the Churchlands point out, it can't be essentially right for it fails to account for a great deal of what such a theory should cover: mental illness, creative imagination, sleep, three-dimensional vision, memory, and much more. These phenomena are just as mysterious as they ever were. In contrast, they envisage the prospect of a fully-matured neuroscience that would discard the propositional attitudes in favor of materially-based categories of mental ontology. Instead of a smooth intertheoretical reduction of the concepts of folk psychology to those of neuroscience, on the pattern of the reduction of thermodynamics to statistical mechanics, the concepts of folk psychology may be so wrong as to require complete elimination; such was the case with the concepts of alchemy as a consequence of the rise of the chemistry of Dalton and Lavoisier. Such a turn of events may seem too farfetched a prospect for common sense to take seriously, but remember that common sense once held a geocentric conception of the universe and believed that heat was a fluid. Commenting on our attachment to the "idea that behavior is explicable in terms of the propositional attitudes of the agent," Fodor (1981, p. 122) has said: "Any sensible ethologist contemplating any *other* species would surely take such considerations as prima facie evidence that the framework of an intentional explanation is innate." But the innateness of a belief does not guarantee its truth as a firefly duped by a femme fatale's signal flashes learns to its cost. (For defenses of the commonsense view against the Stich and Churchland positions see Double [1985] and Clark [1987].)

COGNITIVE ETHOLOGY

My reason for conducting my philosophical tour mainly in the region of folk psychology is that we have, for the most part, taken this theory for granted in cognitive ethology. For example, when Donald Griffin (1976) elected to "concentrate on images, intentions, and awareness of objects and relationships in the outside world [in] attempting to come to grips with the question of possible mental experiences in animals" (p. 6), he was clearly assuming the categories of folk psychology. Daniel Dennett (1983) was doing the same thing when he proposed a way of assessing the degree of intentionality underlying the alarm-calling of vervet monkeys. I think it is well for us to be aware of the theoretical status accorded to folk psychology by much current philosophy and the doubts that have been raised about it. There are at least three reasons. First, if we are to draw on the philosophers for help in trying to come to terms with animal mentality, we need to know what the relevant issues are from their points of view and where they stand on them. Second, if we want cognitive ethology to establish and maintain contact with developments in cognitive science, we may need to revise basic assumptions about the nature of our enterprise. Third, if the conception of folk psychology as a theory is right, and the meanings of the terms we take from it are given by how those terms are placed in the network of that theory, we have a problem in that a large part of the network appears to be missing when we apply the terms to animals. The problem may call for conceptual analysis of ethological usage along the lines that Stich followed in his treatment of the folk psychological concept of belief.

Even our descriptive terms include words about which it is questionable how much of what they mean when they are applied to humans is carried over when they are applied to animals. In a book called *The Explanation of Behaviour,* Charles Taylor (1964) pointed out that describing behavior as action normally implies intention where describing it as movement implies only causation. Thus, to say that I saluted is to assume that I was conforming to a ritual and doing so intentionally, while to say that my arm went up is to assume no more than that nerves fired and muscles contracted. Does the same contrast apply between behavior categorized as action and behavior categorized as movement when we are describing animals? For example, do we conceive soliciting as in a category different from blushing? The problem posed by using terms rooted in human contexts in talk about animal behavior is that links to language are often lacking in the transfer. As Searle (1984, p. 81) observed: ". . . many animals have conscious mental states, but as far as we know, they lack the self–referentiality that goes with human languages and social institutions." But even where there is language possession there may be difficulties. The interconnectedness of concepts and customs can create barriers to communication between people of different cultures. For the same reason Wittgenstein (1958, p. 223) said: "If a lion could talk, we could not understand him."

However, evolutionary common sense tells us that our mentality has ancestral animal roots and historical explanation in terms of survival value. The last philosopher I shall mention will probably appear more congenial to you than any of the others, for she takes her stand on a naturalistic position from which intentionality is viewed as related to the notion of function in the sense in which we use the word to refer to survival value or adaptive significance. Ruth Millikan (1984, 1986) argues against computational theories of the mind in which mentality appears hermetically sealed inside the head without a clear way to get the world in and behavior out. Her solution is to unmesh mental states from the network of the theory of folk psychology and to apply to them the kinds of considerations that bear on the structures and physiological mechanisms of the body. Organs such as the heart and the kidneys have what Millikan calls their "proper" (p. 2ff) functions — pumping blood in the case of the heart and cleansing the blood in the case of the kidneys — which constitute their raisons d'etre, that is to say account for their existence in teleonomic or evolutionary terms. Similarly, beliefs and desires serve to represent states of affairs that can affect an organism's interests, vital or otherwise. Thus, the proper function of a belief is to map onto the world in a way that makes it true and hence provide the basis for other true beliefs and for desires that can be fulfilled through behavioral means. Just as a heart can fail to realize its proper function through malformation or pathological condition so a belief can fail to serve its proper function because its contents do not map onto the world (i.e., it is false) or because the inferences into which it enters are invalid. But the fact that there are failures emphasizes that for proper functions to be served the conditions of production and setting must conform to species norms that reflect evolutionary history. Realization of proper function may even be the exception rather than the rule as in the case of individuals of r-selected species most of whom die before reproducing; or sperm, most of which fail to achieve fertilization; or desires, most of which remain unfulfilled, perhaps, for most of us.

The notion of proper function also bears on the question of behavioral description and what calls for ethological explanation. A grass-pulling herring gull may be facing towards Atlantic City, making its shadow move, damaging a growth of *Spartina patens,* and doing an indefinite number of other things that can be ignored in treating the behavior as a biological category. The proper function and the biologically relevant features of behavior are not always obvious. Indeed, the signalling behavior of animals is more often than not problematic both with regard to immediate function and the "sign vehicle" (Hailman, 1977; Morris, 1946) effecting it.

However, in the waggle dance of the honeybee we have a case in which the connection between behavioral form and proper function has been made beautifully clear and which can be likened to the relationship between a belief and its mapping onto the world. According to Millikan, the bee's dance can be considered a case of intentionality, because it is about a state of affairs in the world. Moreover, it is referentially opaque; although we can tell what a bee's dance is about — nectar obtainable three quarters of a mile to the west — we cannot assume that that is what it means to the bees. In addition, the dance has the further intentionalistic property that it can refer to states of affairs that do not exist, as Gould and Gould (1986) demonstrated. Although the performance of the honeybees is sophisticated, Millikan doubts whether a dancing bee's state (or that of its recipients) constitutes belief (e.g., that there is nectar at a specific place) or desire (e.g., that the other bees follow the directions to the place) ". . . it is unlikely that there is any distinction *within* the performing bee to correspond to the distinction between belief and desire — unlikely that the bee either believes or desires anything in the human way" (Millikan, 1986, p. 72). In humans beliefs and desires can be uncoupled from one another and combined in an indefinite number of ways with other beliefs and desires, and again Millikan doubts whether bees can do anything like this. However, there is the fact that the bee dance can be used to transmit information about prospective hive locations instead of food locations (Lindauer, 1971): also, there is Gould's report that when bees were told that there was nectar in the middle of a lake they ignored the news as though it were too unlikely to be true. These observations suggest that there may be more intentionality to the bees' performance than even Millikan concedes. Be that as it may, it should already be apparent that Millikan's approach comes into closer contact with the phenomena and concepts of ethology than that of any of the other philosophers I have mentioned and yet has equally close contact with the concerns of those philosophers even though she is highly critical of the fix that she thinks they have got folk psychology into. As with the other positions discussed in this paper, I have been able to give only the merest sketch of Millikan's thesis, which she develops in rich detail in a substantial book that includes language as one of the "biological categories" (Millikan, 1984, p. 17ff). I hope that what I have said is sufficient to encourage some of you to read it.

In the meantime, the questions I began with remain: How do we get a handle on the mental states of animals? What differences does language make? What are the differences between human and animal mentality? How does confusion about intentionality cloud the issues? Ruth Millikan suggests some ways in which we may come to grips with them. The experimental studies of Gould, Cheney, Marler, Ristau, Seyfarth and others exemplify ways in which questions about animal mentality in the terms of folk psychology can be pursued empirically, and thus extend to animals a theory of intentionality divested of anchorage in linguistic forms. Although we take common sense as our point of departure, it may be that we shall have the prospect of returning to help put common sense to the test.

REFERENCES

Austin, J. L. (1962). *Sense and sensibilia.* Oxford: Clarendon Press.
Boden, M. A. (1972). *Purposive explanation in psychology.* Cambridge, MA: Harvard University Press.
Brentano, F. (1874). *Psychologie vom Empirischen Standpunkt* (Psychology from an Empirical standpoint). Leipzig: Meiner.
Chisholm, R. M. (1967). Intentionality. In P. Edwards (Ed.), *The encyclopedia of philosophy.* New York: Macmillan.
Churchland, P. S. (1978). Fodor on language learning. *Synthese, 38:* 149–159.
Churchland, P. S. (1982). Mind-brain reduction: New light from the philosophy of science. *Neuroscience, 7:* 1041–1047.
Churchland, P. S. (1986). *Neurophilosophy.* Cambridge, MA: M.I.T. Press.
Churchland, P. M. (1979). *Scientific realism and the plasticity of mind.* Cambridge: Cambridge University Press.
Churchland, P. M. (1981). Eliminative materialism and propositional attitudes. *Journal of Philosophy, 78:* 67–90.
Churchland, P. M. (1985). Reduction, qualia, and the direct introspection of brain states. *Journal of Philosophy, 82:* 8–28.
Churchland, P. M., & Churchland, P. S. (1981). Functionalism, qualia, and intentionality. *Philosophical Topics, 12:* 121–145.
Clark, A. (1987). From folk psychology to naive psychology. *Cognitive Science, 11:* 139–154.
Cummins, R. (1983). *The nature of psychological explanation.* Cambridge, MA: M.I.T. Press.
Dennett, D. C. (1969). *Content and consciousness.* London: Routledge & Kegan Paul.
Dennett, D. C. (1978). A cure for the common code. In D. C. Dennett (Ed.), *Brainstorms.* Cambridge, MA.: M.I.T. Press.
Dennett, D. C. (1981). Three kinds of intentional psychology. In R. Healey (Ed.), *Reduction, time, and reality.* Cambridge: Cambridge University Press.
Dennett, D. C. (1983). International systems in cognitive ethology: The "Panglossian Paradigm" defended. *Behavior and Brain Sciences, 6:* 343–390.
Dennett, D. C. (1986). The logical geography of computational approaches: A view from the East Pole. In M. Brand & R. M. Harnish (Eds.), *The representation of knowledge and belief.* Tucson: University of Arizona Press.
Double, R. (1985). The case against the case against belief. *Mind, 94:* 420–430.
Fodor, J. A. (1975). *The language of thought.* New York: Crowell.
Fodor, J. A. (1981). *Re-presentations.* Cambridge, MA.: M.I.T. Press.
Fodor, J. A. (1987). *Psychosemantics.* Cambridge, MA.: M.I.T. Press.
Gould, J. L., & Gould, C. G. (1986). Invertebrate intelligence. In R. J. Hoage & L. Goodman (Eds.), *Animal intelligence.* Washington, D.C.: Smithsonian.
Griffin, D. R. (1976). *The question of animal awareness.* New York: Rockefeller.
Hailman, J. P. (1977). *Optical signals.* Bloomington: Indiana, University Press.
Hofstadter, D. R., & Dennett, D. C. (1981). *The mind's I.* New York: Basic Books.
Korner, S. (1959). *Conceptual thinking.* New York: Dover.
Lindauer, M. (1971). *Communication among social bees.* Cambridge, MA: Harvard University Press.

Mach, E. (1914). *The analysis of sensations.* Chicago: University of Chicago Press.

Millikan, R. G. (1984). *Language, thought, and other biological categories.* Cambridge, MA: M.I.T. Press.

Millikan, R. G. (1986). Thoughts without laws; cognitive science with content. *Philosophical Review, 95:* 47–80.

Morris, C. W. (1946). *Sign, language, and behavior.* New York: Braziller.

Nagel, T. (1974). What is it like to be a bat? *Philosophical Review, 83:* 2–14.

Premack, D. (1986). *Gavagai! or the future history of the animal language controversy.* Cambridge, MA.: M.I.T. Press.

Quine, W. V. O. (1960). *Word and object.* Cambridge, MA.: M.I.T. Press.

Russell, B. (1912). *The problems of philosophy.* London: Hutchinson.

Ryle, G. (1949). *The concept of mind.* London: Hutchinson.

Searle, J. R. (1980). Minds, brains, and programs. *Behavioral and Brain Sciences, 3:* 417–457.

Searle, J. R. (1983). *Intentionality.* Cambridge: Cambridge University Press.

Searle, J. R. (1984). *Minds, brains and science.* Cambridge, MA.: Harvard University Press.

Sellars, W. (1956). Empiricism and the philosophy of mind. In K. Gunderson (Ed.), *Minnesota studies in the philosophy of science 7.* Minneapolis: University of Minnesota Press.

Stich, S. (1983). *From folk psychology to cognitive science.* Cambridge, MA.: M.I.T. Press.

Taylor, C. (1964). *The explanation of behaviour.* London: Routledge & Kegan Paul.

Wittgenstein, L. (1958). *Philosophical investigations.* Oxford: Blackwell.

3 HOW IS COGNITIVE ETHOLOGY POSSIBLE?

Jonathan Bennett
Syracuse University

ABSTRACT

Cognitive ethology cannot be done well unless its proximate philosophical underpinnings are got straight; this paper tries to help with that. Cognitive attributions are essentially explanatory—if they did not explain behavior, there would be no justification for them—but it doesn't follow that they explain by providing causes for events that don't have physical causes. To understand how mentalistic attributions do work, we need to focus on the quartet: sensory input, belief, desire, and behavioral output. We also need to be able to study classes of sensory inputs—one-shot deals are uninterpretable. The crucial guiding rule is, roughly: The animal's behavior shouldn't be explained by attributing to it the belief that P unless the behavior occurs in sensory circumstances belonging to a class whose members are marked off in some way that involves the concept of P and not in any way that is lower than that. The higher\lower distinction can be understood so that the guiding rule is helpful not only in deciding what thoughts to attribute to an animal but also in deciding whether to attribute any thoughts at all.

INTRODUCTION

My title asks: By what right can one pass from premises about behavior to conclusions about minds? What ultimately is going on when such inferences are made? An impatient but not unreasonable answer might be the following: these are philosophical questions, which means that we ethologists need not worry about them. We *do* infer mentalistic conclusions from behavioral premises, and there are evidently public standards for doing this, agreed controls governing the inferences, shared bases on which we can rationally debate whether those data support that conclusion, and so on. We can maintain this going concern and get what sensible people will regard as solid results without digging down into its philosophical underlay. Similarly, a physicist can get on with his physics without addressing the problem of the philosophical sceptic: What entitles you to be sure that there is a physical world?

Although it is not unreasonable, that answer is wrong. It is not true that cognitive ethology is being conducted on the basis of shared agreed upon standards and controls. On the contrary, the field is more tangled and disputed than it needs to be because everyday working and arguing standards are insecure and idiosyncratic; the reason for this is that some underlying philosophical issues have not been properly addressed. I apologize for the dogmatic tone of this statement, but the issue is urgent and important. What is at stake is the integrity of cognitive ethology as a field of intellectual endeavor; and because I *do* believe in it and think it important, I want to see it equipped with solid enough foundations to support a respectable, coherent, disciplined practice.

That doesn't mean that the foundations need to be explored all the way down. For example, I see no reason why cognitive ethologists have to concern themselves with the issue of mental/material dualism; they can be agnostic about whether inferences from behavioral premises to mentalistic conclusions start inside the physical realm and end outside it. But some foundational issues have to be faced.

MIND AS EXPLANATORY

We look at behavior and conjecture that the animal has certain thoughts. Minimally, we conjecture that it wants X and thinks that what it is doing is a way to get X. (I assume without argument that belief and desire — thinking that P and wanting it to be the case that Q — lie at the heart of the cluster of cognitive states that we might attribute to animals.) The first question to be faced is this: In attributing cognitive states to the animal, do we purport to explain its behavior? Yes, for two reasons.

1. The first is strategic. Our inferences from behavior to cognitive states are intelligible if the conclusions are meant to explain the behavior. For then our procedure falls into the familiar pattern of an inference to the best explanation, like the inference from the fact that the lights went out to the conclusion that a fuse has blown. If, on the other hand, our attributions of

mentality don't purport to explain what they are based on, it is hard to see what the "basing" can consist of.

It might be suggested that what is going on is aesthetic; we look at various specimens of animal behavior and ask ourselves "Don't we feel comfortable applying such and such cognitive language on the basis of this?" If cognitive ethology were in that way merely a matter of inviting one another to respond to the stimuli of animal behavior with the utterance of mentalistic sentences, it would not be a fit activity for competent adults. Anyway, cognitive ethologists clearly don't see their work in that way; on the contrary, they look for conclusions that are supposed to have some chance of being true because they are intellectually supported (not just aesthetically or poetically encouraged) by the behavioral data.

Well, then, perhaps cognitive attributions to animals are just ways of codifying facts about their behavior: "When an animal behaves thus and so, in such and circumstances, we call that 'believing that there is a predator in the undergrowth' " — on an analogy with "When an animal has such and such behavioral features we call it a 'rodent' " or "When a painting is made thus and so, we call it a 'fresco' ". This would reduce the language of cognition to a mere system for classifying facts about behavior. Such a system would be worth having only if mentalistic language could make descriptions of behavior shorter and more compact without loss of content. But clearly the language of cognition does not serve in that role: the required equations, with mentality on one side and behavior on the other, don't exist. And cognitive ethologists don't accord it that role. They think (rightly) that facts about what an animal thinks and wants can help to *explain* how it behaves; and such facts couldn't do that if they were themselves really just facts about how animals behave.

Given those failures, I conclude that what we say about the minds of animals is meant to help explain how they behave.

2. The second reason for this conclusion is more specific and detailed. The link between thought and behavior essentially requires that the former include desire: No information about what an animal thinks, remembers, concludes, or suspects has the slightest bearing on its behavior except in combination with facts about what it wants. And the concept of desire — or its parent concept, namely goal or purpose — is *essentially* explanatory. Some theorists have not seen this. They have tried to explain how one might arrive at the conclusion that an animal's behavior has G as a goal with this being understood as purely descriptive of the animal, untouched by any suggestion that the animal behaves as it does *because* G is its goal. Such attempts to analyze the concept of desire as purely descriptive and in no way explanatory have all failed so radically as to suggest that the project cannot be carried through because desire is essentially an explanatory concept (Nagel, 1979; Tolman, 1932, pp. 10, 13, 21.)

THE CAUSAL SNARE

Let us take it, then, that in attributing beliefs and desires to animals we are trying to explain their behavior. What kind of explanation can this be?

The most natural answer is: causal explanation. That was Descartes' view of the matter. He thought that we could be entitled to attribute thoughts to others only if their behavior could not have been caused purely by the states of their bodies; because he thought that the behavior of nonhuman animals could all be physicalistically explained, he was unwilling to credit them with having any thoughts at all.

His contemporary Arnauld (1964–1976, vol. 7) predicted that Descartes would have trouble convincing people that the behavior of other animals could be explained in purely physical terms:

> For at first sight it seems incredible that it can come about, without the assistance of any soul, that the light reflected from the body of a wolf onto the nerves of a sheep should move the minute fibres of the optic nerves, and that on reaching the brain this motion should spread the animal spirits throughout the nerves in the manner necessary to precipitate the sheep's flight. (p. 205)

Descartes certainly wasn't entitled to be dogmatic about this. But nor was it reasonable to be confident that he was wrong, and intuitions of incredibility were worthless—as Spinoza said a few years later—given how little was known about how animals, human and other, are built and how they function. It has been made easier for us than it was for Spinoza to see this, helped as we are by microscopic knowledge of the brain's complexity and by a shift from a mechanical to a chemical and electrical understanding of neural processes.

So if we go Descartes' way, we ought to give up cognitive ethology; the physical causes of animal behavior probably suffice to explain it all, leaving no gaps that have to be filled from outside the physical realm. We don't have to like cognitive ethology to dislike this approach. For one thing, it ties the notion of mentality to a Cartesian dualist understanding of it, according to which mind is something that lies right outside the physical world and causally intrudes into it. Also, it puts the belief that people have thoughts at the mercy of the claim that their behavior cannot be physicalistically explained. Descartes thought that it couldn't, but it would be rash of us to agree with him and foolish to make that agreement our only basis for supposing that people think!

ANOTHER KIND OF EXPLANATION

I conclude that in attributing beliefs and desires to animals we must be offering noncausal explanations of their behavior. How can this be?

Well, what is needed are fairly reliable generalizations relating beliefs and desires to behavior. The core idea is as follows (Bennett, 1976, chapters 2–4). To say that an animal is behaving with the achievement of G as its goal is to say that it is in a condition C such that: whenever it is in condition C it does whatever it thinks will achieve G. That, though vastly too simple, is the seed crystal from which a complete behavior-based theory of belief and desire can be grown. A crucial fact about it is that it ties the notion of an animal's wanting something or having it as a goal to its falling under some general truth — something to the effect that whenever so-and-so obtains the animal does such-and-such. It is precisely because a generalization must lie in the background of any desire that the attribution of desires can be explanatory: Why did the animal do A? Because it thought that doing A would achieve G, and it was in a condition C such that whenever it is in condition C it will do whatever it thinks will achieve G. Bringing its behavior under that kind of generalization is not causally explaining the behavior. Causal explanations of behavior must always be neurological if materialism is true, and they are probably so even if materialism is false. That is, even if there are mentalistic facts that are entirely additional to anything belonging to the world of matter and things in space, it seems reasonable to suppose that the causes of such facts are always facts about brains. The alternative to this is to suppose that physical causal chains have gaps in them — gaps that are plugged by the intrusion of mental events. That is too much to swallow.

Anyway — and this is the main point — we can hold that mentalistic explanations can be genuinely explanatory and worthwhile without being forced to suppose that they are causal. The reason for this has been well enough expressed in the literature, and I shall merely sketch it here (Bennett, 1976, section 21; Dennett, 1987, pp. 25–28.)

Let us suppose that every move that an animal makes can be fully causally explained in physiological terms (mostly neural ones). Here is the threat we have to meet:

A mentalistic explanation of an animal's behavior involves concepts that are superficial and relatively local. Ex hypothesi there is always a properly causal explanation, using concepts that go deeper and spread wider through the physical world — concepts of neurophysiology that ultimately reach down into chemistry and physics. The latter kind of explanation is surely preferable to the former. Granted, we may sometimes have a mentalistic explanation of something an animal does and not be able to explain it physiologically, and that may give explanations of the former kind a weak sort of legitimacy. But that is the best case we can make for explaining behavior mentalistically — namely, that we sometimes have to use those explanations faute de mieux — so we ought to be a little embarrassed, apologetic, reticent about them, as we should about anything that we would jettison if we were smarter and more knowledgeable.

That is a good try, but it's not good enough. The fact is that our mentalistic explanations involve groupings that would be missed altogether by neurophysiological explanations. The various things that an animal does because it thinks they would lead to food may have no significant neural common factor or anyway none that they don't share with many episodes that have nothing to do with nutrition; similarly for all its moves aimed at escaping from predators, at getting sexual satisfaction, at caring for its young, at attracting a mate, and so on. Thus, mentalistic explanations of behavior bring out patterns, commonalities, regularities, that would slip through the net of the most densely informed and theoretically supported neurological explanations. If we are interested in those patterns (Why shouldn't we be?), that entitles us to be unapologetically interested in the explanations that correspond to them.

Consider a situation in which an animal is threatened by a predator, and its behavior is being predicted by us, in mentalistic terms, and by a superhumanly calculating physiologist who has magical ways of knowing pretty exactly what the animal's detailed brain-states are at this moment. If our cognitive account of the animal is good enough, we may be able to predict that it will climb the nearest tree, say; but if we are less well-informed, we may be in a position to predict only that the animal will behave in some way that increases its chances of escaping the predator; we might know that much without knowing any more. For example, we may not be able to rule out the possibility that the animal will lie motionless and silent. Now the superhuman physiologist may be able to predict that the animal will move just exactly thus and so: it will climb that tree in that precise manner every moment of each limb being precisely predicted. But if the physiologist isn't quite that good and can only approximate to a perfect prediction, he won't be able to predict that the animal will improve its chances of escaping the predator. He will be able to predict that the animal will make approximately such-and-such movements, which means that it will go towards the tree and then make climbing-like movements; but for all he can tell, the animal may not quite get to the tree, or may get there and move like a climber but not hold on tight enough, which means that he cannot predict that the animal will do something that is likely to save it from the predator.

The physiologist's inability to predict whether the animal will do anything to improve its chances of escaping matches our inability to say even approximately what kinds of movements the animal will make (e.g. climb, swim, or lie still). Neither basis for prediction is better than the other. They merely cater to different legitimate interests; those interests correspond to different patterns, different classifications of episodes, and that shows up in (among other things) different kinds of spread of approximation.

THE NOTORIOUS TRIANGLE

Behavior shows what an animal thinks only on an assumption about what it wants. Behavior shows what an animal wants only on assumptions about what it thinks. This is the famous belief-desire-behavior triangle. The message that it brings to the cognitive ethologist is: What you must look for to explain your subject's behavior is a cognitive theory that involves both cognitive and conative elements, i.e. that has to do with beliefs and with desires. There is no chance at all of determining one of these first and then moving on to study the other.

But how are we to tackle them both at once? Here is a simple and incorrect recipe for doing so. Attend to a bit of behavior A and think up some belief-desire pair B-D such that if the animal had B-D, it would have done A. Attribute B and D to the animal. Then attend to a second bit of behavior and repeat the process. Continue to do this through all the animal's behavioral history. At the end of this you will have a complete story about what it thought and what it wanted at each moment.

A moment's reflection will show that this libertine procedure is worthless; it is too easy. It allows any given bit of behavior to fall under so many different belief-desire pairs that it isn't interesting or significant to pick arbitrarily on some one of them. The animal climbed the tree because it wanted to get warm and it thought there was a fire up there; or because it wanted to get food and thought the top of the tree was edible; or because it wanted a sexual partner and thought there was one in the tree; or because. . . . One can fabricate such belief-desire explanations at will in perfect conformity with the rule of the libertine procedure; so there is no point in coming up with any of them.

Notice that because the libertine procedure does not connect what the animal thinks or wants at one time with what it thinks or wants at another, the procedure cannot lead us to results that will have predictive value. That is one mark of the fact that these explanations don't explain anything. Another sign of trouble is that the libertine procedure makes no provision for the animal sometimes to believe something falsely.

FROM TRIANGLE TO SQUARE

What the libertine procedure offers us is a glassy surface: because none of our conjectures can run into serious trouble, we are left to skid and slide all over the place with no rough ground on which we can take a stand and no reason to prefer, in a given situation, to attribute one belief-desire pair rather than another. What we need as rough ground is some independent basis for preferring some attributions to others for a particular animal at a particular time.

The way we find this basis is by developing some theory about what the animal is likely to believe when it is in such and such an environment and when its sense organs are in such and such a condition and are oriented in such and such way. This is a theory about the relation between the animal's sensory inputs and its beliefs. When we have that, our theory turns out to have not just the three items in the triangle but four: (a) sensory inputs leading through (b) beliefs and (c) desires to (d) behavioral outputs.

But how are we to get any generalizations about what beliefs the animal is likely to have when it has such and such sensory inputs? To do that, we must see what beliefs are indicated by its behavior, but we have seen that the behavior won't tell us about the animal's beliefs unless we know what it wants. Are we, then, still stuck unless we can get some independent basis for judging the likelihood of various attributions of wants? I think not. All we need is a general assumption to the effect that the animal's desires don't change very quickly. Let's start with the strongest form of that assumption and pretend to be sure that the animal's basic desires are always the same. Then we search for some hypothesis about what those unchanging desires are and some general hypotheses about what the animal is apt to believe in various kinds of environments. We are looking for two bits of theory at once, each under its own constraint (the beliefs must relate systematically to the environments; the desires must always be the same), and together they must satisfy the further constraint of yielding belief-desire attributions that fit the animal's actual behavior.

The idea that the animal's desires are always the same is unrealistic. Let's drop it. Actually, there is no difficulty of principle in allowing that our animal's desires might change slowly over time. That still allows us to proceed in nearly the way I have described, with just a slight weakening of the independent constraint on the attributed desires. But might not some of the desires change quickly. Yes indeed. The animal wanted food an hour ago, but in the interim it has gorged; it wanted to play this morning, but now it is tired; it wanted sex five minutes ago, but now it is recovering from an orgasm. There is no threat to our theory from this kind of desire change, because changes of this kind are caused by and thus correlated with external observable changes in the animal's condition or circumstances. If our no-change-or-slow-change theory gets bogged down, and can't provide enough true predictions, we can then consider the possibility that the animal undergoes some fast changes of desire, and we can watch for the causes of these changes. If we find them, our control over the theory is restored. And if all goes well, we have a theory that predicts as well as explains. In principle, we can predict what our animal is going to do in the next minute or two because we know (a) what the belief-affecting features of its present environment are and how they affect its beliefs, and (b) what its long-term desires are and what, if any, features of its present circumstances are likely to alter those; so we have a basis for saying what it now thinks and wants, and from this we can infer what it will do.

(What if the animal's basic desires change rapidly with no external indications that this is going on? (The resultant behavior will indicate, too late for prediction, that it *has* gone on.) So far as I can see, the behavior of such an animal would be entirely unpredictable and therefore unexplainable. Such an animal, if there were one, would have to lie outside the purview of the cognitive ethologist.)

That four-point procedure is what saves ethology from the threat of complete and hopeless indeterminacy—the threat that any thought-want attribution can be challenged by some equally well-supported rival because a different belief attribution can always be made safe with help from an appropriate shift in the attributed desire. That is the threat to which we would be open if we followed the libertine procedure; but the anchoring of beliefs not only to behavioral outputs but also to sensory inputs gives us an independent grip, putting gravel under our feet so that we don't skid uncontrollably.

I don't mean to be offering the assurance of fully determinate results. Daniel Dennett (1987, chapter 2), with help from others, has made an unanswerable case for holding that there could be some indeterminacy: Given two somewhat different accounts of what an animal thinks and believes, there may not always be any fact of the matter as to which is correct. The question of how much determinacy there can be is an empirical one; it's no use pontificating about it before doing the work. I am inclined to agree with Dennett that there is a significant amount, that is, that in cognitive ethology it is inevitable that the data will underdetermine the theory by a good deal. But I see no reason to think, and neither does Dennett, that the underdetermination goes so far as to subvert the whole endeavor in the manner threatened by a careless and panicky look at the belief-desire-behavior triangle.

"HIGHER" AND "LOWER"

There is an impressive amount of disagreement over the conjectures through which ethologists seek to explain animal behavior. All the disagreements seem to have this form: John Doe offers data about animal behavior that he says are best explained by hypothesis H_1 about the animal in question, and Jane Doe says that those data can just as well be explained by hypothesis H_2 which is preferable to H_1 because it attributes less to the animal, is more economical, less generous, in what it says about the animal's mind. I don't have any hard-edged general account of what makes one hypothesis (let us say) "higher" than another, but some species of the genus are easy enough to mark out.

1. One hypothesis is higher than another if it attributes cognitive mentality while the other doesn't. For example, H_1 says that the lizard shot out its tongue because it wanted to catch a fly and thought that this was the way to catch one, whereas H_2 says that the lizard shot out its tongue because it received a visual stimulus of kind K and had been habituated — or is hard-wired — to make that kind of tongue movement on the receipt of that type of stimulus.

2. H_1 is higher than H_2 if the thoughts it attributes are more complex than those attributed by the other. For example, H_1 says "The dog is digging there because it thinks that it buried a bone there earlier and thinks that buried bones stay put", while H_2 says "The dog is digging there because it thinks there is a bone there." We may have evidence that if H_2 is true, H_1 must also be true, that is, the dog thinks that the bone is there now because it thinks that that's where it put the bone and believes that buried bones stay put. But in the absence of extra reasons for that view of the matter, if the behavioral facts are well enough explained by H_2, then it should win out over H_1.

3. If H_2 attributes thoughts that are only about the superficial sensorily given features of things, whereas H_1 attributes thoughts that are not so confined, then H_1 is higher than H_2. For example, H_1 says that the monkey called in that way because it wanted its companions to think there was a leopard nearby; H_2 says that it gave the call because it wanted its companions to climb into trees. Both of these explanations involve cognitive mentality, and neither is clearly much more complex than the other; but H_1 counts as higher because it attributes to the animal a desire to make the others believe something (a thought about a thought) whereas H_1 attributes merely a desire to get the others to do something (a thought about a movement).

I have a few ideas about how to pull all this together into a unitary generic account of what it is for one hypothesis to be higher than another, but they are still too incomplete to be worth presenting. Supposing (as I now shall) that we have a usable notion of higher and lower, and that we agree that we ought always to prefer the lowest hypothesis that will satisfactorily explain the behavioral facts, what use are we to make of this in practice?

TESTING MENTALISTIC HYPOTHESES

Dennett (1983) offered some help with this in his first venture into real-world cognitive ethology. In essence, his offering had two items in it: (a) the principle of rationality, which says that *ceteris paribus* we are entitled to assume that an animal will do what it thinks will achieve its goals, and (b) Lloyd Morgan's canon, which says that *ceteris paribus* we should always prefer the lower to the higher of two mentalistic hypotheses.

The former of these is right. Indeed, it is fundamental to the project of cognitive ethology in a way that Dennett does not bring out. The most elemental move that gets cognitive ethology under way is that of finding principles about what the animal is likely to believe in given kinds of environments and finding goals that can be attributed to it, that will let one reasonably conjecture that the animal does A because it wants G and thinks that doing A will produce G. Without that last part, which is just an application of the rationality principle, neither beliefs nor desires can be connected with behavior at all.

Dennett's other offering is right too. Without it, cognitive ethology is possible but is so unconstrained, so undisciplined, as not to be worth doing.

The two offerings taken together constitute a testing procedure for mentalistic hypotheses. To test hypothesis H, according to which the animal thinks that P and wants G, attend to it in a situation where that thought and that belief would lead a rational animal to do A and see whether it does A. If it doesn't, H is false. If it survives that test, there is another to which it can be subjected. Examine the animal's behavior that might be explained by H, and consider whether some lower hypothesis might explain it just as well. If so, then H is condemned as unacceptable. In my not very satisfactory comments on that paper of Dennett's, I was (without realizing it) struggling with two thoughts at once: (a) Dennett had provided only a negative testing procedure, and cognitive ethologists need help with devising hypotheses in the first place, and (b) Dennett hadn't said enough about what it is for a given hypothesis to fit or cover or prima facie explain a range of behavioral data. He left to mere intuition the decisions about what a given hypothesis has in the way of prima facie rivals. I don't now think that there is much in the first of these two ideas, but there is some force in the second. It would be a pity if we couldn't get beyond Dennett's two-part recipe, so that when an ethologist came up with a mentalistic hypothesis and tried and failed to find any lower rivals to it, he merely sat trembling, hoping that no more ingenious and mean-minded colleague would succeed where he had failed. Could we not at least provide some general guide concerning where and how to look for rivals? I think we can, as I now try to show.

THE GUIDING RULE

For simplicity's sake, let us suppose that our animal's goals don't change, that each of them generates desires that the animal sometimes thinks it can satisfy through its own behavior, and that such beliefs never bring into play two desires that cannot both be satisfied (Bennett, 1976, sections 18–20). Then all we have to look at are the different situations in which this animal thinks there is something it can do that will lead to the satisfaction of one of its desires. Let us look into the class of behavioral episodes in which we think that the animal aims to satisfy desire D, for example, the desire to get food.

Cognitive explanations are not supported if the relevant behavior is all covered by this: Whenever the animal picks up a trace of chemical C in the water, it waves its tentacles and then brings them towards its mouth. That plainly invites explanation in terms of simple stimulus-response triggers giving no purchase to explanation in terms of wants and thoughts. Why? For two reasons: (a) The class of situations in which the behavior occurs can be marked out without reference to anything of the form "evidence that doing A will produce food", and (b) the class of behaviors can be marked out without reference to "getting food". The facts are adequately caught in the statement that whenever the animal has such and such a *stimulus*-kind of input, it produces such and such a *motor*-kind of output.

Here is a first approximation to the contrasting case: The class of behaviors to be generalized over involves inputs whose simplest or only unified description is that in each of them the environment is such that there is something the animal can do that will bring it food; and involves outputs that are united only in that in each of them the animal moves in some way that results in its getting food. But that is only a first approximation. It would be right only if our animal never went wrong about what would bring it food. I am content to use simplifying, idealizing assumptions so that the discussion doesn't get bogged down in details, but the possibility of error is much too important to be idealized away.

So we need to replace that account of the class of inputs by something like this: Each of the relevant environments is, given the animal's perceptual apparatus and its quality space etc., significantly similar to ones in which there is something the animal can do that will bring food. I shall designate as "the comparison set" for a given behavioral episode A the class of environments that (a) are relevantly similar to the one in which A occurs, and (b) are such that in each of them there really is something the animal can do that will bring it food. Then I can give an amended description of the outputs, namely: On each occasion, the animal moves in a way that would bring it food if the environment were a member of the comparison set. Of course in most cases the environment *is* a member of the comparison set, but if we don't make allowance for the possibility of error, our account will be too drastically idealized and oversimplified.

(There might be some slight misperformance on the animal's part — a slip of the paw, a tiny but significant failure of aim — such that even if the environment were as the animal thinks it is, the goal still wouldn't be achieved. But we would want such a behavioral episode to be explainable in terms of the animal's having that goal. So, strictly speaking, I ought to have said . . . moves in a way that would be likely to bring it food if . . . or . . . moves in a way that would nearly bring it food if. . . . That would provide for the possibility of failure of execution, which is different from failure as a result of cognitive error.)

Now, both versions of the input side of the story involve the notion of food-getting behavior: In the simple version, each environment is one where the animal can get food; in the version that allows for error, each environment is significantly like ones in which the animal can get food. The notion of the animal's getting food can't be replaced by anything unitary that doesn't involve that, and that it why it is legitimate to explain these behavioral episodes in terms of the animal's thinking that what it is doing will get it food. If there were some single stimulus kind of sensory input — a particular kind of patch in its visual field, a particular kind of smell, or the like — such that on each relevant occasion the animal received a stimulus of that kind, then these behaviors would not support the attribution of wants and thoughts about getting food. *The getting-food content is justified by the need for the notion of food-getting in characterizing the class of environments in which the behavior occurs.*

My guiding rule applies not only to the question of whether it is all right to attribute content, but also to the question of what content to attribute. Did the monkey want its companions to *believe there was a leopard nearby* or merely to *climb a tree?* (I am assuming that the former is higher than the latter.) To have decent evidence that the former attribution is right, we need a class of behaviors in which it is not always the case that the animal's behavior is apt to get its companions to climb trees. If the monkeys can use the information that a leopard is nearby in various ways, and animal X's warning cries occur when any one of these uses could be made of the information, the relevant class of environments is marked off as containing all and only environments where X can behave in a manner that will get its companions to *behave in a manner appropriate to the information that there is a leopard nearby.* Just as in the earlier example, the class of environments is unified with help from the concept of food-getting, which justifies putting food-getting into the animal's goal and thus its belief, so in this example the class of environments is unified with help from the concept of *behaving in a manner appropriate to the information that there is a leopard nearby;* so we are entitled to put *that* into the animal's goal and into its belief. And that is going to pass muster for the animal's having a goal and a belief concerning the others' *believing* that there is a leopard nearby: in the absence of language, there is no chance of getting nearer than that to thoughts and and wants regarding the beliefs of others.

THE OUTPUT SIDE OF THE STORY

What about the output side? I said that we get from a stimulus-response explanation of the behavior to a cognitive one through the move from (1_i) the case where the relevant inputs belong to a single stimulus-kind to (2_i) the case where they are united only by their similarity to situations where the animal can get food. Could we not also make the ascent from stimulus-response to cognition through a move from (1_o) the case where the relevant outputs belong to a single motor-kind to (2_o) the case where they are united only by their being (to put it briefly) apt for the getting of food?

The move from (1_o) to (2_o) is certainly not needed. If the inputs have the right kind of unity, it doesn't matter if the outputs have a unity of a lower kind. Suppose that in each member of the class of episodes we are interested in, the animal simply utters a warning call — there is no significant variation from call to call, but there is a great variation in the physical kinds of situation in which the call is uttered because the animal takes a wide variety of different states of affairs to be clues to the presence of a predator. There is good enough reason here to say that the animal's warning calls are evidence that it thinks there is a predator nearby even though the relevant complexity is all on the input side, with none in the output. (I here modify slightly the stand I took in Bennett 1976, in the light of a criticism in Peacocke, 1981, p. 216.) I presented just such a case in the preceding section.

Then is the move from (1_o) to (2_o) sufficient on its own to justify the attribution of cognitive content? There is no answer to that question because there couldn't be such a case, that is, one where there is a lower unity in the inputs but only a higher unity in the outputs. If there were, the animal's pursuits of a certain kind of goal would be triggered by some relatively simple kind of stimulus with no significant differences among the occasions on the input side, but would be executed by a variety of different kinds of movements that have in common only their being apt to produce the goal. For example, a certain characteristic kind of smell or sound sometimes leads the animal to run, sometimes to climb, sometimes to dig, and usually the behavior in question leads to its getting food. This is just magic. In the actual unmagical world, appropriate behavioral variation is made possible by matching variation of sensory clues: The animal jumps to the left one time and to the right next time because of differences in what it sees or hears, or smells or feels. But here we have a story that credits the animal with a useful behavioral variation while excluding any possible explanation of how that is managed.

REFERENCES

Arnauld, A. (1964–1976). Fourth objections to the *meditations*. In C. Adam and P. Tannery (Eds.), *Oeuvres de Descartes* (p. 205). Vrin: Paris.

Bennett, J. (1976). *Linguistic behaviour.* Cambridge: Cambridge University Press.

Dennett, D. (1987). *The intentional stance.* Cambridge, MA: M.I.T. Press.

Dennett, D. C. (1983). Intentional systems in cognitive ethology: The "Panglossian Paradigm" defended. *Behavioral and Brain Sciences, 6,* 343–90.

Nagel, E. (1979). Teleology revisited. In *Teleology and other essays* (pp. 275–316). New York: Columbia University Press.

Peacocke, C. (1981). Demonstrative thought and psychological explanation. *Synthese, 49,* 187–217.

Tolman, E. C. (1932). *Purposive behavior in men and animals.* New York: The Century Co., 1932.

PART II:
EVIDENCE FROM THE
LABORATORY AND FIELD

4 COGNITIVE ETHOLOGY AND CRITICAL ANTHROPOMORPHISM: A SNAKE WITH TWO HEADS AND HOGNOSE SNAKES THAT PLAY DEAD

Gordon M. Burghardt
University of Tennessee

ABSTRACT

Cognitive ethologists must keep issues of cognition analytically separate from other mental phenomena such as affect and consciousness. Such is important in considering cognition in reptiles, two examples of which are presented here. Close study of predation in a two-headed rat snake shows how evolutionary constraints might affect all levels of mental activity. Over 5 years the incidence of fighting over which head swallowed prey was not reduced, but the two heads did equally partition energy expenditures. The complex antipredator display of the hognose snake is highly variable even among neonates from the same clutch. They also have the ability to monitor their environment in an apparently adaptive manner when they are in the quiescent death-feign phase. The applicability of intention theory and Griffin's (1984) characterization of conscious awareness to this behavior is considered. Critical anthropomorphism is elaborated as a more general heuristic method related to recent philosophical work on critical realism and evolutionary epistemology. Jacob von Uexküll (1909) is highlighted as a neglected pioneer in the study of animal mentality.

Our anthropocentric way of looking at things must retreat further and further, and the standpoint of the animal must be the only decisive one (von Uexküll, 1909/1985, p. 223).

The early post-Darwinian comparative psychologists were very sympathetic to the kinds of cognitive questions Griffin (1976) posed in his initial attempt to establish a cognitive ethology and break the shackles of a mindless behaviorism (Burghardt, 1985). But these early attempts at comparative cognition fell into disfavor and were disparaged by most psychologists until recently. This probably explains why Griffin did not try to build on them but rather relied on contemporary philosophers in developing his perspective. In what follows I will return to some early students of behavior as well as the contributions of selected philosophers as I consider some aspects of the mentality of reptiles, a phylogenetically important but neglected group.

COGNITION AND REPTILES

A psychologist who studies snakes? That may bewilder the average person but not the ethologist, especially if the research aim is to understand their naturalistic behavior. But one looks in vain in recent books on animal cognition (e.g., Griffin, 1984; Pearce, 1987; Roitblat, 1987; Weiskrantz, 1985) for any examples of awareness or cognition even suggested for reptiles or amphibians. Their brains may be mentioned in passing, but it appears generally accepted that such lower vertebrates are just not where one is going to obtain those fruitful examples that will either convince skeptics or uncover mechanisms (c.f. Dennett, 1987).

There is a history here in which we are caught. Consider George Romanes' book titled *Animal Intelligence* (1882). Romanes was Darwin's protégé whose goal was to construct a phylogeny of mind and consciousness. In his survey Romanes does cover amphibians and reptiles, but it is clear that they were of little interest to him. "On the intelligence of frogs and toads very little has to be said" (p. 254). Note that Romanes didn't say that little *can* be said, which implies a lack of study, but that little needs to be said at all! He did allow some emotions and intellect for reptiles. Perhaps his most telling example is that of an English woman and her family's pet boa constrictor (python?). One day her husband had an apoplectic fit and she rushed off to fetch a doctor. Imagine her surprise when they returned (10 minutes later) to her husband's upstairs bedroom and found the snake stretched out on the master's bed dead as a doornail. Apparently the snake, perhaps not too healthy itself, had crawled upstairs from its downstairs lair and, Romanes speculates, upon the sight of its stricken master, died from the shock. I submit that even today a similar story involving a dog might be sympathetically received and might even stimulate a few tears and stifled sniffles if told with sufficient sincerity.

The week before I gave the talk on which this chapter is based I came across a recent and better documented case (albeit in a tabloid) showing the sensitivity of a reptile that actually saved a human life (McGuire, 1987). A small African boy was standing by a dock watching a tourist boat pass by. The boy fell in. A huge crocodile appeared as a crew member of the boat prepared to dive in to save the child. The crew member hesitated, (understandably), and, to the horror of onlookers on both shore and boat, the boy disappeared underwater with the croc. But then the boy suddenly appeared supine and safe on the back of the croc, which then swam to the shore, flipped the child safely onto the bank, and calmly returned to the deep. I think that such a story about a dolphin, even less documented, would be far more readily accepted. Why is this the case? There are two main reasons: (a) crocs have an image problem in terms of benign behavior and appearance, and (b) their relatively small brains and perceived lack of intelligence would seem to preclude thoughtful altruistic behavior, even if derived from parental responses, as are considered responsible for similar human rescues by dolphins.

This second reason highlights one of the main attractions Griffin's writings have had for me: He particularly discounts the dogma that large brains are critical for cognitive processes — including thought and awareness. He has done this in reference to honeybees and other insects, arguing that "thinking" may make up for a lack of brain tissue sufficient to have all contingencies hard-wired genetically. But Griffin and others have avoided reptiles, which as derivations of the ancestral stock from which both mammals and birds arose, should be, but have not been, studied for the phylogenetic precursors of complex behavior and their underlying mechanisms. Because cognitive abilities are themselves evolved, it is not parsimonious to merely assume such abilities arose *de novo* in endotherms. Reptiles often operate on a different (slower) time scale than endotherms and, to us, they do not seem particularly expressive. These are but two factors, among many others, that might be responsible for their neglect. The relevant work on reptiles is of rather considerable scope and warrants consulting (Burghardt, 1977, 1984, 1988).

COGNITION AND COGNITIVE ETHOLOGY

No one really doubts that virtually all animals can remember the location of food, pay attention to certain sensory cues more than others, or orient themselves in time and space. But now it is again appreciated, as it was by the early comparative psychologists, that such abilities pose questions that go beyond the sophisticated simplicity of traditional conditioning models.

Recently, standard animal learning theory in psychology was rehabilitated and refurbished: Attributes such as memory, attention, concept formation, and perceptual discriminations have been called the core of the new comparative cognition (e.g., Pearce, 1987; Roitblat, 1987). Older views, influenced by more recent information, decision, and optimization theories, have been systematized and given new labels such as representation, working and reference memory, and serial anticipation learning. Note that formally, at least, issues of emotion, consciousness, subjective states, and other experiential processes are not incorporated. Griffin's writings have been more eclectic in this respect (Burghardt, 1985). His early statement on cognitive ethology emphasized awareness and subjective concomitants of mental life (Griffin, 1976); his more recent writings have converged to some extent on the psychologists' focus on learning and thinking, although they still incorporate conscious awareness (Griffin, 1984). To Griffin and many others coming out of ethological and evolutionary traditions (Jolly, this volume; Whiten & Bryne, 1988) anthropomorphism, anecdotes, and the attribution of subjective experience to animals are not the egregious errors behavioristic psychologists thought they had expunged from scientific discourse. Although the behaviorists may not have been totally justified in their position and were undoubtedly compromised by their lack of biological knowledge, it is also fair to say that ethologists jumping into the fray too often have not carefully considered the implications of bandying about common-sense mentalistic terms in relation to animals no matter how obviously valid they seemed to be.

Familiarity with the analyses of prebehavioristic psychologists by all parties in the awareness controversy might have led to more focused arguments that brought out the real issues sooner. Too often protagonists have merely talked without listening, each feeling the other missed the entire point of his or her argument.

Romanes (1883) was only following a long tradition when he divided his phylogeny of mental evolution into three categories: (a) intellect, (b) will, and (c) emotion. McDougall (e.g., 1923) refined this tripartite scheme in his discussion of the three aspects of all mental activity: (a) the cognitive, (b) the conative, and (c) the affective. Will and conative encompass what today is called motivation. Consciousness could be an integral part of all three aspects, as McDougall held, but such ubiquitous consciousness is too diffuse and diverse to be considered a unitary construct capable of direct study. And if mental processes are evolved, as Darwin held, then so are all their components; it should have been apparent that no master key would unlock the mysteries of the animal mind, for this does not exist.

There is thus a contrast between a focus on cognitive processes that, in principle, could be duplicated by the output of a machine or computer and affective (emotional) states, subjective experiences, and so on. The conflation of such analytically separate issues has been a major source of controversy and misunderstanding. Awareness or consciousness is inferred to be present by floating criteria that necessarily differ as a function of which of the above are at issue as well as by species, behavior, context, and a host of other variables. It is also one thing to assert that conscious awareness is essential for all cognition as defined by psychologists, which includes the simplest kinds of learning, and using cognitive functioning as evidence for conscious awareness. Typically, awareness and consciousness—from Romanes to Griffin—are indicated by, but not restricted to, complex behavior involving a choice or decision.

In this chapter "mental" is associated with relatively complex behavior encompassing both subjective states (e.g., consciousness, awareness, feelings) and thought processes. Academic cognitive ethology does seem to be focusing more on the strictly cognitive as opposed to awareness or the affective, as both the difficulties of studying the latter and the lack of a necessary link between the two become apparent (Burghardt, 1985). On the other hand, the focus on the affective has come to the fore in animal welfare issues and is increasingly a major emphasis of applied animal ethology (e.g., Dawkins, 1980), which has itself been greatly influenced by Griffin's writings. Ristau (1983) has explicitly made the point that pain and suffering are the major issues in guiding animal use in experimentation, not cognitive or communicatory abilities.

IM

I spent a year at Rockefeller where I shared my office with IM, a two-headed black rat snake, in Griffin's lab. He was named IM back in 1976 when first found as a juvenile in Oak Ridge; the name was derived from the left head being called "Instinct" and the right head "Mind." The snake's frequent conflicts over prey (Fig. 4.1), usually mice, vividly reminded me of the perennial conflict between these two concepts, both outcasts in respectable discourse after the behavioristic revolution (Burghardt, 1978). Everyone watching IM feed or locomote readily agreed that there was often an obvious conflict occurring between what each of the two heads (i.e., brains or minds) "wanted" to do. In some respects there was perhaps no better subject than an IM for addressing problems of intention, communication, problem solving, decision making, and the locus of control. If a normal snake has cognitive abilities or awareness, did IM allow us to more clearly specify what this means?

Anterior axial bifurcation is anomalous in all vertebrates; it occurs most often in snakes (Cunningham, 1937; Smith & Pérez-Higareda, 1987). Our snake had two equally well-developed and symmetrical heads although the left head was shifted from the main axis (Fig. 4.2). Both were highly responsive to stimuli and often tongue-flicked. Tongue-flicking, associated with chemoreception via the vomeronasal organ, is the primary behavioral measure of curiosity and exploration in snakes (e.g., Chiszar, Carter, Knight, Simonsen, & Taylor, 1976) and many lizards (e.g., Burghardt, Allen, & Frank, 1986). We studied IM to understand the behavioral mechanisms where two genetically identical (presumably) brains control the same body.

Fig. 4.1 IM, a two-headed black rat snake (*Elaphe obsoleta*), struggling with himself over which head will swallow a mouse.

But how to investigate this animal? We tried a number of tactics, but our main problem was that we had just one unusual animal and many traditional techniques were just not applicable or safe. It made me aware of the need for more scientifically viable techniques for studying a single subject — a need also recognized by the animal welfare movement (Still, 1982). Too often the stigma attached to anecdotes has led to scientists worshiping at the altar of large N's and disparaging extensive data from only one or a few subjects.

We carried out experiments on the interaction between the two heads involving prey-trailing, olfactory arousal, and locomotor decision making. Additionally, for the first 5 years virtually all the snake's feedings were recorded involving over 400 prey (small rodents, primarily mice). Among the variables measured were prey size, striking head, strike latency, part of prey struck, occurrence and duration of constriction and conflicts between heads, ingesting head, prey swallowing direction, and ingestion latency. Although short-term shifts in head dominance were frequent over the years, and there was a 20-fold increase in the snake's weight), the behavior of the snake was remarkably consistent (Burghardt & Batts, 1981).

Relative prey size was the most important influence on the feeding sequence. The left head struck significantly more often at smaller prey, and the right head struck more at larger prey. Both heads also frequently struck

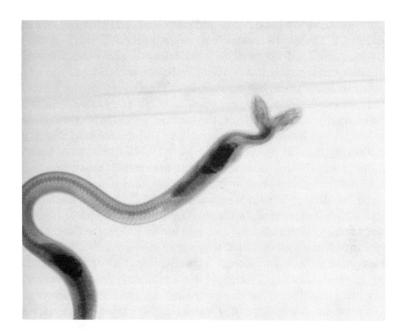

Fig. 4.2 A radiograph of IM showing the arrangement of both heads and a barium sulfate injected mouse just swallowed by the left head and another mouse eaten earlier.

simultaneously. Regardless of whether one or both heads struck, both heads often simultaneously attempted to swallow the prey, frequently lengthening ingestion from minutes to an hour or more. If the heads were aware of this delay and that the food was going to the same place, one head should give up and allow the other to swallow. But competition between the heads was never extinguished or reduced significantly although what head "won" could be predicted from knowing prey size, striking head(s), where the prey was struck, and so on. But notice the conflation here; being aware of something doesn't mean that one is able to adaptively modify one's behavior — even with human beings. But a frequently postulated function of awareness is that it allows the animal the ability to modify behavior in a way that strictly hard-wired responses do not. But even if the snake had showed a reduction in conflicts over time, a strict conditioning interpretation could have been proposed with rapid ingestion as the reinforcer. Certainly snakes do typically swallow prey as quickly as physically possible. This appears functional due to the need to shorten the period when a snake is most vulnerable to predators.

In addition, a close look at the data revealed that the two heads partitioned their prey resources by size such that each head ingested virtually the same mass of food over the years and spent almost identical times handling it (Table 4.1). This was accomplished through different thresholds by each head for striking, constriction, and other behavior. Thus, although behaviorally the conflicts were not reduced and the snake did not seem to learn the obvious, long-term monitoring of the behavior showed that the two heads partitioned resources so that equivalent amounts were ingested with equal effort. Thus, the message from IM is that different measures of adaptive behavior lead to contrary results (see also discussion of decision theory later in this chapter).

Is the lack of apparently rational behavior between IM's two heads any more surprising than that found in split-brain humans (Gazzaniga, 1972)? Perhaps a better analogy is with identical twins. My twin daughters are 30 months old and it is clear that, while they frequently cooperate, the most rational (or mutually optimal) solution for sharing is often not taken. Yet, as with all normal children this age, they are often perceptive, aware, and even introspective although we do not expect children to be as rational as adults are supposed to be. The focus on optimality models (variously defined) is often considered to be the major achievement of behavioral ecology. But the entire ethology of a species as well as cognitive, physiological, and other limitations must be considered in discussions of optimal or rational behavior. For example, it might be relevant to know that a snake will attack food held in another animal's jaws and compete for it, even if other easily obtainable prey is lying around the cage. Such food kleptoparasitism is widespread but little understood (Burghardt & Denny, 1983); the nature of its neural wiring and adaptive function might preclude a two-headed snake from overcoming this competing behavior system in developing overt "rational" cooperation between the two heads.

Today the emphasis is often on how genetically related conspecifics tend to cooperate for mutual genetic benefits, whereas unrelated animals compete. We tend to ignore the frequent disputes among organisms in forced proximity regardless of relationship. In the case of IM we may be seeing the

TABLE 4.1
Prey Ingestion Data for a Two-headed Rat Snake over a 5-year Period

Head	Search Time[a] (hr)	Handling Time[b] (hr)	Total Time Cost[c] (hr)	Prey Ingested (g)	Profitability[d] (g/hr)
Left	4.21	17.58	21.37	1260.7	58.99
Right	3.32	20.00	22.40	1310.6	58.51

[a]Strike Latencies
[b]Ingestion Latencies
[c]Search Time + Handling Time
[d]Prey Ingestion/Total Time Cost

importance of prior evolutionary history as an important constraint on altruistic and cooperative behaviors—constraints holding all mental processes on leashes of varying lengths. All two-headed snakes are monsters with no evolutionary history for dealing with the problems faced by having a siamese sibling. Given the unprecedented problems facing our own species today, IM should not be too quickly dismissed as an irrelevant freak!

BEHAVIORISM AND MENTAL CONSTRUCTS

Part of the controversy concerning the use of cognitive constructs in studying and interpreting what animals and humans do is the inability to directly observe the putative processes involved. Both psychology and ethology have long known that many terms such as hunger, aggressivity, timidity, and impulsiveness are organismal attributes inferred from behavioral data. Behaviorists, in particular, have pointed out the limitations of such unitary constructs since different measures often correlate poorly. Yet we use them, with good effect, as heuristic shorthand.

What early ethological critics of behaviorism were most offended by was the nonnaturalistic, even antievolutionary, tendencies of the behaviorists. What behaviorists were suspicious of in the cognitive realm (that to them was inextricably tied to dualism, subjectivism, introspection, and other errors) was the difficulty of testing ideas based on assertion or theoretical constructs impervious to falsification. But behaviorists have also been guilty of posthoc explanations in their meta-theory. Consider how Skinner (1984) responded to analysis of his canonical papers years after they first appeared. No empirical data appearing over a 50-year period led to an explicit admission of any error. Although comprehensive world views (i.e., Skinner's & Freud's) may provide us with a framework for handling all sorts of information, they usually are not capable of formulating tests of their own validity.

Thus I was intrigued with a recent article by Leonard Eron (1987) that looked at the changes in how his research group has interpreted data from a 22-year longitudinal study of the development of aggressive behavior in children. The original study was based on a Hull-Spence learning theory model and the original data seemed to fit it. But as more data accumulated, an operant framework was found to provide an even better fit, and later a social learning approach as espoused by Bandura and Berkowitz was even more enlightening. Finally, the insights of what Eron terms "cognitive behaviorism" were applied and found most useful. Two points about this study are important. First, the ability to apply different formulations to interpreting their findings was due to an explicit focus on behavior. "The methodology, from the beginning, has been essentially behaviorally based:

The variables have been explicitly defined, and the measures have stemmed directly from these definitions. Thus, aspects of the data are relevant to any of these models" (p. 435). The second point is the critical importance of an eclecticism based on (a) being open to better models regardless of the theory behind them and (b) having sufficient knowledge of and interest in diverse approaches to be able to apply them to one's work. The ability of Griffin and others to reinterpret findings established in the literature by noncognitive workers is testimony to the continuing value of a rigorous behavioral approach. It is the lack of such behavioral data, as well as good natural history, that doomed the earlier comparative mentalism (Burghardt, 1985).

It is also probable that in the future we will be able to monitor neural phenomena that directly correlate with independent measures of cognitive processes that occur during decision making, problem solving, and so on. Rapid eye movements during dreams and increased pupil size during problem solving (Hess, 1975) were early examples of this growing area. Although it is true that such correlations do not say anything about the subjective states themselves, they can tell us whether cognitive, conative, or affective processes are present, just as the presence of cones in the retina of vertebrates is a good indication that wavelength discrimination is present. If a species has the ability to discriminate wavelengths, almost everyone would unabashedly say the animal has color vision—even those who know that color is by definition a subjective experience.

THE MAGNIFICENT DISPLAY OF THE HOGNOSE SNAKE

One of the most complex and fast-paced behavioral sequences known for a reptile is the antipredator display of the hognose snake (*Heterodon platirhinos*). Reports of this remarkable behavior go back to the earliest encounters with this animal in eastern America, and the current literature is reviewed by Greene (1988).

When the hognose snake is approached in the field, it may first remain motionless, move off, or emit prolonged conspicuous tongue flicks. If approached more closely (about a meter), it may coil and puff up the body, expand the neck like a cobra, or hiss (or "blow," hence the name blowing adder). The tail may be raised, and the head and neck become dorsalventrally flattened; the latter adds to the appearance of a viper-like triangular head. At this time the snake may lunge and strike, often in a jerky manner. The mouth is rarely if ever open during these lunges, and biting does not occur. If the intruder persists, the snake may attempt to flee, but when touched (and sometimes when not touched), the snake may begin an erratic writhing behavior—often frenetic and violent—and may even bite itself in the process. It defecates (or discharges its cloacal sacs), coils its tail like a pig's, turns over, and finally becomes quiescent: mouth open, tongue extruded, blood coming from mouth, and with no evident breathing. Further defecation may take place at this time. The snake can be carried, poked, and so forth with no signs of life. The only flaw is that if turned right-side up it will turn upside down at once. If human instigators of the behavior leave and later return, they are usually amazed to find the snake gone. The death-feigning and recovery phases are shown in Fig. 4.3.

So here is the behavior of interest; a dramatic performance that appears to have an antipredator function although there seems to be no empirical evidence, not even any convincing anecdotes. Nonetheless, it seems certain the display has a defensive function. At this point we turn to a consideration of the final quiescent stage which many animals exhibit.

DEATH FEIGNING

Darwin (1883), in his posthumously published essay on instinct, discussed some of the many examples of animals becoming immobile and apparently playing dead. This has led to much discussion and the coining of many terms in the literature including animal hypnosis, akinesia, thanatosis, fright paralysis, catalepsy, cataplexy, bewitchment, sham death, and paroxysmal inhibition (Gallup, 1974). Today the favored term is tonic immobility, about which many studies have been published, most of them involving domestic chicks. Tonic immobility and death feigning have been largely ignored in recent treatments of animal cognition or consciousness. The recent chapters by Jones (1987a, 1987b) on chickens are an exception. A possible explanation is tendered in the subsequent paragraphs.

Animals may have the ultimate goal of spreading their genes to the next generation, but staying alive seems to be the immediate problem facing most animals especially young ones. Although finding food and shelter may be critical, nothing produces an acute crisis more threatening to continued existence then a sudden confrontation with a predator. It might be thought that any mental agility an animal has might be most on call at this time. Of course, many effective strategies in this context do not really draw on thinking a great deal: fleeing, motionless crypticity, fighting with sharp teeth and claws, injecting venom, being aposematic (warningly colored). In fact, hesitating to think could be a fatal mistake. Nonetheless, attempting to deceive one's harasser is a risky strategy and paying close attention to what the predator is doing might be critical. Here I refer to displays composed of several stages that are variable and adjusted to circumstances in a nonreflexive way.

Elsewhere in this volume Ristau discusses her work on the broken wing display in ground nesting birds such as plovers that seems to be flexibly

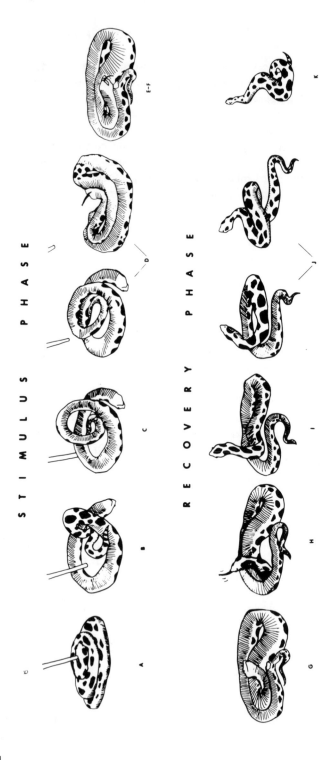

Fig. 4.3 Phases in the death-feigning response of the hognose snake. Phases A–F: writhing to quiescent phase as induced by slight poking of snake with a stick. Phases G–K: typical behavioral sequence of the recovery phase.

adapted to preventing a terrestrial predator from locating her nest and destroying her brood. Here I consider an equally complex behavior that is directed at saving the displayer's life. After all, parents who fail to save their brood can live to breed again.

Darwin clearly related death feigning to escape from predators and thus the operation of natural selection. He was careful to make two points, however. First, most immobile responses by animals do not really look like the animal when dead. The implication is that cessation of motion may lead to the breaking off of an attack by a predator in spite of the victim not looking dead. Indeed this seems substantiated when snakes prey on crickets (Herzog & Burghardt, 1974), when gamecocks fight one another (Herzog, 1978), and when ducks are captured by foxes (Sergeant & Eberhardt, 1975). Based on the analysis of dozens of bear attacks on humans, Herrero (1985) has recommended that when attacked by a grizzly bear, an often effective strategy is to drop to the ground, roll up in a fetal position hiding the head, and remaining motionless – scarcely the way dead bodies are found.

Darwin's second point was that immobility may be a response to excessive fear. ". . . the paralyzing effects of excessive fear have sometimes been mistaken for the simulation of death" (p. 363). The implication is that fear as a postulated mechanism can also be divorced from death feigning.

Although some biologists use the term *letisimulation* instead of death feigning, it is true to say that most have had no problem seeing such responses as adaptive. But they have stayed at the ultimate, evolutionary, and functional levels, albeit without too much experimental data (see discussion of critical anthropomorphism later in this chapter). Psychologists and physiologists have generally ignored the functional aspects and focused on the proximate mechanisms. A long series of studies by Gallup and coworkers (e.g., Gallup, 1974) has established that tonic immobility might well function in a predatory context, but the focus has been on sorting out possible proximate explanations with the probable winner being fear. Now if fear is a motivational process and not just an affective state – the end result of environmental and internal stimulation – then invoking fear only sets the stage for inquiring into the function of fear. Fear can be healthy and not just a paralyzing nonadaptive trait as too often envisioned by the image of a person paralyzed with fear and unable to move from the track as a steam locomotive comes barreling down at high speed.

Fear as both a motivational and emotional process probably derived from predatory or conspecific aggression. Its origin from neonatal separation from parents is less likely because it occurs in reptiles and other vertebrates without parental care although the communicatory expressions of fear could very well be so derived (Burghardt, 1988). Regardless, immobility could have evolved first with the suite of characteristics we term fear evolving later. On the other hand, if fear was present first it could have been n expressed in several adaptive defensive response systems both passive and active. Nonetheless, it seems clear that there is a subset of immobility responses termed death feigning, which is a risky defensive strategy that is both relatively rare and largely separate from tonic immobility as studied in the laboratory. The latter generally involves inversion and physical restraint and no preliminary responses from the animal except perhaps escape attempts. Such immobility responses have been described in many birds and mammals and have been documented in many reptiles (Crawford, 1977).

Lefebvre and Sabourin (1977) have argued that true death feigning is a complex response found only in a few vertebrates such as vultures (Vogel, 1950) and opossums (Franq, 1969) and should not be lumped with simple tonic immobility. In these animals physical restraint is not necessary and detailed associated behaviors are added to the performance — behaviors that are not seen in tonic immobility. Physical contact, even shaking the opossum or vulture does seem necessary according to the original reports, but this is not required for the hognose (although it can facilitate the response). Certainly the behavior of the hognose snake falls into the category of behavior that includes the turkey vulture regurgitating carrion that was not very sweet-smelling to begin with, and the opossum that may presage its death feign with barred teeth but no biting. What the hognose adds is both a vigorous and aggressive but innocuous bluff attack phase and a dramatic "death" prior to the death feign. It is highly possible that the hognose display is an evolutionary elaboration and ritualization of response elements occurring prior to the immobile phase with the feign itself being derived from restraint-induced tonic immobility. For example, in our laboratory we have seen young garter snakes, *Thamnophis marcianus,* engage in head hiding and tail displays when approached. But when touched, especially in the neck region, the animal writhes violently for a brief period, defecates, entirely buries the head in its coils, and arches the curled up tail even higher over its body. Clearly, more comparative work is needed.

In an early influential review (Gilman & Marcuse, 1949), Darwin's death-mimicking view of some instances of immobility was rejected because it involved consciousness and voluntary behavior below the intellectual ability of subhumans or necessitated both a teleological "instinct to feign death" as well as predators that "had an instinct to avoid death-feigning, or dead animals" (p. 162). Much later Ratner (1967) pointed out that only survival of animals performing the behavior was necessary, and no accompanying knowledge, insight, or consciousness by the performer was needed. We can see here a prime example of the confusion between proximate and ultimate (natural selection) explanations. The evolutionary survival view says nothing about the mechanism employed. Thus, how the behavior works cannot be addressed from an adaptive framework alone. Various theories of the mechanism of death feigning, whether they are based on fear, catatonia, hypnosis, spatial disorientation, cerebral inhibition, sign stimulus-fixed action pattern responses, or conscious deception, need to be evaluated in their own right. Also, it may very well be the case that more than one mechanism may be involved simultaneously. Images, goals, and expectations carefully defined can be attributed to aspects of mammalian behavior that cannot be readily incorporated in a behavioristic reinforcement paradigm (Mook, 1987). Why not snakes?

The presumed complexity of an inferred state is important in our judgment of its mental status. Romanes (1883) reflected current prejudice in his rankings of the levels of emotion in animals. Fear was ranked with surprise in the lowest level of emotional development, deceitfulness was 10 units up and in the highest level. Is it thus surprising that today deception in animals is considered one of the highest accomplishments of animal cognition (e.g., Lockard, 1988; Russow, 1986; Whiten & Bryne, 1988). By focusing on fear as an explanation for immobility, psychologists and ethologists have missed the possible cognitive aspects of tonic immobility in general, and death feigning, the ultimate deceit, in particular.[1]

How can we determine whether death feigning involves cognition as well as utilize Griffin's (1984) more ambitious approach?

> . . . a widely applicable, if not all-inclusive, criterion of conscious awareness in animals is *versatile adaptability of behavior to changing circumstances and challenges.* If the animal does much the same thing regardless of the state of its environment or the behavior of other animals nearby, we are less inclined to judge that it is thinking about its circumstances or what it is doing. Consciously motivated behavior is more plausibly inferred when an animal behaves appropriately in a novel and perhaps surprising situation that requires specific actions not called for under ordinary circumstances. . . . the rarity of the challenge combined with the appropriateness and effectiveness of the response are important indicators of thoughtful actions. . . . This . . . criterion of consciousness implies that conscious thinking occurs only during learned behavior, but we should be cautious in accepting this belief as a rigid doctrine. (p. 37)

Note that the basic criterion of consciousness or awareness is "versatile adaptability" in the performance of appropriate and effective responses. That is, conscious awareness is derived from cognitive functioning itself inferred from behavioral observations. The hesitation to invoke learning as

---

[1]Some may argue that deceit and deception are really quite different, the former being necessarily intentional or conscious, but not the latter. Unfortunately for this view, my dictionary (Webster's New Collegiate) defines each in terms of the other. Mitchell (1986) provides a useful typology and historical survey of animal deception.

a necessary concomitant is also important, as we shall see, for the hognose example. Not only did many early writers argue that instinct was accompanied by consciousness (Burghardt, 1985), but it may also be a necessary concomitant in the study of neonate animals. William James (1890) asserted that every instinctive act in an animal with the ability to remember "must cease to be 'blind' after being once repeated, and must be accompanied with foresight of its 'ends' just so far as that end may have gone under the animal's cognizance" (p. 390). I hope to show that many of the characteristics outlined by Griffin apply to the hognose snake's display.

FURTHER CONSIDERATION OF THE MAGNIFICENT HOGNOSE DISPLAY

Preliminary Observations

Erich Klinghammer and I carried out an extensive series of tests on an adult female hognose caught in Indiana before and after she laid a clutch of eggs. In order to test the snake we developed a four-stage procedure. Stage 1 involved approaching to within .5 m and bending down over the snake. Stage 2 involved lightly touching the snake on head or neck with a hand or stick. In Stage 3 we stroked the snake's body, and in Stage 4 we actually lifted up the snake and shook it without turning it over.

One aspect that intrigued us was that the snake remained highly responsive. The literature indicated that habituation of the response was rapid and rarely occurred in captive animals. In contrast we found that the adult female gave the display many times over a 4 month period. The latency to the quiescent phase averaged less than 10 seconds over five separate test sessions involving dozens of tests. However, after the female laid a clutch of 20 eggs the mean latency jumped to 180 seconds and remained much higher than earlier up to the date she was released.

It was also interesting to note that the level of stimulation needed to induce the response declined over the 40 days. On the first day of testing (19 trials), Stage 4 stimulation (picking up) was always necessary. By the last 54 trials Stage 2 stimulation (light touch) was effective on over 70% of the trials. On the other hand, the duration of the time from onset of quiescence to recovery generally declined over time. In short, we see both sensitization or conditioning to the stimulus and habituation of the recovery phase.

Newly Hatched Animals

With Harry Greene's assistance, I carried out a series of experiments out on 40 newly hatched hognose snakes born to females captured in East

Tennessee. We were fortunate to obtain two clutches of eggs from wild-caught hognose snake females. Because others recorded that neonates give the display (see review in Greene, 1988), we decided to record it closely in a standardized protocol derived from our observations on the adult.

Here I will present data on variability among the snakes from one litter. Data were recorded on audio tape by an observer in an adjacent room who monitored the snake's behavior via a closed circuit television system.

Nineteen individually housed snakes were tested on their responses to repeated tests with a human intruder. The temperature in the room was 25 $\pm 1°C$. An escalating series of intrusive behaviors at 10-s intervals was performed, but only to the point that the snake turned itself over. The snake was placed in a square sand-filled arena 100 × 100 × 60 cm high. After 1 min the experimenter approached the snake and bent down over it to a distance of 25 cm (Stage 1). After 10-s a hand moved towards the snake and lightly touched it on the head/neck region (Stage 2). After 10-s more the hand gently stroked the snake's body (Stage 3), and after another 10-s the snake was lifted and shaken slightly for 5 sec but not inverted (Stage 4).

Once the snake was motionless the time of the following recovery behaviors were noted: breathing resumed, tongue retracted, mouth closed, first tongue-flick, head raised, head turned over, bouts of tongue-flicking, partial and then full body righting, yawning, and crawling away. Two minutes after the animal recovered and began moving, the test was repeated.

The display sequence on its four phases is shown in Table 4.2. When the snake is first approached, its head may be up and tongue flicks may (but not always) be given. We did not list the fact that the snake may attempt to flee or escape. In fact, escape attempts may also take place during the bluff and "dying" phases also. Given that such behavior is also common as well as individually variable and consistent in other neonate snakes in defensive contexts (Arnold & Bennett, 1984; Herzog & Burghardt, 1986, 1988), it is likely that fleeing is a primitive trait.

It can be seen that each of the four phases consists of 5–11 largely topographically distinct behaviors. Not all snakes exhibited all behaviors. In Table 4.3 the variation of the 19 animals is summarized. They were given varying numbers of trials depending on their responsivity. Note that all snakes showed some important elements of the bluff display but that four never went beyond this to the feign stage. Of the animals who did feign, 73% habituated. But here again great disparities were found with some taking as long as 45 trials whereas others stopped after 2 (the minimum). Some (27%) never habituated although they received between 12 and 60 trials. Now what does such a simple process as habituation have to do with cognition? Pearce (1987) discusses a representation theory of habituation in which habituated responses are due to a lingering representation of the

TABLE 4.2
Antipredator Display Sequence in Hognose Snakes

Preliminary	Bluff	Dying Feign	Death Feign	Recovery
1. head up	1. Head/neck flattening	1. Turn head away	1. Quiescent	1. Resume breathing
2. tongue-flicking	2. Defensive tongue flicks	2. Partial turning over	2. Complete turnover	2. Jaws close
3. flight*	3. Puffing up	3. Begin writhing	3. Mouth open	3. Tongue retracted
	4. Hissing	4. Tail coiling	4. Tongue out	4. Exploratory tongue flicks
	5. Closed-mouth striking	5. Discharge anus	5. No breathing	5. Head raised
	6. Open-mouth striking	6. Open mouth		6. Head upright
	7. Body jerking	7. Tongue hanging out		7. Tongue flicking increases
	8. Tail display	8. Blood on mouth		8. Body partially upright
	9. Head hiding	9. Complete turnover		9. Body completely upright
				10. Yawn
				11. Snake moves away

Note. Flight behavior may also occur during the Bluff and Dying Feign phases.

70

TABLE 4.3
Antipredator Response Variation in Hognose Snakes

			Death Feigners			
			Habituation After (no. of trials)			
Response	Total	No Habituation	(2–3)	(8–15)	(29)	(45)
Bluff–No Death Feign	4	—	—	—	—	—
Bluff + Death Feign	15	4[a]	3	6	1	1

[a]After 12, 20, 41, or 60 trials.
Note. The sample consisted of 19 snakes that were tested at 3 weekly intervals after they hatched.

eliciting stimulus. Such internal representations are, in fact, what cognitive psychologists mean by "images" (Mook, 1987). What these data could mean is that the imaging ability of the snakes varied greatly. But most habituation studies only deal with a simple or solitary response measure, while here we had several.

What specific elements of the display were shown in the various phases, and were there any differences between those that only bluffed and those that both bluffed and feigned? First consider the bluff phase (Table 4.4). Of the four most common response components, the percentage of trials in which hissing and striking were seen did not differ, but the feigners were tested an average of more than 5 times as often. On the other hand, the two most common components, flattening and puffing, did significantly differ with the bluff-only animals performing both more frequently. Thus flattening and puffing habituated most in the bluff phase. Because animals were given repeated tests, it was clear that many feigners cut short the embellishments of the bluff and went quickly into the feign. Indeed, rapid conditioning or sensitization was noted in that with some individual snakes

TABLE 4.4
Selected Response Components of Hognose Snake Neonates During Bluffing Phase

Behavior	% Snakes Displaying	Feigners (n = 15) % (306) Trials	Bluffers (n = 4) % (15 Trials)	$p < .05$[a]
Bluffing				
Flattening	100	34.6	93.3	*
Puffing	95	22.5	46.7	*
Hissing	89	22.2	26.7	
Striking	74	12.4	13.3	

[a]Mann-Whitney U test based on individual response rate.

the mere approach of the observer or the waving of his hand 30 cm above the snake would lead to the death feign.

Table 4.5 gives data on the feigning and quiescent stages. The few bluff-only snakes often performed some elements of the feigning phase but never reached the quiescent phase. What is intriguing here is that the feigners showed significantly increased percentages of every behavior but the following two: (a) Bleeding from the mouth was rare, although seen at least once by three feigners, and (b) all snakes defecated at least once, but defecating occurred more often in the bluff-only animals in the feigning phase. Although it makes sense that with repeated trials there would be less material to evacuate, I am also inclined to interpret this result as an indication that defecation is not a part of the evolved sequence but a more ancestral primitive (pleisomorphic) character that was incorporated into the display. Most colubrid snakes will defecate or emit highly odoriferous cloacal secretions when handled.

In the feign phase the most common grouping of behaviors was quiescence and complete turnover. However, open mouth, extruded tongue, and cessation of respiratory movements were seen in about half of the animals.

Close encounters with predators are probably rare challenges in the total scheme of any animal's life and thus satisfy another of Griffin's (1984) criteria. But more than that, it is clear that the defensive behavior of the hognose is a complex affair that is highly variable in its specifics across members of even the same litter. Such variability, I submit, is common

TABLE 4.5
Selected Response Components in Hognose Snake Neonates
During Feigning and Death Feign Phases

Behavior	% Snakes Displaying	Feigners (n = 15) % (306 Trials)	Bluffers (n = 4) % (15 Trials)	$p < .0-5^a$
Feigning				
Turn head away	79	75.5	6.7	*
Partial turnover	89	56.5	13.3	*
Writhing	84	73.5	6.7	*
Discharge anus	100	17.3	73.3	*
Open mouth	79	57.5	0.0	*
Tongue out	74	24.2	0.0	*
Blood on mouth	16	1.3	0.0	
Complete turnover	84	74.5	6.7	*
Feign				
Quiescent	79	92.2	—	
Complete turnover	79	74.2	—	
Mouth open	63	28.4	—	
Tongue out	47	15.0	—	
No breathing	47	9.8	—	

[a]Mann-Whitney *U* test based on individual response rate.

among the complex responses of animals in which we are most likely to look for mental processing of information. But any such processing is thus tied in with genetic variation (Arnold & Bennett, 1984) as well as nonspecific environmental variation and may have adaptive value in its own right. But to satisfy Griffin's most emphasized criterion we must demonstrate individual "versatile adaptability to changing circumstances" in the hognose performance, and this I hope to demonstrate below.

But demonstrating versatile adaptability in a rare natural behavior that dances upon a substrate of genetic and ontogenetic variation is not a simple task. We can not reliably deal with either genetic or ontogenetic variation if we focus on isolated fortuitous observations in either natural or captive conditions (e.g., Jolly, this volume, Whiten & Bryne, 1988) or study in great detail one or two individuals as in Alex the gray parrot (Pepperberg, this volume) or the one or two chimps used in language studies by various laboratories (often with conflicting results always attributed to methodological not individual variation). The difficulties in carrying out field experiments add additional complexities, but often pay off as shown by chapters in this volume.

CRITICAL ANTHROPOMORPHISM

In addressing issues of possible mechanisms in behavior, especially mentalistic ones, I have advocated the use of a critical anthropomorphism in which various sources of information are used including: natural history, our perceptions, intuitions, feelings, careful behavior descriptions, identifying with the animal, optimization models, previous studies and so forth in order to generate ideas that may prove useful in gaining understanding and the ability to predict outcomes of planned (experimental) and unplanned interventions (Burghardt, 1973, 1985). Lockwood (1985) discussed aspects of anthropomorphism in some detail and his "projective anthropomorphism" embraces the only kind of traditional anthropomorphism I include in critical anthropomorphism. Lockwood provides some sensible ground rules, even though they have all been around since at least the 19th century (e.g., Morgan, 1894). He and I both call for prediction as the benchmark for validating the anthropomorphic stance.

Why do I use the term critical anthropomorphism when so much else is incorporated? Because, as I argue below, creative research on animal behavior is derived from, but goes beyond, the anthropomorphic stance even if it is not recognized or admitted.

"Is *all* that we see or seem but a dream within a dream?" (Poe, 1827)

In my own thinking, the development of the concept of critical anthropomorphism was influenced by my interest (and teaching) in sensory processes and perception. Philosophers have long debated various versions of subjectivism (idealism, solipsism) and direct (naive) realism (Mandelbaum, 1964). The former is the view, alien to all but philosophers (e.g., Berkeley, Hume) and dreamers of various sorts, that nothing may really exist "out there," or, if it does, we can never know about it: Our sense organs reflect nothing about "true" reality. All we can know from sense perception is our own state of consciousness, state of mind, or ideas. Thus I can only have direct evidence of my own consciousness and not that of other beings; in fact I can never prove that out there really exists. Nothing exists for sure — perhaps not even ourselves. This clearly nonsensical view has not been disproved easily (cf. Descartes "I think therefore I am"). But the opposing position, that our senses give us accurate direct information reflecting some objective reality, *is* easily disproved by visual illusions, hallucinations, and conflicting eye witness reports of murders and UFOs. Nonetheless, some influential and recent philosophers (e.g., Ryle) have, because of their problems with subjectivism, embraced direct realism.

Mandelbaum (1964) convincingly argues for the concept of radical critical realism, which basically holds that whereas "we do not have the right to identify *any* of the qualities of objects as they are directly experienced by us with the properties of objects as they exist in the physical world independently of us, . . . some may more accurately mirror physical properties than do others" (p. 221). Unlike many philosophers, Mandelbaum believes scientific data, especially neurophysiology, are important and that there is continuity between the sciences and common sense. What this means to me is that because we get along in the world OK most of the time, there is a good match between our perceptual systems and the out there even if our senses (or interpretation) can be wrong — sometimes embarrassingly or fatally wrong. We can strengthen the argument by showing that other species having different sensory abilities and perceptual worlds (von Uexküll, 1909/1985) also interact with the out there in a way that works.

When evolutionary factors are brought into the picture (which Mandelbaum does not do) the case is even more convincing. Karl Popper and Donald Campbell (see Radnitzky & Bartley, 1987; especially Campbell, 1987) recently developed an evolutionary epistemology based on critical realism, natural selection, and the trial and error methods of modern science. These writers explicitly acknowledge the reality and importance of animal mental processes.

Transdiction

What is the possibility of knowledge about events, such as those going on in another animal's brain, which are, as von Uexküll pointed out (see subsequent paragraphs), forever closed to us as direct experiences? This raises the issue of *transdiction:* "The question of how observed data can serve as grounds for inferences to objects or events which not only have not yet been observed, but which cannot in principle be observed" (Mandelbaum, 1964, p. 63). The appropriateness of this issue to how we characterize animal minds is uncanny, especially when it is realized that Mandelbaum was discussing the physical sciences and the challenges facing Newton, Boyle, and other 17th century thinkers in the controversy over atomic theory. Certainly the possibility of ever seeing an atom must have seemed highly remote until recently.

In parallel with critical realism, I thus propose that critical anthropomorphism is our best way to gather evidence that mental states and processes in animals do exist independently of our observational and operational procedures. However, as with critical realism, any specific attribution may later be shown in error. We are dealing with probabilities not certainties as is true of all science.

Critical anthropomorphism is not just an eclectic approach to science in general. For example, critical anthropomorphism is not useful in dealing with nonliving entities. If our car stops dead on the highway or the turn signal start acting erratically, we do not ask ourselves what we would do if we were a car faced with this problem. Many people are attached to their cars and even give them names, but I suggest that there is a basic difference between how we deal with cars and pets.

Another example would be to put yourself in the place of an engineer who is trying to develop a defensive response to an enemy's missile system. I dare say that he would not try to empathize with the missile or put himself in the missile's place. To answer a question about understanding an aspect of missile control the engineer would be more likely to say, "Well if I were the *designer* of this missile or writing the software program for its control with a given goal or objective, I would start off by solving it in this way."

Note that when we apply this to an animal we are in danger of falling into the creationist trap and asking not about the animal's mind, behavior, or genes, but about the animal's designer or god!

Recently, a seemingly different position has been taken, which has been well-publicized. I now turn to intention analysis.

INTENTIONALITY AND THE HOGNOSE SNAKE

Dennett (1983) has vigorously argued for the role of intentionality in animal behavior. Intention movements have been part of ethology for decades (e.g., Heinroth, 1911/1985) as has expectancy in animal psychology (Roitbalt, 1987). Although it may appear so, intentionality is not necessarily a conscious state. Similarly, intention movements in core ethology were meant as descriptive statements allowing behavior prediction. In defining communication, I found intent on the part of the signaler an essential notion, but concomitant consciousness was not necessary (Burghardt, 1970).

Dennett (1983) and others (e.g., Ristau, 1983, 1986) suggest that the *intentional stance,* in posing questions about animal behavior is potentially more useful than strictly behavioristic approaches based on 0 order statements. To illustrate this approach I have listed in Table 4.6 intentional statements from a hognose snake's perspective that ascend in level of cognitive complexity from 0 to 4th order. The number of underlined words in each statement is the key that determines its order.

This kind of intentional thinking is not new and is a kind of attribution analysis we use with people all the time. My favorite example is this 4th order 15-word beauty from Robert G. Ingersoll (1884/1902) a famous and outspoken 19th century American anticleric and defender of the oppressed. "The clergy know, that I know, that they know, that they do not know" (p. 348). Although the same word *know* is used four times, the meaning is clear in each context. It should also be clear why Ingersoll's promising political career (he was Attorney General of Illinois and ran for governor) did not progress very far.

Can intentional analysis be experimentally applied to the hognose snake? What is the chance of verifying its beliefs, fears, desires, and thoughts? Dennett (1983) ultimately admits that we can never be certain, but this is also true of critical anthropomorphism as analogous to critical realism

TABLE 4.6
Possible Intentional Stance Deception Statements in
Hognose Snakes Derived From Dennett (1983)

Order	Statement
0	Hognose snake performs certain responses to specific stimuli (any variation due to effects of genes, physiology, or conditioning of a reflexive action).
1	Hognose snake *believes* stimulus is a potential danger (predator).
2	a) Hognose snake *wants* predator to *believe* snake is poisonous (bluff stage), ill (feigning), or dead (quiescence). b) Hognose snake *fears* predator *knows* that snake is really harmless, healthy, or alive.
3	Hognose snake *wants* predator to *think* that it (snake) *believes* that the predator has won (is in control of the situation), and thus will contest no more.
4	Hognose snake *fears* that the predator *will discover* that it (snake) *believes* that the predator *thinks* it is poisonous, ill or dead.

applied to mental processes. But Dennett's anecdotal evidence derived from primates doesn't seem even uncritically plausible beyond the second order. What Dennett does claim is that thinking in intentional terms allows interesting ideas to be generated even if they can't be proven in the traditional sense. "Today we are interested in asking what gains in perspicuity, in predictive power, in generalization, might accrue if we adopt a higher-level hypothesis that takes a risky step into intentional character-ization" (p. 347). Krebs and Dawkins (1984) do this imaginatively by considering animals coevolved mind readers and manipulators although, as discussed below, they use machine and nervous system metaphors to make their "intentions" more palatable.

So, if I were a hognose snake in the presence of an enemy would I remain motionless for a longer time if the threat remained present than if it moved away? I think I would. Some experiments will be summarized here (see Burghardt & Greene, 1988, for details); that could be derived from this anthropocentric view. First, what if a stuffed owl, a potential predator, was clearly visible to the snake while it was feigning death?

Six neonate hognose snakes were selected for the experiment. Each was tested twice in succession under each condition in a balanced design. The recovery of snakes was monitored in the presence or absence of a mounted screech owl attached to a tripod 1 m from the quiescent snake. After the snake was motionless, the latencies of various recovery behaviors were noted until the animal crawled away. Only log-transformed data for the final crawling away times are presented here. A repeated measures analysis of variance (stimulus x order) showed that recovery stimulus condition was a significant factor (Fig. 4.4A).

Thus a question posed from the intentional stance was confirmed. But to even begin to carry out the owl experiment, we had to know many other things, and that is why the intentional stance can at best be a component of critical anthropomorphism. We needed to know the details of the snake's behavior repertoire and possible predators; we also had to have experience working with the species in the laboratory as well as familiarity with the defensive personality of these specific snakes so we could select appropriate ones to test.

Regardless, let us proceed. If I were a hognose snake in the presence of a predator, I might stay motionless longer if the predator appeared to be paying attention to me than if it seemed to have lost interest.

In a subsequent experiment with the same animals, recovery behavior in three conditions was recorded: (a) in the presence of a person looking directly at the snake from a meter away, (b) with a person in the same position but with the eyes averted from a direct gaze at the snake, and (c) in a control condition in which the person moved out of sight as soon as the snake became quiescent. The human "predator" had an enhancing effect on

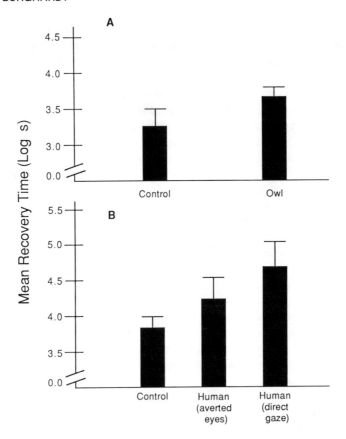

Fig. 4.4 A) Recovery latency (+ 1 standard error) from onset of death feign in hognose snake neonates in the presence or absence of a stuffed owl. B) Recovery latency from death feign in hognose snake neonates in the presence of a human being gazing directly at the snake, a human being in same position averting the eyes, or the absence of a person. (Adapted from Burghardt & Greene, 1988.)

the response with the direct gaze condition producing the longest recovery times (Fig. 4.4B).

These results show that both the presence of the owl and the direct human gaze significantly retarded recovery times over the respective control conditions. The gaze averting human condition gave intermediate results. These results also suggest that neonate hognose snakes possess good visual acuity and can use this ability in a rather sophisticated way to adaptively modify their behavior. This use of subtle cues is an example of mind reading (*sensu* Dawkins & Krebs, 1984). Mitchell (1986) suggested there were 4 levels of deception. The combined data on the hognose shows that it is at his level II and perhaps even his level III.

In the traditional tonic immobility paradigm with chicks and anoles, comparable recovery latency differences have been obtained in similar experiments (Arduino & Gould, 1984; Gallup, Cummings, & Nash, 1972; Hennig, 1977). Thus, there is functional continuity in this aspect of predator induced immobility across both tonic immobility and the more complex antipredator system of *Heterodon platirhinos*. And, in fact, these two snake experiments were carried out in 1974 prior to either Griffin's or Dennett's writings and were derived from studies in the chicken tonic immobility literature, intuition (Burghardt, 1973), and a belief that snakes should be examined for the same abilities found in higher vertebrates. Use of the literature is an explicit and essential aspect of critical anthropomorphism and keeps ethology an accumulating science.

Although we have demonstrated a continuity among immobility responses here, restraint-induced tonic immobility as found in chicks may merely reduce the probability of attack while the animal awaits an opportunity to escape. In *Anolis* lizards recovery is more rapid if there are nearby habitat features (cover) suitable for escape (Hennig, Dunlap, & Gallup, 1976).

Future useful experiments to evaluate the extent and flexibility of the hognose antipredator system might include:

1. Does the snake track changes in gaze fixation by the predator? This could also be measured by recovery time.
2. Does the snake monitor changes in the distance of the predator? Some pilot data indicates that this is so.
3. Because the snake may be moved during the quiescent stage, say by a raptor, does it evaluate the appropriateness of potential escape routes in the new location, or is assessment done prior to feigning death?
4. Other studies could involve the occurrence of any learning components, discrimination among potential predators, their postures, and probable next response.

Vogel (1950) notes that individual differences, context, and opportunity for escape are important factors in death feigning by vultures. Developmental questions can also be addressed; in both vultures (Vogel, 1950) and opossums (Franq, 1969) the behavior is not seen in neonates and develops around the time of independence from the parents. In short, experimental attention to these convergent behavior patterns in diverse unrelated taxa are needed as well as comparative studies on the eastern hognose snake and its relatives.

There are other antipredator tactics in reptiles that merit imaginative experimental study. Lizards, in addition to showing classical tonic immobility, also often have another defensive mechanism not available to snakes. The tail may easily be separated from the body when grabbed; the tail wiggles rapidly and often attracts the attention of the predator while the lizard escapes (Congdon, Vitt, & King, 1974). Herzog and Drummond (1984) found that tail autonomy in geckos (*Phyllodactylus lanei*) greatly inhibits tonic immobility (and thus the animal flees) whereas jerking hard on a limb, which does not automotize, does not inhibit a lizard going immobile and may actually increase the duration of the immobile phase. The reader might want to analyze this response in light of Griffin's (1984) criteria also. The intentional stance here would seem to be rather forced, however.

Another type of defensive behavior in lizards that poses some cognitive questions is the tail wagging response performed by many fast-running lizards when they spot a predator at some distance. The tail is slowly raised and waved in a manner obvious to the intruder. A current favored hypothesis (Dial, 1986) is that this display functions to alert the predator to the fact that it has been spotted. The message in effect is "I see you. Don't waste your time and mine by engaging in pursuit as I'm fast, and you've lost the element of surprise." This would seem a prime area for research based on critical anthropomorphism and the intentional stance.

DECISION MAKING

Most of the questions posed above concerning IM's feeding behavior and the hognose snake's defensive responses involve decision making—exhibiting one response rather than another. Thus, decision theory is relevant. Decisions can be looked at from three standpoints (Mook, 1987)—not mutually exclusive but analytically useful. The first standpoint is to look at *how* decisions are made and try to determine or approximate the cognitive operations or calculations that the actor performs to reach its decision. The second standpoint is the *descriptive* one that focuses on whether or not the results of the actor's actions maximize some outcome either proximately (food intake, predator avoidance) or ultimately (reproductive fitness). The third standpoint is the normative one; that is, what *should* the actor do to maximize the likelihood of obtaining some result? In other words, what, theoretically, is the best response from the options available to the actor?

It is clear that these three ways of approaching decisions must be kept separate as we tried to do with the feeding behavior of IM. In the hognose snake, for instance, even if the snake does not make the most rational (to us) response (normative sense) it does not mean that the cognitive apparatus is wanting. It could be that the relevant information is not available to the snake. On the other hand, "Behavior that is normatively rational can be produced by mechanisms that are not rational at all" (Mook, 1987 p. 339). This leads to the idea that rules of thumb govern most behavior (even in human beings), for they may be most efficient in terms of sensory, neural, and energetic constraints.

PREMONITIONS OF COGNITIVE ETHOLOGY

". . . animals construct nature for themselves according to their special needs" (von Uexküll, 1909/1985, p. 234).

Jacob von Uexküll, in his concern with the environmental perceptual world (*Umwelt*) and innerworld of animals, was a pioneering cognitive ethologist. He called for empirical data (as did Griffin) to substantiate his concepts on the mental life of organisms. Central to von Uexküll's views was the relationship between the surroundings of an organism that are both perceived and biologically meaningful (it's environment or *Umwelt*) and its internal representation or counterworld (*Gegenwelt*), which arises when a nervous system intersperses neural excitation and motor systems between the external world and behavior. In these animals

No external stimulus transformed into excitation signs penetrates any longer directly to the motor networks. These networks receive all their excitations only second hand — from a new world of excitation originating in the central nervous system that is erected between the environment and the motor nervous system. All actions of the muscular equipment can now only be related to them and can only be understood through them. The animal no longer flees from the stimuli that the enemy sends to him, but rather from the mirrored image of the enemy that originates in a mirrored world. (p. 234)

This is the concept of the counterworld and schemata, remnants of which were retained in the configurational innate schema of Tinbergen and Lorenz (Tinbergen, 1951) but became progressively devoid of von Uexküll's content. Template conceptions in bird song learning (Marler & Mundinger, 1971) are contemporary relatives of his concept. Interestingly, von Uexküll and the *Unwelt* concept are mentioned in the evolutionary epistemology of Campbell (1987), which was heavily influenced by Konrad Lorenz. But as no reference to von Uexküll is cited, it seems his position was derived from Lorenz rather than von Uexküll's early seminal writings.

Von Uexküll's vision is further shown in this passage:

> If we possessed the capability of holding the brains of animals before our mind's eye, as we can hold a glass prism before our physical eye, then our environment would appear just as changed before us. There might not be anything more charming or interesting than such a world through the medium of various counterworlds. Unfortunately, this vision is denied us and we must make do with a tedious and imprecise reconstruction of the counterworlds as they become probable to us by detailed and difficult experiments. One guiding thought gives us hope of constructing something useful from this uncertain material, and that is the certainty that nature and animal are not, as it might appear, two separate things, but that they together constitute a higher organism. . . . (p. 234)

This passage is a remarkable presaging of Whitehead's theory of organic mechanism put forth as an alternative to the essentially incompatible and equally untenable doctrines of materialistic mechanism and vitalistic mentalism (Whitehead, 1926: 109–112, 151–152). In the context of this chapter I view the opposition as the perennial one between those who view understanding animals and their behavior as exclusively a matter for reductionistic analysis ultimately based on principles of molecular and submolecular action and those who see a holistic emergentism as the ultimate key. Cognitive ethologists are caught in this clash of scientific approaches. Whereas 20 years ago it seemed that reductionism held all the cards, increasing dissatisfaction has occurred over the years. From the biosphere approach of the Gaia hypothesis and deep ecology to neuroscientists and psychologists who point to numerous examples where mental states and information can profoundly influence physiological functioning and physical health (e.g., Sperry, 1988), there is growing dissatisfaction. Some resolution of conflict between reductionistic and holistic perspectives is urgently needed in science if the world is to survive. For dealing with the immediate issue of animal mentality, the following observations may be pertinent.

Most explanations that rely on a mentalistic or higher order interpretation will eventually be interpretable on what seems to be a 0 order level. Beach (1955) made this point in relation to instinct, but he drew the wrong conclusion. von Uexküll knew that his experiments could determine the environmental cues used by a sea urchin, jellyfish, or octopus to construct its perceptual world. But unless one began with the idea that animals have such a world, the critical experiments would not have been done. Much of the breakthrough findings in animal behavior have originated in speculations concerning counterworlds, motivations, thoughts, instincts, alien sensory abilities, manipulation, and so forth.

Thus, the paradox, as I see it, is that the important reductionistic answers are to nonreductionistic, holistic, even metaphoric speculations posed by those with enough imagination to move beyond the dogma of the time (Kekule's benzene ring based on snakes is, naturally, a congenial example). I think this has been true of the most creative psychological thinkers such as Freud, Piaget, and Lorenz. These pioneers do not need disciples but scientists committed to properly testing the ideas and moving science forward. The answers will almost always allow the skeptic to believe that they are nothing good old reductionistic science can't handle, but what this good old science can't handle is the larger context in which their favored phenomena operate.

To return to cognitive ethology, critical anthropomorphism has been essential for progress in understanding animal behavior, even if it has not been formally recognized (Burghardt, 1985). What is perhaps needed now is a more formal development that incorporates multilevel diverse threads in ethology, not only from nerve cells to ecosystems, but a more careful look at the psychological processes used in developing research questions. Lorenz's writings on this topic may be his most important legacy (see especially Lorenz, 1981, chapter 2).

SOME FINAL THOUGHTS

Fabre (e.g., 1918) and more recently Gould and Gould (1986) provide many examples of how invertebrates, especially, get caught in endless (do) loops, such as the wasp that keeps starting at the beginning of a sequence if interrupted. The persistent conflicts over prey in IM the two-headed snake are comparable. But these data may tell us little either about subjective worlds or intelligence. They do tell us about the specificity of cognitive processes and the constraints involved. Are not many humans caught in loops and webs from alcoholism, smoking, or marital discord in which the participants are all too conscious and aware of what is going on but are unable to extricate themselves. August Strindberg's (1901/1960) two part play on marriage, *The Dance of Death,* is perhaps the most depressing play on human interaction ever written! The point is that it is just not valid for anyone observing destructive stupid behavior to conclude that the humans or nonhumans are nothing but unaware machines. Remember that in other contexts such people can be very creative and adaptable.

I think the answer lies in combining what we *can* learn about cognition, motivation, affect, and the evolutionary and ecological constraints that variously enter each and every response system. Thus, after the analytical separation that I urged earlier, the mind must be put together again. Like the term instinct, which also covers many disparate behavioral events, it will turn out that knowing more may make the label mind less useful in specific situations. But the phenomena will still exist. Ecosystem and biosphere will likewise remain useful concepts even if, as is unlikely, we can account for all events in a reductionistic manner. The danger of using a term rather than analysis to explain or predict events is now well understood and should not be invoked reflexively. But we need to combine reductionistic and mentalistic perspectives with care. Krebs and Dawkins (1984) provocatively describe animal communication as involving mind reading at the same time that they repeatedly assert that animals are but complex machines. They cover themselves by defining mind reading as their use of "statistical laws to predict what an animal will do next" and, for the animal, its use of "fine clues by which other animals' behavior may be predicted" (p. 386). Similar views have been expressed for years. It is the mind reading idea, surely a product of critical anthropomorphism, that provides the conceptual power in their discussion that may stimulate imaginative research.

Today, at 14 years of age, IM's two heads still fight over prey. I have become convinced that the two behavioristic outcasts, instinct and mind, have much in common and that they are intimately connected. Thus, the term cognitive ethology was particularly prescient in my opinion, because it joined ethology, originally focused on the analysis of instinct, with the cognitive processes the early ethologists often acknowledged but just didn't know how to deal with (cf. Thines, 1987).

The opening quote to this chapter by von Uexküll asserted that the central concern has to be with the other organism and not with anthropocentrism or, I would extend it, egocentrism, as in asserting one knows the mind of another human because of our own self-knowledge, subjective feelings, awareness, etc. But no one, including von Uexküll, can escape the fact that we are human, and we have to begin our work acknowledging this. The balance has to be between critically using our own internal as well as external perceptual faculties and the ultimate benchmark of publicly assessable and testable events. Animals are useful in this endeavor if for no other reason than that verbal statements are not present to confuse the uncritical and those untrained in separating various channels or signals.

Sacks (1985) tells the amusing story of patients with aphasia such that the verbal information contained in speeches heard on television was separated from the nonverbal and emotional information; only the latter could be comprehended. During a televised speech by President Reagan these patients found the president's tone, facial expressions, and gestures false and ridiculous. On the other hand, a nearly blind woman with tonal agnosia who was unable to perceive expressive emotional content and could only focus on the words, stated that the president was "not cogent," did not speak "good prose" and had improper word use. "Either he is brain damaged or has something to conceal" (Sacks, 1985, p. 80).

Sacks' closing paragraph is chilling in its implications. "Here then was the paradox of the President's speech. We normals — aided, doubtless, by our wish to be fooled, were indeed well and truly fooled (*'Populus vult decipi, ergo decipiatur'*). And so cunningly was deceptive word-use combined with deceptive tone, that only the brain-damaged remained intact, undeceived" (p. 80).

Does this example imply that a balanced common sense middle ground, between those focused on only what can be seen directly and those trusting their intuitions and empathy, is the most off-course? No, it suggests only that those resistant to analytical and heuristic separation of the two will be misled. But, of course, we are now back to anecdotes, this time by Sacks. Critical anthropomorphism and replication are needed for the study of mental patients as well as animals, indeed, perhaps in all areas of ethology and psychology.

Animals such as reptiles that are difficult to relate to may be among the most illuminating for study. I return, for a moment, to the hognose snake's display. I pointed out that deception was at the top of both Romanes' and modern hierarchies of animal mental abilities. But the next step is self-deception or lying to oneself. Is this uniquely human (Lockard, 1988)? Self-deception is touted as a new key to understanding much human behavior: A basic idea here is that persons convinced that erroneous information is true make the most convincing liars. Now if the snake is trying to convince another animal (or an experimenter) that it is, in fact, dead, then the best way to accomplish this may be to not have any doubts or engage in any conscious activity that might show hesitation or spoil the ruse. Our difficulty in finding unequivocal evidence of conscious awareness may be due to the evolution of mechanisms countering any signs of it — ultimately against awareness itself!

Ah well — perhaps the hognose snake is out of place in a book on the mental gymnastics of plovers and primates, but I suggest that after years of vertebrate class warfare, reptiles will not play dead forever!

CONCLUSIONS

The following paragraphs outline some important concepts covered in this chapter.

1. Issues of consciousness and subjective states in animals must be kept analytically separate from established areas in psychology represented by cognition, motivation, and emotion. Although consciousness may enter into these phenomena, they are not isomorphic.

2. Making choices was considered a mark of consciousness in early comparative psychology. Psychologists now realize that decision making can be approached from the how (mechanism—includes cognitive processes), descriptive, and normative routes. The two-headed snake's failure to learn to stop competing with itself for food showed that an apparently normative (rational) outcome was not obtained. However, using a descriptive approach it was shown that the two heads did partition their food resources equally. The mechanisms employed involved differential responses by the heads to prey size, different thresholds for constriction, and so on.

3. Griffin has characterized conscious awareness in animals as associated with cognitive processes involving adaptive response, variability, and context specificity. I argued that descriptive and experimental data on death feigning in the hognose snake met his criteria. Readers can decide whether the snake is consciously aware. By posing the problem with a snake rather than a chimp, the study of animal consciousness is less affected by uncritical anthropomorphic biases.

4. Regardless of the answer we reach concerning our ability to understand conscious awareness or other putative phenomena in animals, the issue of how we devise research questions is too little studied, and reductionistic and behavioristic approaches are often assumed to be the best, if not exclusive, methods to follow.

5. The history of the study of tonic immobility demonstrates at least two major points. One is that proximate and ultimate issues are confused unless one sees beyond immediate causation. Today, this is not a controversial issue among ethologists. The second is that the label given to the proximal causal process, in this case fear or deception, can influence the very nature of the questions asked.

6. Dennett's intentional stance was proposed as a way of asking questions beyond the 0 (stimulus-response) order. His analysis of animal behavior, primarily of primates, sometimes relies heavily on anthropomorphically treated anecdotal evidence. Yet it can also lead to interesting questions, as I listed for the hognose snake.

7. *Critical anthropomorphism* is proposed as a heuristic method implicitly used by the most creative animal psychologists, ethologists, and behavioral ecologists to formulate research agendas that result in publicly verifiable data that move our understanding of behavior forward. This is true even if the analogies, intuitions, intentions, holistic ideas, and postulated mental processes are either proved erroneous or are untestable directly.

8. Reductionistic methods are critical for testing and evaluating ideas, but the history of animal behavior has shown that the most

paradigm-shaking insights have come about by refusing to be bound by the accepted mechanistic views of the day. Thus the ultimate paradox too rarely appreciated. We must be open to new phenomena considered improbable by current scientific wisdom, yet use all we know of current rigorous scientific methods to test these seemingly unlikely possibilities. Critical anthropomorphism provides a way to combine our human characteristics and abilities with various kinds of knowledge and keep the question-asking in bounds but still creative.

ACKNOWLEDGMENTS

These data were collected over several years, and I am indebted to Erich Kling-hammer, Harry Greene, and Marilla Davis for their help with the hognose snakes and to Bruce Batts, Brian Bock, and many students for their help with IM. Thanks also to the Radiology staff at Rockefeller University. Support for the studies reported here were graciously provided by research grants from the National Institute of Mental Health, the National Science Foundation, and the Science Alliance at the University of Tennessee. Harold A. Herzog, Jr. and Matthew Kramer, in addition to the editors, made useful suggestions on early drafts. Helen Hahn kindly drew Fig. 4.3.

REFERENCES

Arduino, P. J., & Gould, J. L. (1984). Is tonic immobility adaptive? *Animal Behaviour, 32,* 921–923.
Arnold, S. J., & Bennett, A. F. (1984). Behavioral variation in natural populations. III: Antipredator displays in the garter snake *Thamnophis radix. Animal Behaviour, 32,* 1108–1118.
Beach, F. A. (1955). The descent of instinct. *Psychological Review, 62,* 401–410.
Burghardt, G. M. (1970). Defining "communication." In J. W. Johnston, Jr., D. G. Moulton, & A. Turk (Eds.), *Communication by chemical signals* (pp. 5–18). New York: Appleton-Century-Crofts.
Burghardt, G. M. (1973). Instinct and innate behavior: Toward an ethological psychology. In J. A. Nevin & G. S. Reynolds (Eds.), *The study of behavior: Learning, motivation, emotion, and instinct* (pp. 322–400). Glenview, IL.: Scott, Foresman and Co.
Burghardt, G. M. (1977). Learning processes in reptiles. *Biology of the Reptilia, 7,* 555–681.
Burghardt, G. M. (1978). Closing the circle: The ethology of mind. *Behavioral and Brain Sciences, 1,* 562–563.
Burghardt, G. M. (1984). On the origins of play. In P. K. Smith (Ed.), *Play in animals and humans* (pp. 5–41). London: Basil Blackwell.
Burghardt, G. M. (1985). Animal awareness: Current perceptions and historical perspective. *American Psychologist, 40,* 905–919.
Burghardt, G. M. (1988). Precocity, play, and the ectotherm–endotherm transition: Profound reorganization or superficial adaptation. In E. M. Blass (Ed.), *Handbook of behavioral neurobiology, Vol. 9* (pp. 107–148). New York: Plenum.

Burghardt, G. M., Allen, B. A., & Frank, H. (1986). Exploratory tongue flicking by green iguanas in laboratory and field. *Chemical Signals in Vertebrates, 4,* 305–321.

Burghardt, G. M., & Batts, B. (1981, June). *Are two heads better than one: Feeding behavior in a bicephalic rat snake.* Paper presented at the annual meeting of the Animal Behavior Society, Knoxville, TN.

Burghardt, G. M., & Denny, D. (1983). Effects of prey movement and prey odor on feeding in garter snakes. *Zeitschrift für Tierpsychologie, 62,* 329–347.

Burghardt, G. M., & Greene, H. W. (1988). Predator simulation and duration of death feigning in neonate hognose snakes. *Animal Behaviour, 36,* 1842–1844.

Campbell, D. T. (1987). Evolutionary epistemology. In G. Radnitzky & W. W. Bartley, III (Eds.), *Evolutionary epistemology, rationality, and the sociology of knowledge* (pp. 47–89). La Salle, IL: Open Court.

Chiszar, D., Carter, T., Knight, L., Simonsen, L., & Taylor, S. (1976). Investigatory behavior in the plains garter snake (*Thamnophis radix*) and several additional species. *Animal Learning and Behavior, 4,* 273–278.

Congdon, J. D., Vitt, L. J., & King, W. W. (1974). Geckos: Adaptive significance and energetics of tail autonomy. *Science, 184,* 1379–1380.

Crawford. F. T. (1977). Induction and duration of tonic immobility. *Psychological Record,* (Suppl. 1), 89–107.

Cunningham. B. (1937). *Axial bifurcation in serpents.* Durham, NC: Duke University Press.

Darwin, C. (1883). Instinct. In G. J. Romanes, *Mental evolution in animals* (pp. 355–384). London: Kegan Paul, Trench, Trubner, & Co.

Dawkins, M. S. (1980). *Animal suffering.* London: Chapman & Hall.

Dennett, D. C. (1983). Intentional systems in cognitive ethology: The "Panglossian paradigm" defended. *Behavioral and Brain Sciences, 6,* 343–355.

Dennett, D. C. (1987). Eliminate the middle toad. *Behavioral and Brain Science, 10,* 372–374.

Dial, B. E. (1986). Tail display in two species of iguanid lizards: A test of the "predator signal" hypothesis. *American Naturalist, 127,* 103–111.

Eron, L. D. (1987). The development of aggressive behavior from the perspective of a developing behaviorism. *American Psychologist, 42,* 435–442.

Fabre, H. F. (1918). *The wonders of instinct.* New York: Century.

Franq, E. N. (1969). Behavioral aspects of feigned death in the opossum *Didelphis marsupialis. American Midland Naturalist, 81,* 556–568.

Gallup, G. G., Jr. (1974). Animal hypnosis: Factual status of a fictional concept. *Psychological Bulletin, 81,* 836–853.

Gallup, G. G., Jr., Cummings, W. H., & Nash, R. F. (1972). The experimenter as an independent variable in studies of animal hypnosis in chickens. *Animal Behaviour, 20,* 166–169.

Gazzaniga, M. S. (1972). One brain—two minds? *American Scientist, 60,* 311–317.

Gilman, T. T., & Marcuse, F. L. (1949). Animal hypnosis. *Psychological Bulletin, 46,* 151–165.

Gould, J. L., & Gould, C. G. (1986). Invertebrate intelligence. In R. J. Hoage & L. Goldman (Eds.), *Animal intelligence: Insights into the animal mind* (pp. 21–36). Washington, DC: Smithsonian Institution Press.

Greene, H. W. (1988). Antipredator mechanisms in reptiles. *Biology of the Reptilia, 16,* 1–152.

Griffin, D. R. (1976). *The question of animal awareness: Evolutionary continuity of mental experience.* New York: Rockefeller University Press.

Griffin, D. R. (1984). *Animal thinking.* Cambridge: Harvard University Press.

Heinroth, O. (1985). Contributions to the biology, especially the ethology and psychology of the Anatidae (D. Gove & C. J. Mellor, Trans.). In G. M. Burghardt (Ed.), *The foundations of comparative ethology* (pp. 246–301). New York: Van Nostrand Reinhold. (Partial Reprint from *Verhandlungen des V. Internationalen Ornithologen-Kongresses, Deutsche*

Ornithologische Gesellschaft, 1911, 589–702).

Hennig, C. W. (1977). Effects of simulated predation on tonic immobility in *Anolis Carolinensis:* The role of eye contact. *Bulletin of the Psychonomic Society, 9,* 239–242.

Hennig, C. W., Dunlap, W. P., & Gallup, G. G., Jr. (1976). The effect of distance between predator and prey and the opportunity to escape on tonic immobility in *Anolis carolinensis. Psychological Record, 26,* 313–320.

Herrero, S. (1985). *Bear attacks: Their causes and avoidance.* New York: Winchester Press.

Herzog, H. A., Jr. (1978). Immobility in intraspecific encounters: Cockfights and the evolution of "animal hypnosis." *Psychological Record, 28,* 543–548.

Herzog, H. A., Jr., & Burghardt, G. M. (1974). Prey movement and predatory behavior of juvenile western yellow-bellied racers, *Coluber constrictor mormon. Herpetologica, 30,* 285–289.

Herzog, H. A. Jr., & Burghardt, G. M. (1986). Development of antipredator responses in snakes. I: Defensive and open-field behaviors in newborns and adults of three species of garter snakes *(Thamnophis melanogaster, T. sirtalis, T. butleri). Journal of Comparative Psychology, 100,* 372–379.

Herzog, H. A. Jr., & Burghardt, G. M. (1988). Development of antipredator responses in snakes. III: Stability of individual and litter differences over the first year of life. *Ethology, 77,* 250–258.

Herzog, H. A., Jr., & Drummond, H. (1984). Tail autonomy inhibits tonic immobility in geckos. *Copeia,* 763–764.

Hess, E. H. (1975). *The tell-tale eye.* New York: Van Nostrand Reinhold.

Ingersoll, R. G. (1902). Orthodoxy. In C. P. Farrell (Ed.), *The works of Robert G. Ingersoll* (Vol. 2, pp. 341–427). New York: Dresden. (Original work published 1884)

James, W. (1890). *Principles of Psychology* (Vol. 2). New York: Holt.

Jones, R. B. (1987a). Social and environmental aspects of fear in the domestic fowl. In R. Zayan & I. J. H. Duncan (Eds.), *Cognitive aspects of social behaviour in the domestic fowl* (pp. 82–149). Amsterdam: Elsevier.

Jones, R. B. (1987b). The assessment of fear in the domestic fowl. In R. Zayan & I. J. H. Duncan (Eds.), *Cognitive aspects of social behaviour in the domestic fowl* (pp. 40–81). Amsterdam: Elsevier.

Krebs, J. R., & Dawkins, R. (1984). Animal signals: Mind-reading and manipulation. In J. R. Krebs & N. B. Davies (Eds.), *Behavioral ecology: An evolutionary approach* (pp. 380–402). Sunderland, MA: Sinauer Associates.

Lefebvre, L., & Sabourin, M. (1977). Response differences in animal hypnosis: A hypothesis. *Psychological Record,* (Suppl. 1), 77–87.

Lockard, J. S. (1988). Origins of self-deception: Is lying to oneself uniquely human? In J. S. Lockard & D. L. Paulhus (Eds.), *Self-deception: An adaptive mechanism?* (pp. 14–22). Englewood Cliffs, NJ: Prentice-Hall.

Lockwood, R. (1985). Anthropomorphism is not a four letter word. In M. W. Fox & L. D. Mickley (Eds.), *Advances in animal welfare science 1985/86* (pp. 185–199). Washington, DC: Humane Society of America.

Lorenz, H. Z. (1981). *The foundations of ethology.* New York: Springer-Verlag.

Mandelbaum, M. (1964). *Philosophy, science, and sense perception: Historical and critical studies.* Baltimore: Johns Hopkins Press.

Marler, P., & Mundinger, P. (1971). The study of behavioral development. In H. Moltz (Ed.), *The ontogeny of vertebrate behavior* (pp. 389–450). New York: Academic Press.

McDougall, W. (1923). *Outline of psychology* (2nd ed.). London: Methuen.

McGuire, M. (1987, June). Crocodile saves drowning boy! *World Weekly News,* p. 9.

Michell, R. W. (1986). A framework for discussing deception. In R. W. Mitchell & N. S. Thompson (Eds.), *Deception: Perspectives on human and nonhuman deceit.* (pp. 3–40). Albany: SUNY Press.

Mook, D. C. (1987). *Motivation: The organization of action.* New York: W. W. Norton.

Morgan, C. L. (1984). *An introduction to comparative psychology.* London: Arnold.

Pearce, J. M. (1987). *An introduction to animal cognition.* Hillsdale, NJ: Lawrence Erlbaum Associates.

Poe, E. A. (1827/1959). A dream within a dream. In R. Wilber (Ed.), *Poe* (pp. 53–54). New York: Dell.

Radnitzky, G., & Bartley, W. W., III. (Eds.). (1987). *Evolutionary epistemology, rationality, and the sociology of knowledge.* La Salle, IL: open Court.

Ratner, S. C. (1967). Comparative aspects of hypnosis. In J. E. Gordon (Ed.), *Handbook of clinical and experimental hypnosis* (pp. 550–587). New York: Macmillan.

Ristau, C. A. (1983). Language, cognition, and awareness in animals? In J. A. Sechzer (Ed.), *The role of animals in biomedical research. Annals of the New York Academy of Sciences, 406,* 170–186.

Ristau, C. A. (1986). Do animals think? In R. J. Hoage & L. Goldman (Eds.), *Animal intelligence: Insights into the animal mind* (pp. 165–185). Washington, DC: Smithsonian Institution Press.

Roitblat, H. L. (1987). *Introduction to comparative cognition.* New York: W. H. Freeman.

Romanes, G. J. (1882). *Animal intelligence.* London: Kegan Paul, Trench, Trubner, & Co.

Romances, G. J. (1883). *Mental evolution in animals.* London: Kegan Paul, Trench, Trubner, & Co.

Russow, L. M. (1986). Deception: A philosophical perspective. In R. W. Mitchell & N. Thompson (Eds.), *Deception: Perspectives on human and nonhuman deceit* (pp. 41–51). Albany: SUNY Press.

Sacks, O. (1985). *The man who mistook his wife for a hat and other clinical tales.* New York: Summit.

Sergeant, A. B., & Eberhardt, L. E. (1975). Death feigning by ducks in response to predation by red foxes *(Vulpes fulva). American Midland Naturalist, 94,* 108–119.

Skinner, B. F. (1984). The canonical papers of B. F. Skinner [Entire issue]. *Behavioral and Brain Sciences, 7.*

Smith, H. M., & Pérez-Higareda, G. (1987). The literature on somatodichotomy in snakes. *Bulletin of the Maryland Herpetological Society, 23,* 139–153.

Sperry, R. (1988). Psychology's mentalistic paradigm and the religion/science tension. *American Psychologist, 43,* 607–613.

Still, A. W. (1982). On the number of subjects used in animal behaviour experiments. *Animal Behaviour, 30,* 873–880

Strindberg, A. (1960). The dance of death. In E. Sprigge (Trans.) *Five plays of Strindberg* (pp. 125–235). New York: Doubleday & Co.

Thines, G. (1987). The scientific assessment of animal subjective experiences: From Buytendijk's animal psychology to animal welfare. In R. Zayan & I. J. H. Duncan (Eds.), *Cognitive aspects of social behaviour in the domestic fowl* (pp. 2–18). Amsterdam: Elsevier.

Tinbergen, N. (1951). *The study of instinct.* Oxford: Clarendon.

Uexküll, J. von (1909/1985). Environment [Umwelt] and inner world of animals (C. J. Mellor & D. Gove, Trans.). In G. M. Burghardt (Ed.), *The foundations of comparative ethology* (pp. 222–245). New York: Van Nostrand Reinhold. (Reprinted from *Umwelt und Innenwelt der Tiere,* 1909, Berlin: Jena).

Vogel, H. H., Jr. (1950). Observations on social behavior in turkey vultures. *Auk, 67,* 210–216.

Weiskrantz, L. (Ed.). (1985). *Animal intelligence.* Oxford: Clarendon.

Whitehead, A. N. (1926). *Science and the modern world.* Cambridge: Cambridge University Press.

Whiten, A., & Bryne, R. W. (1988). Tactical deception in primates. *Behavioral and Brain Sciences, 11,* 233–273.

5

ASPECTS OF THE COGNITIVE ETHOLOGY OF AN INJURY-FEIGNING BIRD, THE PIPING PLOVER

Carolyn A. Ristau
The Rockefeller University

ABSTRACT

Interest in the scientific investigation of animal mental states has been rekindled recently in several disciplines: philosophy of mind, experimental and comparative psychology, and Griffin's creation of the new enterprise of cognitive ethology. As an approach to this problem, in the present research a low-level intentional stance was assumed (as described by Dennett, 1983, 1987; Bennett, 1976, this volume; Searle, 1980). I suggest that for some species, a bird engaged in injury feigning wants to lead an intruder away from its offspring and acts as needed (within limits) to achieve that end. Field experiments were conducted with piping plovers and Wilson's plovers using human intruders to approach the eggs or young. Data were gathered on each bird's direction of display, monitoring of the intruder, and flexibility of behavior in response to changing behavior by the intruder. Other experiments investigated the birds' responsiveness to attention of an intruder (interpreted as direction of intruder's eye gaze) and the birds' ability to learn to discriminate between potentially "safe" versus "dangerous" intruders.

INTRODUCTION: SOME PHILOSOPHICAL PROBLEMS

Donald Griffin (1976, 1984, 1985, this volume) has been particularly influential in rekindling interest in the possibility that animals may have mental experiences including awareness, purposes, and consciousness and that such experiences are amenable to scientific investigation. "Cognitive ethology" (Griffin, 1976) is a beginning exploration of the mental experiences of animals particularly as they behave in their natural environment in the course of their normal lives.

Cognitive ethology differs from most previous studies of animal cognition — interpreted broadly to include animal learning and discrimination studies — in its emphasis on possible animal mental states and interest in matters such as deception and communication. Most prior animal studies focused on laboratory based experiments whereas many studies in cognitive ethology have, to date, emphasized the importance of observations of naturally occurring behavior and of experimentally based field studies. Lab research in cognitive ethology has emphasized both cognitive and biological/evolutionary significance. In a similar vein, comparative psychologists have emphasized an experimental but biologically based approach.

There are important contributions from the considerable history of experimental, comparative, and developmental psychology. For example, developmental psychologists, in studying children who are nonverbal or "differently" verbal from adults, confront many of the same methodological and interpretative difficulties that cognitive ethologists encounter when studying nonhuman animals. (Michel, this volume). The ape and other animal cognition and artificial language projects have, at least in some of the research, applied techniques of experimental psychology in attempts to deal with issues in communication and attribution of mental states (reviewed in Pepperberg, this volume; Ristau, 1983b, in press; Ristau & Robbins, 1982). All the areas mentioned can contribute to the field of cognitive ethology with respect to useful methodologies, principles, and general phenomena — for example from the area of learning theory and can alert researchers to possible pitfalls which have entrapped others.

The major philosophical problem facing work in cognitive ethology is, as Bennett (1985) phrased it, drawing conclusions about the minds of animals from premises about behavior in the circumstances in which the animals are behaving. We need a conceptual theory — an analysis of mentalistic terms that relates them to patterns of behavior. Indeed any study of mental processes, not just cognitive ethology, faces these problems. We do not, however, have any such theory. And there is also the problem of awareness. It is a hotly disputed matter whether animals, to which one might apply concepts of intentions, belief, and desire, are aware of those beliefs or whether they even experience beliefs or desires as opposed to the terms being a useful functionalist stance for an experimenter to assume.

Though solid theories do not exist, useful approaches do. One is the intentional stance, proferred by philosophers such as Jonathan Bennett (1976, this volume), Daniel Dennett (1978, 1983, 1987), and John Searle (1980) (See discussion of philosophical approaches in Beer's chapter "From Folk Psychology to Cognitive Ethology," this volume.) *Intentional* is a philosophical term meaning "aboutness" and reference. It does not mean "on purpose," although "wants it to be the case that" is an intentional phrase. Other intentional phrases are "thinks that," "believes that," and "wants it to be the case that." Conventional "appropriate" scientific explanation is phrased at the zero order of intentional analysis without recourse to any mental state. Among possible first order intentional analyses is a description in terms of purpose (e.g., An organism wants it to be the case that x, where x could be a response such as organism B to follow). Bennett (1976) and others have noted the importance of a transition among various species from rudimentary "registrations" and "goals" to full-fledged "beliefs" and "desires" characteristic of at least some human activity.

What might be some if not criteria, then descriptive properties of purposeful behavior? Among others, the psychologists Tolman (1932) and Griffin have particularly noted persistence to the goal including variation in behavior to achieve the goal should the path to the goal be obstructed. Griffin (1985, p. 37) specifically suggests that a criterion of conscious awareness in animals is "versatile adaptability of behavior to changing circumstances and challenges." Margaret Boden (1983), in considering animal behavior from the vantage point of artificial intelligence, also stressed appropriate variation in behavior to overcome obstacles.

I will draw upon these ideas in proposing suggestive evidence for a purposive interpretation of distraction behavior exhibited by a number of species of ground nesting birds when intruders approach the eggs or young (Ristau, 1983a). I particularly chose to study birds not because a purposive interpretation for their behavior is clear-cut or because we are easily able to empathize with their possible communications and mental states (as we seem to with apes and our pet dogs), but because it is difficult to do either. These very obstacles may help us to specify the evidence for such an interpretation more carefully and to suggest possible levels in the transition from rudimentary to more full-fledged knowledge and purposes (or beliefs and desires as termed by many philosophers). I have chosen to study a behavior that, like many behaviors human and otherwise, is a mixture of some fixed genetically transmitted elements and more flexible behaviors.

THE INJURY FEIGNING PLOVERS

The Plovers' Behaviors Toward Intruders

I shall concentrate on the piping plover *Charadrius melodus* and also include data from Wilson's plover *C. Wilsonia,* two shorebirds which typically nest on beaches or sand dunes of the eastern United States. Both parents incubate the eggs for about 4 weeks. At this point precocial young hatch; they can run freely and feed themselves on their first day. The young are able to fly in another 3 weeks.

The nest, eggs, young, and adult are all extremely well-camouflaged on the sand. The nest, like that of many birds that perform distraction displays, is simply a scrape on the ground sometimes lined with commonly found sand-colored shells. In some regions the nest may be further hidden because it is located among light grasses. Because the nest is easily accessible to predators, protection of the eggs depends on camouflage, preventing potential predators' knowledge of the nest's location, and keeping them out of the nest's vicinity.

In order for a plover to be conspicuous special behaviors or vocalizations are required. During incubation and before the young can fly, both parents of both species perform distraction displays to intruders which move along the ground. (See review of various species' behavior in Gochfeld, 1984.)

There are several different kinds of distraction behaviors. The bird, especially piping plovers, may peep loudly while walking and keeping apace or ahead of the intruder. The plover may also fly conspicuously and slowly exposing its underside and bright wing stripes as it circles within about 30 meters and returns again to the vicinity of the predator. As it flies or walks at a distance from its young, it can be heard to vocalize a "peep" or "peep-lo." This is, in fact, often what first attracts the human's attention to the cryptically colored bird against the sandy beach. Sometimes the plover may engage in false brooding that is, sit down with feathers slightly fluffed, wriggling as it does so giving the appearance of sitting on a nest when, in fact, there are no eggs in that particular location. Or it may merely pace back and forth in the general vicinity of a human, seeming to eye the presumed predator as it does so.

On some approaches of an intruder, the bird may do a gradation of broken-wing displays (BWD), which may perhaps begin with a fanning tail and gradually increase the awkwardness of walk until it has one and then both wings widely arched, fluttering, and dragging. It may then vocalize loud raucous squawks as well. The broken-wing display is usually made while the bird is moving forward along the ground, although stationary displays are also made. The full display, as made by piping plovers, consists of outstretched widely arched wings that flutter and drag along the ground. The bird presents a convincing case for being injured, and the observer often trudges hundreds of meters after the bird only to see it suddenly fly away with agility. At that point one is far from the nest or young.

Note that the plover does not always make a broken-wing display (BWD) when its offspring are approached by a ground-moving object. In the course of my experiments conducted on Long Island, New York in 1983, parents gave broken-wing displays during approximately 40% of the close approaches to the nest. In other cases the plover left the nest cryptically with a silent low run. It may also silently hide in hollows with its tail towards the intruder making it very difficult to be seen.

Furthermore, a related species, the killdeer *C. vociferous,* only rarely performs broken-wing displays at the approach of grazing animals such as cattle, which do not eat eggs but may accidentally trample the nest. Instead, when cattle come quite close to the nest, the killdeer may lunge in a cow's face thereby startling it and causing it to veer away. (Armstrong, 1947; Graul, 1975; Walker, 1955). A somewhat similar set of reactions to mammals occurs among southern lapwings in Africa (Walters, 1980). Cattle and horses were typically ignored until the animal approached within about 5 meters of the nest or young. At such times, the parent bird either lunged with a characteristic defensive posture, wings spread wide and held low, or else did a brief mild distraction display. In short, at least some species which perform broken wing displays exhibit flexibility in their use of the behavior.

But precisely what is it that the bird is doing? Is this a stereotyped reflex, a fixed action pattern (FAP), or possibly a disorganized "hysterical" behavior as some have termed it? (Skutch, 1976, p. 403).

Does the bird have to do it? Can it control initiation or stopping of the BWD? Can the behavior be construed as intentional? What is evidence for the existence of an intention? Finally, can we answer any of these questions in a satisfying way?

It will be important to distinguish between "intentional" meaning "on purpose" and the philosophical use of the term to mean "aboutness"—a mark of the mental. I shall discuss both meanings.

What Are Some Possible Hypotheses About the Plover's Behavior?

Note that the following hypotheses are not mutually exclusive; it is quite possible that some combination may finally prove to be the most satisfactory.

Reflexive or Fixed Action Pattern Response

The bird's behavior is a reflex or an FAP which occurs when the parent bird is in a certain hormonal condition and is in the presence of an intruder and the plover's nest or young. A reflex is a simple stimulus-response connection in which a specific input is inevitably followed with little or no intervening processing by a unitary output. For example, the human knee-jerk response or the eye-blink response to a puff of air are reflexes. Complex behaviors are considered to be constructed by a chain of reflexes. In contrast, a fixed action pattern, a concept developed by the ethologists Lorenz and Tinbergen (1951), is described in a recent textbook as follows:

The distinguishing characteristics of the behavior are the innate and stereo-typed coordination and patterning of several muscle movements which, when released, proceed to completion without requiring further sensory input. In terms of its almost total independence of feedback, the fixed-action pattern represents an extreme class of prewired behavioral performances which have come to be known as 'motor programs.' (Gould, 1982, p. 37)

For either a reflex or an FAP, there are several possibilities about the direction in which the plover makes a broken-wing display. In all cases, given the complexity of the motor acts involved, an FAP seems a more reasonable construct than does a reflexive interpretation. The possible directions are the following:

1. The BWD is made in random directions. This hypothesis predicts that the displaying bird should be just as likely to display toward as away from the nest or young.
2. The displaying bird merely goes away from the nest or young.
3. The displaying bird merely goes away from the intruder.
4. The displaying bird moves away from both the nest or young and the intruder. This hypothesis requires that the plover must know the location and movements or trajectories of the young and the intruders in order to respond appropriately. That is no small feat. (And it is difficult to conceive of as reflexive or an FAP.)

Conflict Behavior

Earlier investigators often interpreted the broken-wing display to be the result of conflicting motivations. The displaying bird's behavior was thought to be "convulsive," "deliriously excited," and "its behavior patterns were more or less disorganized" (Skutch, 1976, p. 403). If the bird's behavior were indeed so disorganized, one would predict random directions of display or at least inconsistent leading away from the nest or young.

Approach/Withdrawal Tendencies

This point of view, espoused by students of Schneirla (1959), is similar to the conflict hypothesis but emphasizes more orderly behaviors by the bird than those predicted by a simple conflict hypthesis. It is hypothesized that the bird would make a broken-wing display at the point of conflict. Not one of the many possible predicted behaviors suffices to account for the complexity of the observed behaviors.

Pre-programmed Sequence of Behavior

According to this hypothesis, the bird behaves according to a programmed sequence of behavior in which stimuli such as direction of
movement of the intruder, size of intruder, nearness to nest, and so forth
determine the response of the parent bird. At least for the piping and
Wilson's plovers, the variability observed in their behavior does not lend
itself to an interpretation of a rigidly programmed sequence of behavior. If
we allow for great flexibility in that programming, we are including the
possibility of learning (see Learning), and if we allow reprogramming, we
might well be talking about purposeful behaviors. Recognize, however, no
program yet exists that adequately accounts for the behavior of a whole
animal in the real world, so the kind of "super" program that could include
descriptions of intentional behavior is not plausibly included as part of the
hypothesis of pre-programmed behavior.

Learning

Plovers might be able to learn about various aspects of a situation. This
might include the ability to distinguish potential predators from those that
are not. We have investigated that possibility in work discussed in section
IV and in detail in Ristau (1986). Except for a simple reflexive interpretation
of the plover's behavior and the conflict hypothesis, none of the other
hypotheses necessarily preclude the possibility of learning.

An explanation of all the complexities of the parent bird's behavior in
terms of operant conditioning is not viable if only because the infrequent
interactions with predators are not likely to provide the extensive learning
history required. A plover may, however, over one or more breeding
seasons learn to improve its strategy for effective use of a BWD.

Intentional or Purposeful Behavior

The plover wants to lead the intruder away from the nest or young. It
behaves so as to achieve this objective, which might include using the
broken-wing display. I do not mean to imply that every plover has
independently thought of or learned to make a BWD. The BWD is exhibited
throughout the species and is undoubtedly an evolved genetically transmitted behavior. (There is no direct evidence for this assertion for no studies
have been made of the ontogeny of the BWD.) However, strategies for its
effective use may well be learned both directly and by observation. The fact
that a behavior or some aspect of it is learned or genetically prewired does
not preclude the possibility of conscious thinking associated with it (see
Griffin, 1984, 1985). The hypothesis of purposeful behavior requires that

the plover must know the location and movements of young and intruders. In the next section, this hypothesis is discussed more fully.

Evidence Needed to Evaluate the Hypothesis: The Plover Wants to Lead the Intruder Away from Nest/Young

Based on the previous discussion concerning descriptive characteristics of intentional behavior, I propose the following observable behaviors as suggestive evidence in support of the following hypothesis: The plover wants to lead the intruder away from nest/young. I can make no claim that these are necessary and sufficient conditions for intentional behavior. I have not succeeded where centuries of philosophical thought have failed, that is, in proposing unassailable connections between observable behaviors and accompanying mental states. In evaluating the hypothesis, I will concentrate on broken-wing displays because they are very conspicuous and easily observed; other behaviors may also distract a predator.

1. The direction in which a bird moves during BWDs made in different encounters between intruders, nest or young, and parents should usually be appropriate or adequate to accomplish the objective of leading the intruder away. However, one should not expect that the parent bird will always move in a correct direction; in fact completely accurate performance might well be suspect. Neither is it required that the displaying bird move in an optimal direction.
2. The displaying birds should monitor the intruder to determine the intruder's attention, location, and behavior, particularly whether it is following the displaying bird.
3. Once the intruder's behavior is monitored, the displaying bird, if necessary, should modify its own behavior in a variety of ways in response to the intruder's behavior so as to achieve the goal of leading an intruder away. For instance, if the intruder is not paying attention to the displaying bird, as indicated either by eye gaze or failure to follow, the plover should try to gain the intruder's attention by loud vocalizing or by flying or walking into the visual field of the intruder. As one example, the displaying bird could reapproach the intruder to try again from a closer distance to attract the intruder's attention. If the intruder stops following, the bird could increase the intensity of its display or stop displaying and change its behavior.
4. The bird should exhibit appropriate flexibility of behaviors in other circumstances. For example, it should not make BWDs before eggs

are laid or after young can fly safely away. If we encounter a parent away from nest or young (e.g., feeding on its favorite mud flat), it should not make BWDs. If predators destroy the eggs or the eggs hatch and the young leave the nest, parents should no longer make BWDs leading away from the nest site. Flexibility could extend to other aspects of the bird's behavior, for example, the ability to learn which intruders are potentially dangerous and which are not.

Methods

The data being reported were gathered in the breeding season of 1982 on piping plovers and Wilson's plovers on a barrier island off the coast of Virginia. In that work, human intruders approached the nest or young, walked in the area of offspring, stopping at the nest and at other locations, and either followed or did not follow the displaying adult. Directions of the intruder's initial approach and changes in movements were varied so as to make the intruder's behavior unpredictable to the birds. Observations of the birds' behavior and of the location and direction of movement of the birds, chicks, and intruder were recorded by means of audio dictations and often videotape as well. Directions were given in compass points such as northeast or north northeast, which was the most precise specification of direction used. One observer was frequently located in a portable blind, while the other also functioned as an intruder. Sometimes both observers were the intruders.

Results

The reported data are drawn only from interactions in which the locations and directions of intruder, displaying birds, and nest or all chicks could be determined. The data derive from 19 different experimental sessions and from 10 birds which were members of 4 different pairs of piping plovers and 2 different pairs of Wilson's plovers. Data are combined for sessions with one and two intruders and for the stages of incubation and unfledged young. In 45 instances of broken-wing displays, the data were sufficiently detailed for analysis.

Evidence that the Plovers Make Broken-Wing Displays in a Direction "Appropriate" to Lead Intruders Away from the Nest or Young

Definitions of "Appropriate Direction". The first question I asked was whether the bird was displaying in a direction so as to cause an intruder to move toward or away from the offspring. In 44 out of 45 cases (98%), the bird's direction of display would have caused an intruder who followed it (i.e., went to the locations of the displaying bird) to get further from the young at the end of the period of injury-simulating display than at the beginning. One can also use a more stringent definition of the intruder moving away from eggs or young. Would the intruder ever, in the course of following the displaying bird, pass closer to the offspring? By those requirements, in 39 of the 45 cases (87%), the most direct path by which an intruder could have followed the displaying bird would never bring it closer to the nest or young. These data indicate that the birds' direction of display is adequate to get an intruder further from offspring.

Where in the Intruder's Visual Field does the Bird Make Broken-Wing Displays?   If the bird is displaying in order to attract the intruder's attention, one would expect the bird to be selective about where it displays; it should display where the intruder will see it. With respect to location, 44 of the 45 BWDs were made in front of the intruder rather than behind, that is, within a 180 degree arc of the intruder's visual field. The one possible exception occurred when an intruder was searching for young (very near them) and moving in a somewhat unpredictable fashion. The parent made a BWD to the side of the intruder, directed away from the young, and headed opposite to the general trend of the intruder's movement toward the chicks. In this situation, because the intruder was moving in a zigzag fashion, she was likely to turn so that sometimes the BWD would be within her visual field, and sometimes it would not.

These data do not determine which intruder characteristics the bird was responding to because, in most cases, the intruder was moving so that direction of movement, eye gaze, and facial and body orientation could be cues for the bird. When the intruder was stationary, it is conceivable the bird opted to display with respect to remembered direction of intruder movement rather than simply direction of eye gaze.

Positioning by the Bird Before Making a BWD.   Another question examined in detail was the location of the bird when it began its broken-wing displays. If this behavior is a reflex that is elicited whenever an intruder approaches closely enough, one might expect the display to occur wherever the bird is located. However, the bird always moves before displaying. Sometimes the bird moves by flying, which is an easily and accurately observable form of locomotion. One can argue that by flying to a location rather than walking, a slower form of locomotion, it is probably important to the plover to get to that location rapidly. In all 13 cases of flying, the bird's new position was closer to the intruder than was its position before flight. One would not expect such positioning if, as some have suggested, the bird were attempting to get away from the intruder.

Furthermore, in 11 of those 13 cases, not only was the bird closer to the intruder, but it was closer to the front of the intruder than it had been, that is, more directly in the center of the intruder's visual field and/or the path of the moving intruder.

Evidence that Birds Making a BWD Monitor the Intruder's Behavior

To engage in these various behaviors strongly suggests the birds are monitoring the intruders. Are they? How can one determine what a plover is monitoring? Plovers have eyes that are placed laterally with both frontal and side (temporal) foveas so they can see can see over a wide field. It would be difficult to specify exactly what they are attending to within that field. They cannot, however, see behind them. Observations, photographs, and videotapes show that as a plover is making a broken-wing display while moving away from an intruder, it often turns its head sharply back over its shoulder its eye toward the intruder. The change in head/eye orientation strongly suggests monitoring of the intruder.

Modification of Displays in Response to Changing Intruder Behavior

Further indications of intentionality are provided by the behaviors of plovers when intruders do not follow the displaying bird. Detailed information is available in 36 of the 45 total cases of broken-wing displays. In five instances the intruder followed the displaying bird, and in all five cases the bird continued its display and did not stop to move closer to the intruder. Because five is a small number of cases, I looked through the data in 1983, 1984, and 1985 and found 12 additional cases (with adequate data) when the intruder followed the displaying bird; the bird did not reapproach the intruder in any of these cases.

In 31 cases of the original data set, the intruder did not follow the displaying bird or ceased to follow it. It seems sensible to expect that a bird that was not sensitive to the intruder's response to its display would simply continue what it was doing, that is, making a BWD. However, the bird did not typically do this. In 17 of these 31 instances (55%) when the intruder did not follow the display, the bird stopped its display and reapproached the intruder by either flying or walking closer. In nine instances (29%), the bird either continued to make a BWD or increased the intensity of the display, for example, by flapping its wings more vigorously or vocalizing raucously while displaying. Of the remaining five cases, after displaying, (a) the bird flew to the location of the young (three instances), (b) flew away (one instance), or (c) in one other case did not reapproach or fly.

Summary

In summary, the use of intense distraction displays, at least by the plovers in this study, indicates that they usually perform the displays in a direction that would cause an intruder following them to get further away from the threatened nest or young. Furthermore, the birds monitor the intruder's approach and modify their behavior in response to changes in intruder locomotion. I interpreted the data as providing at least suggestive evidence for the purposive nature (or first order intentional analysis) of the birds' behavior. I don't mean to claim that it is the very flexible, fully cognitive, fully conscious, purposeful behavior we humans sometimes have. (Of course, conscious intention is almost impossible to demonstrate in a totally unequivocal fashion even in other human beings, but these data are the beginnings.)

To those who are discomforted by attempts to study "consciousness" in animals, recognize that even taking the stance of purposeful or intentional behavior without ever implying consciousness is a fruitful enterprise. The stance led me to design experiments that I had not otherwise thought to do, that no one else had done, and that revealed complexities in the behavior of the piping plover's distraction behavior not heretofore appreciated. I invite readers to adopt the stance of intentional behavior and to help delineate the levels and kinds of knowledge and purposiveness an organism might have.

THE GAZE EXPERIMENTS

Is a piping plover responsive to the attention of an intruder to its nest area — defined here as the direction of gaze of the intruder? To investigate this question experimentally, we conducted a series of very simple experiments on Long Island beaches New York in 1984 and 1985.

In each experiment there were two human intruders. They were dressed differently so as to aid the birds in distinguishing between them. One intruder always looked towards the dunes while the other intruder always looked away from the dunes and towards the ocean. Note that on Long Island the piping plovers' nests are located in the dunes. Matched pairs of trials were conducted such that within each pair the intruders walked, one at a time, along the same path which was parallel to the dunes and within 15-25 meters south of the dunes. As they walked, the intruders actively scanned either the dunes or the ocean and turned their heads as well as their eyes from side to side as they did so. In addition, during some of the sessions, about five meters *before* an intruder was due south of the nest on the walk, the intruder sat down and continued scanning either the dunes or the ocean for approximately 45 seconds.

Each trial began when a parent plover was incubating eggs. The incubating bird almost always left the nest when an intruder walked by (one exception). The data consisted of the duration of time a bird remained off the nest when each type of intruder walked by. (The underlying assumption is that a bird will remain off the nest longer for a more threatening human intruder than for a less threatening one.) Adequate data were available for a total of 50 trials (25 matched pairs); 11 different birds served as subjects. Results indicated that the birds stayed off the nest longer when the intruder gazing towards the dunes walked by than when an intruder walking along the same path but looking towards the ocean walked by. (Results were statistically significant by a Chi squared analysis applied to (a) the number of birds which stayed off the nest longer for the "looking toward" gazer as compared to those who stayed off longer for the "looking away" gazer and (b) the total number of trials [summed across all birds] during which birds stayed off the nest longer for the looking toward condition as contrasted to the looking away condition.") (Ristau, in prep.)

In brief, even at a fairly great distance from the nest (15-25 meters), the gaze of an intruder towards the general area where the nest is located (the dunes) in contrast to a gaze in the opposite direction causes a parent plover to behave differently. The birds act in a more intense or aroused fashion (stay off the nest longer) for walkers looking towards the nest region than away.

These results strongly suggest that the plovers are sensitive to at least one measure of the intruder's attention — direction of eye gaze towards their eggs. Note that Burghardt (this volume) has shown that hognose snakes engage in death feigning longer (or more precisely, take longer to fully recover from death feigning) in the presence of an intruder 1 meter away who is looking directly at them, than in the presence of an intruder who has his eyes averted. The snakes feign death an even shorter time when the human intruder leaves. The snake experiments differ from my work with the plovers in several respects: (a) the intruder is much closer to the animal in Burghardt's research (1 meter for the snakes vs. 15-25 meters for the plovers); (b) the snake experiments were done in the laboratory whereas the plover experiments were conducted in the field; (c) the intruder is stationary in the snake experiments and moving in the plover study, and (d) importantly, the human intruder is staring at the snake but scanning the general location of the plover's nest/eggs. However, because my experiments were started when the plover was incubating its eggs, the plover was, at least initially, occasionally within the gaze of the intruder scanning the nest region.

Gallup, Cummings, and Nash (1972) also found (in laboratory experiments) that chickens engage longer in tonic immobility in the presence of a human who is staring at them vs. not looking at them. Similar results have been obtained for anoles (Hennig, 1977): (the reader is also referred to a general review and discussion of this phenomenon by Arduino and Gould, 1984). Tonic immobility is also termed death feigning, though it is not as complex a behavior sequence as that of the hognose snake. Comparative research is especially important in order to better understand the limitations and differences in abilities that comprise similar but possibly differently complex behaviors.

Several experiments with plovers would be of interest. To determine more precisely the effect on the parent bird's behavior when an intruder gazes towards the eggs vs. to the parent plover, one would want to conduct the gaze experiments when a parent is in the area but is not incubating the eggs. Under natural conditions, this is a rare event; it typically happens only when there is a nest exchange (one bird relieves the other of incubation duties) or when the parent is involved in a territorial encounter with another bird or is interacting with an intruder. Very infrequently the parent might be nearby feeding leaving the nest unincubated for a brief time. Except perhaps for the last scenario, none of these conditions are adequate for conducting the proposed experiments. To have an intruder either gaze at or away from a displaying adult has, as yet, been impracticable because sufficiently precise observations could not be obtained without the observer becoming an intruder.

Another series of potential experiments arise from the observation that the piping plovers' eggs are better camouflaged when not being incubated than during incubation. Presumably, degree of egg camouflage and tendency to leave the eggs in the presence of an intruder coevolved. Might, however, each bird also be able to assess egg conspicuousness and modify its behavior accordingly? Pertinent evidence could be gathered by brightly and conspicuously marking the camouflaged eggs of a bird species which leaves the nest during an intruder's presence. Does the bird then alter its behavior adaptively as the parent of its now noncamouflaged eggs by remaining on the nest longer, for example, or increasing its likelihood of attacking the intruder or of making a broken-wing display rather than relying on camouflage to deter predation?

CAN BIRDS DISCRIMINATE BETWEEN SAFE AND DANGEROUS INTRUDERS?

Introduction

The plover does not display to all objects or intruders which move along the ground. To leave the nest and to display to intruders requires energy of the parents and possibly endangers the eggs which may heat or cool beyond tolerable limits while the parents are not tending them. Getting involved with a nondangerous intruder may deflect attention from a real predator to whom eggs or young may fall prey. Therefore, the stakes are high for the plover to know when an intruder is potentially dangerous and when not.

How do the birds come to know this? They could be innately equipped to respond to sign stimuli of predators, or they could be learning to discriminate potential predators from benign intruders, possibly guided by innate constraints.

There is information from the laboratory and the field that suggests many species of birds can learn to discriminate between intruders of possible danger to the eggs or young and those which are not. Depending upon the stage of development of their young, parents should behave differently to predators that eat eggs or young or both. Evidence supporting this derives from aggressive mobbing behavior. Sordahl (1980) observed that avocets (*Recurvirostra americana*) and stilts (*Himantopus himantopus*) that had eggs frequently mobbed gulls, predators that eat the eggs and very young chicks of these shorebirds. When the avocets and stilts had young, they mobbed gulls far less frequently and mobbed herons (which eat young) more frequently. Stilts do not mob Franklin's gulls (*Larus pipixcan*), which are almost entirely insectivorous (Bent, 1921), although they do, in another geographic region, mob the egg-eating Laughing gulls (*L. atricilla*) (Dinsmoor, 1977). Laughing gulls are very similar in appearance to Franklin's gulls.

In a laboratory mobbing experiment, European blackbirds (*Tordus merula*) learned to mob innocuous honeyeaters by observing another blackbird apparently mobbing a model of a stuffed honeyeater, an avian species not typically found locally. The "teacher" blackbird was actually mobbing a stuffed owl, carefully hidden from the "student's" view by partitions. Further experimentation indicated that the students could in turn teach seven generations the unusual mobbing behavior (Curio, Ernst, & Vieth, 1978).

Occasional field observations indicate that some avian species behave differently depending on the kind of danger the intruder poses to the eggs. Only rarely does the killdeer *C. vociferous* (close relatives of piping plovers) perform broken-wing displays at the approach of grazing animals such as cattle, horses, or goats which do not eat eggs but may accidentally trample the nest. Instead, when a cow comes quite close to the nest, the killdeer may lunge in a cow's face thereby startling it and causing it to veer away. (Armstrong, 1947; Graul, 1975; Walker, 1955).

Other laboratory experiments indicate that pigeons (*Columba livia*) could learn to make distinctions between various classes of objects, drawings, and living organisms which were displayed on photographic slides. Among the discriminations a pigeon could learn were photographs of: (a) tree from nontree items (including celery stalks) (b) fish from nonfish; (c) water (drops, puddles, and pools) from "nonwater" (Herrnstein & de Villiers, 1980); (d) oak leaves from other species of leaves (Cerella, 1979); (e) the letter "A" in various typesets from the number "2" (Morgan, Fitch, Holman, & Lea, 1976); and (f) even a particular person in a variety of poses and attire from other people (Herrnstein, Loveland, & Cable, 1976). Note that this list includes both "natural" categories a pigeon might be innately predisposed to make (or to have experienced even in captivity) as well as quite arbitrary ones (e.g., the letter A). The pigeons could also, with training, make yet more arbitrary distinctions; for example, they could learn to peck more frequently at one of two sets of slides, each of which were randomly selected photos of fish and nonfish. Such differential responding required far more training than did the same set of slides separated into fish vs. nonfish piles, but it could be done.

Our own observations from the field as well as those of others note that birds habituate to certain humans and not to others, again indicating a discrimination. For example Bent (1921) reported that a farmer regularly plowing his field does not disturb a killdeer nest a few feet away, but a stranger entering the field and located much further from the nest does arouse the bird. Likewise, W. H. Drury (personal communication, 1983) noticed that birds once trapped by him became very wary and highly responsive to him. They did not, however, react strongly to another human dressed in Drury's clothing who was not associated with the trapping.

Methods

Overview of Methods

With this body of data and suggestive observations in mind, we designed the following experimental situation to determine if the piping plovers in their natural environment could learn to discriminate between two intruders, one of whom had acted benignly or safely towards the eggs and parent bird while the other behaved more dangerously. (I find a note here to myself asking whether I really want to phrase this question in terms of how the parent plovers may construe the events or, more cautiously, in terms of an intruder who walks at a considerable distance from the nest and does not look at the bird or nest vs. an intruder who approaches closely to the nest and hovers over it. As you can see, I have chosen the plover's point of view which is, after all, the motivation for doing the experiment. I am, however, careful to define "safely" and "dangerously" in terms of the operations used in the experiment. And the reader will note that later in the discussion section I proceed carefully when discussing the possible meaning of dangerous to a plover, and I consider other empirically defined variables that should be studied when exploring the notion of danger.)

Intruders were chosen who differed in characteristics unlikely to arouse the parent plovers differentially. Thus the intruders were all humans who wore distinctively different clothing. In the rare case when one intruder was much larger than the other and therefore a potentially more threatening stimulus, that larger intruder was conservatively chosen as the safe intruder.

The distinctively dressed humans each walked safely by a nest containing eggs (at a considerable distance from the nest) and did not pay attention to the nest or to the parent bird. These pretests were conducted to verify that the plovers did not react differentially to various humans used in the experiments initially. One intruder then closely approached the nest approximately twice and acted in a way that we hoped would appear to the parent bird to be dangerous or threatening (the dangerous approaches). In the posttest trials, each intruder once again walked safely by the nest several times and payed no attention to the nest or parent (See Figure 5.1.) Would the parent birds now react differently to the previously dangerous intruder as compared to the intruder who had acted only safely?

If the plovers can learn to discriminate between human intruders, it is most probable that they are able normally to learn an even simpler discrimination between different species of nonhuman intruders which have

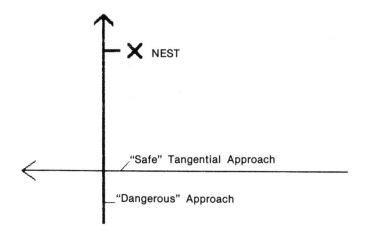

Fig. 5.1 Diagram of safe and dangerous approaches to the nest. Vertical arrow indicates the path walked by the dangerous intruders. The path passes close (4 meters) by the nest (X) and includes a portion during which the intruder more closely approaches the nest and hovers over it. The horizontal arrow indicates the path walked by each of the intruders as they walk tangentially past the nest at a much greater distance (12–32 meters).

behaved in differentially threatening ways towards the plovers' nest or young.

The Sites

The safe-dangerous experiments were conducted on sand beaches in Long Island, New York. Most of the beaches were wide with the ocean to the south and a line of low grassy dunes to the north. All plover nests were located in the dunes on the side nearest the ocean. An area around each nest approximately 60 by 80 meters was marked with distinctive objects set 10-15 meters apart. Maps were made of the areas with notations of the markers and were used during and after the experiments to indicate locations and movements of the birds and intruders. Because even inexpensive wooden stakes proved to be too great a temptation to the acquisitive nature of the beach goers, we used garbage markers such as brightly colored, used, plastic laundry detergent containers, a discarded fan, a deflated faded pink beach ball, empty whiskey containers, and old tires; these were chosen so as to be easily visible but unlikely to be collected by passersby. (However even these appeared to have occasional aesthetic value or else inspired altruistic acts of beach cleaning, for one beach user was caught in the act of removing a carefully placed bright red container, and children too often favored the deflated old beach ball over their own bouncy new ones.)

Experimental Methods

Each bird served once as a subject in a completed experimental session (In one case of uncertain identity, the bird or its mate participated in a second discrimination.) During the course of each experiment, a plover's nest was approached in two distinct ways designated as safe or tangential and dangerous or near. In safe intrusions, a human walked by the nest at a distance of 12-32 meters and did not look at the nest but looked straight ahead. In dangerous (near) intrusions, a human walked towards the nest on a path 4 meters to one side of it. The intruder looked at the nest during the entire approach. Then the dangerous intruder paused about 30 seconds upon reaching the edge of the dunes and, again, when directly opposite the nest, both times with body and face oriented to the nest. Next the dangerous intruder walked nearer the nest to a distance of 2 meters or less and acted so as to appear to be searching for eggs, moving the head and body from side to side while looking towards the nest area. Finally, the dangerous intruder turned, left the immediate area of the nest, and resumed walking past the nest on a path 4 meters from it and over the dunes. Both the safe and dangerous intrusions were made at similar rates of walking and with a similar gait.

As noted, the safe and dangerous intruders were dressed distinctively to aid the birds in forming a discrimination. The intruders wore light or dark colored slacks, differently colored and patterned shirts, blouses, jackets, shorts, bathing suits, hats, wigs, sunglasses, satchels, and different hair styles. The apparel for any given pair of intruders differed in as many ways as practicable, for example, both would never wear skirts at the same time. Tape recorders and walkie-talkies (if used) were typically hidden under an intruder's clothing and in satchels so as not to incriminate the observers who also used the same equipment. The observers always wore approximately the same clothes, army green or denim pants and dark shirts, which the intruders never wore. When possible, different persons functioned as observer(s) and intruders, but when not possible, care was taken that the intruder changed costume before resuming a post as observer or videotape operator.

Data Collection

Ongoing observations were dictated simultaneously onto audio cassettes by the intruder and by an observer at the observer station 30-60 meters from the nest. Data consisted of time to the nearest second and descriptions in real-time of the intruder's and bird's behavior, including their movements and locations. Videotapes of the proceedings were also frequently made at the observer station. Necessary coordination was done via walkie-talkies. Each plover in a pair was individually identified by the size and shape of the neck ring.

Scheduling of Trials

A trial consisted of either a safe (tangential) or dangerous (near) approach. Each session occurred over the course of a single day; it began with pretests consisting of two or more tangential approaches — one half by the person designated safe and the other half by the person scheduled to do a dangerous approach. Trials were run in pairs such that within any pair, both persons walked along paths that were equidistant from the nest.

In the next phase, one intruder (not both) made approximately two dangerous approaches (range 1–4) separated in time by about 5 minutes. Posttests followed in which each person made a series of tangential approaches at different distances from the nest. As in the pretest, trials were paired with respect to distance. The sequence of trials in the posttest was systematically varied in order to control for possible order effects. Interruptions caused some experimental sessions to be discontinued before completion. The interruptions included weather changes such as rain, thick fog, onset of cold or very hot temperatures (both of which are stresses upon the developing fetus), and other disturbances such as frequent nest exchanges (incubating bird is relieved by mate) and boundary disputes.

Hierarchy of Responses Made by Incubating Bird to an Intruder

Dramatically different responses of an incubating bird to the tangential approach of an intruder are to remain on the nest or to get off. Other possible behaviors, arranged in hierarchical order from the most aroused or disturbed to the most calm, are listed in Fig. 5.2.

Three categories of the bird's behavior are to some extent dependent on each other and should be considered alternate rather than hierarchical categories. These (listed in Fig. 5.1 under "Gets OFF Nest") are distance of bird off the nest, time off the nest, and distance of intruder from the nest when the bird leaves the nest.

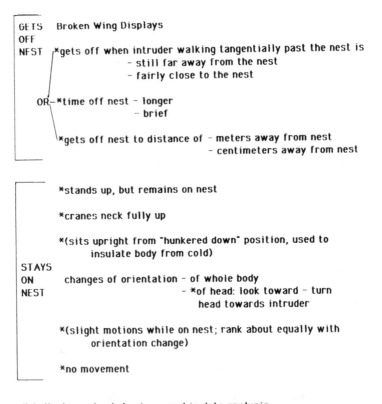

GETS OFF NEST   Broken Wing Displays

*gets off when intruder walking tangentially past the nest is
  - still far away from the nest
  - fairly close to the nest

OR—*time off nest – longer
              – brief

*gets off nest to distance of – meters away from nest
                              – centimeters away from nest

STAYS ON NEST

*stands up, but remains on nest

*cranes neck fully up

*(sits upright from "hunkered down" position, used to insulate body from cold)

changes of orientation – of whole body
                       – *of head: look toward – turn head towards intruder

*(slight motions while on nest; rank about equally with orientation change)

*no movement

* indicates avian behaviors used in data analysis
( ) indicates avian behaviors not originally on this list

Fig. 5.2 Hierarchy of behaviors by incubating bird in response to intruder. Behaviors are listed from the most aroused (top) to the least aroused (bottom).

The bird's behavior was compared for matched pairs of trials in which the safe and dangerous intruder walked along paths at equal distances from the nest. Relative arousal of the bird's behaviors was determined from the hierarchy of incubating bird's behavior. If the bird reacted more intensely to a tangential walk by the dangerous intruder than by the safe one, the score for the comparison was "+". If the safe person elicited more arousal, the score was "−." Approximately equal behaviors were scored "0".

The birds' scores were then summarized over all the pairs of trials during an entire experimental session to determine whether a given bird had learned the discrimination.

Results

The primary question being asked is whether piping plovers exposed to approximately two dangerous intrusions near the nest can then discriminate between that dangerous intruder and a distinctively dressed safe intruder who has only walked by the nest at a safe distance. By comparing the birds' reactions to the intruders when each intruder later walks safely by the nest in a posttest, I determined whether the birds discriminated, that is, whether they acted in a more aroused manner to the previously dangerous intruder than to the safe intruder.

Sixteen complete experimental sessions were conducted, each within the course of one day, with at least 15 different piping plovers serving as subjects (possibly 16 due to the one case of uncertain identity). The birds were members of 11 different pairs of plovers; nine birds were male, five were female, and sex was uncertain in one session. An additional six sessions had to be aborted before completion.

A total of 196 tangental walks were made by intruders; 69 were pretest tangents and 127 were posttest tangents. Forty matched pairs of posttest trials (80 tangents) could be used in the analyses. The remaining posttest tangents could not be used due to interruptions, nest exchanges or boundary disputes, or because a comparable tangent was not available in the data for the other intruder.

Do the Birds Discriminate Between Dangerous and Safe Intruders?

The data indicate that birds are able to discriminate between intruders. There are at least two ways to consider the data: (a) The total number of matched pairs of trials on which birds responded more strongly to the previous "dangerous" intruder than to the "safe" intruder (see Fig. 5.3) and

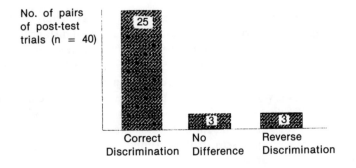

No. of pairs
of post-test
trials (n = 40)

Correct Discrimination   No Difference   Reverse Discrimination

corrected data $\chi^2 = 31.23$, p < .001 (change = 10.3)

Fig. 5.3 Do piping plovers discriminate between safe and dangerous intruders (a comparison of matched pairs of posttest trials)?

(b) the number of individual birds that responded more strongly to the previously dangerous intruder than to the safe intruder.

Comparing Responses on Total Number of Matched Pairs of Posttest Trials

Birds responded more strongly to the dangerous intruder than to the safe one in 25 pairs or 81% of the 31 pairs of posttest trials (corrected data). The difference was dramatic in 13 of the 25 pairs of trials (52%) in that the bird left the nest at the approach of the previously dangerous intruder but not to the safe one. In the remaining 12 of the 25 pairs, the birds responded differentially but less dramatically (Fig. 5.4). In only 3 of 31 tests did the birds make a reverse discrimination and respond more intensely to the safe intruder than to the dangerous one. The birds showed no difference in their behavior to the safe and dangerous intruders on 3 pairs of posttest trials (corrected data) or on 12 pairs if we consider the data uncorrected for reaction distance.[1]

With or without the correction procedure, the results are significant by a Chi-squared analysis (see Fig. 5.3) ($p < .001$).

---

[1]In some posttest trials, the incubating bird made no observable response to either the safe or dangerous intruder when they were walking along paths very distant from the nest (i.e., beyond the bird's reaction distance). At closer distances during that session, the same birds did react differentially to the same intruders. Under such conditions, as long as the pairs of trials on which the birds made no response were the farthest paths walked in that session, those farthest trials were discounted in one analysis of the data. This analysis was termed "data corrected for reaction distance." An analysis including those data was also always done.

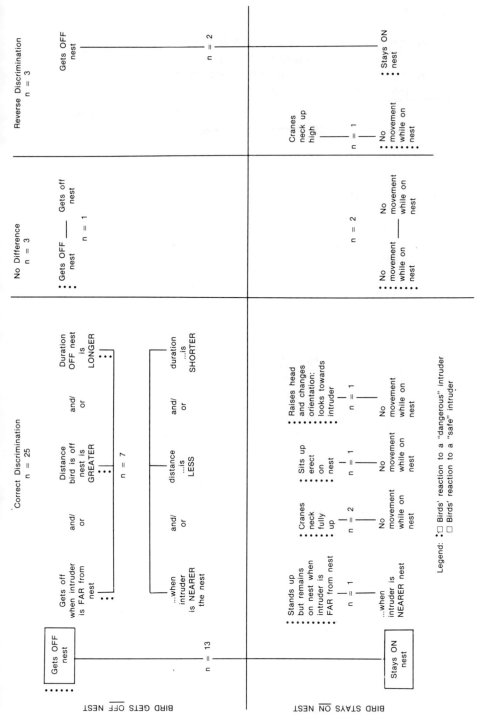

Fig. 5.4 Details of birds' behaviors on posttest trials with dangerous vs. safe intruders.

113

Comparing the Total Number of Birds that
Responded more Strongly to the Previously
Dangerous Intruder than to the Safe Intruder (or did
not Differentiate Between Either)

Thirteen different birds served as subjects in 14 different completed experimental sessions (data corrected for reaction distance). (See Fig. 5.5.) Of those 13 birds, 11 different birds made a total of 12 correct discriminations (i.e., 11 first discriminations), another bird did not discriminate, and one other bird made a reverse discrimination. Comparing the number of correct first discriminations made by each bird (11) to the number of completed sessions in which no discrimination was made (1) and to the number of reverse discriminations (1) yields statistically significant results: χ^2 (2, N = 13) = 15.39, p < .001. Even using data uncorrected for reaction distance yields statistically significant results χ^2 (2, N = 15) = 11.20, p < .01.

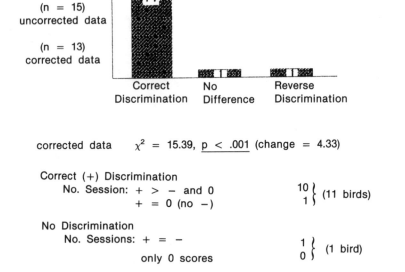

corrected data χ^2 = 15.39, p < .001 (change = 4.33)

Correct (+) Discrimination
    No. Session: + > − and 0   10 } (11 birds)
                 + = 0 (no −)   1

No Discrimination
    No. Sessions: + = −   1 }
            only 0 scores   0 } (1 bird)

Reverse Discrimination
    No. Session: − > +   1   (1 bird)

Total No. of Different Birds   13

Fig. 5.5 Do piping plovers discriminate between safe and dangerous intruders (an analysis by birds)?

The single incident of a reverse discrimination is particularly interesting. In that experiment, which was conducted on hatching day, each bird received fewer than the usual number of approaches, that is, each was approached closely by the dangerous intruder only once rather than twice as was typical. Perhaps most important, it was the only case in which there were two prior aborted experiments in which the roles of safe and dangerous intruders were reversed, that is, the person now safe had previously been dangerous in both the aborted attempts and vice versa. This was necessitated by the lack of enough different persons to function as intruders. (Note that each dressed differently than they had during the "aborted" experiment.) Nevertheless, one bird in the pair correctly discriminated, while the other made a reverse discrimination.

Do Other Intruder Characteristics Account for Differential Responding by the Plovers?

Analysis of the plovers' behavior towards intruders during pretest trials (i.e., before dangerous approaches to the nest had been made) indicates that the discriminations made by the plovers could not be accounted for by any differences observed in the pretest trials either with respect to the particular persons functioning as the safe and dangerous intruders or with respect to the particular clothing worn by intruders.

Discussion

In brief, piping plovers (*Charadrius melodus*) did discriminate between dangerous and safe intruders in the great majority of tests. Recall that 11 birds made correct discriminations, 1 made a reverse discrimination under particularly interesting conditions, and either 1 (corrected data) or 3 (data uncorrected for reaction distance) made no discrimination.

There are several possible reasons why a few piping plovers did not show evidence of forming the discrimination. First, for reasons of wildlife conservation, the dangerous activity performed by the intruder was purposefully not actually dangerous; the eggs were not touched and the intruder's stay near the nest was comparatively brief (about 30-60 seconds).

Furthermore, of all the piping plovers in the world, the birds in this study are probably among those most habituated to humans. Such habituation can be advantageous in these experiments insofar as the birds may respond to some humans as nonthreatening thereby permitting unobtrusive observation by humans. Furthermore, these birds may have already learned that it is beneficial to discriminate between humans who are likely to pose a threat and those who are not.

Another possible hindrance to forming a discrimination is that the experiments were performed under less than ideal conditions. Ideally, the intruders should not have to function as observers as well or have any previous experience with the birds or associate in the presence of the birds with each other or the other team members.

These experiments raise the possibility of observational learning — learning in which a different organism is rewarded or punished or gains information, and the observer, merely through observing the situation, alters its own behavior in accordance with those factors. Such learning is considered quite complex and is difficult to demonstrate in many animals. In my experiments, there was one session with sufficient data to determine that a mate not incubating the eggs could learn to discriminate between safe and dangerous intruders. In that case the mate was not a passive observer; it did interact with the intruder.

It is also plausible that neighboring birds can learn which intruders may be dangerous. On several occasions during the 1983 field season, neighboring birds appeared on the territory during a dangerous intrusion. And in other experimental procedures, in years when more nest sites were closer together, neighboring birds would sometimes walk along with an intruder who had passed through several territories. In their neighbor's territory, the birds could observe experimental interaction and might witness the resident plover engaging in antipredator behaviors to the intruder. It seems plausible such an experience could teach the neighboring plovers to be wary of that particular intruder.

Finally, one must consider whether it is appropriate to label intruders as "safe" and "dangerous". Would some other more minimal description of the intruders' behavior suffice? It is, of course, not clear whether a plover can form a concept such as "safe" or "dangerous". Yet in their natural world the plovers must react to some set of animals (and possibly humans) as potential predators and others as nonthreatening.

What mechanism might underlie the plovers' discrimination? Classical conditioning might be occurring such that the plover becomes more highly aroused when an intruder is close to the nest. That dangerous intruder, even at a distance, becomes a conditioned stimulus for arousal. Simultaneously, the plover could be habituating to some degree to the safe intruder who does not come close to the nest on repeated walks past the nest.

The present set of experiments do not, however, determine which aspects of the intruders' behavior are most critical to the plover's reacting in a more aroused way to the dangerous intruder. That intruder not only approached the nest area much more closely than did the safe intruder, it could also be considered as knowing the location of the nest while the safe intruder did not. To determine whether each of these factors has significance for the plovers would require additional experiments. (a) One possible sort of experiment would require that different intruders walk near the nest, one look toward it while the other, following an identical path and with equal duration near the nest, either look away from it (see Gaze experiments, p. 102–104 for a related experiment in which intruders walked fairly far from the nest) or else search unsuccessfully (i.e., look in various directions on the ground without appearing to look at the nest), and (b) intention of the intruder (or at least its past history of behavior) also may be a variable in that in the present experiments, in addition to being near the nest and knowing where it is located, the intruder also acted so as to appear threatening (i.e., the intruder hovered over the eggs). The sort of experiment which might reveal the importance of such differences would require giving the plover knowledge that one intruder is dangerous, that is, allow the plover to observe the intruder smashing another plover's eggs, and then have that intruder and one who has walked benignly by another's nest walk safely by the plover's own nest. Intention might also be determined by having an intruder in one case, walk close to the plover's nest and hover over it (i.e., an attempt to appear interested or potentially dangerous) and in the other case, although very close by, become interested in some object or piece of equipment located near the nest.

Even these suggested experiments are only initial explorations of a plover's beliefs or knowledge about an intruder, and as results are gathered, yet more fine-tuning of the research must be done.

There are also a host of other more obvious empirical manipulations that can be done to examine perceived dangerousness of an intruder including varying intruder size, speed of approach, direction of approach (we have gathered data on this question which await analysis). With the exception of the last, these are of less theoretical significance.

Summary

Ground nesting shorebirds, piping plovers (*Charadrius melodus*), can learn to discriminate between distinctively dressed safe and dangerous intruders. In these experiments, the discrimination was achieved after the plovers experienced usually only two approaches (range 1–4) by an intruder (the dangerous intruder) who walked near the nest (2 meters or less). A plover was considered to have discriminated between the intruders by responding in a more aroused way when the dangerous intruder walked tangentially by the nest than when the safe intruder walked by. Relative arousal was measured by ranking the observed behaviors according to a hierarchy of behaviors that reflect arousal. The most frequent and most dramatic difference in the bird's behavior was the bird's leaving the nest when the dangerous intruder walked tangentially by while remaining on the nest for a tangential walk by the safe intruder.

The experiments strongly suggest the plovers would be able to distinguish similarly between animals who may be potential predators and those who are not by having even brief experiences with a predator walking near its nest in an attentive fashion. Possibly even mates not incubating during a dangerous approach to the nest or neighboring birds who observe and interact with an intruder/predator could learn to make the discrimination.

DISCUSSION

The Benefits of Limited Anthropomorphism and of using an Intentional Stance

One may question why we should describe the way animals behave in terms of an intentional stance, that is, with respect to goals or beliefs and desires as philosophers use the terms. J. Bennett (this volume) has discussed this issue by focusing on the explanatory value of beliefs and desires and other mental states in understanding behavior. He, in fact, extends the ideas developed by Grice (1967), Dennett (1978, 1983, 1987) and Bennett (1976) to emphasize the importance of grounding the beliefs, desires, and behavior in the environment. When a simple, "triggered" stimulus-motor response description of behavior does not suffice, Bennett argues that an explanation may be needed in terms of a class of situations which are characterized by the organism's having certain beliefs and desires which make possible a variety of behaviors to achieve the goal.

Some, such as Burghardt (this volume), consider an intentional stance a possibly useful heuristic device in suggesting experiments to be done and emphasizes that it should be considered just one of many possible approaches; he underscores the need for empirical data. I couldn't possibly disagree. Of course other approaches should be followed and, of course, every scientist needs empirical data. Yoerg and Kamil (this volume) go a step further and state that anything that helps provoke a scientist to design experiments is OK — in that limited way. Thus, any sort of event might be the seed for a reasonable experiment, but the method of conjuring up an experiment should not be confused with the appropriate interpretation of the experiment or with a useful theoretical approach. For example, they suggest one may wish to imagine how an organism might feel or think when one makes field observations or designs an experiment, but that is not evidence that the organism actually feels that way. Their statements are also very sensible, but there are several other issues to be considered in conjunction with them.

Among these issues we should examine why it should be fruitful to be anthropomorphic in at least a limited way or to use an intentional stance when designing experiments or interpreting observational data. Why do these approaches work? Griffin and others propose that the approach of anthropomorphism works because animals may indeed have mental states including mental experiences. He uses several arguments to support his claim; most relevant here is the continuity of nature and of evolution. It is highly unlikely given all the continuities between humans and other organisms that humans alone should be aware or conscious, and have thoughts, purposes, beliefs, and desires. It is more likely that creatures other than humans should have a mind. The anthropomorphism, of course, should be limited. Another organism is not a human; it lives in different circumstances and sometimes has quite different sensory apparati. (See also Burghardt's ideas about critical anthropomorphism, this volume.)

Why should an intentional stance be particularly useful? Recall that, in Dennett's view, an intentional stance need not imply consciousness. The stance can be applied to a thermostat, a chess-playing computer program, a plover, or a human (a snake too? — see Burghardt, this volume) Other philosophers, for example, Searle (1980), distinguish between the derived intentionality of a thermostat or a computer program (intentionality derived from its designer) and the intrinsic intentionality of a human and perhaps a plover. A human actually does want a vacation or a dinner, whereas it is simply a useful strategy to deal with a chess-playing computer program to say it wants to bring its queen out early.

An intentional stance, at least the first level, can include a purposive interpretation of behavior (e.g., my studies in which I suggested that the plover wants to lead the intruder away from its nest). Because I took that stance, predictions about the plover's behaviors were made and experiments were designed to test the predictions.

Many ethologists who may not wish to deal with questions of animal mentality might opt to describe the plovers' injury feigning in terms of its function; the behavior functions to lead an intruder away from the nest. It has evolved to have that function. As proposed by the ethologist Tinbergen (1951), the function of a behavior is one of the four kinds of explanations of behavior scientists seek to answer. (The other three "whys" of behavior are evolution, ontogeny, and proximate mechanism — the last typically phrased in terms of physiological information; note the absence of any mentalistic explanation.) The concept of "proper function" (Millikan, 1984, 1986) of a behavior or a morphological structure, as developed by Millikan is related to this ethological formulation. (Millikan's ideas are described in Beer, this volume)

It appears to me that a purposive or functional interpretation of behavior is useful because we may have struck upon an organizational principle of organisms. This is a most important point that I wish to emphasize. At an extreme level, the blowfly, upon encountering a sucrose solution with the chemoreceptors on its feet, extends it proboscis and imbibes the solution.

We may say of the blowfly that its goal or the function of its behavior was to drink the sugar. At other extremes, there are the cases of the plover leading an intruder away from its nest or the human wanting dinner. For the blowfly, or some other organism, if you prefer, the proboscis extension and drinking behavior is probably under little if any voluntary control whereas there is extensive voluntary control, at least at the human end, for how to go about getting dinner. The degree of flexibility is a most important characteristic of the behaviors that are described as purposeful, and they may vary in interesting ways ontogenetically and across species. The description of the blowfly's behavior may be made in terms of the stimulus-response triggers as discussed by Bennett (this volume) whereas that of the plover and the human appear to be better described by goals (desires) to be accomplished by a variety of behaviors.

Design by Evolution or Conscious Design?

The preceding discussion may lead us to ask how we can determine whether a given behavior was designed by evolution or is a product of conscious design. How do we gather data about this issue? In some ways, the question is a misleading one. Both the particular behavior (consider a human smile) and the ability to plan to use the behavior can be the result of evolution. Wanting a vacation is not evolved; wanting dinner is a mixture of an innate need to obtain nourishment and learned cultural aspects of what dinner consists of. In the case of the piping plovers, the broken-wing display is most likely an evolved behavior, because it occurs in many ground-nesting species of birds and presumably at some point in all adult plovers with eggs or young. (Note, however, that there have been no developmental studies of the ontogeny of the BWD and occurrence of use; such studies conducted with birds in the field, such as the piping plover, would be quite formidable.) It is not likely that each plover conjured up the behavior. Yet the plover appears to have the ability to use the BWD and other antipredator behaviors flexibly, adjusting its behavior appropriately to the intruder's behavior. It acts in a variety of ways, sometimes exhibiting what are to the observer novel behaviors which function to keep the intruder away from the nest or young (see Ristau, 1986). In short, the plover appears to be using the behavior purposefully.

Purposefully or adaptively? The previous discussion suggests both might be reasonable answers. Usually, however, someone asking this question is most interested in whether the behavior could merely be an evolved set of actions which are evoked in the presence of certain stimuli and which have survived through evolution because of their adaptive functions in reproductive success. This encompasses the question asked in an earlier section, "Is the behavior a reflex or a fixed action pattern?" The arguments weighing in against such a simple interpretation of the behavior center about the variability and flexibility in use of the display, the complexity of the array of behaviors utilized along with the BWD in keeping an intruder away from the nest, the sensitivity of the bird's behavior to the intruder's behavior, and the apparent novelty of behaviors observed. The proponent of an FAP or some other motor program of behavior would have to specify the relevant stimuli and resultant actions that, taken together, describe the highly variable behaviors actually observed in the piping plover. The behaviors, although they are different, can be understood in terms of a plover wanting to lead an intruder from the nest or young.

How to Prove that a Creature or Machine is Conscious?

Of course one cannot prove this position. This is the philosophical problem of "other minds." The extreme sollipsistic position is that only one's own mental experience exists; that is all one can have direct evidence for. The external world and other organisms do not exist. (Berkeley, 1939) A less extreme version is that one can have direct evidence only for oneself as a conscious being; consciousness is a phenomenological experience. One can experience only one's own consciousness, never that of another. Therefore one can prove only one's own consciousness. Nevertheless, one assumes that there is a continuity in nature and therefore between oneself and at least other humans. Furthermore it is plausible that humans and other creatures evolved to have senses that were, by and large, veridical with the external world if only because substantial information about the external world must be veridical if creatures are to be able to survive in it. One therefore concludes there is an external world, usually adequately represented by sensing organisms at least to the extent that they can gather information with survival value.

By this line of reasoning, the consciousness of any being but oneself can never be proved. One can, however, gather suggestive evidence for the existence of conscious beings. (See Yoerg and Kamil [this volume] who decry suggestive evidence for consciousness and want definitive criteria; that is philosophically impossible by the above reasoning.) Suggestive evidence is easiest within the human species; shared language about events and experiences helps to verify that we have approximately the same meanings for most of our words. (This presumed shared knowledge also has its limitations, e.g., see Quine's [1960] discussion of the meaning of "Gavagai" to the native language user/teacher and the new language learner.) Some mysteries always exist; I can never know that your experience of the color red is exactly like mine or, in philosophical terms, that our qualia are the same. However psychophysical experiments in which different persons judge intensities of a light, loudness of a sound, and so on strongly suggest that most of us share at least some similar important aspects of our perceptions. Similarly, tests such as the Osgood Semantic Differential (Osgood, Suci, & Tannenbaum, 1957) in which subjects rate words, including perceptual experiences such as red, along various dimensions (e.g., heat, power, etc.) again suggest perceptual similarities (or at the very least, shared cultural associations for color and other words).

In determining whether other creatures have conscious experiences, we can begin by analyzing what behavioral evidence, other than language, leads us to conclude that another human is having a particular kind of conscious experience (that is, the sort of thing we do in our normal daily life — attribution of mental states including feelings and purposes to another). Ethological evidence is of primary importance; a person blushes, averts eye gaze, perhaps especially in contexts in which we have behaved similarly, and we conclude that he or she is feeling embarrassed and we associate certain likely consequent behaviors and emotional turbulence with that state. It becomes much more difficult when species lines are crossed but, in essence, we boot strap downwards, beginning with species such as chimpanzees and continuing, with more difficulty to others. But this procedure, though not impossible, is fraught with danger. We must study the life of another species in its natural surroundings so we can draw reasonable analogies and avoid unlikely comparisons. For example, although direct eye gaze in humans occurs both in very intimate and very aggressive contexts, for most other primates, direct eye gaze occurs in agonistic situations, not more intimate ones. We must therefore, be particularly cautious about the analogies we attempt to make concerning the use of eye gaze in most other primate species,

Methodology

How then should one undertake studies using a limited or critical anthropomorphic approach or an intentional stance?

1. Empirical data are essential. Discussions of the possible mind states of animals without reference to their sensory and cognitive capabilities will be limited. It would be most useful to gather data so as to be descriptive of the organisms' behavior even to scientists uninterested in a mentalistic approach.
2. A hypothesis or stance and alternative interpretations must be specified as clearly as possible. Hypotheses must be falsifiable. Evidence must include not only data in support of a (mentalistic) hypothesis, but data which disconfirm simpler alternative interpre-

tations. Precisely how the empirical data disconfirm alternative explanations must be carefully delineated.

3. In applying an intentional stance one should look for gaps in intentionality; that is, deviations from the expected behavior of a fully rational creature which, indeed, even we humans are not. One should look for errors and limitations of abilities in order to specify them more precisely.

4. Comparative studies are most useful. In this way, one can accumulate evidence about the different kinds of abilities. In particular, the degree of flexibility exhibited by different species may reveal differences along the continuum from rigidly programmed control of behavior to more voluntary control (Ristau, 1988). If we consider a potentially purposive behavior, the flexibility could be observed in terms of the breadth of stimuli to which the organism is responsive in achieving its goal; the situations or contexts in which the behavior can occur; and the ability to overcome obstacles in achieving the goal, particularly with respect to the variety and novelty of responses utilized.

Are Piping Plovers Intentionalist Creatures?

This is a tough question to answer. Remember that the philosophical meaning of intentional does not mean on purpose, although purposeful behavior and "wants it to be the case that" are among various intentional idioms. For a plover to be intentional it must be shown to have mind states. An intentional creature will have beliefs and knowledge, and it will act in accordance with them. Its behavior, such as a broken-wing display, will not simply appear, like a reflex or fixed action pattern, only in the presence of certain very specific stimulus. An intentionalist plover would be aware of its goal, and alters its behavior in ways appropiate to achieve its goal. There may be other and better ways of stating all this. I am simply exploring the possible application of an intentional stance to an animal's behavior—in this case, the piping plover.

It is for the previously mentioned reasons that I examined the ability of the piping plovers to attempt to continue to attract an intruder's attention and to cause the intruder to follow it away from nest/young as part of a body of evidence needed to indicate that the plover had a goal achievable by a variety of means. (Other behavioral flexibilites are discussed in Ristau, 1986). The plover is sensitive to many aspects of its environment including the attention paid by the intruder to its general nest area (defining attention in terms of direction of intruder's eye gaze). To begin to investigate the plover's knowledge/beliefs about its environment, the safe-dangerous experiments were conducted, which showed that a piping plover could learn to discriminate between two persons. These experiments are only a beginning in the exploration of whether and to what extent plovers are intentional creatures. The results so far suggest that they are. It will be important and most interesting to explore the limits of their abilities as well. They most assuredly are not the intentional creatures humans are, they are most likely far more limited than chimpanzees, and yet are probably interestingly different from snakes and blowflies. Whether critical aspects of the differences can be most profitably examined using an intentional stance to guide us remains an unanswered question.

Continuing the Dialogue

Most important is to continue the dialogue between scientists with different viewpoints and to establish more interaction with philosophers of science and of mind with whom we share concerns over similar issues. Using an intentional analysis, for example, is but one possible approach to the study of the animal and human minds. It is unlikely that any present viewpoint or theoretical orientation is totally correct. It behooves us to be open-minded, to learn from each other, and to explore.

ACKNOWLEDGMENTS

I would like to thank the following for their help in the 1982 field season: The Harry Frank Guggenheim Foundation for financial support; The Virginia Coast Reserve of The Nature Conservancy for permission to use their land; The Marine Science Consortium of Wallops Island, Virginia for living and office accomodations; David Thompson for help in initial preparations; and Laura Payne for help in observations. For subsequent field seasons, I thank the Mashomack Preserve of the Nature Conservancy on Shelter Island, New York, its Director, Michael Laspia for living and office accomodations and supportive services, and both the Morton Wildlife Refuge and the town of Southampton, Long Island for permission to use their land for research. I am grateful to the Whitehall Foundation for financial support of the research and the Edna Bailey Sussman Fund and Barnard College for support of research assistants. I am also indebted to Margaret McVey who was my colleague during most of the 1983 field season and to Elysia Hellen, William Langbauer, and Terry Metwijn for help in field work and preliminary data analysis for that season. For subsequent seasons, I thank my research assistants Angela Greer, Margaret Mosteller, Karen Seidler, Samuel Hellings, Peter Sherman, Kim Pietrzak, Crista Diels, Randi Massey, Rachel Larson, Salila Shivde, and Angelica Landrigans. I thank Daniel C. Dennett for philosophical insights, Stevan Harnad for his helpful discussions and in particular Donald R. Griffin for his work in cognitive ethology, constructive comments on a longer manuscript from which this paper is drawn, and for his continued encouragements.

REFERENCES

Arduino, P. J., & Gould, J. L. (1984). Is tonic immobility adaptive? *Animal Behaviour, 32,* 921–923.

Armstrong, E. A. (1947). *Bird display and behaviour.* London: Lindsay Drummond.

Bent, A. C. (1921). Life histories of North American gulls and terns. *U.S. National Museum Bulletin, 113,* 1–345.

Bennett, J. (1976). *Linguistic behaviour.* Cambridge: Cambridge University Press.

Bennett, J. (1985) Paper presented at seminar.

Berkeley, G. (1939). *A treatise concerning the principles of human knowledge.* In E. A. Burtt (Ed.). *The English philosophers from Bacon to Mill.* N.Y.: The Modern Library. Reprinted from (1710)

Boden, M. (1983). Artificial intelligence and animal psychology. *New Ideas in Psychology, 1,* 11–33.

Cerella, J. (1979). Visual classes and natural categories in the pigeon. *Journal of Experimental Psychology: Human Perception and Performance, 5,* 68–77.

Curio, E., Ernst, U., & Vieth, W. (1978). The adaptive significance of avian mobbing. II. Cultural transmission of enemy recognition in blackbirds: Effectiveness and some constraints. *Zeitschrift für Tierpsychologie, 48,* 184–202.

Dennett, D. C. (1978). *Brainstorms.* Cambridge, MA: Bradford Books.

Dennett, D. C. (1983). Intentional systems in cognitive ethology: The 'Panglossian paradigm' defended. *Behavioral and Brain Sciences, 6,* 343–390.

Dennett, D. C. (1987). *The intentional stance.* Cambridge, MA: Bradford Books.

Dinsmoor, J. J. (1977). Notes on avocets and stilts in Tampa Bay, Fla. *Florida Field National, 5,* 25–30.

Gallup, G. G., Jr., Cummings, W. H., & Nash, R. F. (1972). The experimenter as an independent variable in studies of animal hypnosis in chickens. *Animal Behaviour, 20,* 166–169.

Gochfeld, M. (1984). Antipredator behavior: Aggressive and distraction displays of shorebirds. In J. Burger & B. L. Olla (Eds.), *Shorebirds: Breeding behavior and populations* (pp. 289–377). New York: Plenum.

Gould, J. L. (1982). *Ethology: The mechanisms and evolution of behavior.* New York: W. W. Norton.

Graul, W. D. (1975). Breeding biology of the mountain plover. *Wilson Bulletin, 87,* 6–31.

Grice, H. P. (1967). Logic and conversation. William James Lectures, Harvard University. In P. Cole & J. L. Morgan (Eds.), *Studies in syntax* (Vol. 3). New York: Academic Press.

Griffin, D. R. (1976). *The question of animal awareness* (2nd ed.). New York: Rockefeller University Press.

Griffin, D. R. (1984). *Animal thinking.* Cambridge, MA.: Harvard University Press.

Griffin, D. R. (1985). Animal consciousness. *Neuroscience and Biobehavioral Reviews, 9,* 615–622.

Hennig, C. W. (1977). Effects of simulated predation on tonic immobility in *Anolis carolinensis:* The role of eye contact. *Bulletin of the Psychonomic Society, 9,* 239–242.

Herrnstein, R. J., & de Villiers, P. A. (1980). Fish as a natural category for people and pigeons. In G. H. Bower (Ed.), *The psychology of learning and motivation,* Vol. 14 (pp. 59–95). New York: Academic Press.

Herrnstein, R. J., Loveland, D. H., & Cable, C. (1976). Natural concepts in pigeons. *Journal of Experimental Psychology: Animal Behavior Processes, 2,* 285–302.

Jolly, A. (1985). *The evolution of primate behavior* (2nd ed). New York: Macmillan.

Millikan, R. G. (1984). *Language, thought and other biological categories.* Cambridge, MA: Bradford Books.

Millikan, R. G. (1986). Thoughts without laws; cognitive science without content. *Philosophical Review, 95,* 47–80.

Morgan, M. J., Fitch, M. D., Holman, J. G., & Lea, S. E. G. (1976). Pigeons learn the concept of an "A." *Perception, 5,* 57–66.

Osgood, C. E., Suci, G. J., & Tannenbaum, P. H. (1957). *The measurement of meaning.* Urbana: Univ. of Illinois Press.

Quine, W. V. O. (1960). *Word and Object.* Cambridge, MA: M.I.T. Press.

Ristau, C. A. (1983a). Intentionalist plovers or just dumb birds? [Commentary on Dennett, D. C. Intentional systems in cognitive ethology: The 'Panglossian paradigm' defended]. *Behavioral and Brain Sciences, 6,* 373–375.

Ristau, C. A. (1983b). Symbols and indication in apes and other species? [Review of Can a chimpanzee make a statement?]. *Journal of Experimental Psychology: General, 112,* 498–507.

Ristau, C. A. (1988). Thinking, communicating, and deceiving: Means to master the social environment. In G. Greenberg & E. Tobach (Eds.), *Evolution of social behavior and integrative levels* (pp. 213–240). Hillsdale, NJ: Lawrence Erlbaum Associates.

Ristau, C. A. (in press). Animal language and cognition research. In A. Lock and C. R. Peters (Eds.), *The handbook of human symbolic evolution* (pp. XX). London: Oxford University Press.

Ristau, C. A. (1986). Intentional behavior by birds? The case of the "injury feigning" plovers. *Manuscript submitted for publication.*

Ristau, C. A. (in preparation). Piping plovers are responsive to direction of intruder's gaze.

Ristau, C. A., & Robbins, D. (1982). Language in the great apes: A critical review. In J. S. Rosenblatt, R. A. Hinde, C. Beer, & M. C. Busnel (Eds.), *Advances in the study of behavior,* Vol. 12, (pp. 141–255). New York: Academic Press.

Schneirla, T. C. (1972). An evolutionary and developmental theory of biphasic processes underlying approach and withdrawal I. In L. R. Aronson, E. Tobach, J. S. Rosenblatt & D. S. Lehrman (Eds.), *Selected writings of T. C. Schneirla* (pp. 297–339). San Francisco: W. H. Freeman & Company. Reprinted from *Nebraska symposium on motivation,* 1959, (pp. 1–42).

Searle, J. R. (1980). Minds, brains and programs. *Behavioral and Brain Sciences, 3,* 417–457.

Skutch, A. F. (1976). *Parent birds and their young.* Austin: University of Texas Press.

Sordahl, T. A. (1980). *Antipredator behavior and parental care in the American Avocet and Black-Necked Stilt (Aves: Recurvirostoidae).* Unpublished doctoral dissertation, Utah State University, Logan, Utah.

Tinbergen, N. (1969). *The study of instinct.* New York: Oxford University Press. (Original work published 1951).

Tolman, E. C. (1932). *Purposive behavior in animals and men.* New York: Appleton-Century.

Walker, J. (1955). Mountain plover. *Audobon, 57,* 210–212.

Walters, J. (1980). *The evolution of parental behavior in lapwings.* Unpublished doctoral dissertation, University of Chicago, Chicago, Illinois.

6 TRUTH AND DECEPTION IN ANIMAL COMMUNICATION

Dorothy L. Cheney
Robert M. Seyfarth
University of Pennsylvania

ABSTRACT

The evolution of animal signals is currently a matter of some controversy. One hypothesis argues that signals typically function to communicate accurate information about subsequent behavior. An alternate hypothesis claims that signals are often attempts to mislead, bluff, or deceive and that selection has favored skeptical recipients able to detect such deception. We review evidence that bears on these hypotheses and pay particular attention to communication among group-living animals. We consider evidence that animals (a) change the meaning of signals, (b) vary the rate of signalling and thus withold or conceal information, (c) signal false information, or (d) respond skeptically to the signals of others. Field experiments on vervet monkeys suggest that animals are skeptical recipients, and that the detection of deception is determined by the ways in which animals compare signals based upon their meaning.

INTRODUCTION

The "truthfulness" of animal communication is controversial because in some cases animal signals appear to provide accurate and reliable information to those nearby, while in other cases they do not. As one of the many examples of truthful signalling, consider the courtship display of the smooth newt (*Triturus vulgaris*). After copulation, male smooth newts require a number of hours to replenish their supply of spermatophores (Halliday, 1976). When a male meets a female, therefore, he may have a great deal of sperm available or very little. If a male encounters a female, he gives a courtship display that includes a variety of tail movements called "fanning." The rate at which the newt performs this display is strongly correlated with how much sperm he eventually deposits, and thus fanning provides the female with accurate information about the male's suitability as a mate (Halliday, 1983).

There are numerous other examples of signals that provide others with accurate information about an individual's resources, its intentions, or aspects of its environment. Male mockingbirds with larger song repertoires have better quality territories (Howard, 1974); the "play face" of many primates accurately signals that aggression is unlikely (e.g., Walters, 1987); and the alarm calls of many birds (e.g., Marler, 1956), prairie dogs (e.g., Hoogland, 1983), ground squirrels (e.g., Dunford, 1977; Leger & Owings, 1978; Sherman, 1977) and monkeys (e.g., Struhsaker, 1967; Seyfarth, Cheney, & Marler 1980) provide accurate information not only about the presence of a predator, but also about whether the predator in question is an eagle, snake, or a carnivore.

At the same time, there is evidence that other animal signals provide inaccurate information, and in this sense apparently function to deceive other individuals. We use here a functional definition, defining a deceptive signal as one that provides others with false information. Whether any animal is conscious of its own attempts to deceive, and thus practices deception in the human sense, remains an open question (Griffin, 1984; Woodruff & Premack, 1979). Setting aside the question of conscious awareness, however, there are many instances in which animals behave as if they may be attempting to deceive one another. The threat displays of many species are generally poor predictors of subsequent behavior, and hence cannot be used by recipients to determine whether an opponent is likely to attack (Caryl, 1979; Hinde, 1981). In scorpionflies, a male can only copulate with a female if he first provides her with the gift of a dead insect. Some males catch insects on their own while others steal insects by approaching males who already have them and adopting the posture and behavior of females (Thornhill, 1979).

Similarly, polygamy in the pied flycatcher has been interpreted as an example of a successful attempt by males to deceive females (Alatalo, Carlson, Lindberg, & Ulfstrand, 1981). In this species, males sometimes hold two separate territories that can be separated by as many as 3.5 km. One explanation for these widely dispersed territories is that they prevent females from determining if a male is already mated. Secondary females have lower reproductive success than monogomously mated females, so females would be predicted to avoid already mated males. However, females may not be able to detect whether a male already has a mate if the male holds more than one territory and his territories are widely dispersed.

By the time the secondary female has laid her eggs and the male has returned to his first female, it is too late in the season for the female to start another clutch.

The study of deception in animal communication is a young one, and many unresolved issues remain. For example, there have really only been the most preliminary of analyses on the rate at which animals might be expected to signal truthfully (as opposed to unreliably) or on the effects of context. More important, there is still very little consensus on whether deceptive or unreliable signals ever occur at all or how flexible animal signals really are. Do animals really have the ability to modify their signals? If so, how flexible is the production of different signals?

In this paper we review some of the evidence for deceptive communication and the detection of unreliable signals among animals. We concentrate in particular on communication among group-living animals and on signals of intention and the environment because these signals offer the widest scope for modification.

In some cases, of course, signals cannot easily be falsified. In particular, signals that reflect or are tied to some physiological state — such as body size or reproductive condition — are usually reliable simply because they are difficult to modify. But this is not necessarily true of signals that convey information about the environment or about the signaller's intentions. In fact, there are good reasons for predicting that animals seldom ought to communicate precisely about their intentions except in cooperative interactions.

THEORETICAL BACKGROUND

A variety of theories have attempted to explain why deceptive signals might occur or even become common. Maynard Smith and Price (1973) argue that in any population in which animals use threat displays to signal their intentions, natural selection will favor those individuals who "cheat" and threaten others at the highest level of intensity (falsely signalling imminent attack) regardless of their actual intentions (see also Caryl, 1979; Krebs & Dawkins, 1984; Maynard Smith, 1979, 1984). Building on this argument, Andersson (1980) offers a scenario of how deceptive signals might actually evolve. Originally, a movement or posture (such as the lunge of a monkey) is an effective threat display because it reliably predicts subsequent attack. Over time, however, the display gains increasing use as bluff, presumably because signallers find that the display alone is sufficient to deter opponents even if it is not followed by an actual attack. As the frequency of bluffing increases, skeptical recipients note that the display is no longer an accurate predictor of attack, and the display loses its effectiveness. Signallers respond by introducing a new display, which predicts attack more reliably than the old one. This signal, too, however, will eventually be used as bluff. Continuing competition between deceptive signallers and skeptical recipients ultimately produces a proliferation of displays with each display becoming less effective the more often it is used as bluff (Andersson, 1980; Paton, 1986). Although Andersson's theory has not yet been adequately tested, the general point that displays about intention are signals of assessment, and therefore seldom signal precise courses of action, is an important one.

Given the theoretical arguments that deceptive signalling should be evolutionarily successful, and empirical evidence that animals sometimes — but not always — signal false information, we need to specify the conditions under which deceptive signalling can succeed and be beneficial to the signaller. Conversely, it will be necessary to identify those factors that constrain deception and give animals no choice other than to signal accurate information.

CONSTRAINTS ON THE USE OF DECEPTIVE SIGNALS

Although there are both theoretical reasons why animals should signal inaccurate information and empirical evidence that they occasionally do so, a number of factors place limits on the ability of animals to deceive one another.

Social Constraints

The first constraint arises from a species' social structure. Species that live in stable social groups face special problems in any attempt at deceptive communication. If individuals recognize one another and remember past interactions, deceptive communication should be far easier to detect than in species like the previously mentioned scorpionfly which rarely encounter each other. In groups, deceptive signals will probably have to be more subtle and occur at lower frequencies if they are to go undetected. Equally important, if animals live in social groups in which some degree of cooperation is essential for survival, the need for cooperation may also reduce the rate at which unreliable signals are given. Indeed, it has been argued that bluffing about one's intentions cannot evolve under these conditions (van Rhijn & Vodegal, 1980). Because social animals act as both signallers and recipients, mutual cooperation, even if based on skepticism, may be more evolutionarily stable than mutual exploitation (Axelrod & Hamilton, 1981; Markl, 1985).

Unfortunately, both the risk of detection and the need for cooperation are likely to make deception in social groups both rare and difficult to study. Observational studies will almost by necessity be anecdotal simply because most forms of deception will occur at low rates. Constraints imposed by social structure suggest that many of the theoretical arguments about deception, which assume no individual recognition and little memory of previous interactions (e.g., Maynard Smith, 1974, 1982; Krebs & Dawkins, 1984), may not be applicable to a wide variety of group-living animals.

Constraints Imposed by the Need to Invent New Signals

Deception will also be constrained by a signaller's ability both to control and to invent new signals. As many authors have pointed out, some signals cannot be faked because they reflect and depend on some physiological attribute (e.g., size or age). For example, male toads (*Bufo bufo*) fight for access to females, and the larger males typically win. Because fights usually take place in murky pond water or at night, visual cues are absent and males use auditory signals to assess the size of their opponent. Larger males have larger vocal cords, and hence give peeps with a lower fundamental frequency or pitch. When a male hears his rival peeping, he is more likely to continue fighting if the rival's pitch is higher and less likely to continue fighting if the rival's pitch is lower than his own (Davies & Halliday, 1978, 1979). Because their acoustic features are so closely linked to anatomical structures that cannot be altered, signals like the toads' peeps will always be truthful (Maynard Smith, 1984, 1986).

On the other hand, signals that are not dependent on physiological attributes, but instead function as cues to probable courses of action or the possession of a resource, are at least potentially open to deceit. Further, in the scenario created by Andersson (1980), where novel threat displays are always more effective than old ones, deception will be limited by the signaller's ability to create novel signals. In any species there will probably be few behavior patterns associated with attack and fewer still that can be separated from attack to serve an independent signal function (Andersson, 1980; Moynihan, 1970).

Even those displays that are tightly linked to some physiological attribute cannot be entirely divorced from motivation, however, because many additional factors — like possession of a territory or mate — might influence the willingness of an animal to fight. Even when information about each opponent's physiological state is evident, therefore, fights may escalate slowly and involve numerous displays that permit the evaluation of less accessible motivational information (Markl, 1985).

The Assessment of Meaning

Finally, deception will be constrained by the skill with which receivers can assess the meaning of signals and can incorporate this information into what they have learned about the signaller from past interactions. Although the assessment of meaning has received little attention, it is considered in some detail in the subsequent paragraphs.

DECEPTION THROUGH SILENCE

East African vervet monkeys (*Cercopithecus aethiops*) give acoustically different alarm calls to different predators, and each call type elicits a different escape response from those nearby. Alarm calls given to leopards (called leopard alarms) cause others to run into trees, while alarm calls given to eagles (eagle alarms) cause others to look up or run into bushes. Leopards take vervet monkeys by hiding in bushes and attacking them on the ground but cannot capture vervets when they are in trees. By contrast, eagles can take monkeys either on the ground or in trees; the only safe refuge from eagles is in a bush. Different predator hunting strategies call for different escape responses and acoustically different alarm calls that signal different sorts of danger (Seyfarth et al., 1980; Struhsaker, 1967).

Given this vocal repertoire, the adaptive significance of false alarms seems obvious. A vervet monkey could spot a leopard in a bush, wait until a rival approached the bush, then give an eagle alarm and watch the rival run into the bush and be eaten. Curiously, however, vervet monkeys do not seem to do this (personal observation); possibly such deceptive alarm-calling is too easy to detect when an an obviously different predator is visible. Although a false alarm might dispatch a rival, it is more likely that other group members would easily recognize the mismatch between alarm-call type and predator and cease paying attention to the caller.

There is a more subtle strategy, however — one that is almost as effective as outright deception and much less easy to detect. The vervet monkey could spot a predator and simply remain silent, giving an alarm call only if it or its kin were in imminent danger. There is now some suggestion that deception by withholding information occurs regularly in vervet monkeys and that it may also be widespread in other species.

In vervet monkeys, where adult males and adult females can be ranked in stable linear-dominance hierarchies (Cheney, Seyfarth, Andelman, & Lee, 1988), high-ranking individuals are significantly more likely to give alarm calls than are low-ranking individuals. Films of scanning behavior give no indication that high-ranking individuals have better vantage points or spend more time looking for predators. Instead, results suggest that low-ranking animals spot predators equally often but simply fail to warn others in their group (Cheney & Seyfarth, 1985).

Similarly, it is well known that when a predator is nearby ground squirrels (*Sciuridae*) with kin are more likely than those without kin to give alarm calls (Dunford, 1977; Sherman, 1977). Because we have no reason to believe that animals with kin spend more time scanning or are more likely to spot predators than animals without kin, such data provide indirect evidence that some individuals see predators but do not inform others.

Numerous other studies of nonhuman primates have reported similar instances of apparent withholding or concealment of information from others (see examples in Jolly, this volume; Ristau, 1988). Most examples are anecdotal, which is not surprising given that we might expect deception in social animals to be relatively infrequent (see previous discussion).

Hans Kummer reports observing a female hamadryas baboon who spent 20 minutes gradually shifting her way in a seated position toward a rock where she began to groom a subadult male–an act that would not normally be tolerated by the dominant adult male. From his resting position, the dominant adult male could see the back and head of the female but not her arms. The subadult male sat in a bent position and was also invisible to the adult male. What made Kummer doubt that this arrangement was accidental was the exceptionally slow, inch-by-inch shifting of the female (Kummer, 1982; see also Whiten & Byrne, 1988).

The captive rhesus monkeys (*Macaca mulatta*) studied by de Waal (1986) also provide examples of animals apparently deceiving others by witholding information. In de Waal's study, dominant monkeys often behaved aggressively toward subordinates if the latter failed to respond to threats with submissive behavior. Dominant animals were rarely aggressive, however, if it appeared that the subordinate had not noticed the original threat. Under these conditions, subordinates frequently ignored threats (by sitting very still and looking down at the ground or up in the air) that they had almost certainly seen.

Further examples come from de Waal's study of captive chimpanzees (1982, 1986). In one case, a young male, Dandy, walked over a place where experimenters had hidden some grapefruit underneath the ground. Because Dandy did not react in any way, the experimenters assumed that he had not noticed the fruit. Over 3 hours later, however, when the other chimpanzees were asleep, Dandy walked straight to the spot, dug up, and ate the grapefruit. De Waal has also described a number of instances in which male chimpanzees concealed their penises behind their hands when dominant males interrupted their courtship.

Finally, chimpanzees in the wild that come upon a fruiting tree have been observed to give loud pant hoots that attract other individuals if the tree has a great deal of fruit. However, there is some evidence that they remain silent if only a little food is available (Wrangham, 1975).

What do these anecdotes tell us? They suggest, although they clearly do not prove, that nonhuman primates do not simply monitor physical aspects of their world — like the location of a food item or another individual — but that the animals also monitor and predict the mental states of animals and the consequences of their own behavior on the behavior of others.

What is presently lacking is a method for systematically observing the frequency and consequences of such apparent attempts at deception. More important, we need some way of discriminating between explanations which posit that animals have the ability to monitor the thought processes of others and simpler interpretations that do not rely on complex mental processes. For example, it might easily be argued that Hans Kummer's female baboon concealed her grooming of the subadult male simply because she had learned from past experience that this reduced the aggression of the dominant male. Choosing between simpler and more complex explanations becomes particularly problematical whenever we attempt to compare apparent deception across species. House sparrows, for example, also modify the rate at which they utter food calls, apparently according to whether or not the food supply is divisible (Elgar, 1986). Intuitively, we are inclined to believe that chimpanzee food calls are governed by different mechanisms than those of house sparrows, yet in the absence of any systematic information about the flexibility and modifiability of calls in each of these species, we are left simply with two very similar patterns of behavior.

Those taking an entirely functional or evolutionary perspective (e.g., Krebs & Dawkins, 1984) might argue that the mechanisms underlying the food calls of chimpanzees and house sparrows are not really relevant as long as the calls function to allow callers to manipulate others. Mechanisms become more important, though, if we wish to use deception as a means to study the mental states and capacities of animals. Moreover, some knowledge of the proximate mechanisms underlying deceptive behavior may well be essential if we are ever to understand the extent to which animals can use their communicative signals to manipulate each other.

More systematic evidence that animals deceive others by withholding information can be found in experiments on vervet monkeys and on jungle fowl (*Gallus gallus*). Vervet monkeys were studied in an indoor-outdoor enclosure that allowed some members of the group to be temporarily separated from others. Upon seeing a predator, adult females gave alarm calls at significantly higher rates if they were with their juvenile offspring than if they were with an unrelated juvenile of the same age and sex. Males gave significantly more alarm calls if they were with a female than if they were with another male (Cheney & Seyfarth, 1985).

Cockerels also appear to have the ability to withold or modulate signals depending upon social context (Gyger, Karakashian, & Marler, 1986; Marler, this volume). When cockerels were presented with silhouettes of aerial predators, they alarm-called significantly less when they were alone than when they were accompanied by a mate or another female. Thus alarm-calling was not simply a reflexive response but was modulated according to whether or not an audience was present. This result did not occur because of the behavior of the audience. When a baffle was erected so that the male, but not the females, could see the predator, males still called significantly less when alone than when the female audience was present. Similar results were obtained when the males were in the presence of chicks.

Interestingly, this audience effect was species-specific. Males were tested alone, with their mates, and with a familiar female bobwhite quail as an audience. Again, there were significantly more alarm calls when males were in the company of their mates than when they were alone or with the quail female. By contrast, there was no difference between the males' alarm-calling when they were alone and when they were with the quail.

These experiments suggest that animals may have an intent to communicate that depends crucially on the appropriate social context. The issue of intention in communication is important not just for what it potentially reveals about an animal's mind (e.g., Dennett, 1987) but also because it reveals the constraints within which communication operates. Clearly, there will be far wider scope for the manipulation of signals (and the deception of others) if animals are not only able to modify call production but also to predict the consequences of their signals on the behavior of others.

Although the witholding of information clearly has the potential of misleading others to the signaller's personal gain, it could be argued that signal concealment cannot strictly be interpreted as deception unless the signaller intends to manipulate others or unless others have the expectation of being informed. Not only are these issues difficult to study, but they also demand far greater cognitive abilities on the part of animals because they require that animals have some ability to attribute motives or intentions to others.

Nevertheless, at least in the case of nonhuman primates, it does seem at least theoretically possible to investigate the extent to which individuals expect information from other group members. For example, in *Cebus apella,* the dominant adult male is the primary individual in each group to inform others of aerial predators and to call adult females to palm nuts, which he alone seems to be strong enough to open (C. van Schaik, personal communication, 1987). It might be possible to test females' expectation of information by presenting females with predators or palm nuts out of the sight of the dominant male and investigate whether his apparent failure to inform them affects their subsequent relationship with him.

Finally, a study by Woodruff & Premack (1979) illustrates how withholding information can appear as an early rudimentary form of deception among animals that eventually practiced more explicit forms of deceit. In these experiments a chimpanzee was first shown two containers, one with food hidden inside. The chimpanzee was then introduced to two different trainers, neither of whom knew the location of the food. One was a "cooperative" trainer: If the chimpanzee signaled which container held the food, the trainer collected the food and shared it with the chimp. The second trainer was "uncooperative": When shown the location of the food, he ate the food himself. Over time, chimpanzees were tested with each trainer in trials where chimp and trainer alternately served as sender and recipient of information. When interacting with the cooperative trainer, chimps from the very beginning were able both to produce and to comprehend accurate cues about the location of food. When interacting with the uncooperative trainer and playing the role of sender, after many trials chimpanzees began to deceive this trainer. They first did so by withholding information — turning their backs and sitting motionless so that the trainer was given no clue as to where the food was hidden. Only later, after considerably more trials, did some of the chimpanzees signal falsely to the trainer by gesturing or pointing to the wrong container (Woodruff & Premack 1979).

To summarize, in social species where individual recognition, the memory of past interactions, and presumably the detection of false signals are well developed, witholding information provides an effective means by which animals can deceive one another without being detected. Just as silence may be difficult for conspecifics to detect, however, it may also be difficult for observers to detect. The frequency of deception through silence may therefore have been underestimated by previous reviews of deception in animal communication.

SIGNALLING FALSE INFORMATION

While signal concealment provides an indirect means of deception, more explicit deceit occurs when one individual actively falsifies the information it conveys to another. The falsification of signals potentially provides a much wider scope for deception than concealment. It also carries implications for animals' cognitive abilities, particularly their ability to attribute knowledge and motives to others.

Explicit falsification can occur when an individual grossly distorts information as in the case of the male scorpionfly that mimics a female in order to deprive another male of his nuptial gift (Thornhill, 1979). It can also occur when a stimulus is present, but an individual signals false information about it. De Waal (1986), for example, describes how one male chimpanzee that was injured in a fight with his rival limped for a week afterward but only when his rival could see him. Such active falsification is clearly more complex than simple concealment because it demands that the signaller not just withold something from his rival but that he also actively distract his rival from one feature of the environment to an entirely different one (Byrne & Whiten 1988; Jolly, this volume).

Similarly, on six different occasions Frans de Waal (personal communication, 1987) observed chimpanzees making false overtures for reconciliation. They invited their opponent toward them with a friendly gesture only to turn aggressive at the last second when the opponent approached to within arm's reach. Similar behavior has been observed in baboons and vervet monkeys, and there are numerous accounts of chimpanzees actively leading rivals away from a hidden food source or feigning ignorance of the food source (Goodall, 1971, 1986; de Waal, 1982; Byrne & Whiten, 1988).

Monkeys and apes may also falsify vocal signals. There is anecdotal evidence, for example, that male vervet monkeys occasionally give alarm calls when no predators are present, although these false alarm calls have not yet been investigated systematically. On a number of occasions, males have been observed to give leopard alarm calls during intergroup encounters or when an immigrant male is approaching their group. Such calls are at least temporarily highly effective, since they invariably cause others to flee. Given the ability of vervets to give false alarm calls in these inappropriate contexts, it is even more puzzling that vervets never seem to mislabel actual predators with inappropriate alarm calls (see previous discussion).

As with signal concealment, these anecdotes of signal falsification are potentially subject to overinterpretation. For example, if accounts of false reconciliation are considered alone, it can certainly be argued that attacks were the result of conflicting tendencies to show aggression and appeasement rather than any intention of the signaller to deceive his rival.

However, the literature now contains many similar examples which, taken together, illustrate a wide variety of techniques for concealment or falsification. The data are particularly rich in the case of chimpanzees. The variety of gestures used to deceive or conceal information is crucial, because this indicates that the chimps' behavior cannot be explained simply in terms of displacement activity or a ritualized display. Through their number and variety these anecdotes gain in persuasive power and suggest at least the possibility of some degree of intentional falsification of signals and of the attribution of knowledge and motives to others.

There are also numerous examples from Old World monkeys that suggest the possibility of deception in "triadic interactions." These occur when one animal manipulates a rival by using other animals as social tools For example, Kathy Rasmussen (Byrne & Whiten, 1988) describes a situation in which one male baboon recruited three other males in a fight against a rival in order to obtain the rival's female. The male approached his rival and then screamed as if he had been attacked. Three other males converged on the rival until the rival "cracked", chased them, and left his female. At this point, the first male (who had not joined the coalition) quickly ran up to the female and chased her in the opposite direction.

This example is again subject to a variety of interpretations. It is possible, for example, that the other males knew very well that the first male had not been attacked but came to his aid because they regularly cooperated with him in a reciprocal exchange of alliances (e.g., Packer 1977; Seyfarth & Cheney, 1984). One could test these two hypotheses by noting the timing and frequency of fights and coalitions between males and the consequences of these interactions for each of the participants. Whatever its underlying causes, however, the use of other individuals as "social tools" is of interest if only because such examples are so common among Old World Monkeys. As Byrne and Whiten (1988) have pointed out, the frequency of their use in monkeys only accentuates the puzzling dearth of comparable examples of apparent deception in triadic interactions among apes.

The ability to use a variety of signals and contexts to signal false information is of great interest to those interested in the cognitive abilities of animals because such human-like deception demands that individuals be able to attribute knowledge and beliefs to others and to understand that other individuals' knowledge and beliefs may be different from their own. They must also be able to predict the consequences of their own behavior on others and to modify their behavior accordingly. In children, these abilities apparently do not emerge until approximately 4 years of age (Wimmer & Permer, 1983), suggesting that they may demand skills that do not exist in nonhuman species.

At the same time, we must be careful not to exaggerate the abilities of nonhuman primates prematurely. Before we conclude that apparent signal falsification in monkeys and apes indicates an ability to impute mental states to others, we should remind ourselves that the ability to modify and falsify signals is not restricted to nonhuman primates. In fact, there is evidence that signal falsification may be quite common in birds.

Munn (1986a, 1986b) studied mixed species flocks of birds in the Amazon basin and found that within each flock the members of one species (either *Thamnomanes schistogynus* or *Lanio versicolor*) led flock progressions and were the first to give alarm calls to predators. These birds also, however, frequently gave alarm calls when no predator was present. Such false alarms were especially common when a member of the sentinel species and a member of another species were chasing an insect. Typically, false alarms caused the other individual to hesitate briefly whereupon the sentinel grabbed the prey. Similarly, Moller (1988) found that 63% of all alarm calls given by great tits in winter foraging flocks were false and were emitted when no predator was present. False alarm calls were seemingly given with the intent of driving away more dominant individuals from concentrated food sources and allowed callers to gain access to feeding perches from which they otherwise might be excluded. Subordinate birds gave false alarm calls to both dominant and subordinate individuals. Dominant birds, however, gave false alarm calls to other dominant individuals but not to subordinate individuals whom they could supplant in threat displays.

If they are analyzed from a functional perspective, these alarm calls are clearly deceptive because they falsely manipulate the recipient's behavior to the signaller's benefit. What information do they reveal, however, about the signallers' ability to assess the knowledge and probable responses of others? No doubt any analysis of such calls will be influenced by the fact that they are given by birds rather than by apes simply because we are usually less inclined to attribute complex cognitive abilities to birds than to primates.

Part of the problem of investigating attribution in animals is method-ological; it is exceedingly difficult to study attribution solely by observing the effect of signals on those nearby. A first step, however, would be to examine the proximate mechanisms underlying such false alarm calls. For example, do sentinel species ever use other signals to manipulate flock members? How often can false alarm calls be given before the recipients cease to respond? In other words, how flexible is the behavior of signallers and recipients? How easily can the signallers modify their signals to falsify information? Under what circumstances do recipients detect deceptive signals?

Investigation of these proximate questions is essential if we are ever to understand the mental capacities of animals or the limits to animal deception. In the case of avian false alarm calls, the behavior of the deceitful signallers can probably not be interpreted as truly deceitful unless it can be shown that the birds are capable of using other signals and of modifying the rate of their signals to manipulate other flock members.

DETECTION OF DECEPTION AND THE ASSESSMENT OF SIGNAL MEANING

The degree to which animals can deceive one another depends crucially on how recipients assess the meaning of signals. If one animal provides another with false information, how does this affect the recipient's subsequent behavior? The success or failure of a deceptive signal will depend on (a) the ability of the recipient to discover that the signal is false, (b) whether, once the recipient has identified a signal as false it continues to be skeptical about the same signal, and (c) whether, once the recipient has identified one signal as false, the recipient's skepticism expands, and he begins to doubt the signaller's credibility in other quite different spheres of interaction.

To take a commonplace example, suppose a friend offers you advice about the stock market. You follow his suggestions, and you lose substantial amounts of money. Fairly quickly you will begin to doubt your friend's expertise, and you will cease paying attention to his suggestions. Now suppose your friend offers you advice about which banks offer the best interest rates on their savings accounts. Whether or not you follow his new advice will depend crucially on how you assess the meaning of his statements and how you classify what we might call spheres of meaning in the world around you.

In this example, because dealing in stocks and dealing with banks concern fairly similar issues (or, we might say, fall within the same sphere of meaning), you may well transfer skepticism about your friend's knowledge of the stock market to skepticism about his knowledge of banks. Because his information was false in one context, you assume it will also be false in other closely related contexts within the same domain. On the other hand, despite past events you may still be willing to consider your friend's advice about restaurants because communication in these two domains deals with quite different spheres of meaning.

This discussion is meant to illustrate an important point: The spread of deception in any population depends crucially on how animals assess the meaning of signals, and how signals are classified on the basis of their meaning. If an individual successfully uses bluff in a threat display, can it also deceive others in courtship? Can it falsely inform others about predators?

Similarly, if a recipient learns that a particular individual is deceptive in his threat displays, how does this affect the recipient's subsequent behavior? Will it begin to doubt everyone's threat displays, or will its skepticism be limited to one individual? Will the recipient be skeptical only in the domain of aggression, or will it also begin to doubt the signaller when he signals about food or alarm calls? The limits to deception will be set—to a considerable extent—by the skill with which recipients can take information gained in one sphere of meaning and accurately transfer it to other spheres. Deception thus depends crucially on how animals classify signals according to their meaning. Conversely, as we suggest later, experiments in the study of deception can reveal how animals categorize events in the world around them.

An Experimental Test of the Response to Unreliable Signals

To test these ideas, we designed an experiment in which a vervet monkey was made to be an unreliable signaller. We then examined whether this unreliability affected the willingness of other monkeys to respond to the same (or different) individual when it signalled about either similar or different information.

The subjects for our experiments were vervet monkeys living in six social groups in Amboseli National Park, Kenya. All groups had been observed continuously since 1977 (Cheney & Seyfurth, 1987). The animals were habituated to close-range observation on foot and could be recognized individually.

Within the study area groups of vervet monkeys occupied ranges that averaged 23 hectares in size and were actively defended against incursions by other groups (Cheney, 1981, 1987; Cheney & Seyfarth, 1987). Intergroup encounters usually began with the exchange of a loud trill call, the "wrr" vocalization between females and juveniles in the two opposing groups. This call appears to function to alert both the members of the females' own group and the other group that the other group has been spotted. When such initial vocalizations occurred, groups could be separated by as much as 200 m. Although many encounters involved only the exchange of wrrs, 54% ($N = 348$) escalated to include threats, chases, or even physical contact. When groups came together under these conditions, females and juveniles often gave an acoustically different call, the intergroup "chutter" (Cheney, 1981, 1987; Cheney & Seyfarth, 1988).

Although 'wrrs" and 'chutters' both occur during intergroup interactions, they were given together in only 27% of all intergroup encounters. Moreover, when chutters and wrrs did occur in the same encounter, they were usually given by different individuals; they were given by the same individual in only 3% of all encounters. These acoustically different calls, therefore, appear to have broadly similar referents, even though they do not always occur simultaneously or in precisely the same context (Fig. 6.1). This raises the following question: If a monkey learns that individual X gives an intergroup wrr when no other group is around, will it also doubt the reliability (and cease responding to) X's chutter? Will monkeys transfer their skepticism from one type of intergroup call to another type of intergroup call?

Vervet monkeys in Amboseli also give acoustically different alarm calls to different predators, with each call evoking a different escape response (see previous discussion). In other words, in addition to having acoustically different calls that refer to roughly the same external stimulus (the wrrs and

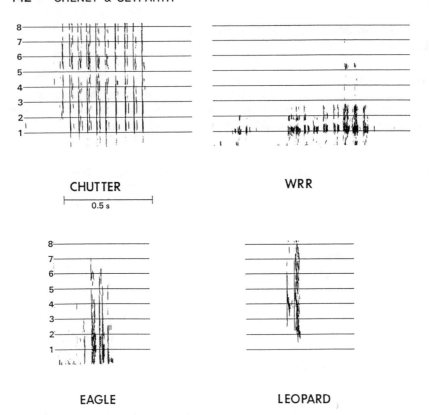

Fig. 6.1   Chutter and wrr vocializations given by adult female SN and alarm calls to eagles and leopards given by adult female AM. Horizontal lines show frequency in units of 1 kHz.

chutters previously described), the monkeys also have acoustically distinct calls that refer to different stimuli and evoke very different responses. This raises the following question: when confronted with an unreliable signaller, how broadly will monkeys extend their skepticism? If a monkey learns that individual X gives eagle alarms when there no eagles are around, will it also cease responding to individual X's leopard alarms? Will skepticism be transferred to calls of different meaning?

Procedure

To test whether monkeys would transfer skepticism from one call type to another we used a habituation/dishabituation procedure (e.g., Eimas, Sigueland, Vusczyh, & Vigonito, 1971). On day 1 a subject was played the chutter of individual X in order to establish the baseline strength of the subject's response to X's chutter. Then, on day 2, the subject heard X's wrr repeated eight times at roughly 20 minute intervals. Because there was no other group present at the time, we predicted that the subject would rapidly cease responding to X's wrr. In other words, it would come to regard X's wrr as an unreliable signal. Finally, roughly 20 minutes after the last playback in the habituation series, the subject heard X's chutter again. If the subject had come to regard X's wrr as unreliable, and if the subject treated wrrs and chutters as having roughly similar meaning, then the subject should have transferred its skepticism to other intergroup calls by X and therefore respond much less strongly than it had on day 1 to playback of X's chutter.

To test whether monkeys would transfer skepticism when the calls had different referents, we repeated the procedure described above using X's alarm call given to leopards and X's alarm call given to eagles.

Third, to determine whether subjects would transfer habituation across individuals as well as across call types, we varied the test procedure by playing a different individual's call following the habituation trials. On day 1, we established baseline data on the strength of a subject's response to X's chutter. On day 2 the same subject heard Y's wrr eight times. After habituating to Y's wrr, the subject was tested to see if it would also habituate to X's chutter. If subjects also attended to the identity of the signaller they should have been less likely to transfer habituation to the chutter in this case because presumably only animal X had been made unreliable.

Finally, to determine whether individuals would transfer skepticism across both individuals and call types, we tested whether habituation to Y's eagle alarm call would cause subjects to habituate to X's leopard alarm call.

Results

Results (Cheney & Seyfarth, 1988) are summarized in Figs. 6.2-6.5. When calls had the same referent and were given by the same individual, subjects did habituate across call types. In other words, if a subject had learned that X's intergroup wrr was unreliable, the subject also treated X's chutter as unreliable (Fig. 6.2). In contrast, when calls had the same referent but came from different individuals, habituation was not transferred (Fig. 6.3). In other words, if a subject had learned that individual X's wrr was unreliable, it did not transfer its skepticism to individual Y: Y's chutter still elicited the same response as it did under normal conditions.

When the two calls had different referents, skepticism was also not transferred (Figs. 6.4 and 6.5). If a subject had learned that X was unreliable when signalling about leopards, it still responded both to X's eagle alarms (different referent, same signaller) and to Y's eagle alarms (different referent, different signaller).

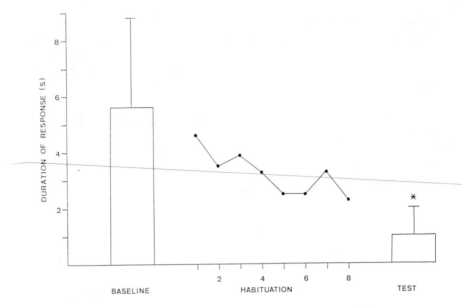

Fig. 6.2 The duration of responses shown by 10 subjects to playback of a given individual's intergroup chutter following repeated exposure to that individual's wrr (test) compared with their responses to the same chutter in the absence of such exposure (baseline). Histograms show means and SD for all subjects. The mean duration of subjects' responses during the eight habituation trials is also shown. * = *P* < 0.01 when baseline and test conditions are compared. (From Cheney & Seyfarth, 1988).

The failure of monkeys to transfer habituation from one alarm call type to another did not occur simply because alarm calls, unlike intergroup vocalizations, are signals that are too costly to ignore. If this were true, monkeys should have taken longer to habituate to repeated presentation of the same alarm call than to repeated presentation of the same intergroup call. This, however, was not the case. Habituation occurred at equal rates to alarm and to intergroup vocalizations (Cheney & Seyfarth, 1988).

In summary, vervets treated two acoustically different calls as being the same only when they had the same broad referent and were given by the same individual. If either the call's meaning or the signaller's identity was changed, the two calls were treated as different. Vervets therefore appear to attend both to the signaller's identity and the signal's meaning when assessing the reliability of a call. When asked to compare two vocalizations, vervet monkeys make judgments about them according to their meaning rather than simply according to their acoustic properties.

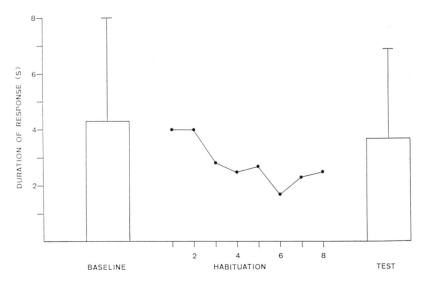

Fig. 6.3 The duration of responses shown by 10 subjects to playback of a given individual's chutter following repeated exposure to a *different* individual's wrr (test) compared with their responses to the same chutter in the absence of such exposure (baseline) (Cheney & Seyfarth, 1988).

DISCUSSION: DECEPTION AND THE ASSESSMENT OF MEANING

As suggested earlier, in any group-living species in which animals might attempt to deceive one another, selection should favor recipients who can transfer information about the reliability of a particular signaller from one context to another. In other words, the detection of unreliable signals will be influenced by the ways that animals assess the meaning of signals. In the case of vervets and probably other species as well, animals seem to recognize spheres of meaning and are able to transfer information gained in one sphere to another closely related one. In our experiments, for example, vervets seemed to judge intergroup wrrs and intergroup chutters as sufficiently similar that habituation to one call produced habituation to the other.

Note that in these experiments vervet monkeys appear to be comparing calls not on the basis of their acoustic features but according to their referents. After habituating to an individual's wrr, subjects also habituated to the same individual's chutter even though these vocalizations are quite different acoustically. Results contradict the view (e.g., Morton 1977) that animals respond to acoustic signals primarily according to the signals'

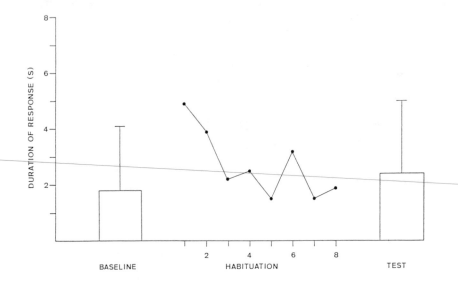

Fig. 6.4 The duration of responses shown by nine subjects to playback of a given individual's leopard (or eagle) alarm call following repeated exposure to that individual's eagle (or leopard) alarm call (test) compared with their responses to the same alarm call in the absence of such exposure (baseline). (Cheney & Seyfarth, 1988).

physical properties. Instead, results suggest that vervet monkeys (and perhaps many other species as well) process information at a semantic as well as an acoustic level (Cheney & Seyfarth, 1988).

The experiments on vervet monkeys do not demonstrate deception through signal falsification. Rather, they investigate the potential scope for deception by testing the skepticism of recipients and the ability of recipients to transfer such skepticism to other contexts. Classification of signals according to their meaning suggests that, if an individual monkey tries to deceive others by falsely signalling the presence of another group with a chutter, animals will soon recognize that this chutter is no longer reliable and the signaller will no longer be able to deceive using any of his intergroup calls even though their acoustic properties might be quite different. On the other hand, the signaller could continue to deceive others by giving false alarm calls, because – to vervets at least – an animal that is unreliable when signalling about one event is not automatically regarded as unreliable when signalling about a completely different event. Vervet monkeys seem to view leopard and eagle alarm calls as so different in meaning that – at least in our experiments – experience gained in one sphere was not transferred to another.

The ways in which vervet monkeys assess the meaning of signals thus

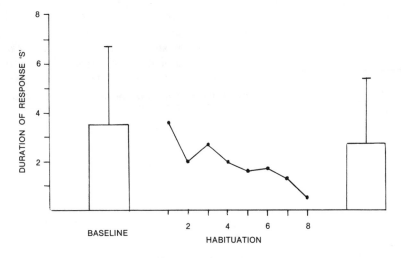

Fig. 6.5 The duration of responses shown by nine subjects to playback of a given individual's leopard (or eagle) alarm call following repeated exposure to a *different* individual's eagle (or leopard) alarm call (test) compared with their responses to the same alarm call in the absence of such exposure. (Cheney & Seyfarth, 1988).

places a constraint on the ability of signallers to deceive, but it also provides them with opportunities. Because of the way recipients assess meaning, a monkey who has been detected deceiving others in one domain can now no longer expect to succeed in deception unless he moves to a new domain.

At least two additional factors may affect the responses of recipients to signals. First, it is highly probable that the relative costs of responding or failing to respond to a potentially false signal strongly influence whether or not a recipient continues to attend to unreliable signals. For example, although recipients who respond to false alarm calls may incur costs in the form of wasted energy or decreased feeding opportunities, the cost of failing to respond to an alarm call is potentially so high that they may continue to attend to such calls even when they are skeptical of the signaller's reliability. In contrast, because the cost of failing to respond to a food call is far less, recipients may become skeptical of false food calls at a much faster rate. Thus, the frequency of false signals may be much higher in some circumstances than in others simply because recipients cannot always afford to become skeptical.

It is also possible that the failure of recipients to transfer skepticism across very different spheres of meaning is related less to their ability to generalize across widely disparate contexts than to the ways in which they assess the motives of the signaller. To return to the example of the unreliable friend's advice about stocks, suppose that you and your friend are in a building together when he suddenly shouts "Fire!". Whether or not you heed his advice and run for the nearest emergency exit will depend to a large extent on how you perceive your friend's motives. If you perceive your friend as merely incompetent in financial matters, you will probably follow his advice because ineptitude in one sphere does not necessarily imply ineptitude in another totally distinct one. If, however, you are beginning to suspect that your friend is maliciously trying to drive you to financial ruin or worse, you may well decide that your friend's warning is simply another deceptive ruse and ignore his advice.

In the case of vervet monkeys, some degree of cooperation among group members is essential for individual survival. Thus it seems unlikely that an individual will be regarded as intentionally deceptive unless many aspects of his behavior become unreliable. In the experiments described above, an individual was made to be unreliable in a single context for only a few hours. Assuming for the moment that vervet monkeys are capable of making such judgements, it seems more likely that the experiments caused the signaller to be regarded as having made a mistake rather than as being deceitful. A signaller that is regarded as mistaken may be attended to for longer and in a wider variety of different contexts than a signaller who is regarded as intentionally deceitful.

Clearly, whether or not we can talk in terms of intentions and attributions in any nonhuman species is a controversial issue. However, assumptions about intentions and attributions are often implicit in much of the debate about the function of deception in animal signals. We should be aware of these assumptions, but we should also be hopeful that eventually we will be able to use communication to gain a window on animals' minds.

SUMMARY

The manipulation of others through false or unreliable signals can potentially take a number of forms. Among group-living animals, one of the most effective means of deceiving others is through silence — by withholding information that might be beneficial to others. This is the method of deceptive communication least likely to be detected. More direct manipulation can occur through active falsification of signals. Signal falsification will be most effective if it occurs at low rates and if the circumstances surrounding successive acts of deception are varied; for example, if a false food call is subsequently followed by a false alarm call rather than simply by another false food call. Variation in the context of deception, at least in vervet monkeys, allows individuals to maintain the highest rates of deceptive signalling without producing permanent skepticism among others in their group.

At present, we have no evidence that any animal species regularly varies the rate and context of false signals. Through more systematic observations and experiments it should eventually become possible to determine whether the intriguing anecdotes reported in the literature do at least in some cases represent intentional signal falsification as well as to specify more precisely the constraints under which deceptive communication acts.

REFERENCES

Alatalo, R. V., Carlson, A., Lundberg, A., & Ulfstrand, S. (1981). The conflict between male polygamy and female monogamy: The case of the pied flycatcher, *Ficedula hypoleuca*. *American Naturalist 117*, 738–753.

Andersson, M. (1980). Why are there so many threat displays? *Journal of Theoretical Biology 86*, 773–781.

Axelrod, R., & Hamilton. W. D. (1981). The evolution of cooperation. *Science, 211*, 1390–1396.

Byrne, R., & Whiten, A. (1988). Towards the next generation in data quality: A new survey of primate tactical deception. *Behavioral and Brain Sciences, 11*, 233–273.

Caryl, P. G. (1979). Communication by agonistic displays: What can games theory contribute to ethology? *Behaviour, 68*, 136–169.

Cheney, D. L. (1981). Intergroup encounters among free-ranging vervet monkeys. *Folia primatologica, 35*, 124–146.

Cheney, D. L. (1987). Interactions and relationships between groups. In B. B. Smuts, D. L. Cheney, R. M. Seyfarth, R. W. Wrangham, & T. T. Struhsaker (Eds.), *Primate societies*. Chicago: University of Chicago Press.

Cheney, D. L., & Seyfarth, R. M. (1985). Social and non-social knowledge in vervet monkeys. *Philosophical Transactions of the Royal Society, London, Series B, 308*, 187–201.

Cheney, D. L., & Seyfarth, R. M. (1987). The influence of intergroup competition on the survival and reproduction of female vervet monkeys. *Behavioral Ecology and Sociobiology, 21*, 375–386.

Cheney, D. L., & Seyfarth, R. M. (1988). Assessment of meaning and the detection of unreliable signals by vervet monkeys. *Animal Behaviour, 36*, 477–486.

Cheney, D. L., Seyfarth, R. M., Andelman, S. J., & Lee, P. C. (1988). Reproductive success in vervet monkeys. In T. H. Clutton-Brock (Ed.), *Reproductive success*. Chicago: University of Chicago Press.

Davies, N. B., & Halliday, T. R. (1978). Deep croaks and fighting assessment in toads *Bufo bufo*. *Nature, London, 274*, 683–685.

Davies, N. B., & Halliday, T. R. (1979). Competitive mate searching in common toads, *Bufo bufo*. *Animal Behaviour, 27*, 1253–1267.

Dennett, D. (1987). *The intentional stance*. Cambridge, MA: M.I.T Press/Bradford Books.

Dunford, C. (1977). Kin selection for ground squirrel alarm calls. *American Naturalist, 111*, 782–785.

Eimas, P. D., Siqueland, P., Jusczyk, P., & Vigorito, J. (1971). Speech perception in infants. *Science, 171*, 303–306.

Elgar, M. A. (1986). House sparrows establish foraging flocks by giving chirrup calls if the resources are divisible. *Animal Behaviour, 34*, 169–174.

Goodall, J. (1971). *In the shadow of man.* Boston: Houghton Mifflin.

Goodall, J. (1986). *The chimpanzees of Gombe: Patterns of behavior.* Cambridge: Harvard University Press.

Griffin, D. (1984). *Animal thinking.* Cambridge: Harvard University Press.

Gyger, M., Karakashian, S. J., & Marler, P. (1986). Avian alarm calling: Is there an audience effect? *Animal Behaviour, 34,* 1570–1572.

Halliday, T. R. (1976). The libidinous newt. An analysis of variations in the sexual behaviour of the male smooth newt, *Triturus vulgaris. Animal Behaviour, 24,* 398–414.

Halliday, T. R. (1983). The study of mate choice. In P. Bateson (Ed.), *Mate choice.* Cambridge: Cambridge University Press.

Hinde, R. A. (1981). Animal signals: ethological and games theory approaches are not incompatible. *Animal Behaviour, 29,* 535–542.

Hoogland, J. L. (1983). Nepotism and alarm-calling in the black-tailed prairie dog, *Cynomys ludovicianus. Animal Behaviour, 31,* 472–479.

Howard, R. D. (1974). The influence of sexual selection and interspecific competition on mockingbird song (*Mimus polyglottis*). *Evolution, 28,* 428–438.

Krebs, J. R., & Dawkins, R. (1984). Animal signals: Mind reading and manipulation. In J. R. Krebs & N. B. Davies (Eds.), *Behavioural ecology, an evolutionary approach* (2nd ed.). Sunderland, MA: Sinauer Associates.

Kummer, H. (1982). Social knowledge in free-ranging primates. In D. R. Griffin (Ed.), *Animal mind – human mind.* Berlin: Springer/Verlag.

Leger, D. W., & Owings, D. H. (1978). Responses to alarm calls by California ground squirrels. *Behavioral Ecology and Sociobiology, 3,* 177–186.

Markl, H. (1985). Manipulation, modulation, information, cognition: Some of the riddles of communication. In B. Holldobler & M. Lindauer (Eds.), *Experimental behavioral ecology and sociobiology.* Sunderland, MA: Sinauer Associates.

Marler, P. (1956). The voice of the chaffinch and its function as a language. *Ibis, 98,* 231–261.

Maynard Smith, J. (1974). The theory of games and the evolution of animal conflict. *Journal of Theoretical Biology, 47,* 209–221.

Maynard Smith, J. (1979). Game theory and the evolution of behaviour. *Proceedings of the Royal Society of London, Series B, 205,* 475–488.

Maynard Smith, J. (1982). *Evolution and the theory of games.* Cambridge: Cambridge University Press.

Maynard Smith, J. (1984). Game theory and the evolution of behavior. *Behavioral and Brain Sciences, 7,* 95–125.

Maynard Smith, J. (1986). Ownership and honesty in competitive interactions. *Behavioral and Brain Sciences, 9,* 742–744.

Maynard Smith, J., & Price, G. R. (1973). The logic of animal conflicts. *Nature, London, 246,* 15–18.

Moller, A. P. (1988). False alarm calls as a means of resource usurpation in the great tit *Parus major. Ethology 79,* 25–30

Morton, E. S. (1977). On the occurrence and significance of motivation-structural rules in some bird and mammal sounds. *American Naturalist, 111,* 855–869.

Moynihan, M. (1970). The control, suppression, decay, disappearance and replacement of displays. *Journal of Theoretical Biology, 29,* 85–112.

Munn, C. (1986a). Birds that "cry wolf." *Nature, London, 319,* 143–145.

Munn, C. A. (1986b). The deceptive use of alarm calls by sentinel species in mixed-species flocks of neotropical birds. In R. W. Mitchell & N. S. Thompson (Eds.), *Deception: Perspectives on human and nonhuman deceit.* Albany: SUNY Press.

Packer, C. (1977). Reciprocal altruism in *Papio anubis. Nature, London, 265,* 441–443.

Paton, D. (1986). Communication by agonistic displays: II. Perceived information and the definition of agonistic displays. *Behaviour, 99,* 157–175.

van Rhijn, J. G., & Vodegal, R. (1980). Being honest about one's intentions: An evolutionary stable strategy for animal conflicts. *Journal of Theoretical Biology, 85,* 623–641.

Ristau, C. A. 1988. Thinking, communicating and deceiving: Means to master the social environment. In G. Greenberg & E. Tobach (Eds.). *Evolution of social behavior and integrative levels.* (pp. 213–240). Hillsdale, NJ: Lawrence Eolbaum Associates.

Seyfarth, R. M., & Cheney, D. L. (1984). Grooming, alliances, and reciprocal altruism in vervet monkeys. *Nature, London, 308,* 541–543.

Seyfarth, R. M., Cheney, D. L., & Marler, P. (1980). Vervet monkey alarm calls: Semantic communication in a free-ranging primate. *Animal Behaviour, 28,* 1070–1094.

Sherman, P. (1977). Nepotism and the evolution of alarm calls. *Science, 197,* 1246–1253.

Struhsaker, T. T. (1967). Auditory communication among vervet monkeys (*Cercopithecus aethiops*). In S. A. Altmann (Ed.), *Social communication among primates.* Chicago: University of Chicago Press.

Thornhill, R. (1979). Adaptive female-mimicking behavior in a scorpionfly. *Science, 205,* 412–414.

de Waal, F. (1982). *Chimpanzee politics.* New York: Harper & Row.

de Waal, F. (1986). Deception in the natural communication of chimpanzees. In R. W. Mitchell & N. S. Thompson (Eds.), *Deception: Perspectives on human and nonhuman deceit.* Albany: SUNY Press.

Whiten, A., & Byrne, R. (1988). The manipulation of attention in primate tactical deception. In R. Byrne & A. Whiten (Eds.), *Machiavellian intelligence: Social expertise and the evolution of intellect in monkeys, apes, and humans.* London: Oxford University Press.

Wimmer, R., & Permer, G. (1983). Beliefs about beliefs: Representation and constraining function of wrong beliefs in young children's understanding of deception. *Cognition, 13,* 103–128.

Woodruff, G., & Premack, D. (1979). Intentional communication in the chimpanzee: The development of deception. *Cognition, 7,* 333–362,

Wrangham, R. W. (1975). *The behavioural ecology of chimpanzees in the Gombe National Park, Tanzania.* Unpublished doctoral dissertation, University of Cambridge.

7

A COMMUNICATIVE APPROACH TO ANIMAL COGNITION: A STUDY OF CONCEPTUAL ABILITIES OF AN AFRICAN GREY PARROT

Irene M. Pepperberg
Northwestern University

ABSTRACT

An African Grey parrot has been taught to use the sounds of English speech to identify, request, refuse, categorize, and quantify more than 80 different objects and to respond to questions concerning categorical concepts of color and shape. The parrot, Alex, has now been trained and tested on relational concepts of *same* and *different*. He learned to reply with the correct English categorical label ("color", "shape", or "mah-mah" [matter]) when asked "What's same?" or "What's different?" about pairs of objects that varied with respect to any combination of attributes. He performed equally well on pairs of novel and familiar objects, and special trials demonstrated that his responses were based upon the question being posed as well as the attributes of the objects. These results are compared with the findings of other studies on animal cognition and interspecies communication.

INTRODUCTION

The study of animal cognition encompasses topics as disparate as the numerical competencies of laboratory rats (e.g., Davis & Bradford, 1986) and the foraging behaviors of hummingbirds (Kamil, 1978). What is common to studies of animal cognition is that the research is performed not just to learn what the animal can do or be trained to do, but also how and why the animal does what it does, and how its behavior may develop or change (e.g., Galef, 1984). Cognitive studies test the hypotheses that animal subjects can solve complex problems and make and revise inferences and decisions, both in their natural niches and in the artificially constructed environment of a laboratory (see Kamil, 1984, 1988; Kintsch, 1982).

Because many cognitive abilities, when examined in humans, appear to be mediated by human language, some researchers endeavor to study animal cognition by examining the communication processes of their animal subjects. These investigators may, for example, examine the role of communication in social cognition—how an animal recognizes individuals and relationships between individuals. By examining ways animals communicate with one another, researchers hope to determine not just the information that these behaviors convey but also the conceptual abilities such behaviors may indicate (Beer, 1982a). The inference is that mechanisms underlying social cognition may also be available to mediate cognitive behaviors involved in other tasks, such as involving, memory, information processing, and categorization (see discussions in Cheney & Seyfarth, 1986; Crook, 1983).

The assumption that the same cognitive capacities can be used in widely divergent situations remains to be fully tested (see Galef, 1984; Rogoff, 1984). Investigations of communication patterns in many animals' natural environments, however, do demonstrate connections between communication and cognition (see discussion in Gouzoules, Gouzoules, & Marler, 1985). Studies have shown that signalling systems that even at first appear relatively stereotypic may reveal abilities that can be considered cognitive: Often the ways that signals are employed—the variations in features of signals, in how signals are combined, and in the context in which signals are emitted—serve important functions for transmitting complex information (Markl, 1985).

For example, Beer (1975, 1976, 1982b) has demonstrated that vocal gradations conveying individual variations in meaning exist in what were once thought to be uniform "long calls" of laughing gulls (*Larus atricilla*). Variations in amplitude differentiate calls directed at the gulls' own nestlings from those directed at adults, and also differentiate calls made to younger versus older chicks. These variations appear to have both semantic and pragmatic significance in that the chicks not only distinguish which sets of parental calls are directed towards them, but the chicks also respond differently to the earlier and later calls, even when tested late in the nestling stage. Smith (1986) has shown that variations in context affect the meaning of otherwise identical signals in fly catchers (*Tyrannus tyrannus*); such variations allow for significant expansion of a limited vocal repertoire and enable the birds to elicit and process information so as to begin, reaffirm, test, or alter their relationships. Similarly, Tyack (1983) has demonstrated that differing responses of humpback whales (*Megaptera novaeangliae*) to playback of the same social sounds appear to depend on the number of animals and the sexual composition of the social group hearing the signals.

He suggests that, like tamarins and marmosets (*Saguinus oedipus, Saguinus mystax, Cebuella pygmaea,* Snowdon, 1988), vervets (*Cercopithecus aethiops,* Cheney & Seyfarth, 1986) or rhesus monkeys (*Macaca mulatta,* Gouzoules, Gouzoules, & Marler, 1984), whales may use acoustic signals to define or mediate social relationships. Kroodsma (1981, 1987, 1988) has shown not only that some warblers (*Parulinae, Muscicapidae*) use different songs in different contexts (e.g., mate attraction vs. territorial defense; see also Ficken & Ficken, 1967; Morse, 1970; cf. Lein, 1978) but also that the context in which these warblers learn a song may affect the way that the song is later used. This ability to acquire sensitivity to the contextual appropriateness of the signal suggests some form of information processing.

Other studies have demonstrated additional capacities similarly interpreted as cognitive (see Gouzoules et al., 1985). For example, some species vary their alarm calls with respect to the identity of the predator or the immediacy of the danger; often, too, the degree to which the alarm is heeded is related to which individual has done the signalling (Cheney & Seyfarth, 1985; Leger & Owings, 1978; Leger, Owings, & Boal, 1979; Leger, Owings, & Gelfand, 1980; Owings & Hennessy, 1984; Owings & Virginia, 1978; Robinson, 1980, 1981). Some studies (e.g., Dittus, 1984; Marler, Dufty, & Pickert, 1986; Pflumm, Comtesse, & Wilhelm, 1984; Snowdon, 1988) provide evidence that the rate and number of food calls of several species varies with the preference rankings of the food involved: Preliminary analyses of these variations suggest that they express degrees of excitation concerning the quality of the source rather than specific information about its identity, but more detailed analysis of the calls and their context could prove otherwise.

Although the study of natural communication systems has therefore provided scientists with some insight into the cognitive capacities of various animals, other investigators have chosen an alternative approach. They have been training animal subjects to use human-based codes (e.g., nonvocal codes such as American Sign Language or artificial forms of communication based on rules presumed to underlie human systems; see von Glasersfeld, 1977) as a means through which to assess cognitive competence. With such techniques, researchers have examined conceptual abilities of several great apes (chimpanzees, *Pan troglodytes:* Fouts, 1973a; Gardner & Gardner, 1984; Gillan, 1982; Premack, 1976, 1983; Rumbaugh, 1977; Savage-Rumbaugh, Rumbaugh, Smith, & Lawson, 1980; gorillas, *Gorilla gorilla:* Patterson, 1978; an orangutan *Pongo pygmacus:* Miles, 1978, 1983); marine mammals; (dolphins, *Tursiops touncatus:* Herman, Richards, & Wolz, 1984; Herman & Forestell, 1985; Reiss, Markowitz, Firestein, & Mullen, 1981; Sea lions, *Zalophus californianus: Schusterman & Krieger, 1986); and a parrot (Pepperberg, 1978, 1981, 1983, 1987a,*

1987b, 1987c, 1988a, 1988b, 1988c). To assess the impact of interspecies communication on the study of animal cognition, intelligence, and communicative intent, it is helpful to view the relevant work within a historical perspective—in particular, within the context of the changes in philosophies and methodologies that have governed the study of behavior in the last century.

"Animal Intelligence"—
A Brief Historical Perspective

Early observers of animal behavior believed in the existence of sophisticated communicative and cognitive capacities of their subjects (see Darwin, 1872; Romanes, 1882), but their lack of objectivity, the anecdotal nature of much of their evidence, and their failure to examine alternative, less sophisticated explanations of the behaviors they observed often led to overinterpretation of many phenomena (see review in Burghardt, 1984). The response of the scientific community was to canonize the cautionary tenets of Morgan (1894) and to welcome the advent of strict behaviorism (e.g., Watson, 1929). Although experimental designs improved considerably, the search for parsimonious explanations of animal behavior led researchers to ignore potentially productive and informative areas of research, particularly with respect to the mechanisms underlying these behaviors. Only recently has scientific interest again shifted (Beer, 1982a, 1982b, this volume; Dennett, 1983; Griffin, 1981, 1985), and a synthesis of careful experimental technique and wide-ranging curiosity engendered interest in cognitive approaches to both psychology and ethology—an interest based on the premise that animals do indeed have complex, cognitive abilities that are analogous, if not necessarily homologous, to those of humans (Snowdon, 1988).

Despite increased sophistication in experimental design, research into animal cognitive abilities, particularly with respect to the use of interspecies communication as an investigative tool, has not been free of controversy. Results that suggest mental and behavioral continuity across species run counter to the arguments of scientists who base their research interpretations on the existence of qualitative (as opposed to quantitative) differences in the capacities of human and nonhuman animals (Premack, 1978; see discussion in Kamil, 1988). Specifically, some researchers propose that (a) possession of, or ability to acquire, "human language" (or at least a specific human-based linguistic code) is just such a qualitative difference, and (b) "language" is necessary if an organism is to organize and process information for certain complex cognitive tasks (see Macphail, 1985, 1987; Premack, 1983; cf. Marschark, 1983). Consequently, the study of comparative cognition through interspecies communication has been sidetracked by arguments about whether nonhuman subjects in these communication programs have, in fact, mastered various aspects of human language.

The controversy can be summarized as follows: After nonhuman subjects had demonstrated behaviors such as tool use (see Beck, 1980) and cooperative hunting (Goodall, 1968; Teleki, 1973; more recently, see Boesch, 1986), language became one of the few remaining defining lines between human and animal abilities. Through the mid-1960s, the possibility that animals could participate in even simple forms of two-way communication was frequently discounted (e.g., Chomsky, 1966); basic communicative tasks such as labeling were supposed to be beyond the reach of even "closely" related species such as chimpanzees. In accordance with these views, Struhsaker, whose study was the first to suggest that vervets used different signals to refer to different predators and possibly different social situations, was careful to refer to his findings as "Information on and *impressions of* [italics added] the conditions evoking the sounds and the communicative function of the sounds . . ." (Struhsaker, 1967, p. 323). The results of a study by Hayes and Nissen (1956/1971), which demonstrated that a chimpanzee could acquire only a limited number of vocal labels, were widely cited as evidence of the inferiority of animal abilities. (For a review of other early projects, see Kellogg, 1968.) When the Gardners, Premacks, and Rumbaughs, using widely divergent but equally innovative techniques, showed that, at the least, associative (and possibly referential; e.g., Lock, 1980) labeling was within the range of nonhuman primates, researchers like Bronowski and Bellugi (1970) rightly countered that labeling alone was not language. Lenneberg (1971) subsequently developed a set of criteria by which to judge if an animal's acquired communicative behavior could be considered language, but he declared, within the same article, that a demonstration of even these accomplishments would not be sufficient. By the mid-1970s, it appeared as though "language" was to be defined as that part of human communication that animals were incapable of achieving: As apes in the various projects demonstrated one or more of the characteristics initially thought to define language (e.g., reference, conversational skills, simple syntax), critics searched for additional criteria ". . . to safeguard human uniqueness" (Miles, 1983, p. 45; see also Fouts, 1973b).

Unfortunately, such debates on the degree to which these animals had acquired human language (e.g., Sebeok & Rosenthal, 1981) obscured what should have been the truly important issue, that is, that the techniques developed in these communication programs enabled researchers to examine those cognitive (and not necessarily linguistic) abilities in animals that were not observable using the more traditional paradigms (see Griffin, 1978, 1985; Pepperberg, 1986, 1987c, 1988a, 1988c; Premack, 1983; Savage-Rumbaugh et al., 1980). Thus, although direct comparisons of acquisition and use of linguistic forms by animal and human subjects may in themselves be interesting and valid (Fouts, 1974), it is the worth of the communication code for the study of comparative cognition that should be the focus of interest. There is value in a system that (a) enables researchers to query their animal subjects in as direct a manner as they now query human participants in related studies; (b) enables researchers to communicate to their subjects, in the most efficient manner possible, the precise nature of the questions being asked; (c) takes into account the animals' natural predispositions to respond within a social context not entirely unlike their field situation (see Menzel & Juno, 1982, 1985); and (d) facilitates comparisons not just between humans and other animals but between various animal species (Pepperberg, 1987b).

Interspecies communication is, moreover, not just a viable but a particularly powerful means of studying animal cognition. An open, arbitrary system that makes use of subtle variations to create an enormous variety of signals allows researchers to examine the nature and not just the extent of the information perceived by the subject. The flexibility of the system allows for novel and possibly innovative responses that may demonstrate even greater competence than the required responses of traditional (e.g., operant) paradigms. Whether or not the animal subjects do possess (or demonstrate) advanced cognitive capacities, a two-way communication system allows researchers to explore such possibilities in a most efficient manner.

COGNITION IN THE GREY PARROT: ABILITIES OF A NONPRIMATE, NONMAMMALIAN SUBJECT

Choice of a Psittacine Subject

For over a decade, my students and I have been teaching a nonmammalian, nonprimate subject, an African Grey parrot, to communicate via the sounds of English speech so that we may examine an avian capacity for advanced cognitive and communicative abilities. When I began the present study, other projects using interspecies communication employed as their subjects animals that had either a close phylogenic relationship to humans (like great apes) or were known for their large brain-to-body-weight ratios (like cetaceano: see review in Morgane, Jacobs, & Galaburda, 1986). The choice of a parrot as a subject was, however, not surprising when viewed within the context of contemporary ornithological research.

For many years, scientists had been examining and categorizing the vocal behaviors of various birds, and these researchers had found a number of interesting parallels in the development of human speech and avian vocalizations (Marler, 1970, 1973; Nottebohm, 1970, 1975; Petrinovich, 1972; Thorpe, 1974); subsequent work lent further support to the initial findings (Dooling & Searcy, 1981; Marler & Peters, 1977; Nottebohm, 1981; Payne, Thompson, Fiala, & Sweany, 1981; Shiovitz & Lemon, 1980; Pepperberg, 1985). For example, researchers learned that, for both birds and humans, adult forms of communication are often preceded by a practice period: For a short time, immature subjects appear to experiment — with little regard for meaning — with the sounds that will eventually be employed for intentional communication (Baldwin, 1914; Brown, 1973; de Villiers & de Villiers, 1978; Kroodsma, 1974; Lenneberg, 1967; Marler, 1970, 1973; Marler & Peters, 1982; Mowrer, 1950; Nottebohm, 1970, 1975; Thorpe, 1974). Furthermore, many initially inchoate vocalizations contain messages whose exact meanings appear to be acquired by learning (Baptista, 1983; Brown, 1973; Kroodsma, 1987, 1988; Mebes, 1978; Morse, 1967, 1970; Mundinger, 1970; Shiovitz & Lemon, 1980); at first, a subject may have only a general sense of the usefulness of an utterance, not of what it actually "means", and will occasionally overgeneralize to inappropriate situations. Thus a human child may for a time call all animals "doggie" (Brown, 1973; cf. Bowerman, 1978, 1982) or an immature bird may employ variations of adult song patterns not in the normal adult repertoire (Kroodsma, 1974; Marler & Peters, 1982). In both avian and human subjects, imitative learning of some vocalizations has been found to play a role in certain aspects of normal development; the processes of repetition and imitation seem, at least in the early stages of acquisition, to be self-rewarding and reinforcing (Lovaas, Varne, Koegel, & Lorsch, 1977; Markl, 1985; Marler, 1970; Mattick, 1972; Mowrer, 1950, 1952, 1958; Weir, 1962). Furthermore, for both birds and humans, social interactions appear to influence what exactly can be learned (Bandura, 1971a, 1971b; Baptista & Petrinovich, 1984, 1986; Furrow & Nelson, 1986; Harris, Jones, Brookes, & Grant, 1986; Kroodsma & Pickert, 1984a, 1984b; Pepperberg, 1985, 1988a; cf. Gleitman, Newport, & Gleitman, 1984). Finally, there exists the possibility that specific neural structures subserve vocal learning, production, and storage in various species (Bottjer & Arnold, 1985; Kroodsma & Canady, 1985; Nottebohm 1985; Nottebohm, Kasparian, & Pandazis, 1981; Paton & Nottebohm, 1984; Paton, Manogue, Nottebohm, 1981; A. Smith, 1978; Walker, 1981).

This last point is of particular interest because birds lack a significant cerebral cortex — the "organ" generally accepted as ". . . essential for the discriminative adaptations that make intelligent behavior possible." (Cobb, 1960, p. 383; see also Geschwind, 1979). Nevertheless, laboratory studies have shown that certain birds (notably parrots [*Amazona ochrocephala, Psittacus erithacus*]; crows [*Corvus americanus, Corvus corax, Corvus cornix*]; jackdaws [*Corvus monedula*]; ravens [*Corvus corax ruficollis*]; jays [*Cyanocitta cristata, Garrulus glandarius*]; and mynahs [*Gracula religiosa*]) are capable of acquiring complex vocal and nonvocal behaviors that (a) many scientists believe are co- or prerequisites for referential communication and (b) suggest cognitive capacities comparable to those of some primates (Benjamini, 1983; Boosey, 1947, 1956; Braun, 1952; Dücker, 1976; Dücker & Rensch, 1977; Geschwind, 1965; Gossette, 1967; Gossette, Gossette, & Reddell, 1966; Kamil, 1984; Kamil & Hunter, 1970; Koehler, 1943, 1950, 1953; Lögler, 1959; Mackintosh, Wilson, & Boakes, 1985; Mowrer, 1950, 1954; Pastore, 1954a, 1954b, 1955, 1961; Premack, 1978; Rensch & Dücker, 1973; G. Smith, 1971; Stettner & Matyniak, 1968; Thorpe, 1964, 1974; Zorina, 1982). It appears that different, equally well-developed parts of the brain—areas known to be in the striatal regions—subserve such intelligent behaviors in birds (Cobb, 1960; Hodos, 1982; Krushinskii, 1965; Nauta & Karten, 1970; Stettner, 1974).

Among the reasons for the choice of a parrot as a subject (for a full discussion, see Pepperberg, 1981) was also the knowledge that the training demands in the laboratory would be analogous to naturally occurring tasks: (a) The ability of parrots to engage in vocal learning has its origins in their behavior in the wild (Nottebohm, 1970; Nottebohm & Nottebohm, 1969), and (b) a significant portion of communication within psittacine communities, both in the wild and in aviary settings, appears to be conducted vocally (Busnel & Mebes, 1975; Mebes, 1978; Power, 1966a, 1966b). Even some of the nonvocal forms of communication such as aggressive displays or mutual preening and courtship feeding are often accompanied by specific vocalizations (e.g., Dilger, 1960; Serpell, 1981).

My project was not the first to attempt vocal communication with a parrot. Mowrer (1950, 1952, 1958), using standard laboratory techniques such as shaping and food reinforcement, had investigated the possibility that a parrot might actually be able to understand the meaning of the words and phrases it could be taught to repeat. It was Mowrer's lack of success that reinforced the popular belief that parrots could do little more than mimic the sounds of human speech (Fromkin & Rodman, 1974; Lenneberg, 1973). The possibility existed, however, that Mowrer's failure was due not to any inherent limitations in his avian subjects but rather to the use of inappropriate training procedures. It was my hypothesis that alternative nontraditional training methods might facilitate communication with a nonprimate, nonmammalian subject. In particular, I believe that the relative success of my project (Pepperberg, 1981, 1983, 1987a, 1987c, 1988b, 1988c; Pepperberg & Kozak, 1986) derives from the recognition that functional acquisition of a nonspecies–specific communication code by a parrot is an instance of *exceptional learning*[1] that, in order to occur,

---

[1]*Exceptional learning* refers to behavior that is regulated (some researchers might even say inhibited) by (a) limited sensitive phases during which learning capacities are maximal and (b) sensory templates that act to restrict attention to a subset of the auditory environment. Even

requires both intense social interaction and referential contextually-relevant modeling (Pepperberg, 1986, 1988a). What follows, therefore, is a brief description of the methods and some results of this project.

The Subject and Our Training Procedure

The experimental subject has been an African Grey parrot named Alex. He was approximately 13 months old when he was obtained from a pet store in the Chicago area in June 1977. Prior to this date, he had received no formal vocal instruction. Alex is allowed free access to the laboratory room while trainers are present (approximately 8 hrs/day); at other times he is confined to a cage (approximately 62 × 62 × 73 cm) and the desk upon which it rests. Water and a standard psittacine seed mix (sunflower seeds, dried corn, kibble, oats, etc.) are continuously available throughout the day. Fresh fruits, vegetables, specialty nuts (cashews, pecans, almonds, walnuts) and toys are used in training and are provided upon his vocal requests.

Several training procedures are employed in this project, but one feature they all have in common is the consistently exclusive use of intrinsic reinforcers—each correct identification is rewarded by a relevant, different reinforcer, that is, the object to which the targeted label or concept refers, rather than any single, extrinsic item. Thus, if Alex correctly identifies a cork, that is what he receives. This procedure insures, at all times and at every interaction, the closest possible association of the label or concept to be learned and the object or task to which it refers (Pepperberg, 1978, 1981).

Often, programs designed to develop communicatory skills rely on extrinsic rewards. In such programs, all correct identifications for food or nonfood items or appropriate responses to various specific commands are rewarded with the acquisition of a single, particular food that neither directly relates to the skill being taught nor varies with respect to the specific task being targeted. Because such extrinsic rewards may actually act to delay label or concept acquisition by confounding the label of the exemplar to be learned with that of the food reward (Greenfield, 1978; Miles, 1983; Pepperberg, 1978), Alex never receives extrinsic rewards. On occasion, he will be rewarded with the right to request vocally a more desirable item than that which he identified, but he never automatically receives, for example, a slice of banana when he identifies a cork; the banana must specifically be requested ("I want banana"), and trainers will not respond to such a request until the appropriate prior task is completed. Interestingly, studies with

those birds that easily acquire and reproduce elements of allospecific vocalization systems learn referential use of these allospecific vocalizations only under specific situations (for details, see Pepperberg 1985, 1986, 1988a).

severely retarded children provide preliminary evidence that using extrinsic reinforcers makes it difficult for the subjects to extrapolate knowledge that has thus been acquired to situations in which the extrinsic reinforcer is absent (e.g., Lovaas, 1977), and that the ease of learning is often related to the degree to which the stimulus and reinforcer are related (Saunders & Sailor, 1979).

The primary training system, called the model/rival, or M/R technique, was based on a protocol developed by Todt (1975), an ethologist interested in social learning in parrots. Todt's procedures, in turn, derive much from the work of Bandura (e.g., 1971a) on social modeling. The M/R procedure involves three-way interactions between two competent human speakers and the avian student. M/R training is used primarily to introduce new labels and concepts but also aids us in shaping correct pronunciation.

During M/R training, humans demonstrated to the bird the types of interactive responses that are desired. A typical interaction involved the following: Alex is seated on his gym, his cage, or the back of a chair, and observes two humans handling some objects in which he already demonstrated an interest. In the presence of the bird, one human acts as a trainer of the second human. The trainer presents an object, asks questions about the object (e.g., "What's here?", "What color?", "What shape?"), and gives praise and the object itself as a reward for a correct answer. Disapproval for incorrect responses (erroneous answers that are similar to those being made by the bird at the time: unclear vocalizations, partial identifications, etc.) is demonstrated by scolding and temporarily removing the object from sight. The second human acts as a model for the bird's responses, as a rival for the trainer's attention, and also allows the parrot to observe the process of "corrective feedback" (see Goldstein, 1984, p. 390; Vanayan, Robertson, & Biederman, 1985). The model is asked to try again or talk more clearly if the response was (deliberately) incorrect or garbled. An excerpt from a training session on the label "five" is presented in Table 7.1 (Pepperberg, 1988b). Unlike the modeling procedure developed by Todt (and several other researchers; see Goldstein, 1984), this protocol also involves repeating the interaction while reversing the roles of the human trainer and model, and, occasionally, includes the parrot in the interactions. Our protocol thus demonstrates that the interaction is indeed a "two-way street": (a) one person is not always the questioner and the other always the respondent, and (b) the procedure can be employed to effect changes in the environment. Inclusion of role reversal in M/R training appears to counteract what would be, for our project, the drawbacks associated with Todt's method: Todt's birds were exposed only to pairs of individuals maintaining their respective roles, and his birds did not transfer their responses to anyone other than the human who posed the questions. In contrast, Alex responds to, interacts with, and learns from all of the trainers with whom he comes

TABLE 7.1
Excerpt of a Model/Rival (M/R) Training Session

I (acting as trainer)   Bruce, what's this?

B (acting as model/rival)   *Five* wood.

I That's right, *five* wood. Here you are . . . *five* wood. (Hands over five wooden popsicle sticks. B begins to break one apart, much as Alex would.)

A 'ii wood.

B (now acting as trainer, quickly replaces broken stick and presents the five sticks to Alex)   Better . . . (briefly turns away then repositions himself in visual contact with Alex) . . . How many?

A No!

B (Turns from Alex to establish visual contact with the PI.)   Irene, what's this? (presents sticks)

I (Now acting as model/rival)   'ii wood.

B Better . . . (turns then resumes eye contact) . . . How many?

I *Five* wood (takes wooden sticks) . . . *five* wood. (Now acts as trainer, directs gaze to Alex, and presents sticks to him) . . . How many wood?

A Fife wood.

I OK, Alex, close enough . . . *fivvvvve* wood . . . Here's *five* wood. (Places one stick in the bird's beak and the other within his reach.)

Note.   The aim of the session was to review and improve pronunciation of the label five. B refers to Bruce Rosen, one of the secondary trainers, I to the PI (principal investigator), and A to the parrot Alex. This portion of the session lasted approximately 5 minutes.

Note.   From "An Interactive Modeling Technique for Acquisition of Communication Skills: Separation of 'Labeling' and 'Requesting' in a PsiHacine Subject by I.M. Pepperberg, 1988, *Applied Psycholinquistics, 9,* p. 63. Copyright 1988 by Cambridge University Press. Reprinted by permission.

in contact. If there are indeed parallels between the mechanisms for learning in birds and humans (e.g., Marler, 1970; Petrinovich, 1972), this finding in itself may have important clinical applications (Sonnenschein & Whitehurst, 1984; Weisberg, Stout, & Hendler, 1986).

In light of the importance of social interaction in training, why do we use any reinforcements other than social? With children, for example, parental approbation ("yes," "good," even "hmm") can sometimes act as an effective nonreferential (extrinsic) reward (see Bowerman, 1978 for a review). My students and I do, in fact, find such approbation useful in maintaining an established behavior and in directing Alex's attention during training. Approbation alone, however, does not provide the contextually relevant rewards that appear necessary to effect acquisition of a targeted behavior in a nonspecies-specific communication code.

After Alex has begun to produce a new label in the presence of a new exemplar, we use an additional procedure to clarify his pronunciation. We present the new exemplar to him along with a string of "sentence frames" — phrases like "Here's your paper!" and "Such a big piece of paper!". The target word "paper", is thus consistently stressed and is the one most frequently heard, but it is not presented as a single, repetitive utterance. This combination of a particular form of vocal repetition and the physical action of presenting the object resembles the behavior parents sometimes use when introducing labels for new items to very young children (Berko-Gleason, 1973, 1977; de Villiers & de Villiers, 1978). The procedure appears to have two effects: (a) Alex hears the label employed in normal productive speech so that he experiences the label in the way in which it is to be used, and (b) he learns to reproduce the emphasized targeted label without associating simple word-for-word imitation of the trainers with reward.

Initial Results

The effects of our training have been significant. Over the course of the experiment, Alex acquired a vocabulary consisting of labels for (a) more than 30 objects: paper, key, grain, chair, grape, wood, cracker, hide (rawhide chips), peg wood (wooden clothes pins), back, knee, cork, corn, nut, gym, carrot, scraper (a metal nail file), walnut, shower, shoulder, banana, water, tray, rock (a lava stone), pasta, chain, wheat, popcorn, chalk, banerry (apple), gravel, box, block, and grate (a nutmeg grater); (b) seven colors: rose (red), green, blue, yellow, orange, grey, and purple; and (c) five shapes: 2-corner (football shape), 3-corner (triangle), 4-corner (square), 5-corner (pentagon), and 6-corner (hexagon). He uses the labels 2, 3, 4, 5, and "ssih" (six) to distinguish between appropriate numbers of objects; has acquired functional use of the phrases "come here," "wanna go X"(X = chair, gym [a construction of wooden dowel rods, which he preferred to his cage], knee, shoulder, back [to his cage] and, occasionally, out), "no" to refuse unwanted attention, objects, training or tests, "want Y" (Y = cork, nut, etc.), and what appears to be functional use of "yeah." Alex is beginning to use phrases such as "What's this?", "What color?", and "What shape?" to initiate interactions. He combines these vocalizations routinely to identify more than 100 objects including those that differ somewhat from the training exemplars; for example, pieces of paper (white, unlined index cards) vary in shape as do those of hide, wood, and cork. Clothes pins ("peg wood") are correctly identified even though they may be considerably chewed, and the shades of his color objects vary somewhat as they are, with the exception of keys, hand-dyed with food colors.

Alex has averaged scores of about 80% over more than 300 identification tests (for test procedures and results, see Pepperberg, 1981). For all tests administered, he correctly identified 80.3% of all objects shown to him on the first try; his score was 80.2% when all responses to all presentations were included. Alex is considered to have mastered a label by correctly identifying the particular object during testing with an accuracy of 80%.[2]

The remainder of this chapter will focus on one set of Alex's achievements: his capacity for categorization with respect to color, shape, and material, and his comprehension of abstract concepts of *same* and *different*.

Categorization Abilities

The degrees to which a nonhuman subject can perform categorization and comprehend the related concept of same/different have been widely discussed as possible measures of cognitive capacity (Premack, 1976, 1983; Savage-Rumbaugh et al., 1980; Thomas, 1980). Determining what constitutes a category and learning the labels for particular instances of a category are complex tasks that are likely to draw upon more sophisticated capacities than, for example, encoding meanings of single labels or of simple sentences of invariant agent-action-object order (Rice, 1980; for detailed discussions of this point, see Herman, 1988; Schusterman & Gisiner, 1988). As reviewed and described by de Villiers and de Villiers (1978), acquiring, for example, both the category *color* and the actual labels for colors means that a subject: (a) can distinguish color from other categories such as size, material, or shape; (b) can isolate certain colors as focal points and others as variants of these; (c) understands that each color label is part of a class of labels that are linked under the category label *color*; and (d) can produce each label appropriately. Because progress on such a categorization task seems to be affected by caretaker input (Rice, 1980), determination of Alex's competence in these areas was a reasonable training goal for our project.

Interestingly, it was Alex's responses to questions concerning object identification that provided the first indication of a limited concept of category. During instruction on labels for novel exemplars, there would typically be a generic pattern to Alex's incorrect identifications; for example, initial errors on clothes pins ("peg wood") were "wood" and colored keys were often labeled simply "key" (Pepperberg, 1981, 1983). My students and I therefore decided to examine the extent to which this behavior might generalize.

Our first step in testing Alex's categorical capacity was to examine his ability to identify unfamiliar objects with respect to color or shape. At the time, the labels "color" and "shape" had not been the focus of targeted instruction but had been employed in vocal exchanges when appropriate.

---

[2]Because Alex's food preferences changed considerably over short time periods, we do not formally test his ability to label food items. However, we have good contextual evidence that food labels are referential: He will refuse foods other than those he has requested and repeat his initial request (see Pepperberg, 1987b, 1988b).

Thus, when Alex omitted a color or shape marker, examiners would ask, "What *color X?*" or "What *shape Y?*" to elicit the appropriate response (Pepperberg, 1981, 1983). During free (nontesting, nontraining, nontaping) periods, we subsequently presented Alex with objects for which he could produce color or shape but not material labels (e.g., rose pens, green plastic paper clips, tinted dog biscuits, variously shaped buttons) and queried him as to "What color?" or "What shape?" In all cases, he identified correctly, on the first attempt, the colors or shapes of these items (see Pepperberg, 1981). Although interesting, Alex's responses to such questions under these conditions suggested only that he could extrapolate the color or shape markers then in his repertoire ("rose", "green", "blue", "three-corner", "four-corner") to unfamiliar items, not that he had necessarily acquired an understanding of the actual words or the relationships of these specific instances of color and shape to the labels "color" and "shape". It is possible that he might not have even attended to the queries but may have simply viewed each object and produced all the relevant information.

We have since examined Alex's capacity to learn something about categorical concepts and have found that he is able not only to recognize instances of four different categories (color, shape, material, and quantity), but that he has acquired, through various procedures, a limited under-standing of the concept of category; for example, he understands not only what is or is not "green" or "3-corner", but that green and 3-corner represent different categories of markable attributes of any given exemplar. This is a significant finding because research with children has shown that subjects capable of learning that exemplars in one particular set are labeled "green" and in another set "red" may still not realize that there exists an overall concept of "greenness" or "redness" that can be generalized to objects not in these sets (Rice, 1980).

We examined Alex's concept of category by testing his ability to respond to queries of "What color?" *or* "What shape?" when presented with objects having both color *and* shape {(e.g., objects such as a green wooden triangle or a rose rawhide square that represented various combinations of five colors, four shapes, and three different materials [wood, rawhide and metal (keys)]}. Alex's scores were better than 80%. Note that such identifications required that Alex answer on the basis of color *or* shape and not provide all the relevant information; that is, he had to produce answers such as "five-corner wood" *or* "grey hide" (Pepperberg, 1983). The results suggested that he was able to associate labels representing two categorical concepts ("color" | "shape") with those labels representing the various instances of these categories (e.g., "blue", "2-corner") rather than merely respond to the particular instances of color or shape: He could view items that could be described relevantly in more than one way, decode from our question which of two categories was being targeted, decide which of several color or shape labels was correct, and then produce, based on the question posed, the label for the particular instance of that category (Pepperberg, 1983).

The test employed was rather strong, for it actually involved reclassification of objects; that is, Alex was required to classify the same object with respect to color at one time and shape at another. Reclassification is not only thought to be a more difficult task than simple classification, but flexibility in changing the basis for classification is also thought to indicate the presence of "abstract aptitude" (Hayes & Nissen, 1956/1971, p. 90).

Another important point is that Alex's tests never included strings of questions on color and shape or questions for which a single response (e.g., "yellow" or "3-corner") would be correct; rather, one or two such questions on color and shape were randomly inserted into his standard identification tests. Intermingling different types of questions on tests prevented "expectation cuing" (Pepperberg, 1983, p. 182; see also Terrace, 1979): In single-topic tests, contextual information (the homogeneous nature of questions that have a relatively restricted range of answers) could be responsible for a somewhat better performance than would otherwise result from a subject's actual knowledge of the topic. Alex, however, had to be ready to employ any response from his entire repertoire because a given test could involve queries on total object identification as well as either color or shape (Pepperberg, 1983), and later tests also included questions on the quantity of a collection (Pepperberg, 1987a).

Concepts of Same and Different[3]

Once a subject has demonstrated some capacity for categorization, studies can be performed to examine its abilities on the more abstract concepts of similarity and difference. There is significant debate in the literature concerning exactly what has been demonstrated in the various animal studies purporting to examine same/different (e.g., Premack, 1983; Edwards, Jagielo, & Zentall, 1983). The debate is important because researchers continue to argue that there exist species-specific differences in the abilities of nonhumans (e.g., Rumbaugh & Pate, 1984), and comprehension of the abstract, relational concept of same/different has often been singled out as a concept not typically attributable to nonprimates (Mackintosh et al., 1985; Premack, 1978, 1983).

According to Premack, comprehension of same/different is not the same as being able to respond to match-to-sample and oddity-from-sample, but

---

[3]Portions of this section have been excerpted from "Acquisition of the same/different concept by an African Grey parrot (*Psittacus erithacus*): Learning with respect to categories of color, shape, and material" by I. M. Pepperberg, 1987, *Animal Learning & Behavior, 15,* p. 423–432 Copyright 1987 by Psychonomic Society, Inc. 1987c. Reprinted by permission.

rather involves the ability to use arbitrary symbols to represent the relationships of sameness and difference between sets of objects. That is, for generalized match-to-sample or oddity-from-sample, the subject demonstrates its understanding of the concept simply by showing a savings in the number of trials needed to respond to B and B as a match after learning to respond to A and A as a match (and, likewise, by showing a savings in trials involving C and D after learning to respond to A and B as nonmatching). But, according to Premack, demonstrating comprehension of "same" requires that a subject be able not only to recognize that two independent objects, A_1 and A_2, are blue, but that there is only a single attribute, the category color, that is shared, and that this attribute, or sameness, can be immediately extrapolated and symbolically represented not only for two other blue items but for two novel independent green items, B_1 and B_2, that have nothing in common with the original set of As. Likewise, the subject would have to demonstrate a concept of difference that could also be extrapolated to two entirely novel objects. Premack (1978, 1983) proposed that such abilities are likely to be limited to primates, and, because of the requirement for symbolization, are most readily demonstrated by nonhuman primates that have undergone some form of language training (cf. Reese, 1972).

The results of early studies appeared to support Premack's claim. For example, some pigeons trained on match-to-sample or oddity-from-sample tasks actually learned little about the nonmatching alternative; that is, they acquired a concept of "same" but not of "different" (see discussions in Edwards et al., 1983; Zentall, Edwards, Moore, & Hogan, 1981). And, although corvids were able to transfer matching *and* oddity rules to new stimulus sets (Mackintosh et al., 1985: *Corvus monedula, Garrulus glandarius,* and *Corvus frugilegus*), such transfer did not examine labeling the relations "same" and "different". Recently, however, researchers (Edwards et al., 1983; Zentall et al., 1981; Zentall, Hogan, & Edwards, 1984; Santiago & Wright, 1984; Wright, Santiago, & Sands, 1984; Wright, Santiago, Urcuioli, & Sands, 1984) have demonstrated that pigeons (*Columba livia*) can show same/different concept transfer including use of symbols to represent "same" versus "different". Although the pigeons scored above chance, their level of transfer to novel items was lower than that for primates. These experiments therefore suggested that a nonprimate's use of symbols for "same" and "different" might not be fully comparable to that of language-trained chimpanzees, humans, or even appropriately trained monkeys.

Few other studies have investigated concepts of same/different in avian subjects, even though natural behaviors of individual recognition, vocal dueling, and song matching (e.g., Beecher, Stoddard, & Loesche, 1985; Falls, 1985; Falls, Krebs, & McGregor, 1982; Kroodsma, 1979) would make categorization based on similarity or difference seem an adaptive trait in many birds. Starlings (*Sturnus vulgaris*), cowbirds (*Molothrus ater*), and mockingbirds (*Mimus polyglottos*) appear capable of classifying novel series of tones as ascending or descending — that is, same or different from ascending or descending reference series — but only for sequences that lay within the range of frequencies used in training (Hulse & Cynx, 1985). In laboratory studies on the ability of several species (Park & Dooling, 1985; budgerigars, *Melopsittacus undulatus;* Stoddard & Beecher, personal communication, 1986: cliff swallows, *Hirundo pyrrhonota* and barnswallows, *Hirundo rustia) to discriminate similarities and differences in vocalizations of allo-specifics, the avian subjects appeared to respond on the basis of unique characteristics of individual vocalizations. Other studies (Shy, McGregor, & Krebs, 1986: great tits, Parus major)* have demonstrated the ability of birds to recognize test songs as similar to or different from one particular training song (comparable to visual categorization by pigeons, e.g., Herrnstein, 1984), but none of these studies has shown (a) actual labeling of the relation of sameness or difference in transfer to entirely different exemplars, or (b) labeling which *aspects* are same or different for the calls or songs of various other species.

The present study was therefore undertaken to see if our African Grey parrot, previously taught a categorization task based on comprehension and production of vocal labels, could use additional vocal labels to demonstrate symbolic comprehension of same/different.

For the reasons previously discussed, the task designed for Alex would have to be functionally equivalent to that used with Premack's chimpanzees. The task would have to insure that: (a) the symbolic concepts tested would be more abstract than those examined in standard conditional discrimination paradigms; (b) the subject would be given explicit, equal training on concepts of both "same" and "different"; (c) the findings could not be dismissed as stimulus-specific associations; and (d) first-trial transfer test results could be examined for their significance.

To take into account these constraints and Alex's history with respect to use of vocal labels, the following task was designed. Alex was to be presented with two objects that could differ with respect to three categories: color, shape, or material (e.g., a blue wooden pentagon and a rose rawhide pentagon; a yellow wooden triangle and a grey wooden triangle). He would then be queried "What's same?" or "What's different?" The correct response would be the label of the appropriate category — not the specific color, shape, or material marker — that represented the correct response (e.g., "color", not "yellow"). Therefore, to be correct, Alex would have to (a) attend to multiple aspects of two different objects; (b) determine, from a vocal question, whether the response was to be on the basis of similarity or difference; (c) determine, based on the exemplars, what was same or different (e.g., were they both blue, or triangular, or made of wood), and (d) produce, vocally, the label for this particular category. Thus, the taskrequired, at some level, that Alex perform a feature analysis of the two objects: Correct responses could not be made on the basis of total physical similarity or difference of the objects (see Premack, 1983).

In comparison, most research on the same/different concept in animals uses (a) a two-choice design in which the subject indicates only whether pairs do or do not match, (b) a topographically similar (and therefore more easily acquired) response for both answers (e.g., lever pressing or key pecking; see Michael, Whitely, & Hesse, 1983), and (c) "same" pairs that are identical in all dimensions and "different" pairs that are different with respect to most if not all dimensions. This would be equivalent to asking Alex to view two objects and simply respond "same" or "different", the latter response being correct when any two objects differed in any way. Alex, however, must respond with the vocal label of one out of three dimensions that is same or different for each pair of objects depending upon the question he is asked; this is a considerably more difficult task. Note, too, that McClure and Helland (1979) have shown that even chimpanzees will not respond "different" as reliably for pairs of objects differing on only one of three dimensions as for pairs differing on two dimensions.

Alex's responses on tests were unlikely to be made on the basis either of absolute physical properties or by learning the answer to a given pair: He would be trained on a subset of familiar exemplars (objects that were red, green, blue, triangular or square, wood or rawhide) so that the number of objects not used in training would provide a large number of permutations of question topic, correct response, and combination of exemplar attributes for testing.[4] Moreover, because Alex's response would be a category label rather than a specific object or attribute label, we could perform additional tests using totally novel objects with unknown labels. Alex would thus have to be able to transfer between like and unlike pairs of colors, like and unlike pairs of shapes, and like and unlike pairs of materials, all of which would vary from the training exemplars. In other

---

[44]There were approximately 70 different possible objects (food items were rarely used), 3 possible correct responses, and two different questions for the same/different task alone. For example, if we asked "What's same?", desired the response to be "color", and chose a round green key as one of the exemplars, this key could be paired with 2-, 3-, 4-, 5-, or 6-cornered objects of paper, wood, or rawhide; 3-, 4-, or 6-cornered objects of plastic, plus objects such as green clothes pins, wooden or plastic cubes or spheres, plastic boxes and cups, and so forth. A similar set of permutations existed for responses of "shape", "matter", and the question "What's different?" In addition, Alex was concurrently being tested on numerical concepts ("How many?") and additional labels ("What's this?", "What color?", etc.).

words, he would have to demonstrate transfer among stimulus domains as well as among various instances of each domain. Premack (1976, pp.354–355), for example, stresses the importance of such transfers in determining that the behavior is not just stimulus generalization.

We also planned to conduct probes to examine whether Alex was responding to the content of the questions (i.e., differentially processing "What's same?" vs. "What's different?") and not just responding to variations in the physical characteristics of the objects themselves. That is, during the standard (nonprobe) trials, Alex could, by looking at the objects, have determined the *one* attribute that was same or different and simply responded on that basis. Thus, at random intervals, probes were to be administered in which Alex would be asked questions for which either of *two* category labels could be the correct response; that is, he would be shown a yellow and a blue wooden triangle and asked "What's same?" If he were ignoring the content of the question and answering on the basis of the attributes and his prior training, he would respond as if we had asked "What's different?" and give the one wrong answer. If, however, he were indeed answering the question posed, he would have two possible correct responses.

In sum, after training, Alex was to be given a series of questions involving, in random order, pairs of objects that were familiar but not used in training, pairs in which one or both exemplars were totally novel objects, and probes to examine if he were indeed processing the content of the questions. And, as always, questions on same/different would be inserted randomly into tests for other concepts so that Alex would never experience a string of questions on the same topic or for which the same answer would be correct (Pepperberg, 1987a, 1987b, 1987c).

The results of these experiments would not only provide information on Alex's concept of same/different, but the data would also provide additional evidence for comprehension of categorical concepts; that is, the ability to recognize that two novel objects (e.g., pink and white plastic triangles) differed with respect to the category color even though the colors were untrained and the specific combinations of color, shape, and material for each exemplar, as well as for the pair, had never before been seen on a test. Correct responses would suggest that Alex was not responding to specific instances of color, shape, and material but rather was responding on the basis of the categorical concepts.

The results of our study (Fig. 7.1) indicated that Alex had acquired some concept of same/different (Pepperberg, 1987c). His scores for tests on objects that were familiar but had not been used in same/different training (e.g., had been used in a study of numerical competence, Pepperberg, 1987a) were 99/129 = 76.7% correct for all trials, 69/99 = 69.7% on first

FAMILIAR OBJECTS

WHAT'S SAME?

CORRECT RESPONSE

	C	S	M
C	**16**	4	3
S	2	**16**	2
M	2	2	**16**

ALEX'S RESPONSE

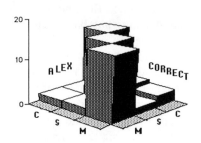

WHAT'S DIFFERENT?

CORRECT RESPONSE

	C	S	M
C	**17**	3	3
S	2	**16**	1
M	2	4	**18**

ALEX'S RESPONSE

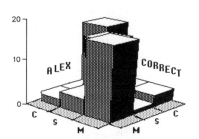

Fig. 7.1 Histogram of results for questions of "What's same?" and "What's different?" for pairs of objects that differed somewhat from training exemplars. The correct responses lie on the diagonal; the off-diagonal elements are the errors. C = color, S = shape, and M = Matter.

Note. From "Acquisition of the Same/Different Concept by an African Grey Parrot (*Psittacus erithacus*): Learning with Respect to Categories of Color, Shape and Material" by I.M. Pepperberg, 1987, *Animal Learning and Behavior, 15,* p. 428. Copyright 1987 by Psychonomic Society. Reprinted with permission.

trial performance, $p < .0001$ on binomial test with a chance value of $1/3$.[5] Note that choice of $1/3$ was conservative in that it ignored the possibility that Alex could have said any number of vocalizations besides "color", "shape", and "matter". In all cases, the first single word that Alex uttered was one of these category labels, although he produced other phrases that encoded requests for other objects or actions (e.g., "I want X"; see Pepperberg, 1987a, 1987b).

Alex's score on transfer tests containing entirely novel objects was $96/113 = 85\%$ on all trials, $79/96 = 82.3\%$ on first trial performance, $p < .0001$ with chance value again of $1/3$ (Fig. 7.2). In these pairings, one or both objects incorporated colors, shapes, or materials for which Alex might not even have labels. His scores for pairs containing one versus two totally novel objects (respectively 86% and 83% for first trials, $p < .0001$) differed little.

It is interesting to compare the results for Alex's responses for objects that were totally novel with his responses for those that were more similar to the training exemplars: Alex's scores look considerably better for the former set than the latter. The subjects of most studies, in contrast, usually perform less well on transfer tests. Based on the test for differences in proportions at the .05 confidence level, Alex's scores were not, however, significantly better for questions involving novel exemplars versus familiar ones when the results are examined for all trials and were only just significantly better when the results are examined for first trial performance only. The higher scores on novel items might be due to our use of intrinsic rewards: Remember that Alex received the objects themselves as his primary reward; therefore there was some inherent incentive to pay closer attention to both the objects and to the response when these reward objects were new items that were potentially interesting to chew apart, to try to eat, or to use for preening.

The results of the probes demonstrated that Alex was indeed processing the questions as well as responding to the physical properties of the objects. The data are presented in Fig. 7.3; his score was $55/61 = 90.2\%$ on all trials, $p = .00001$, chance of $2/3$ and $49/55 = 89.1\%$ on first trial performance, $p < .0001$.

---

[5]Our test protocol employs a correction procedure (see Pepperberg, 1981, 1987c for full details of the test protocol) in which Alex is re-presented with a question when he makes an error on the first trial. We therefore report the results of his first trials separately from the results of all trials administered. It is also sometimes the examiner, rather than Alex, who is corrected: In about 1 in 20 trials, an examiner would err and scold Alex for a correct response. Alex would repeat his response despite his having learned a lose-shift strategy. The examiner would then recognize his/her error, and the bird would get his reward. Note that although this is not a formal blind test, it produced the same results. For descriptions of other blind tests, see Pepperberg, 1987c.

NOVEL OBJECTS

WHAT'S SAME?

CORRECT RESPONSE

	C	S	M
C	**17**	3	3
S	1	**16**	0
M	2	1	**17**

ALEX'S RESPONSE

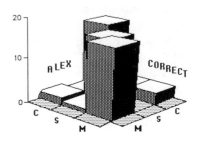

WHAT'S DIFFERENT?

CORRECT RESPONSE

	C	S	M
C	**15**	1	3
S	1	**16**	2
M	0	0	**15**

ALEX'S RESPONSE

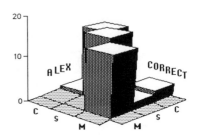

Fig. 7.2 Histogram of results for questions of "What's same?" and "What's different?" for novel pairs of objects that differed significantly from training exemplars. Key is the same as in Fig. 7.1.

These data indicate that at least one avian subject, an African Grey parrot, has shown symbolic comprehension of the concept of same/different. The conditions of the tests, although not identical to those used by Premack (1976, 1983), were at least as rigorous as those used in Premack's initial study with chimpanzees. Comparisons between the results for primates and nonprimates are therefore possible despite the somewhat differing protocols.

Unlike the production task most frequently employed with the language-trained chimpanzees (in which the animals responded with the labels "same" and "different"), Alex's task was one of symbolic comprehension of the labels "same" and "different" (i.e., responding to questions of "What's

QUESTION   COMPREHENSION?

WHAT'S SAME?

CORRECT RESPONSE

		C	S	M
ALEX'S RESPONSE	**C**	**10**	0	0
	S	0	**11**	0
	M	1	2	**11**

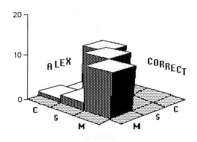

WHAT'S DIFFERENT?

CORRECT RESPONSE

		C	S	M
ALEX'S RESPONSE	**C**	**8**	1	0
	S	0	**7**	2
	M	0	0	**8**

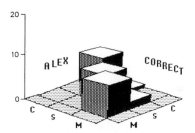

Fig. 7.3 Histogram of results of probes to learn if Alex was responding on the basis of the experimenters' questions or on the basis of physical variations of objects and his previous training. Key is the same as in Fig. 7.1.

same?" and "What's different?"). Alex, however, similarly had to respond symbolically on the basis both of (a) the instances of the categorical classes the objects represented and (b) the symbolic relationship (the labels "same" or "different") requested by the experimenter—and not on the basis of whether two items looked alike. Alex, like the chimpanzees, was also presented with the object pairs—including objects never before tested—simultaneously, rather than successively. According to Premack (1983, p. 127), it is more difficult to answer a question about the relationship between two exemplars that are presented at the same time than it is to answer about two items that are presented on two different occasions: In Premack's view, animals that are trained on successive match-to-sample (or oddity-from-sample) may not have any concept of same/different, but rather are likely to be responding on the basis of "old" versus "new" or "familiar" versus "unfamiliar"; that is, whether or not they had recent experience with the objects. It is therefore unlikely that the task presented to Alex could be interpreted as a forced-choice conditional discrimination of the type generally used to determine nonhuman conceptual abilities.

Although these findings present additional evidence for Alex's comprehension of concepts of categorical classes, determination of the extent of his abilities is still incomplete. For example, he has just begun to respond appropriately to questions of "What's the color of the metal key?" or "What shape is the green wood?" for collections of differently colored and shaped exemplars of various materials (see Essock, Gill, & Rumbaugh, 1977; Granier-Deferre & Kodratoff, 1986). It is also not yet clear if he can learn to respond directly to analogic "relations between relations" (Premack, 1976, p. 133); for example, whether the relation between A_1 and A_2 is (same/ different) as that between B_1 and B_2 (Premack, 1983). Alex has, however, gone beyond match-to-sample or oddity-from-sample: He comprehends the vocal symbols "same" and "different" and a more abstract concept of category than in our previous study (Pepperberg, 1983). Alex's responses were not stimulus-specific: He performed as well on entirely novel objects as he did on familiar ones including those for which he had no labels. Thus he appeared to learn the task in terms of the concepts and labels of "color", "shape", and "material" — a capacity once thought to be limited to humans and nonhuman primates (Premack, 1983).

CONCLUSION

Several comparisons have been made between the abilities of a parrot and those of other animals (including humans), and I have placed a certain emphasis on the use of a vocal, human-based code to examine these abilities. The rationale of the work, however, has not primarily been to discover whether a nonprimate, nonmammalian subject can acquire "human language", and the emphasis on two-way communication should not overshadow the main issue: that Alex's acquisition, even if only to a limited extent, of a mutual, explicit representational system allows us to investigate most efficiently the interspecies similarities and differences among and between various subjects. Our approach is a first step along a path indicated by Donald Griffin in 1985:

> Perhaps it is time to consider tentatively a substantial revision in the way which we think about animals and their behavior. I do not claim that the

correctness of this cognitive approach to ethology can yet be established by satisfactory evidence. But I believe that it can lead to fruitful working hypotheses to be tested by scientific methods. Even if such investigations eventually disconfirm these hypotheses, or more likely fail to settle the matter conclusively, the effort promises to improve and enrich our understanding of animals and of the relationship between human and animal thinking. (p. 479)

ACKNOWLEDGMENTS

The work described in this chapter was supported by grants from the Harry Frank Guggenheim Foundation and the National Science Foundation, BNS 8014329, 8414483, and 8616955. Preparation of this chapter was supported in part by grant BNS 8616955. I thank Alan Kamil, Donald Kroodsma, and Nicholas Thompson for postconference discussions, Anthony Wright and Thomas Zentall for comments on the study of same/different, Larry Kimball for assistance with the figures, and Jeff Galef, Donald Griffin, and Carolyn Ristau for critiques of an earlier version of the manuscript.

REFERENCES

Baldwin, J. M. (1914). Deferred imitation in West African Grey parrots. *Proceedings of the IXth International Congress of Zoology* (p. 536). Monaco.

Bandura, A. (1971a). Analysis of modeling procedures. In A. Bandura (Ed.), *Psychological modeling* (pp. 1–62). Chicago: Aldine–Atherton.

Bandura, A. (1971b). Psychotherapy based upon modeling principles. In A. E. Bergin & S. L. Garfield (Eds.), *Psychotherapy and behavioral change: an empirical analysis* (pp. 653–708). New York: John Wiley & Sons.

Baptista, L. F. (1983). Song learning. In A. H. Brush & G. A. Clark, Jr. (Eds.), *Perspectives in ornithology* (pp. 500–506). Cambridge: Cambridge University Press.

Baptista, L. F., & Petrinovich, L. (1984). Social interaction, sensitive phases, and the song template hypothesis in the white-crowned sparrow. *Animal Behaviour, 32,* 172–181.

Baptista, L. F., & Petrinovich, L. (1986). Song development in the white-crowned sparrow: Social factors and sex differences. *Animal Behaviour, 34,* 1359–1371.

Beck, B. B. (1980). *Animal tool behavior.* New York: Garland.

Beecher, M. D., Stoddard, P. K., & Loesche, P. (1985). Recognition of parents' voices by young cliff swallows. *Auk, 102,* 600–605.

Beer, C. G. (1975). Multiple functions and gull displays. In G. Baerends, C. G. Beer, & A. Manning (Eds.), *Function and evolution of behaviour* (pp. 16–54). Oxford: Clarendon Press.

Beer, C. G. (1976). Some complexities in the communication behavior of gulls. *Annals of the New York Academy of Science, 280,* 413–432.

Beer, C. G. (1982a). Study of vertebrate communication—Its cognitive implications. In D. R. Griffin (Ed.), *Animal mind—human mind* (pp. 251–268). New York: Springer-Verlag.

Beer, C. G. (1982b). Conceptual issues in the study of communication. In D. E. Kroodsma & E. H. Miller (Eds.), *Acoustic communication in birds. Vol. 2: Song learning and its consequences* (pp. 279–310). New York: Academic Press.

Benjamini, L. (1983). Studies in the learning abilities of brown-necked ravens and herring gulls. I. Oddity learning. *Behaviour, 84,* 173–194.

Berko-Gleason, J. (1973). Code switching in children's language. In T. E. Moore (Ed.), *Cognitive development and the acquisition of language* (pp. 159–167). New York: Academic Press.

Berko-Gleason, J. (1977). Talking to children: some notes on feedback. In C. E. Snow & C. A. Ferguson (Eds.), *Talking to children: Language input and acquisition* (pp. 199–205). Cambridge: Cambridge University Press.

Boesch, C. (1986, July). *Cooperation in hunting in wild chimpanzees.* Paper presented at the XIth International Primatological Society Congress, Göttingen, Germany.

Boosey, E. J. (1947). The African Grey parrot. *Aviculture Magazine, 53,* 39–40.

Boosey, E. J. (1956). *Foreign bird keeping.* London: Iliffe Books, Ltd.

Bottjer, S. W., & Arnold, A. P. (1985). The ontogeny of vocal learning in songbirds. In E. M. Blass (Ed.), *Developmental psychobiology and neurobiology, Vol. 8* (pp. 129–161). New York: Plenum Press.

Bowerman, M. (1978). The acquisition of word meaning: An investigation of some current conflicts. In N. Waterson & C. E. Snow (Eds.), *Proceedings of the Third International Child Language Symposium: The Development of Communication* (pp. 263–287). New York: Wiley.

Bowerman, M. (1982). Reorganization processes in lexical and syntactic development. In E. Wanner & L. R. Gleitman (Eds.), *Language acquisition: The state of the art* (pp. 319–346). Cambridge: Cambridge University Press.

Braun, H. (1952). Über das Unterscheidungsvermögen unbenannter Anzahlen bei Papagein [On the ability of parrots to distinguish the size of groups] *Zeitschrift für Tierpsychologie, 9,* 40–91.

Bronowski, J., & Bellugi, U. (1970). Language, name, and concept. *Science, 168,* 669–673.

Brown, R. (1973). *A first language: The early stages.* Cambridge, MA: Harvard University Press.

Burghardt, G. M. (1984). Animal awareness: Current perceptions and historical perspective. *American Psychologist, 40,* 905–919.

Busnel, R. G., & Mebes, H. D. (1975). Hearing and communication in birds: The cocktail party effect in intra-specific communication of *Agapornis roseicollis. Life Science, 17,* 1567–1570.

Cheney, D., & Seyfarth, R. (1985). Social and non-social knowledge in vervet monkeys. *Philosophical Transactions of the Royal Society, London, B308,* 187–210.

Cheney, D., & Seyfarth, R. (1986). The recognition of social alliances by vervet monkeys. *Animal Behaviour, 34,* 1722–1731.

Chomsky, N. (1966). *Cartesian linguistics.* New York: Harper & Row.

Cobb, S. (1960). Observations in the comparative anatomy of the avian brain. *Perspectives in Biology and Medicine, 3,* 383–408.

Crook, J. H. (1983). On attributing consciousness to animals. *Nature, 303,* 11–14.

Darwin, C. (1872). *The expression of emotions in man and animals.* London: Murray.

Davis, H., & Bradford, S. A. (1986). Counting behavior in rats in a simulated natural environment. *Ethology, 73,* 265–280.

Dennett, D. C. (1983). Intentional systems in cognitive ethology: The "Panglossian paradigm" defended. *Behavioral and Brain Sciences, 6,* 343–390.

de Villiers, J. G., & de Villiers, P. A. (1978). *Language acquisition.* Cambridge, MA: Harvard University Press.

de Villiers, P. A., & de Villiers, J. G. (1979). *Early language.* Cambridge, MA: Harvard University Press.

Dilger, W. C. (1960). The comparative ethology of the African parrot genus *Agapornis.*

Zeitschrift für Tierpsychologie, 17, 649–685.

Dittus, W. P. J. (1984). Toque macaque food calls: Semantic communication concerning distribution of food in the environment. *Animal Behaviour, 32,* 470–477.

Dooling, R. J., & Searcy, M. H. (1981). A comparison of auditory evoked potentials in two species of sparrow. *Physiological Psychology, 9,* 293–298.

Dücker, G. (1976). Erlernen von drei verschniedenen Positionen durch Vogel [Birds learn about three different ordinal positions] *Zeitschrift für Tierpsychologie, 42,* 301–314.

Dücker, G., & Rensch, B. (1977). The solution of patterned string problems by birds. *Behaviour, 62,* 164–173.

Edwards, C. A., Jagielo, J. A., & Zentall, T. R. (1983). Same/different symbol use by pigeons. *Animal Learning & Behavior, 11,* 349–355.

Essock, S. M., Gill, T. V., & Rumbaugh, D. M. (1977). Language relevant object- and color-naming tasks. In D. M. Rumbaugh (Ed.), *Language learning by a chimpanzee* (pp. 193–206). New York: Academic Press.

Falls, J. B. (1985). Song matching in Western Meadowlarks. *Canadian Journal of Zoology, 63,* 2520–2524.

Falls, J. B., Krebs, J. R., & McGregor, P. K. (1982). Song matching in the great tit (*Parus major*): The effect of similarity and familiarity. *Animal Behaviour, 30,* 997–1009.

Ficken, M. S., & Ficken, R. W. (1967). Singing behavior of Blue-winged and Golden-winged warblers and their hybrids. *Behaviour, 28,* 149–181.

Fromkin, V., & Rodman, P. 1974. *An introduction to language.* New York: Holt, Rinehart, & Winston.

Fouts, R. S. (1973a). Acquisition and testing of gestural signs in four young chimpanzees. *Science, 180,* 978–980.

Fouts, R. S. (1973b). Capacities for language in the great apes. *Proceedings IXth International Congress of Anthropological and Ethnological Science.* The Hague: Mouton.

Fouts, R. S. (1974). Language: Origins, definitions, and chimpanzees. *Journal of Human Evolution, 3,* 467–482.

Furrow, D., & Nelson, K. (1986). A further look at the motherese hypothesis: A reply to Gleitman, Newport, & Gleitman. *Journal of Child Language, 13,* 163–176.

Galef, B. G., Jr. (1984). Reciprocal heuristics: A discussion of the relationship of the study of learned behavior in laboratory and field. *Learning and Motivation, 15,* 479–493.

Gardner, B. T., & Gardner, R. A. (1984). A vocabulary test for chimpanzees. *Journal of Comparative Psychology, 98,* 381–404.

Geschwind, N. (1965). Disconnexion syndromes in animals and man. Part 1. *Brain, 88,* 237–294; 585–644.

Geschwind, N. (1979). Specialization of the human brain. *Scientific American, 241,* 180–199.

Gillan, D. J. (1982). Ascent of apes. In D. R. Griffin (Ed.), *Animal mind—human mind* (pp. 177–200). New York: Springer-Verlag.

Gleitman, L. R., Newport, E. L., & Gleitman, H. (1984). The current status of the motherese hypothesis. *Journal of Child Language, 11,* 43–79.

Goldstein, H. (1984). The effects of modeling and corrected practice on generative language and learning of preschool children. *Journal of Speech and Hearing Disorders, 49,* 389–398.

Goodall, J. van Lawick (1968). The behavior of free-living chimpanzees in the Gombe Stream Reserve. *Animal Behaviour Monographs, 1,* 161–311.

Gossette, R. L. (1967). Successive discrimination reversal (SDR) performance of four avian species in a brightness discrimination task. *Psychonomic Science, 8,* 17–18.

Gossette, R. L., Gossette, M. F., & Reddell, W. (1966). Comparison of successive discrimination reversal performances among closely and remotely related avian species. *Animal Behaviour, 14,* 560–564.

Gouzoules, S., Gouzoules, H., & Marler, P. (1984). Rhesus monkey (*Macaca mulatta*) screams: Representational signaling in the recruitment of agonistic aid. *Animal Behaviour,*

32, 182-193.

Gouzoules, S., Gouzoules, H., & Marler, P. (1985). External reference and affective signaling in mammalian vocal communication. In G. Zivin (Ed.), *The development of expressive behavior: Biology-environment interactions* (pp. 77-101). New York: Academic Press.

Granier-Deferre, C., & Kodratoff, Y. (1986). Iterative and recursive behaviors in chimpanzees during problem solving: A new descriptive model inspired from the artificial intelligence approach. *Cahiers de Psychologie Cognitive, 6,* 483-500.

Greenfield, P. M. (1978). Developmental processes in the language learning of child and chimp. *Behavioral and Brain Sciences, 4,* 573-574.

Griffin, D. R. (1978). Prospects for a cognitive ethology. *Behavioural and Brain Sciences, 1,* 527-538.

Griffin, D. R. (1981). *The question of animal awareness.* New York: Rockefeller University Press.

Griffin, D. R. (1985). Epilogue: The cognitive dimensions of animal communication. In B. Hölldobler & M. Lindauer (Eds.), *Experimental behavioral ecology and sociobiology* (pp. 471-482). Stuttgart & New York: Fischer-Verlag.

Harris, M., Jones, D., Brookes, S., & Grant, J. (1986). Relations between the non-verbal context of maternal speech and rate of language development. *British Journal of Developmental Psychology, 4,* 261-268.

Hayes, K. J., & Nissen, C. H. (1956/1971). Higher mental functions of a home-raised chimpanzee. In A. Schrier & F. Stollnitz (Eds.), *Behavior of nonhuman primates, Vol. 4* (pp. 57-115). New York: Academic Press.

Herman, L. M. (1988). The language of animal language research: Reply to Schusterman and Gisiner. *Psychological Record, 38,* 349-362.

Herman, L. M., & Forestell, P. H. (1985). Reporting presence or absence of named objects by a language-trained dolphin. *Neuroscience & Biobehavioral Reviews, 9,* 667-681.

Herman, L. M., Richards, D., & Wolz, J. (1984). Comprehension of sentences by bottlenosed dolphins. *Cognition, 16,* 129-219.

Herrnstein, R. J. (1984). Objects, categories, and discriminative stimuli. In H. L. Roitblat, T. G. Bever, & H. S. Terrace (Eds.), *Animal cognition* (pp. 233-261). Hillsdale, NJ: Lawrence Erlbaum Associates.

Hodos, W. (1982). Some perspectives on the evolution of intelligence and the brain. In D. R. Griffin (Ed.), *Animal mind—human mind* (pp. 33-56). New York: Springer-Verlag.

Hulse, S. H., & Cynx, J. (1985). Relative pitch perception is constrained by absolute pitch in songbirds (*Mimus, Molothrus,* and *Sturnus*). *Journal of Comparative Psychology, 99,* 176-196.

Kamil, A. C. (1978). Systematic foraging by a nectar-feeding bird, the Amakihi (*Loxopx virens*). *Journal of Comparative and Physiological Psychology, 92,* 388-396.

Kamil, A. C. (1984). Adaptation and cognition: Knowing what comes naturally. In H. L. Roitblat, T. G. Bever, & H. S. Terrace (Eds.), *Animal cognition* (pp. 533-544). Hillsdale, NJ: Lawrence Erlbaum Associates.

Kamil, A. C. (1988). A synthetic approach to the study of animal intelligence. In D. W. Leger (Ed.), *Nebraska symposium on motivation: Comparative perspectives in modern psychology, Vol. 35.* Lincoln: University of Nebraska Press.

Kamil, A. C., & Hunter, M. W. III. (1970). Performance on object discrimination learning set by the Indian Hill mynah, *Gracula religiosa. Journal of Comparative and Physiological Psychology, 13,* 68-73.

Kellogg, W. N. (1968). Communication and language in a home-raised chimpanzee. *Science, 162,* 423-427.

Kintsch, W. (Rapporteur) (1982). Comparative approaches to animal cognition: State of the art report. In D. R. Griffin (Ed.), *Animal mind—human mind* (pp. 375-389). New York: Springer-Verlag.

Koehler, O. (1943). Zähl-Versuche an einem Kolkraben und Vergleisch-versuche an Menschen [Studies on counting by a raven and comparable experiments with humans] *Zeitschrift für Tierpsychologie, 5,* 575–712.

Koehler, O. (1950). The ability of birds to 'count.' *Bulletin of Animal Behaviour, 9,* 41–45.

Koehler, O. (1953). Thinking without words. *Proceedings of the XIVth International Congress of Zoology,* 75–88.

Kroodsma, D. E. (1974). Song learning, dialects, and dispersal in Bewick's wren. *Zeitschrift für Tierpsychologie, 35,* 352–380.

Kroodsma, D. E. (1979). Vocal dueling among male Marsh Wrens: Evidence for ritualized expressions of dominance/subordinance. *Auk, 96,* 506–515.

Kroodsma, D. E. (1981). Geographical variations and functions of song types in warblers (*Parulidae*). *Auk, 98,* 743–751.

Kroodsma, D. E. (1987, July). *Song development in birds.* Paper presented at the meeting of the Association for the Study of Animal Behaviour, St. Andrews, Scotland.

Kroodsma, D. E. (1988). Song types and their use: Developmental flexibility of the male blue-winged warbler. *Ethology, 79,* 235–247.

Kroodsma, D. E., & Canady, R. (1985). Differences in repertoire size, singing behavior, and associated neuroanatomy among marsh wrens have a genetic basis. *Auk, 102,* 439–446.

Kroodsma, D. E., & Pickert, R. (1984a). Sensitive phases for song learning: Effects of social interaction and individual variation. *Animal Behaviour, 32,* 389–394.

Kroodsma, D. E., & Pickert, R. (1984b). Repertoire size, auditory template, and selective vocal learning in songbirds. *Animal Behaviour, 32,* 395–399.

Krushinskii, L. V. (1965). Solution of elementary logical problems by animals on the basis of extrapolation. *Progress in Brain Research, 17,* 280–308.

Leger, D. W., & Owings, D. H. (1978). Response to alarm calls by California ground squirrels: Effects of call structure and maternal status. *Behavioral Ecology & Sociobiology, 3,* 177–186.

Leger, D. W., Owings, D. H., & Boal, L. M. (1979). Contextual information and differential responses to alarm whistles in California ground squirrels. *Zeitschrift für Tierpsychologie, 49,* 142–155.

Leger, D. W., Owings, D. H., & Gelfand, D. L. (1980). Single-note vocalizations of California ground squirrels: Graded signals and situation-specificity of predator and socially evoked calls. *Zeitschrift für Tierpsychologie, 52,* 227–246.

Lein, M. R. (1978). Song variation in a population of Chestnut-sided warblers (*Dendroica pensylvanica*): Its nature and suggested significance. *Canadian Journal of Zoology, 56,* 1266–1283.

Lenneberg, E. H. (1967). *Biological foundations of language.* New York: John Wiley & Sons.

Lenneberg, E. H. (1971). Of language, apes, and brains. *Journal of Psycholinguistic Research, 1,* 1–29.

Lenneberg, E. H. (1973). Biological aspects of language. In G. A. Miller (Ed.), *Communication, language, and meaning* (pp. 49–60). New York: Basic Books.

Lock, A. (1980). *The guided reinvention of language.* London: Academic Press.

Lögler, P. (1959). Versuche zur Frage des [Experiments to determine the ability of a Grey parrot to count, and comparable experiments on humans]. 'Zähl'-Vermögens an einen Graupapagei und Vergleichsversuche an Menschen *Zeitschrift für Tierpsychologie, 16,* 179–217.

Lovaas, O. I. (1977). *The autistic child: Language development through behavior modification.* New York: Irvington.

Lovaas, O., Varne, J. W., Koegel, R. L., & Lorsch, N. (1977). Some observations on the non-extinguishability of children's speech. *Child Development, 48,* 1121–1127.

Mackintosh, N. J., Wilson, B., & Boakes, R. A. (1985). Differences in mechanisms of intelligence among vertebrates. *Philosophical Transactions of the Royal Society, London,*

B308, 53–65.

Macphail, E. M. (1985). Vertebrate intelligence: The null hypothesis. *Philosophical Transactions of the Royal Society, London, B308,* 37–51.

Macphail, E. M. (1987). The comparative psychology of intelligence. *Behavioral and Brain Sciences, 10,* 645–695.

Markl, H. (1985). Manipulation, modulation, information, cognition: Some of the riddles of communication. In B. Hölldobler & M. Lindauer (Eds.), *Experimental behavioural ecology and sociobiology* (pp. 163–194). New York: Fischer-Verlag.

Marler, P. (1970). A comparative approach to vocal learning: Song development in white-crowned sparrows. *Journal of Comparative and Physiological Psychology, 71,* 1–25.

Marler, P. (1973). Speech development and bird song: Are there any parallels? In G. A. Miller (Ed.), *Communication, language, and meaning* (pp. 73–83). New York: Basic Books.

Marler, P., Dufty, A., & Pickert, R. (1986). Vocal communication in the domestic chicken: I. Does a sender communicate information about the quality of a food referent to a receiver? *Animal Behaviour, 34,* 188–193.

Marler, P., & Peters, R. (1977). Selective vocal learning in a sparrow. *Science, 198,* 519–521.

Marler, P., & Peters, R. (1982). Structural changes in song ontogeny in the swamp sparrow, *Melospiza georgiana. Auk, 99,* 446–458.

Marschark, M. (1983). A code by any other name . . . *Behavioral and Brain Sciences, 6,* 151–152.

Mattick, I. (1972). The teacher's role in helping young children develop language. In C. Cazden (Ed.), *Language in early childhood education.* (pp. 107–116). Washington, DC: National Association for Education of Young Children.

McClure, M. K., & Helland, J. (1979). A chimpanzee's use of dimensions in responding same and different. *The Psychological Record, 29,* 371–378.

Mebes, H. D. (1978). Pair-specific duetting in the peach-faced lovebird, *Agapornis roseicollis. Naturwissenschaften, 65,* 66–67.

Menzel, E. W., Jr., & Juno, C. (1982). Marmosets (*Saguinus fuscicollis*): Are learning sets learned? *Science, 217,* 750–752.

Menzel, E. W., Jr., & Juno, C. (1985). Social foraging in marmoset monkeys and the question of intelligence. *Philosophical Transactions of the Royal Society, London, B308,* 145–158.

Michael, J., Whitley, P., & Hesse, B. (1983). The pigeon parlance project. *VB News, 2,* 6–9.

Miles, H. L. (1978). Language acquisition in apes and children. In F. C. C. Peng (Ed.), *Sign language and language acquisition in man and ape* (pp. 103–120). Boulder, CO: Westview Press.

Miles, H. L. (1983). Apes and language. In J. de Luce & H. T. Wilder (Eds.), *Language in primates* (pp. 43–61). New York: Springer–Verlag.

Morgan, C. L. (1894). *An introduction to psychology.* London: W. Scott.

Morgane, P. J., Jacobs, M. S., & Galaburda, A. (1986). Evolutionary morphology of the dolphin brain. In R. J. Schusterman, J. A. Thomas, & F. G. Wood (Eds.), *Dolphin cognition and behavior: A comparative approach* (pp. 5–29). Hillsdale, NJ: Lawrence Erlbaum Associates.

Morse, D. H. (1967). The contexts of songs in black-throated green and blackburnian warblers. *Wilson Bulletin, 79,* 64–74.

Morse, D. H. (1970). Territorial and courtship songs of birds. *Nature, 226,* 659–661.

Mowrer, O. H. (1950). *Learning theory and personality dynamics.* New York: Ronald Press.

Mowrer, O. H. (1952). The autism theory of speech development and some clinical applications. *Journal of Speech and Hearing Disorders, 17,* 263–268.

Mowrer, O. H. (1954). A psychologist looks at language. *American Psychologist, 9,* 660–694.

Mowrer, O. H. (1958). Hearing and speaking: An analysis of language learning. *Journal of Speech and Hearing Disorders, 23,* 143–152.

Mowrer, O. H. (1960). *Learning theory and symbolic processes.* New York: Wiley.

Mundinger, P. C. (1970). Vocal imitation and individual recognition of finch calls. *Science, 168,* 480–482.

Nauta, W. J. H., & Karten, H. J. (1970). A general profile of the vertebrate brain, with sidelights on the ancestry of the cerebral cortex. In F. O. Schmitt (Ed.), *The neurosciences second study program: Evolution of brain and behavior* (pp. 7–26). New York: Rockefeller University Press.

Nottebohm, F. (1970). Ontogeny of bird song. *Science, 167,* 950–956.

Nottebohm, F. (1975). A zoologist's view of some language phenomena with particular emphasis on vocal learning. In E. H. Lenneberg & E. Lenneberg (Eds.), *Foundations of language development* (pp. 61–104). New York: Academic Press.

Nottebohm, F. (1981). A brain for all seasons: Cyclic anatomical changes in song control nuclei of the canary brain. *Science, 214,* 1368–1370.

Nottebohm, F. (1985). Neuronal replacement in adulthood. In F. Nottebohm (Ed.), *Hope for a new neurology* (pp. 143–161). New York: NY Academy of Sciences.

Nottebohm, F., Kasparian, S., & Pandazis, C. (1981). Brain space for a learned task. *Brain Research, 213,* 99–109.

Nottebohm, F., & Nottebohm, M. (1969). The parrots of Bush Bush. *Animal Kingdom,* 19–23.

Owings, D. H., & Hennessy, D. F. (1984). The importance of variation in sciurid visual and vocal communication. In J. O. Murie & G. R. Michener (Eds.), *The biology of ground dwelling squirrels* (pp. 169–200). Lincoln: University of Nebraska Press.

Owings, D. H., & Virginia, R. A. (1978). Alarm calls of California ground squirrels (*Spermophilus beecheyi*). *Zeitschrift für Tierpsychologie, 46,* 58–70.

Park, T. J., & Dooling, R. J. (1985). Perception of species-specific contact calls by budgerigars (*Melopsittacus undulatus*). *Journal of Comparative Psychology, 99,* 391–402.

Pastore, N. (1954a). Spatial learning in the canary. *Journal of Comparative and Physiology Psychology, 47,* 288–289.

Pastore, N. (1954b). Discrimination learning in the canary. *Journal of Comparative and Physiological Psychology, 47,* 389–390.

Pastore, N. (1955). Learning in the canary. *Scientific American, 192,* 72–77.

Pastore, N. (1961). Number sense and 'counting' ability in the canary. *Zeitschrift für Tierpsychologie, 18,* 561–573.

Paton, J. A., Manogue, K. R., & Nottebohm, F. (1981). Bilateral organization of the vocal control pathway in the budgerigar, *Melopsittacus undulatus. Journal of Neuroscience, 1,* 1276–1288.

Paton, J. A., & Nottebohm, F. (1984). Neurons born in adult brain are recruited into functional circuits. *Science, 225,* 1046–1048.

Patterson, F. (1978). Linguistic capabilities of a lowland gorilla. In F. C. C. Peng (Ed.), *Sign language and language acquisition in man and ape* (pp. 161–202). Boulder, CO: Westview Press.

Payne, R. B., Thompson, W. L., Fiala, K. L., & Sweany, L. L. (1981). Local song traditions in indigo buntings: Cultural transmission of behavior patterns across generations. *Behaviour, 77,* 199–221.

Pepperberg, I. M. (1978, March). *Object identification by an African Grey parrot (Psittacus erithacus).* Paper presented at Midwest Animal Behavior Society Meeting, W. Lafayette, In.

Pepperberg, I. M. (1979, June). *Functional word use in an African Grey parrot.* Paper presented at the annual meeting of the Animal Behavior Society, New Orleans, LA.

Pepperberg, I. M. (1981). Functional vocalizations by an African Grey parrot *(Psittacus erithacus). Zeitschrift für Tierpsychologie, 55,* 139–160.

Pepperberg, I. M. (1983). Cognition in the African Grey parrot: Preliminary evidence for auditory/vocal comprehension of the class concept. *Animal Learning & Behavior, 11,* 179–185.

Pepperberg, I. M. (1985). Social modeling theory: A possible framework for understanding avian vocal learning. *Auk, 102,* 854–864.

Pepperberg, I. M. (1986). Acquisition of anomalous communicatory systems: Implications for studies on interspecies communication. In R. J. Schusterman, J. A. Thomas, & F. G. Wood (Eds.), *Dolphin cognition and behavior: A comparative approach* (pp. 289–314). Hillsdale, NJ: Lawrence Erlbaum Associates.

Pepperberg, I. M. (1987a). Evidence for conceptual quantitative abilities in the African Grey parrot: Labeling of cardinal sets. *Ethology, 75,* 37–61.

Pepperberg, I. M. (1987b). Interspecies communication: A tool for assessing conceptual abilities in the African Grey parrot *(Psittacus erithacus).* In G. Greenberg & E. Tobach (Eds.), *Language, cognition and consciousness: Integrative levels* (pp. 31–56). Hillsdale, NJ: Lawrence Erlbaum Associates.

Pepperberg, I. M. (1987c). Acquisition of the same/different concept by an African Grey parrot *(Psittacus erithacus):* Learning with respect to categories of color, shape, and material. *Animal Learning & Behavior, 15,* 423–432.

Pepperberg, I. M. (1988a). The importance of social interaction and observation in the acquisition of communicative competence: Possible parallels between avian and human learning. In T. R. Zentall & B. G. Galef (Eds.), *Social learning: Psychological and biological perspectives* (pp. 279–299). Hillsdale, NJ: Lawrence Erlbaum Associates.

Pepperberg, I. M. (1988b). An interactive modeling technique for acquisition of communication skills: Separation of 'labeling' and 'requesting' in a psittacine subject. *Applied Psycholinguistics, 9,* 59–76.

Pepperberg, I. M. (1988c). Evidence for comprehension of "absence" by an African Grey parrot: Learning with respect to questions of same/different. *Journal of the Experimental Analysis of Behavior, 50,* 553–564.

Pepperberg, I. M., & Kozak, F. A. (1986). Object permanence in the African Grey parrot *(Psittacus erithacus). Animal Learning & Behavior, 14,* 322–330.

Petrinovich, L. (1972). Psychological mechanisms in language development. In G. Newton & A. H. Riesen (Eds.), *Advances in psychobiology, Vol. 1* (pp. 259–285). New York: Wiley-Interscience.

Pflumm, W., Comtesse, H., & Wilhelm, K. (1984). Sugar concentration and the structure of the sunbird's song. *Behavioral Ecology and Sociobiology, 15,* 257–261.

Power, D. M. (1966a). Agnostic behavior and vocalizations of orange-chinned parakeets in captivity. *Condor, 68,* 562–581.

Power, D. M. (1966b). Antiphonal duetting and evidence for auditory reaction time in the orange-chinned parakeet. *Auk, 83,* 314–319.

Premack, D. (1976). *Intelligence in ape and man.* Hillsdale, NJ: Lawrence Erlbaum Associates.

Premack, D. (1978). On the abstractness of human concepts: Why it would be difficult to talk to a pigeon. In S. H. Hulse, H. Fowler, & W. K. Honig (Eds.), *Cognitive processes in animal behavior* (pp. 423–451). Hillsdale, NJ: Lawrence Erlbaum Associates.

Premack, D. (1983). The codes of man and beasts. *Behavioral and Brain Sciences, 6,* 125–167.

Reese, H. W. (1972). Acquired distinctiveness and equivalence of cues in young children. *Journal of Experimental Child Psychology, 13,* 171–182.

Reiss, D., Markowitz, H., Firestein, S., & Mullen, J. (1981, December). *A pragmatic approach to symbol-based two-way communication between humans and Tursiops truncatus.* Paper presented at the 4th Biennial Conference on Marine Mammals, San Francisco, CA.

Rensch, B., & Dücker, G. (1973). Discrimination of patterns indicating four and five degrees of reward by birds. *Behavioral Biology, 9,* 279–288.

Rice, M. (1980). *Cognition to language.* Baltimore, MD: University Park Press.

Robinson, S. R. (1980). Antipredator behaviour and predator recognition in Belding's ground squirrels. *Animal Behaviour, 28,* 840–852.

Robinson, S. R. (1981). Alarm communication in Belding's ground squirrels. *Zeitschrift für*

Tierpsychologie, 59, 150–168.

Rogoff, B. (1984). Introduction: Thinking and learning in a social context. In B. Rogoff & J. Lave (Eds.), *Everyday cognition: Its development in social context* (pp. 1–8). Cambridge, MA: Harvard University Press.

Romanes, G. J. (1882). *Animal intelligence.* British Edition; 1906, New York: Appleton.

Rumbaugh, D. M., (Ed.) (1977). *Language learning by a chimpanzee.* New York: Academic Press.

Rumbaugh, D. M., & Pate, J. L. (1984). Primates' learning by levels. In G. Greenberg & E. Tobach (Eds.), *Behavioral evolution and integrative levels* (pp. 221–240). Hillsdale, NJ: Lawrence Erlbaum Associates.

Santiago, H. C., & Wright, A. A. (1984). Pigeon memory: *Same/Different* concept learning, serial probe recognition acquisition, and probe delay effects on the serial-position function. *Journal of Experimental Psychology: Animal Behavior Processes, 10,* 498–512.

Saunders, R., & Sailor, W. (1979). A comparison of the strategies of reinforcement in two-choice learning problems with severely retarded children. *American Association for the Education of the Severely (Profoundly) Handicapped Review, 4,* 323–334.

Savage-Rumbaugh, E. S., Rumbaugh, D. M., Smith, S. T., & Lawson, J. (1980). Reference: The linguistic essential. *Science, 210,* 922–925.

Schusterman, R. J., & Gisiner, R. (1988). Artificial language comprehension in dolphins and sea lions: The essential cognitive skills. *Psychological Record, 38,* 311–348.

Schusterman, R. J., & Krieger, K. (1986). Artificial language comprehension and size transposition by a California sea lion *(Zalophus californianus). Journal of Comparative Psychology, 100,* 348–355.

Sebeok, T. A., & Rosenthal, R. (Eds.) (1981). *The Clever Hans phenomenon: Communication with horses, whales, apes, and people.* New York: New York Academy of Sciences.

Serpell, J. (1981). Duets, greetings, and triumph ceremonies: Analogous displays in the parrot genus *Trichoglossus. Zeitschrift für Tierpsychologie, 55,* 268–283.

Shiovitz, K. A., & Lemon, R. E. (1980). Species identification of songs by indigo buntings as determined by responses to computer-generated sounds. *Behaviour, 74,* 167–199.

Shy, E., McGregor, P. K., & Krebs, J. (1986). Discrimination of song types by male great tits. *Behavioural Processes, 13,* 1–12.

Smith, A. (1978). Lenneberg, Locke, Zangwill and the neuropsychology of language and language disorders. In G. A. Miller & E. Lenneberg (Eds.), *Psychology and biology of language and thought* (pp. 133–149). New York: Academic Press.

Smith, G. (1971). Tool use in parrots. *Aviculture Magazine, 77,* 47–48.

Smith, W. J. (1986). Signaling behavior: Contributions of different repertoires. In R. J. Schusterman, J. A. Thomas, & F. G. Wood (Eds.), *Dolphin cognition and behavior: A comparative approach* (pp. 315–330). Hillsdale, NJ: Lawrence Erlbaum Associates.

Snowdon, C. T. (1988). A comparative approach to vocal communication. In D. W. Leger (Ed.), *Nebraska symposium on motivation: Comparative perspectives in modern psychology, Vol. 35.* Lincoln: University of Nebraska Press.

Sonnenschein, S., & Whitehurst, G. J. (1984). Developing referential communication: A hierarchy of skills. *Child Development, 55,* 1936–1945.

Stettner, L. J. (1974). Avian discrimination and reversal learning. In I. J. Goodman & M. W. Schein (Eds.), *Birds, brain, and behavior* (pp. 194–201). New York: Academic Press.

Stettner, L. J., & Matyniak, K. (1968). The brain of birds. *Scientific American, 218,* 64–76.

Struhsaker, T. T. (1967). Auditory communication among vervet monkeys *(Ceropithecus aethiops).* In S. A. Altmann (Ed.), *Social communication among primates* (pp. 281–324). Chicago: University of Chicago Press.

Teleki, G. (1973). *The predatory behavior of wild chimpanzees.* Lewisburg, PA: Bucknell University Press.

Terrace, H. S. (1979). Is problem-solving language? *Journal of the Experimental Analysis of*

Behavior, 31, 161–175.

Thomas, R. K. (1980). Evolution of intelligence: An approach to its assessment. *Brain, Behavior and Evolution, 17,* 454–472.

Thorpe, W. H. (1964). *Learning and instinct in animals.* London: Methuen.

Thorpe, W. H. (1974). *Animal and human nature.* New York: Anchor Press, Doubleday.

Todt, D. (1975). Social learning of vocal patterns and modes of their applications in Grey parrots. *Zeitschrift für Tierpsychologie, 39,* 178–188.

Tyack, P. (1983). Differential response of humpback whales, *Megatera novaeangliae,* to playback of song or social sounds. *Behavioral Ecology & Sociobiology, 13,* 49–55.

Vanayan, M., Robertson, H. A., & Biederman, G. B. (1985). Observational learning in pigeons: The effects of model proficiency on observer performance. *Journal of General Psychology, 112,* 349–357.

von Glasersfeld, E. (1977). Linguistic communication: Theory and definition. In D. M. Rumbaugh (Ed.), *Language learning by a chimpanzee* (pp. 55–72). New York: Academic Press.

Walker, L. C. (1981). The ontogeny of the neural substrate for language. *Journal of Human Evolution, 10,* 429–441.

Watson, J. B. (1929). *Psychology from the standpoint of a behaviorist.* Philadelphia, PA: Lippincott.

Weir, R. (1962). *Language in the crib.* The Hague: Mouton.

Weisberg, P., Stout, R., & Hendler, M. (1986). Training and generalization of a "yes-no" discrimination with a developmentally delayed child. *Child and Family Behavior Therapy, 8,* 49–64.

Wright, A. A., Santiago, H. C., & Sands, S. F. (1984). Monkey memory: *Same/Different* concept learning, serial probe acquisition, and probe delay effects. *Journal of Experimental Psychology: Animal Learning Processes, 10,* 513–529.

Wright, A. A., Santiago, H. C., Urcuioli, P. J., & Sands, S. F. (1984). Monkey and pigeon acquisition of same/different concept using pictorial stimuli. In M. L. Commons, R. J. Herrnstein, & A. R. Wagner (Eds.), *Quantitative analysis of behavior, Vol. 4* (pp. 295–317). Cambridge, MA: Ballinger.

Zentall, T. R., Edwards, C. A., Moore, B. S., & Hogan, D. E. (1981). Identity: The basis for both matching and oddity learning in pigeons. *Journal of Experimental Psychology: Animal Behavior Processes, 7,* 70–86.

Zentall, T. R., Hogan, D. E., & Edwards, C. A. (1984) Cognitive factors in conditional learning by pigeons. In H. L. Roitblat, T. G. Bever, & H. S. Terrace (Eds.), *Animal cognition* (pp. 389–405). Hillsdale, NJ: Lawrence Erlbaum Associates.

Zorina, Z. A. (1982). Reasoning ability and adaptivity of behaviour in birds. In V. J. A. Novak & J. Mlikovsky (Eds.), *Evolution and environment* (pp. 907–912). Praha: CSAV. (Translation provided by the author).

8
DO ANIMALS HAVE THE OPTION OF WITHHOLDING SIGNALS WHEN COMMUNICATION IS INAPPROPRIATE? THE AUDIENCE EFFECT

Peter Marler
University of California, Davis

Stephen Karakashian
Marcel Gyger
The Rockefeller University Field Research Center

ABSTRACT

Communicative behavior provides a potential window into problems of intentionality in animals. One elementary but neglected aspect of animal communication is the ability to emit or withhold a signal in the presence of the referent for that signal. Little is known about the degree to which this option is open to animals. We reasoned that presence or absence of appropriate signal receivers might influence the decision to withhold a signal. Alarm and food calls were elicited in cockerels by the appropriate external stimulation — overhead hawk models and favored food items — and studied in the presence and absence of an appropriate audience (e.g., a hen). The results demonstrate that, when an animal is in the presence of a signal referent, there is an ability to modulate signal production according to the appropriateness for communication of the caller's social circumstances.

In broadest terms, the theme of intentionality embraces a multitude of topics. Included are issues of action and cognition, systems of belief, and attributions of beliefs to others — all subjects that are difficult to investigate in organisms with which we have no common natural language (Dennett, 1981; Premack, 1986; Premack & Premack, 1983; Premack & Woodruff, 1978). Nevertheless, if intentions are revealed by a manifest concern with the effect of one's actions on others, communicative behavior is the natural subject for investigations of intentionality — the combined operation of beliefs and desires. It is a subject with an extensive literature (e.g., Bennett, 1976; Dennett, 1983; Searle, 1983), but the reflections of linguists and philosophers on intentionality are so often bound up with the exigencies of human language that it is impossible to assess their relevance to the communication of animals (Churchland, 1983). Rather than attempting to paraphrase animal behavior in the propositional terms of human language, zoologists may be well advised to develop their own methodology even though this may call for drastic simplifications, at least in the initial stages.

Under the leadership of Donald Griffin, cognitive ethology has done much in recent years to alleviate the stigma on mental processes in animals as a valid subject for scientific research (Griffin, 1981, 1984, this volume). As he indicates, one widely held view of the signals used in animal communication is that their production is essentially involuntary and reflexive and that they derive from the expression of emotion, affect, and arousal. He characterizes this position as the "groans-of-pain" (GOP) concept of animal communication (Griffin, 1985, p. 615). The GOP position is based more on anthropocentric preconception than on scientific observation. It has the reductionistic advantage, however, of suggesting experimental paradigms for addressing basic questions about animals' intent to communicate. If the GOP interpretation is found to be universally valid, we can conclude that the intent to communicate plays no part in animal communication.

The progress made in ethological studies of animal communication in recent years in specifying the semantic content of vocal signals has been reviewed elsewhere (Cheney & Seyfarth, 1982; Gouzoules, Gouzoules, & Marler, 1984; Marler, 1985; Seyfarth, 1986; Seyfarth, Cheney, & Marler, 1980). Here we restrict our attention to one limited aspect of intentionality; we are concerned not with the beliefs being communicated but with the desire to communicate. For the most part, we leave aside the question of what it is that animals are communicating about and concentrate instead on whether they evince an intent to communicate. In this spirit of reductionistic simplification, we address here one limited aspect of behavior, concerned with the options open to animals (Roitblat, 1983) in relation to the social context in which communication takes place. Do animals have the option to emit signals or withhold them according to the communicative potential of the situation in which they find themselves?

What class of behaviors would be appropriate for such an investigation? We have reasoned that if the GOP view of animal signalling is valid, animals should consistently emit signals while in the presence of the appropriate external referent, say a predator or food, regardless of the social circumstances at the time. Investigation of the impact of social context on the production of such signals thus permits one test of the GOP point of view.

A positive demonstration that an animal has the option to emit or withhold signals would be evidence against the generality of the GOP hypothesis. Manipulation of the presence or absence of an appropriate audience for signal production thus offers an opportunity to explore one of the circumstances in which the withholding of signals might be expected to occur. Why emit a call or perform a visual display if there is no one to hear or see it? If animals prove to have such abilities, this would be consistent with possession of intentions to influence the behavior of companions. Conversely, an animal that displays insensitivity to the social context for signal production would seem to be an unlikely candidate for the possession of intentional communicative behavior.

There is a significant complication lurking here. The production of many animal signals is directly elicited by stimuli received from social companions. Cessation of signalling upon removal of a companion could occur because the companion is in some sense a referent for production of this particular signal. To circumvent this problem, we must identify signalling systems that have nonsocial referents. A companion's role must be that of a signal audience or addressee and not that of a signal referent. It is crucial that these two roles of a companion as a referent and as a signal recipient be dissociated if the role of social context in signal production is to be properly appraised.

This difficulty can be circumvented by focussing on signal systems with primary referents of an environmental nature such as food or a predator. Furthermore, the referent should be experimentally manipulable so that varying probabilities of signal production can be brought under control. The stage is then set for the introduction of a companion, with potential access to the signals produced, as a second variable.

SIGNALS WITH DANGER AS A REFERENT: ALARM CALLS

Domestic chickens have an unusually large vocal repertoire (Baeumer, 1962; Collias, 1987; Collias & Joos, 1953; Guyomarc'h, 1962, 1966; Konishi, 1963). Included within it is an interesting array of alarm calls. Like many birds, chickens have at least two distinct classes of alarm calls, one for aerial predators and one for ground predators (Klump & Shalter, 1984; Marler, 1955). The former are of particular historical interest as the object of efforts by early ethologists to gain experimental control over escape behavior and alarm call production by use of cardboard silhouettes of hawks passing overhead.

We have verified that chickens respond predictably and consistently to small aerial models of raptors like those used in the pioneering experiments of Konrad Lorenz and Niko Tinbergen (Karaskashian, Gyger, & Marler, 1988; Schleidt, 1961). Ours were designed to mimic the silhouette of a hawk soaring at 30-50 meters above the ground. Habituation was minimized by varying the size, the direction of transit, and the particular overhead track along which the model was moved. The same configuration was never repeated in a given experiment. In the open-air compounds in which the birds lived prior to the experiments, red-tailed hawks were the raptors that occasioned most of the aerial predator calls given by cockerels (Gyger, Marler, & Pickert, 1987).

We used a particular strain, the golden sebright bantam, which were bred by fanciers and not subjected to intensive selection for farm use and egg production. Behaviorally, sebrights do not appear to be far removed from the original jungle fowl stock. Birds were fitted with wireless microphones so that even faint calls could be tape recorded and ascribed to a particular caller.

The "ground predator" call of cockerels is a pulsed broad-band cackle, given primarily to foxes, dogs, and other ground living potential predators and sometimes also to hawks and eagles at close quarters either moving or perched nearby (Fig. 8.1a). The "aerial predator" call ranges from a monosyllabic narrow-band whistle (Fig. 8.1c) to a broad-band scream and is typically given to distant objects moving high in the sky overhead (Fig. 8.1b). Some studies have been conducted of the stimulus situations eliciting these calls in free-ranging birds, but much remains to be learned (Gyger, Marler, & Pickert, 1987). In the tests we describe here, only aerial alarm calls were given, all in response to models of hawks. In almost 400 tests, 509 aerial alarm calls were given, and no ground predator calls occurred at all.

Presentation of the presumed referent, an aerial predator, reliably elicits production of a vocal signal specific to the stimulus, the aerial predator call. The stage is thus set for examining the effect of an audience on the cockerel's alarm calling. To explore this we compared call production when males were either alone, or with the mate, or with some other companion present in an adjoining cage. Prior to testing, each male was housed for some weeks with a single female which was regarded, for purposes of this experiment, as his mate.

Audience Effects on Alarm Call Production

First we compared the alarm calling of six cocks when they were alone, with their mates, or accompanied by a different female (actually the mate of another male kept in the same room). Alarm calling occured significantly less when males were alone than when accompanied by a female that was or was not the mate (Fig. 8.2). Most alarm calls were given with a female other than

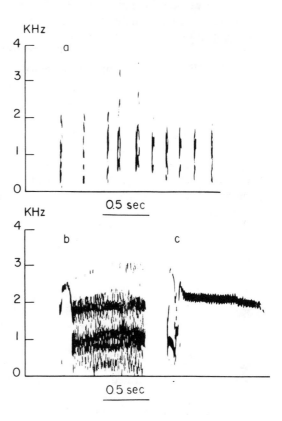

Fig. 8.1 Sound spectrograms of two types of alarm calls used by the domestic chicken: (a) the ground predator call and (b&c) the aerial predator call. The call for terrestrial predators consists of a rapid string of short, loud, broad-band pulses, sometimes ending with a longer cackle (not shown). The call for distant, flying predators has two major parts — a short, soft, wide-band pulse followed by (b) a long trill which may be noisy and wide-band or (c) tonal and whistle-like.

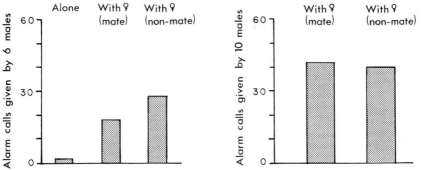

Fig. 8.2 Numbers of aerial alarm calls given by six (left) and ten (right) cockerels: alone, with the mate in an adjacent cage, and with a strange female as an audience. Adapted from Karakashian, Gyger & Marler, 1988 p. 131.

191

the mate as an audience, and although the difference was not significant, we decided to pursue this point further (Karakashian et al., 1988).

We next tested 10 males for alarm calling with females that had been housed in a separate building and were thus completely unfamiliar to the males. When males were tested with these strange females and with their mates, the differences in numbers of alarm calls were negligible. Thus, in this test situation a male is equally likely to alarm call whether his familiar mate or an unfamiliar female is the audience.

The effect of another male as an audience was also examined. In this case we used as the audience an unmated cockerel previously housed in a separate building. Mutual aggressive displays inevitably ensued when they were placed in their test cages, but these waned before the experiment began. Subjects alarm called as frequently with a male as with a female audience (Fig. 8.3). Again, calling was significantly lower in the absence of an audience. As a precaution against effects of individual idiosyncracies of stimulus males, we repeated the experiment with a different design. Each male from 10 male/female pairs was used as the audience for one other male. The result was similar.

The Audience Sees the "Hawk" While the Subject Does Not, and Vice Versa

With the original experimental design, audience birds could see the predator model just as well as the subjects could see it. For example, in the experiments just mentioned, with males as both subject and audience, both were likely to alarm call. Of five presentations in which both males alarmed, subjects called first in three presentations, and the audience first in two of them. This raises the question of whether the response of a subject in this type of experiment is influenced by the behavior of the audience, and in

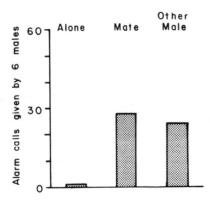

Fig. 8.3 Aerial alarm calling by six cockerels in response to a hawk model: alone, with a mate, or with another male as an audience. Adapted from Karakashian, Gyger & Marler, 1988 p. 131.

particular by any visual or vocal reactions it may give itself to the referent. The next step was to modify the test situation to control who could see the hawk and who could not (Karakashian et al., 1988).

We installed a baffle that obscured the view from the audience cage of one trajectory of the hawk model leaving the other trajectory unobstructed. The cockerel serving as a subject was positioned in such a way that he could see both trajectories all the time. By presenting the hawk on one track or the other, visibility of the predator to the audience bird could be controlled. As before, solitary males alarm called significantly less than with a female audience even when the female was unable to see the model (Fig. 8.4). The male's increased alarm-calling behavior was not triggered or potentiated by fearful behavior of the female when she saw the hawk model.

Intriguingly, in the first experiment of this type, there was more calling when the model was invisible to the female audience than when she could see it, suggesting perhaps that the inattentive behavior of a female unaware of danger actually increased a male's calling. This trend was not significant, but it served to bring to mind one kind of evidence about effects of audience behavior on signal production that could indicate intentions on the signaller's part to elicit certain reactions from an audience.

To follow up on this point we repeated the experiment with more subjects ($N = 24$) and obtained the opposite result. This time the cockerels alarm called more when the female could see than when she could not. Although ideally one would like to manipulate audience behavior in a more direct and controllable fashion, at present we have no evidence that cockerels closely

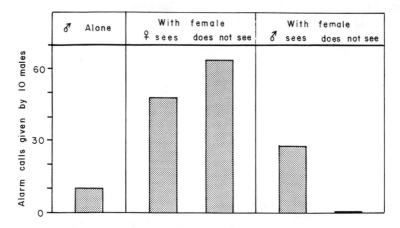

Fig. 8.4 Male aerial alarm calling with the mate as an audience in a situation in which either the male or the female was prevented (by a baffle) from seeing the hawk model passing overhead. Adapted from Karakashian, Gyger & Marler, 1988 p. 132.

monitor audience behavior and curtail or augment signalling accordingly, as would be expected if they had intentions to change the behavior of companions in a particular way.

As a further test of the possibility that fearful behavior of a female audience potentiates male alarm calling, the baffle arrangement was changed so that, while audience females could see the hawk model all the time, male subjects could see it on only half of the trials. Males called only when they could see the hawk despite freezing, monitoring, scanning, and crouching behavior and, in a few cases, even alarm calling by the females, all visible and audible to the male. In fact, it was unusual for females to alarm call with our test paradigm.

Is Another Species Effective as an Audience?

What criteria must a social companion satisfy to serve as an adequate audience for alarm-call production? Will anything animate suffice? Given the risks involved in emitting signals in the presence of a predator and the pressures of kin selection, one might predict that the intent to communicate would at least tend to focus on members of the same species. This proves to be the case. Female bobwhite quail were presented as an audience to cockerels tested for alarm calling. In the first experiment, six cockerels were studied in the presence of a bobwhite female, and responses were compared to those with the mate as an audience (Karakashian et al., 1988). The difference in effectiveness of the two species is clear (Fig. 8.5). The heterospecific audience elicits an increase in the number of male alarm calls, but it is significantly less effective than a sebright hen as an audience.

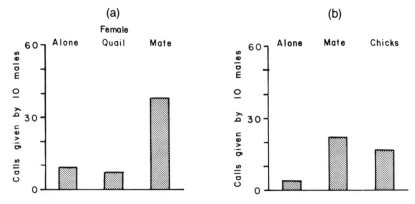

Fig. 8.5 The results of two experiments in which aerial alarm calling of cockerels was evoked by a hawk model: alone, in the presence of a female quail, the mate, or a group of four chicks. Adapted from Karakashian, Gyger & Marler, 1988 p. 133.

A bobwhite quail is only two thirds the size of a female bantam chicken. Might an unspecific effect of stimulus size be responsible for the inadequacy of quail as an audience for male bantams? As a first step in investigating this possibility, males were tested for alarm calling with golden sebright chicks. Responses to the hawk models were compared when males were alone, with their mates, and in the presence of chicks 4–7 days old. Males called significantly more with the chicks than when alone. The difference in the effects of mate and chicks was not significant. Thus the evidence suggests that a signalling bird is sensitive to relatively subtle features of the audience, probably including those that designate members of the same species. (This issue is also discussed in Cheney and Seyfarth, this volume).

Hormonal Effects on Signal Production and Audience Effects

It is clear that readiness to alarm call is strongly affected by the social context in which signal production takes place. Conspecific adults and chicks are both effective as an audience for a cockerel, but gender appears to be unimportant. Other aspects of the audience that have yet to be investigated include physiological condition and breed: For example, is a sebright more or less effective than a silky bantam? A preliminary test with broody hens, that had gone through the process of incubating and hatching eggs, presented both alone and with chicks, revealed that they do indeed constitute an effective audience for male alarm calling (Fig. 8.6). Interest-

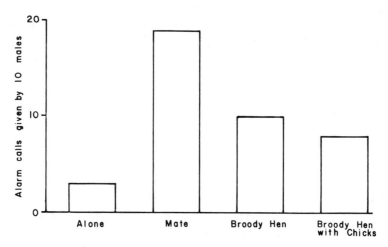

Fig. 8.6 Aerial alarm calling by cockerels: alone, with the mate, with a broody hen, and with a broody hen and chicks as an audience. Adapted from Karakashian, Gyger & Marler, 1988 p. 133.

ingly, the broody hens themselves called much more frequently than laying hens did, suggesting an influence of the physiological state of females on their own readiness to alarm call. We already know that the hormonal state of males has strong effects on their alarm-call production. Castration of males drastically reduces alarm-call rates (Gyger, Karakashian, Dufty, & Marler, 1988). Normal calling rates are reinstated by androgen therapy. On withdrawal of exogenous testosterone sources, alarm-calling rates return to baseline (Fig. 8.7).

Production of aerial alarm calls by males is enhanced by testosterone, but it appears that the effect of an audience is independent of the subject's androgen levels (Gyger, et al., 1988). Thus, despite an overall reduction in calling rates, castrated males still showed higher calling rates in the presence of a hen than when alone. We also noted that, by comparison, food-call production appeared to be unaffected by castration and androgen therapy. The contrast in the hormonal substrates of alarm- and food-calling suggests that the effect of testosterone is selective, and not a facilitation of all vocal production. This is one of several differences between alarm calling and food calling indicating a degree of independence in the physiological control of these two communicative subsystems.

AUDIENCE EFFECTS ON CALLS WITH FOOD AS A REFERENT

Gallinaceous birds such as the domestic chicken are remarkable and perhaps unique in the animal kingdom for the richness and diversity of their systems of food signalling. Food calls are used in at least two contexts: by males when courting females and by adults of both sexes in providing food for young. The calls in both of these situations have been well described in both domestic chickens (Baeumer, 1962; Collias & Joos, 1953; Guyomarc'h, 1962, 1966, 1974; Konishi, 1963; Kruijt, 1964) and in the ancestral red junglefowl (Collias, 1987; Collias & Collias, 1967; Hughes, Hughes, & Covalt-Dunning, 1982; Sherry, 1977; Stokes, 1971).

Upon discovering food, adult males give a particular call that attracts adult females to approach and share the food with them. As a behavioral system food calling satisfies the requirements for study of the audience effect. Calls occur in a social context, and there is a nonsocial external referent for signal production readily brought under experimental control. Moreover, strength of different foods as stimuli for calling can be varied.

Males call most freely with highly preferred foods. Calling rates provide an index of the degree of preference and are minimal with inedible objects, although calling may still occur at an appreciable rate. Experiments in which a hen was released from behind a visual barrier after a male was

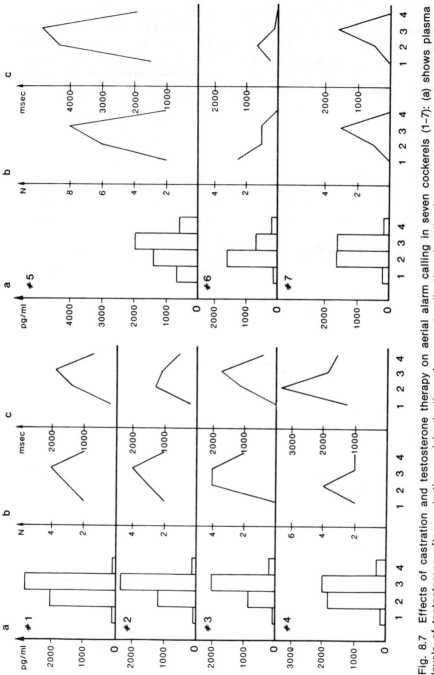

Fig. 8.7 Effects of castration and testosterone therapy on aerial alarm calling in seven cockerels (1–7): (a) shows plasma levels of testosterone after castration and implanting of an empty silastic tube (1), after removing the empty implant and replacing it with a first testosterone implant (2), adding a second testosterone implant (3), and after removal of all implants (4); (b) shows the numbers of aerial alarm calls evoked by the hawk model; and (c) the durations of alarm calling under these four conditions.

presented with food, and allowed to approach him at her own pace suggested that male food calling communicates to the hen information about food quality (Marler, Dufty, & Pickert, 1986a) (Fig. 8.8). The ability of the experimenter to manipulate the strength of the referential stimulus serves to reveal some novel aspects of the audience effect.

A cockerel is significantly more likely to food call if his mate is present than when alone. There is, however, an appreciable baseline level of calling in the absence of an audience. This baseline level is maximal with favored foods (Fig. 8.9a), decreases with less preferred foods and, approaches zero with nonfood items (Fig. 8.9b).

Male food calling is strongly potentiated by the presence of an adult female as an audience (Marler, Dufty, & Pickert, 1986b). In contrast with alarm calling, there is a difference in the effectiveness of a familiar female (the mate) and a strange female. This difference is revealed most readily by comparing male responses to a "strong" and a "weak" food referent (i.e., a nonfood). With a preferred food, there is no difference in the amount of calling with a strange female and with the mate. However, if something

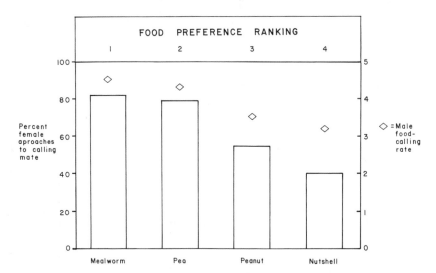

Fig. 8.8   Food calling of cockerels with foods ranging from highly favored (mealworm) to inedible objects (nutshell). Male calling rates in the presence of a hen are indicated by diamonds. Histograms show the percentage of females approaching the calling male after release from an adjacent cage when males were given one of the four foods. A female could hear the male calling but could not see the food until after she had approached him. These are the results from 360 trials, in 275 of which males called. Adapted from Marler, Dufty & Pickert, 1986a pp. 190 & 191.

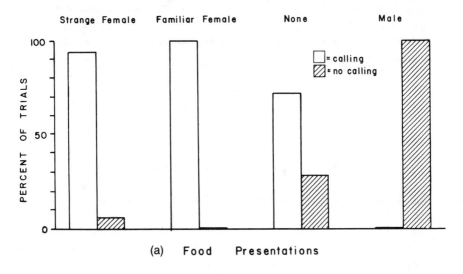

(a) Food Presentations

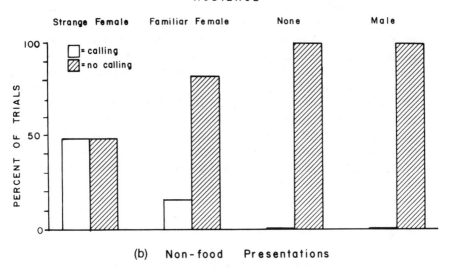

(b) Non-food Presentations

Fig. 8.9 Food calling of cockerels with several kinds of audiences showing that strange and familiar females exert different effects: (a) number of trials in which cockerels food called when given a mealworm (expressed as percent trials) in the presence of strange and familiar females, alone, and with another male as an audience and (b) food calling in the same situations when males were given an inedible object (a piece of peanut shell).

inedible is presented, the male hardly calls at all to his mate but calls at an appreciable rate to the strange female.

In the case of food calling there is a significant effect of audience gender upon signal production. Food calling is actively inhibited by a male audience, so that the incidence of food calling actually falls below the baseline. Thus a cockerel is more ready to communicate information about the presence of food to a female than to another male. This is another striking contrast with alarm calling; in the experimental situation we employed, male and female audiences were equipotential in the facilitation of alarm calling.

ARE AUDIENCE EFFECTS MEDIATED BY AROUSAL?

Before entertaining cognitive interpretations of the audience effect and any potential implications for the existence of intentions to communicate, the possibility must be explored that an audience influences signal production by changing the general arousal level of a signaller. When a signaller, stimulated by a referent, also perceives the presence of an appropriate social companion, perhaps this additional percept results in increased arousal and lowers the threshold of responsiveness to external stimulation in general? If responsiveness to potentially dangerous stimuli were affected in this way, then alarm call production would naturally be potentiated by an audience. Arousal is a ubiquitous phenomenon in animal behavior and undoubtedly influences the occurrence of signal production in many circumstances. Several lines of evidence suggest that this is not a general explanation for the audience effect, however, although it is difficult to exclude completely.

If arousal were a primary factor in the audience effect, calling rates should covary with other measures of arousal. Subjects exposed to a signal referent in the absence of an appropriate companion should call less, be less attentive to referential stimulation, and be less aroused by such stimulation. In the course of some of the alarm-calling experiments we have described, the responses of subjects to the overhead hawk models were videotaped and samples were examined for the occurrence of fearful behavior including freezing, crouching, and visual fixation of the hawk model. We found that whether males called with an audience or without an audience, they frequently showed signs of alarm and always carefully monitored movements of the overhead model.

These preliminary observations suggest that the presence or absence of an appropriate audience has effects not on fearful behavior in general but specifically on signal production. This potential dichotomy between general displays of emotion and arousal in response to a stimulus and the production of signals that bear a specific relationship to that same stimulus is important and merits further investigation. It has significant implications both for the issue of intentionality and in modelling the underlying physiological control of signalling behavior.

Another line of evidence bears on the arousal interpretation of audience effects. A given manipulation of the social context for signal production should have equivalent effects on all signal systems. This is patently not the case. Audience gender is important for food calling and not for alarm calling. Food calling is sensitive to the contrast between a familiar female and a strange one, and alarm calling is not. These differences are difficult to reconcile with an arousal interpretation of audience effects. They make sense, however, if one assumes that the act of signal production is preceded by an appraisal of the appropriateness of the social situation for the initiation of a communicative interaction.

There are reasons to think that such audience effects are widespread. In field research on the downy woodpecker (*Picoides pubescens*) the production of alarm calls was found to be facilitated by presence of the mate but not by a downy woodpecker of the same sex or members of other species (Sullivan, 1985). Captive vervet monkeys also vary rates of alarm calling when they detect a predator as a function of their social circumstances (Cheney & Seyfarth, 1985).

DECEPTIVE SIGNALLING: A POSSIBLE CASE

The indications that an appraisal of the immediate social environment influences an animal's decision to emit or withhold a communicative signal, invite the speculation that animals possess intentions to communicate. Acts of deception are a potentially valuable source of insights into intentionality (Thompson & Mitchell, 1987; Woodruff & Premack, 1979). If animals have the option to withhold signals regardless of the presence of normal referents, perhaps they can also produce them at will thus opening up the possibility of using signals deceptively. In addition to operating in an "honest" mode, perhaps they can signal "dishonestly" when referents are absent. We should thus be prepared to encounter examples of deception in animals, not simply of the passive kind, as in cases of mimicry, but also of an active type. Animals with intentionality should have the option of prevaricating.

A possible case has been found in the food calling of chickens, which is a component in their parental care and also in the "tidbitting" behavior by which a cockerel keeps the flock together and courts females by proferring food items to his companions. In preparation for laboratory investigation of food-calling behavior, we conducted a naturalistic study on several pairs of silver sebrights allowed to forage in natural vegetation in large open-air compounds (Gyger & Marler, 1988). For periods of up to 3 months, each pair was followed for several hours a day. Continuous notes were kept of their behavior, and all vocalizations were tape-recorded by wireless microphones attached to each bird. All circumstances in which food calling occurred were systematically classified together with the kind of object, edible or otherwise, with which calling was associated.

In a majority of cases, food calling appeared to be triggered by objects clearly identifiable as edible. Often these were live-caught insects or spiders. At other times they were plant objects such as seeds or leaves. Some food calling was associated with the food trough where mash was provided. In 45% of the cases of food calling, however, no edible object could be detected. These cases of food calling without an object may constitute a possible case of deception.

When males with animal food objects called, females approached in 86% of the cases and almost always ate the food. As is typical of cockerels during food calling, they usually refrained from eating the food themselves, giving the female prior access. Male calling to less preferred foods elicited female approach more rarely. Females approached only 29% of the time after males called with no detectable food present.

We found the same kind of relationships between male calling, female approaches, and food quality in these free-ranging birds that we had found in the laboratory. Food-calling rate correlated positively both with food palatability and also with the probability that the hen would approach. The correspondence between these field observations and the results of our experimental studies was reassuring, confirming that the move from field to laboratory had left the essential features of food calling interactions intact.

What can we make of the surprisingly large proportion of cases of food calling without food? Are there any indications of dishonesty in the patterns of use perhaps to trick a female into approaching if she wanders too far away? Alternatively, is there anything about the acoustic structure of calls given in this situation to support the notion that different signals are used in calling with food and without food? In this case it might be more appropriate to identify nonfood calling as a distinct signal to a female who has wandered away that she should approach. We therefore focussed our attention on the role of distance between male and female in these naturalistic studies.

We found no relationship between food calling and the degree of separation of the pair at the time. There was no correlation between calling rate and intermate distance, either in the pooled data or when the results were divided into two sets, one with food present and the other without food objects. The calling rates were high with food and low without food, although variation was great.

We feel that these results are most readily accommodated by the hypothesis that the same call is being used in all cases—honestly in some cases and dishonestly in others — and that calling rate correlates better with food quality than with degree of separation from the mate. We were also unable to detect any differences in the acoustic morphology of individual calls, with and without food. Thus, we have been unable to find any indications that we are dealing with two acoustically distinct call types, one associated with food and attraction of the mate to feed, and the other with mate separation and the restoration of social proximity.

When we concentrated our attention on occasions in which females approached the male caller, we found that although the approach rate was always higher (86%) with food than without it (29%) the probability of the pair being reunited bore the same relationship to call rate when food was absent and when it was present. In other words a male calling without food was only likely to be approached by a female on the relatively rare occasions when his calling rate was at the high end of the range for the nonfood situation. Again, the results conform most readily to the assumption that the nonfood calling of a tidbitting cockerel to a hen is a case of dishonest food signalling.

When we explored further, we eventually discovered a correlation between calling behavior and mate separation. The initial distance between mates was significantly greater when calling was initiated in the absence of food than with food (Fig. 8.10). A male is more likely to initiate a food-calling bout without food when the female is far from him than when she is close by. Once calling is initiated, however, the relationships between calling behavior, mate distance, and the probability of the mate approaching the male all appear to follow the same rules whether food is present or absent (Gyger & Marler, 1988).

These different lines of evidence all led us to consider the possibility of dishonest use of this particular signal system employed to bring companions back when they get too far away. According to this interpretation, mate separation tends to favor deceptive signalling. A final relevant point is that in more than half of the cases in which the mates regained proximity, after the male had called without food, she scratched or pecked at the ground in front of him as though she expected to find food there. Many details of the behavior are thus consistent with the assumption that the female is effectively deceived by the male, especially with calling at a high rate, and is led to expect that, on approaching the male, she will find food there.

Not one of these lines of evidence, taken alone, is sufficient to sustain a definitive case for deception and other interpretations are tenable (see the discussion in W. J. Smith, this volume). Yet all of our data are consistent with the proposition that cockerels are capable of both honest and dishonest use of food calling. If the male does have the option to emit or withhold food calls, and his calling is not reflexively controlled by a combination of environmental and social stimuli, then it would appear that some elements of the intention to communicate are indeed present.

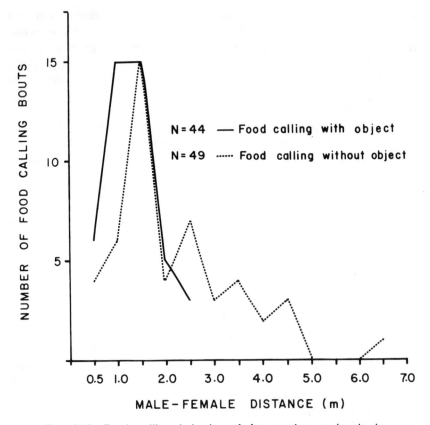

Fig. 8.10 Food calling behavior of free-ranging cockerels in relation to the distance of the mate. The initiation of food calling with a food object occurs at shorter intermate distances (on average) than when food calling occurs without food present.

Perhaps the strongest argument against the deception hypothesis is the large proportion of all food calling under naturalistic conditions made up by calling without food—a total of 45%. We tend to assume that, for deception to succeed, dishonest usage should be a relatively rare event. However, until we learn more of the costs and benefits of behaviors such as this and the extent to which they vary from one situation to another, we can only speculate about where the permissible limits may lie. Certainly the benefits to the female will be high when an honest signal yields access to a rare highly valued food. We must not forget that, food or no food, female approach rates are maximal only with high calling rates which, when honestly used, signify a preferred and valuable food. Recall too that high-rate calling only occurs in a small proportion of the occasions when a male calls but has no food.

There may be analogies with operant schedules for intermittent reinforcement. It has long been known that high rates of operant responding can be sustained with unreinforced responses far outnumbering those that are reinforced especially with variable ratio schedules. Cockerels may turn out to be skilled in the kind of deception in which a Skinnerian indulges by withholding knowledge about which bar press will yield food during variable ratio reinforcement. Females experienced with male food calling behavior may be so effectively conditioned that they come to tolerate high rates of unreinforced approaches.

In the final analysis it must be acknowledged that definitive proof of the existence of intentionality and deception in animals is going to be unusually difficult to obtain. Disproving intentionality is, of course, no less elusive. As Griffin (1985) has so cogently and forcefully argued, it may be scientifically more productive to take the position of an agnostic than that of a skeptic because this is the stance most likely to lead to the creation of new, testable, and potentially illuminating hypotheses.

CONCLUSIONS

We have taken the position that, if a referential signal is optionally withheld in the absence of a suitable audience, this can be taken as evidence of an intention to communicate. The arguments we have presented fall short of proving the validity of this position. It can be argued that we are dealing with behavior that is essentially reflexive but with the complication that signallers are simultaneously responsive both to external referents for signal production and to aspects of concurrent social stimulation. If this argument is valid, there must be reflexive responsiveness to relatively subtle features of a companion such as species, gender, and age. As yet there is no evidence of responsiveness to the behavior of audiences. If evidence should be forthcoming that, for example, a signaller perseveres with alarm calling more with an apparently unreactive audience than with an aroused and fearful one, this could be taken as evidence of intentional communication (Bates, 1976a, 1976b). A reflexive interpretation of the very same phenomena is, however, conceivable. Similarly, with the view of food calling without food as a case of deception, this could be reinterpreted as a reflexive, hard-wired reaction triggered by separation from the mate. Information on the developmental plasticity of audience effects is urgently needed. Until it is available, we have to admit that virtually any "intentional" scenario is potentially reinterpretable in reflexive terms if one is ready to multiply the number of reflexes impinging on signal production. Perhaps it is time to begin to explore the possibility that all aspects of intentionality can be encompassed by reflexive models, as an alternative to cognitive interpretations?

Conversely, there is no evidence to exclude the hypothesis that chickens possess the cognitive capacity to make judgments about the appropriateness of a perceived receiver for a given signal. In our present state of knowledge this remains a valid alternative to reflexive interpretations of the audience effect (Griffin, 1984, 1985). Studies of the ontogeny of audience effects on signal production will be critical in distinguishing between these alternatives.

Regardless of how questions about intentions to communicate in animals are resolved, the data on audience effects demonstrate that birds signalling in the presence of an environmental referent are unexpectedly responsive to the presence and nature of their companions. Responses to the same referent differ from one communicative context to another. Thus, effects of the social context upon referent-dependent signal production in animals open up a novel array of unusually sensitive behavioral assays, both for the quantitative measurement of responsiveness to companions and their behavior and for exploring the nature of the social networks that exist between members of a group.

REFERENCES

Baeumer, E. (1962). Lebensart des Haushuhns, dritter Teil, uber seine Laute und allgemeine Erganzungen [Lifestyle of the domestic chicken, part three, on vocalizations and general characteristics]. *Zeitschrift fur Tierpsychologie, 19,* 394–416.

Bates, E. (1976a). *Language and context: The acquisition of pragmatics.* New York: Academic Press.

Bates, E. (1976b). Intentions, conventions and symbols. In E. Bates (Ed.), *The emergence of symbols: Cognition and communication in infancy* (pp. 33–68). New York: Academic Press.

Bennett, J. (1976). *Linguistic behaviour.* Cambridge: Cambridge University Press.

Cheney, D. L., & Seyfarth, R. M. (1982). How vervet monkeys perceive their grunts: Field playback experiments. *Animal Behaviour, 30,* 739–751.

Cheney, D. L., & Seyfarth, R. M. (1985). Vervet monkey alarm calls: Manipulation through shared information? *Behaviour, 94,* 150–166.

Churchland, P. S. (1983). Dennett's instrumentalism: A frog at the bottom of the mug. *Behavioral and Brain Sciences, 6,* 358–359.

Collias, N. E (1987). The vocal repertoire of the red junglefowl: A spectrographic classification and the code of communication. *Condor, 89,* 510–524.

Collias, N. E., & Collias, E. C. (1967). A field study of the red jungle fowl in North-central India. *Condor, 69,* 360–386.

Collias, N. E., & Joos, M. (1953). The spectrographic analysis of sound signals of the domestic fowl. *Behaviour, 5,* 176–188.

Dennett, D. (1981). Three kinds of intentional psychology. In R. Healey (Ed.), *Reductionism, time and reality.* Cambridge: Cambridge University Press.

Dennett, D. C. (1983). Intentional systems in cognitive ethology: The "Panglossian paradigm" defended. *Behavioral and Brain Science, 6,* 343–390.

Gouzoules, S., Gouzoules, H., & Marler, P. (1984). Rhesus monkey (*Macaca mulatta*) screams: Representational signalling in the recruitment of agonistic aid. *Animal Behaviour, 32,* 182-193.

Griffin, D. R. (1981). *The question of animal awareness.* New York: Rockefeller University Press.

Griffin, D. R. (1984). *Animal Thinking.* Cambridge, Mass., Harvard University Press.

Griffin, D. R. (1985). Animal consciousness. *Neuroscience and Biobehavioral Reviews, 9,* 615-622.

Guyomarc'h, J. C. (1962). Contribution a l'etude du comportement vocal du Poussin de *Gallus domesticus* [Contribution to the study of the vocal behavior of the chicken, *Gallus domesticus.*] *Journal Psychologie norm et Pathologie,* 283-305.

Guyomarc'h, J. C. (1966). Les emissions sonores du Poussin domestique, leur place dans le comportement normal [Acoustic signals of the domestic chicken, and their role in normal behavior.] *Zeitschrift fur Tierpsychologie, 23,* 141-160.

Guyomarc'h, J. C. (1974). Le role de l'experience sur la semantique du cri d'offrance chez le poussin [The role of experience in the semanticity of the food call of the chicken.] *Revue Comparatif. Animaux. 9,* 219-236.

Gyger, M., Karakashian, S. J., Dufty, A. M. Jr., & Marler, P. (1988). Alarm signals in birds; the role of testosterone. *Hormones and Behavior, 23,* 305-314.

Gyger, M., Karakashian, S., & Marler, P. (1986). Avian alarm calling: Is there an audience effect? *Animal Behaviour, 34,* 1570-1572.

Gyger, M., & Marler, P. (1988). Food calling in the domestic fowl (*Gallus gallus*): The role of external referents and deception. *Animal Behaviour, 36,* 358-365.

Gyger, M., Marler, P., & Pickert, R. (1987). Semantics of an avian alarm call system: The male domestic fowl, *Gallus domesticus. Behaviour, 102,* 13-40.

Hughes, M. K., Hughes, A. L., & Covalt-Dunning, D. (1982). Stimuli eliciting food calling in domestic chickens. *Applied Animal Ethology, 8,* 543-550.

Karakashian, S. J., Gyger, M., & Marler, P. (1988). Audience effects on alarm calling in chickens (*Gallus gallus*). *Journal of Comparative Psychology, 102,* 129-135.

Klump, G. M., & Shalter, M. D. (1984). Acoustic behavior of birds and mammals in the predator context. (Parts I & II). *Zeitschrift fur Tierpsychologie, 66,* 189-226.

Konishi, M. (1963). The role of auditory feedback in the vocal behavior of the domestic fowl. *Zeitschrift fur Tierpsychologie, 20,* 349-367.

Kruijt, J. P. (1964). Ontogeny of social behaviour in Burmese red junglefowl (*Gallus gallus spadiceus*) Bonaterre. *Behaviour Supplement, 12,* 1-201.

Marler, P. (1955). Characteristics of some animal calls. *Nature* (London), *176,* 1-6.

Marler, P. (1985). Representational vocal signals of primates. *Fortschritte der Zoologie, 31,* 211-221.

Marler, P., Dufty, A., & Pickert, R. (1986a). Vocal communication in the domestic chicken: I. Does a sender communicate information about the quality of a food referent to a receiver? *Animal Behaviour, 34,* 188-193.

Marler, P., Dufty, A., & Pickert, R. (1986b). Vocal communication in the domestic chicken: II. Is a sender sensitive to the presence and nature of a receiver? *Animal Behaviour, 34,* 194-198.

Premack, D. (1986). *Gavagai! or The Future History of the Animal Language Controversy.* Cambridge, MA: M.I.T Press.

Premack, D., & Premack, A. J. (1983). *The mind of an ape.* New York: W. W. Norton & Co.

Premack, D., & Woodruff, G. (1978). Does the chimpanzee have a theory of mind? *Behavioural Brain Science, 4,* 515-526.

Roitblat, H. L. (1983). Intentions and adaptations. *Behavioral Brain Science, 6,* 375.

Schleidt, W. M. (1961). Reaktionen von Truthuhnern auf fliegende Raubvogel und Versuche zur Analyse ihrer AAM's [Responses of turkeys to flying raptors and experiments on the analysis of their innate release mechanisms.] *Zeitschrift fur Tierpsychologie, 18,* 534–560.

Searle, J. (1983). *Intentionality: An essay on the philosophy of mind.* Cambridge: Cambridge University Press.

Seyfarth, R. M. (1986). Vocal communication and its relation to language. In B. B. Smuts, D. L. Cheney, R. M. Seyfarth, R. W. Wrangham, & T. Struhsaker (Eds.), *Primate societies* (pp. 440–451) Chicago: Chicago University Press.

Seyfarth, R. M., Cheney, D. L., & Marler, P. R. (1980). Vervet monkey alarm calls: Semantic communication in a free-ranging primate. *Science, 210,* 801–803.

Sherry, D. F. (1977). Parental food calling and the role of the young in the Burmese red junglefowl *(Gallus gallus spadiceus). Animal Behaviour, 25,* 594–601.

Stokes, A. W. (1971). Parental and courtship feeding in red jungle fowl. *Auk, 88,* 21–29.

Sullivan, K. (1985). Selective alarm calling by downy woodpeckers in mixed-species flocks. *Auk, 102,* 184–187.

Thompson, N. S., & Mitchell, D. (1987). *Deception.* NY: SUNY at Albany Press.

Woodruff, G., & Premack, D. (1979). Intentional communication in the chimpanzee: The development of deception. *Cognition, 7,* 333–362.

9 ANIMAL COMMUNICATION AND THE STUDY OF COGNITION

W. John Smith
University of Pennsylvania

ABSTRACT

Information provides the basis for anticipating and dealing actively with events. Communicating animals both provide and respond to specially packaged information yielding particularly useful clues to their mental operations. This chapter examines features of communication and cognition that raise problems for designing and interpreting research. First, animals' signals can provide information about a signaller's behavior, identity, and external stimuli to which it is responding. Attempts to understand both mental and social processes are impeded if this diversity of information is not considered or if behavioral information is underestimated or confounded with information about "affect" or "arousal". Second, in moment-by-moment responding animals must continuously select among signals and other stimuli and rank them as focal or contextual. Animals probably generate predictive scenarios based on both current and stored information and compare and select among competing scenarios as events develop. The presence of expected information may lead quickly to "typical case" judgments, but its absence could engender "worst case" predictions. Experimental control of contextual sources of information can create circumstances in which stored information (often not controllable) gains heightened influence. Because context-dependent responding is complex and flexible, investigators must be especially careful in considering the kinds and sources of information that are involved.

Many contributors to this volume have pursued Griffin's suggestion (e.g., 1976, 1985) that behavior involved in communicative events should provide perhaps our most ready access to the mental experiences of nonhuman animals. The behavior of both signallers and individuals responding to signals can indeed provide clues about how individuals represent to themselves the information they process during communication. However, interpreting these clues is a difficult challenge.

Evidence provided in this volume bears significantly on both issues that are fundamental to gaining understanding of how cognitive processes operate in communicating. On the one hand, we need to discover certain basic features of signalling: both how individuals select formalized signals to perform and what their signals "are about"—the referents of signals. On the other hand, we also need to discover how recipients of signalled information devise their responses to it. This issue is not independent of the preceding because the cognitive bases of responding to signals cannot be understood without knowledge of all the kinds of information each signal makes available. The issue is made more complex because responding is context-dependent. Many kinds of information from many sources must be selected, attended to, ranked, and dealt with together by an individual when formulating a response to a signal.

In this chapter I discuss issues of both performing and responding to formalized signals (i.e., to acts specialized to make information available, hereafter simply termed signals). A principal aim is to promote more awareness of methodological and conceptual limitations that restrict the conclusions we can draw from certain kinds of research. For instance, interpretations have been proposed in which individual animals bias, perhaps intentionally, their use of signalling to different "audiences" in order to inform, withhold information from, or even mislead those other individuals. These proposals require the referents of the signals in question to be food or predators (see section on Selective Signalling). If the referents are (or include) behavior, then the interpretations are not likely to be applicable, and in these cases there are reasonable candidates for behavioral referents. Investigation has been hampered, however, by misunderstandings of the ways in which signalling acts correlate with and provide information about other actions of signalling individuals, by a confounding of information about behavior with that about the internal states of signallers, and by a tendency to experiment with responses to signals before completing sufficient research on the signalling individuals. These experiments can be powerful, but their limitations must be understood. Part of the problem arises in underestimating the complexities of context-dependent responding to signals including the use of information from experience (i.e., information stored in memory). Animals responding to signals appear to use information from many sources, and in formulating and testing predictive scenarios they may employ cognitive operations of appreciable complexity.

SIGNALLING

Research on cognition has focused in part on the conditions under which animals signal. Conditions have been construed primarily in terms of stimuli that elicit signalling or of the presence, absence, and behavior of different individuals that could be affected by the signalled information. A major goal of this research has been to understand the extent to which signallers behave selectively. Another goal has been to ask to what extent nonhuman signalling is "symbolic" or emotive, and this has required investigation of referents of signalling. In some papers, behavioral referents have been confounded with or reduced to information about internal states, for example, when seeking to show (via experiments on responses to playback of recorded vocalizations) that external referents have primacy.

Selective Signalling

To what extent do animals have the flexibility to alter their signalling so as to affect other individuals' responses? Griffin has proposed that signallers might sometimes choose which of their signals to perform, selecting them in accordance with the effects each can have.

There are examples of interspecific signalling being adjusted with respect to its effects. For instance, Pepperberg (1981, 1987, this volume) has shown that, at least for English words taught to a parrot in a socially rewarding situation, the parrot has the flexibility to choose among signals. Certain species of birds and snakes have been shown to have selective control over aspects of signalling done toward predators. Plovers (Ristau, this volume) monitor a human near their eggs or chicks and adjust the directions in which they move while performing "distraction displays" such that the responding human is led away. Plovers also adjust the intensity of their actions on the basis of experience with different humans. Hognose snakes monitor the attentiveness of humans who attack them and choose when to terminate their "death-feigning" performances (Burghardt, this volume).

Choice might also be seen if an individual determined whether it signaled in accordance with the presence, absence, or identity of a second individual. "Audience" effects of this sort have been reported in recent work both on vervets and on what are termed "alarm" and "food" calls of domestic fowl. However, the results are subject to more than one interpretation. What appears to be flexibility in these cases may simply be a product of our incomplete understanding of the referents of the signals. That is, it is possible that the signals refer less to predators or food than to behavior the signaller may perform—behavior that differs in probability as interactions are accommodated to different companions. If so, different audiences may not elicit choices about whether to signal. To explain this possibility it is necessary to develop, briefly, a couple of examples.

First, domestic fowl and their jungle fowl ancestors (Collias, 1987; Collias & Collias 1967, 1985; Stokes & Williams, 1971) utter what has been termed a food call as part of a signalling act known as "tidbitting." In experiments with this signalling, Marler, Dufty, and Pickert (1986a) report that the probability of a male with a mealworm uttering the call was affected by other birds: If an unfamiliar rather than a familiar female were present, he was more likely to call, and he would not call in the presence of a male. Further, males called in 67% of the trials in which the only stimulus was a nonfood item; a hen approached in 46% of these cases (Marler, Dufty, & Pickert, 1986b). Marler's interpretation (this volume; Marler et al., 1986b) is that cockerels choose whether to call depending on their audience and may even intentionally choose to deceive, particularly strange females, when no food is present. Both conclusions depend on the assumption that food is the referent of the call.

An alternative possibility is that certain foods, although not necessary, can contribute to satisfying the set of conditions for calling; there may be at least three conditions. Based on descriptions by Stokes and Williams (1971), Collias and Collias (1985), Collias (1987) and others, these are: (a) the sight of an appropriate audience or the sound of another individual uttering this call; (b) some spatial separation between the signaller and its audience; and (c) a feature that keeps the signaller from going to its audience but may not interfere with attracting that audience. This last feature can be positive (e.g., the signaller finds a site with special food and stays there) or negative (e.g., an intervening territorial boundary or the presence of a competitor near the appropriate audience individual). The restraining feature appears to be centrally involved in the "courtship" functions of the signal, which depend on attracting a female to come to a male. (The signal has other functions, in other kinds of events, and all may depend on eliciting approach.)

The consistent correlates of this call may be behavioral. The accounts mention some behavior that is typical of an individual who calls: (a) It stays where it is while calling; (b) it interacts with an individual who joins it (the interaction can take various forms, not including attack); and (c) it may peck at food or other small items if these are present, but will not ingest them during a bout of calling. Thus the call appears to make available information predicting that a calling individual will interact in some positive way with an individual who joins it, although it will not (at least while calling) move to join another individual. (Note that all these predictions are about the caller's *own* behavior, not about the behavior of individuals who may respond.) As with all other animal signals, the predictions of behavior are conditional. That is, what occurs depends on how each event develops, much of which depends on what other participants do.

Under this interpretation, information about food may be made available less by the call itself than by a recipient's memory of experiences in which it was shown and given access to food by a bird who was uttering the call. Whether food or a set of behavior patterns is the referent cannot be resolved on the existing evidence. Food is not a consistent correlate (although perhaps it is of some as yet undescribed variant form of the call). Possible behavioral correlates need more thorough study, and the full range of circumstances within which the call is uttered needs to be considered.

If the call's referents are (or include) behavior patterns, however, when an individual is not likely to perform such behavior it will not utter the call. If that behavior is performed relative to other individuals (e.g., by foregoing approach and yet interacting nonaggressively with them should they approach), then different classes of individuals will elicit the call with different frequencies. Males might not elicit it at all, and females who are not socially bonded to the signaller might elicit it more readily than his mates would.

This is not what has been implied by the term "audience effect", which prejudges the issue. Instead, whether the call is uttered may depend not on an individual's appraisal of the effects calling may have on some other individual's behavior, but on the ways the signaller itself may behave. If the call's referents are behavioral, assessment of effect need not be invoked to explain different propensities to signal in the presence of different individuals.

A second, potentially simpler example involves "alarm calls" of male domestic fowl. These are uttered more in the presence of an audience individual than when a lone cockerel sees danger (Gyger, Karakashian, & Marler, 1986). The authors interpret this difference as evidence that a signaller chooses whether to call (Marler, this volume). That interpretation depends on the assumption that the referent of this vocalization is indeed a predator.

An untested possibility is that the referent is or includes a set of behavior patterns of the signaller. For instance, suppose that a fowl on perceiving a source of danger must choose between fleeing and freezing. A lone individual might do well to freeze, but a cock with an unalerted companion nearby would be at risk if the latter's movements gave away their position. Such a companion should bias the cock more toward fleeing instead of freezing. If the danger were distant and the cock did not flee immediately, it might well vacillate. At this point it might call. This hypothetical construction of the event is basically an elaboration of the *cave* postulate of Dawkins (1976).

By this conjecture, the call has as referents freezing, fleeing, and behaving indecisively (e.g., vacillating and similar behavior, see Smith, 1977: 106–108). Only one such act can occur at a time, and they are listed here in increasing order of their probability of being performed by a signaller after it calls—if the situation does not change. Freezing could become the most probable again if the cock's companion froze or fleeing if the companion fled: The predictions would be conditional.

A companion of either gender should elicit these calls from a cock when danger appears just as Gyger et al., 1986 found. A hen, much more camouflaged than a cock, might almost always be biased much more toward freezing if she saw a passing predator and thus would rarely call— again as was found.

Do cocks and hens behave as suggested here? The best way to detect the correlates that imply behavioral referents is not to make suppositions about what they might be and then test for them but first to observe signallers: to see what fowl do when uttering an alarm or food call. Detailed observation of signallers' behavior is often not an easy task because (a) behavioral correlates are conditional, (b) there are probabilistic relations among the several correlates of any one signal (see Smith, 1977: 127–133), and (c) the kinds of behavior that correlate may not fit our preconceptions and thus may not be immediately recognizable. Preconceived categories of behavior must be questioned continuously and modified or replaced as necessary, and a considerable range of events must be studied. Nonetheless, inferences cannot safely be made about conscious, perhaps manipulative use of signalling without understanding what information is being signalled (or withheld). Any attempt to identify the referents of signals must encompass all reasonable possibilities and explore a full range of alternative explanations of results before it can be used as a basis for investigating cognitive processes.

The Referents of Animal Signalling

Each formalized signal has multiple referents: (a) several kinds of behavior (plus their probabilities and other variables), (b) physical characteristics of the signaller (e.g., its species and other identities), and (c) for some signals, external stimuli to which the signaller is responding. To explore cognitive processes in communicating, or the possibility of deceptive signalling, an ethologist must usually be aware of most or all of the referents of a signal. This requires considerable effort to discover the nature and range of what correlates with performing that signal.

Evidence for each behavioral correlate of a signal may require the most prolonged effort because it develops only after signallers have been observed repeatedly. The behavior can defy accurate description and categorization until it has been seen in many kinds of events. The probabilistic and conditional features of each correlation cannot be grasped without benefit of many and diverse examples. However, if an external stimulus such as a predator or resource is a referent of a signal, then whenever the signal occurs the signaller should have detected the stimulus. (It is assumed that vervets, for instance, do not use their "leopard" call "conversationally". Additionally, in practice it is necessary to allow for inevitable mistakes by signallers in their perception of stimuli. In some cases it may also be necessary to allow for a realistically low level of deceptive intraspecific signalling, but this problem is only beginning to be explored.) The very high correlation between signal and stimulus should make external referents more evident, and perhaps more readily testable, than are behavioral referents.

The search for behavioral referents of signals is being conducted differently in different studies, particularly in cases in which analyses are focused on external correlates of signalling. For instance, in some cases, each category of signal has been found to provide information both about external stimuli to which a signaller is responding and also about the signaller's fleeing, monitoring, approach, and other behavior (Owings & Leger, 1980, working with variant forms of the chatter of California ground squirrels). In yet other cases, attempts have been made either to show that external referents are primary (i.e., are more significant to animals responding to the signal than is information about signaller behavior, see Gouzoules, Gouzoules, & Marler, 1984, 1985) or to suggest that because no single class of behavior such as fleeing inevitably accompanies the signal, "the" referent is external (Gouzoules et al., 1985:85).

Several problems appear in the latter attempts. Misunderstandings over the relations between signals and their behavioral correlates have led to confusion over symbolic and emotive uses of signalling. Related to this problem, information about behavior has sometimes been confounded with (or inappropriately reduced to) information about internal states. Further, experiments have concentrated on the responses animals make to signals, using these responses as sufficient indicators of the primary kinds of information provided by those signals.

Animal Signals as "Symbols"

The referents of animals' signals can be variously categorized. For example, they may be viewed as comprising signalers' behavior or physical characteristics or as external stimuli to which signallers are responding. A different sort of categorization has been an attempt (e.g., Gouzoules, et al., 1985, Marler 1984, Seyfarth, Cheney, & Marler 1980a) to clarify cognitive representations by distinguishing between "symbolic" and "affective" uses of signals (better: symbolic vs. emotive, see Ogden & Richards, 1946). In human communication, symbolic use involves signalling about referents per se, whether these are behavior patterns, physical characteristics, or external stimuli. Human emotive use, on the other hand, involves signals less for informing about referents than as devices for what Ogden and Richards termed evoking feelings and attitudes—closely akin to what traditional ethologists called the "releasing" of emotional states. In practice, both uses of signalling can occur simultaneously because individuals can have emotional responses to symbols.

Many ethologists working with the communication of at least vertebrate animals have recognized limitations both of the releaser concept and of current understanding of emotional (affective) states, and they have found it useful to concentrate largely or wholly on symbolic signalling. Why, then, should the issue of distinguishing symbolic from emotive signalling (which can be viewed both as an issue of referents and of the ways in which recipients of signals respond) arise so recently? The reasons seem to lie both in misunderstandings of the relationships between signals and their behavioral referents and in a failure to realize that a behavioral referent is not just a transform of a motivational or affective state. Involvement of such states in communication might entail considerable emotive use of signals, but providing information about behavior patterns employs animal signals as symbols.

There is some basic misunderstanding over just what the relation is between formalized signals, such as displays, and those other actions of a signaller that are referents of signals. The problem can be seen in a criterion put forth by Marler (1984): "If an alarm call is truly a referential symbol it should be potentially dissociable from acts of fleeing" (p. 354). By dissociable he meant that an individual uttering a call would not always flee. In fact, individuals do not always flee after calling—not just in the case of vervets but in ground squirrels and, indeed, in *any* well-studied case of which I am aware. Fleeing is simply one of several options that become predictable from such a call. Other options may include pausing to monitor or continuing with a previous activity that was interrupted by calling; the particular conditions of each event determine whether escape, monitoring, or some other alternative follows calling (Smith, 1977, 1985). No single class of behavior occurs as the exclusive and inevitable correlate of a signal.

Far from being exceptional, the relation Marler's criterion requires is perhaps universal. It appears that few or no animal signals have one-to-one correlations between their performance and the occurrence of any of their behavioral referents. They cannot. Signals are usually performed while a signaller is selecting among alternative courses of action and, as a result, each signal correlates with more than one kind of behavior. A signal permits prediction of various alternative actions each with a probability of occurring that is relative to the probability of each of the others (Smith, 1977 e.g. pp. 87 and 106–108, plus numerous examples in chapters 3 through 5; the work of ethologists making motivational analyses also supports this conclusion, see chapter 8 and also Hinde, 1985a, 1985b). Which of a signal's behavioral referents is most likely to appear in any particular event can be predicted only approximately without information obtained from sources contextual to the signal, and even then predictions fail if conditions change. Thus, the idea of "severing . . . the link between alarm call and escape behavior" (Seyfarth, Cheney, & Marler 1980a, Seyfarth & Cheney, 1982, Gouzoules et al., 1985:85) is unrealistic. There was no simple one-to-one link to be severed.

Until recently, most of what ethologists learned about the correlates of signalling was about behavior. The main exception was the information supplied about resources by honey bees in their dancing. Nonetheless, external referents were not thought to be unlikely in principle (Smith, 1977:73–74). The literature contained various supposed examples of food calls, hawk alarm calls, and the like. Although there was a dearth of adequately detailed studies, recent work is more convincing. External referents have been studied by Owings and Leger (1980), Seyfarth, Cheney, and Marler (1980a, 1980b), Gouzoules et al. (1984), Dittus (1984) and others, although not all studies are fully definitive.

Does demonstration of correlations between formalized signals and classes of predators or resources imply the discovery of symbolic signaling? No. Symbolic signalling has been shown over and again by demonstration of signals with behavioral referents. Recognizing external referents can add to our understanding of the kinds of information about which animals signal, but it is a fundamental mistake to claim that all of our previous knowledge has been simply about emotive communication. The mistake hinges upon a confounding of information about behavior with that about internal state.

Behavior vs. Internal State

In presenting cases for the discovery of external referents (Seyfarth et al., 1980a, 1980b) or the primacy of such referents (Gouzoules et al., 1984, 1985), the authors assessed the possibility that the signals might also have behavioral correlates. The attempts were marred by the notion that behavioral correlates would entail emotive signalling, and the discussions confounded an individual's actions with the internal states that underlie behavior. This confounding has serious consequences (Smith, 1981) such as diverting attention from the ways in which signalling makes a signaller's behavior more predictable. The confusion also entangles behavioral analyses unnecessarily in constraints inherent in severe limitations of the current understanding of motivational states.

The error perhaps arose because in the earlier traditions of ethology, behavioral correlates of signalling were used predominantly as a basis for inferring underlying motivational (and sometimes just emotional) states. The practice still persists to some extent. Marler (e.g., 1984) has argued that most attempts to identify the emotional states of signallers have not been productive. (He did not deal with the broader issue of motivation, but the case is similar.) Griffin (1985) implied a comparable assessment in labelling this the "groans-of-pain" (p. 620) interpretation of animal signalling.

These criticisms are by no means new. Recognition of inadequacies of the traditional interpretation of signals was basic to the development of an approach that seeks to analyze the information made available by signalling. Neither Marler nor Griffin deals adequately with this "informational" alternative. It is as if turning away from motivational interpretations also requires disregarding the behavioral correlates of signalling. But there is abundant evidence for behavioral correlates. Signalling thus does make information available about the behavior of a signaller. In fact, information about behavior may account for most of the information provided by animal signals. To deal with its significance we need not interpret either motivational or emotional states of signallers.

Informational and motivational perspectives for research differ greatly and have been contrasted by Smith (1977: chapter 8, in which their compatibility is also evaluated). Both perspectives seek correlations between signalling acts and other behavior of signallers, but the results are interpreted differently (and the informational approach also seeks correlations other than behavioral). Motivational analyses ask Tinbergen's causal question about internal states of individual organisms. In this case: What are the immediate causes of signalling behavior? (Cognitive studies also ask this question but shift the focus from motivational states to mental processes.) In contrast, an informational analysis asks what the performance of a signal by one individual makes known or predictable to other individuals. For example: What classes of the signaller's behavior become conditionally predictable when a signal is performed, and how may each be enacted (e.g., how intensely, how stably, in what direction, and with what probability relative to the others). Questions about information and predictability seek to understand what signalling contributes to the organization and running of social interactions. That is, they address social mechanisms rather than the internal workings of individuals.

In the extreme, confounding behavior with internal states takes the following form. First, because behavior is (by definition) motivated, the argument implies that analyses of the information made available about behavioral correlates of signals are nothing more than analyses of motivational causes of signalling and should be reduced to them. Yet the interpretation of signals in terms of their behavioral referents is no more "motivational" than is the interpretation of external referents. Both are attempts to understand the information that can be gleaned from a signal's performance. Neither is directly concerned with the internal states and processes of signalling individuals, even though either can be used in studies of internal mechanisms.

Second, after inappropriately reducing behavior to motivation, the narrower terms "affect" and "emotion" have been substituted (e.g., Green & Marler, 1979; Marler, 1984; Seyfarth, 1984; Seyfarth et al., 1980a). Smith (1985:57–58) has argued that this narrowing of focus from motivation to emotion is inappropriate even for causal analyses. Third, "arousal", a visceral state presumed to underlie emotions, has then been substituted for affect (and all these interpretations even erroneously attributed to me). Proponents of this argument contend that if different signals provide different information about affect, then they must also differ in the level of arousal that underlies each. Tests are then used to show that signals do not differ predictably in the level of arousal they elicit from responders (e.g., Gouzoules, et al., 1985). Note that the tests shift the focus from signallers to responders. These tests, however, do not bear on the initial point of comparing behavioral with external referents. The whole line of argument has gone far astray.

Postulates that signals simply or primarily reflect different levels of arousal are not remotely adequate to account either for the known richness of the behavior correlated with signals (Smith, 1977) or for the complex ways in which signals differ from one another in their sets of behavioral correlates (*message assortment,* p. 176–180). Even supplemental information that signals provide about the "intensity" with which their behavioral referents may be performed (ibid.:133–134) is much more complex than implied by "level of arousal." (Intensity measures differ for different acts and signals, and they need not all vary concordantly: A movement performed with great vigor may nonetheless be incomplete.) Thus, reduction of behavioral referents to any notion as simplistic as levels of arousal is not realistic. It is not appropriate to claim that behavioral referents are secondary or questionable simply because no correlations with arousal levels (of signallers or responders) can be demonstrated.

Responses as Criteria for Primacy of Referents

Gouzoules, Gouzoules, and Marler (1984, 1985:81–82) offered the suggestion that "An external referent is the primary information conveyed . . ." (p. 81) by a signal if, in the absence of all controllable contextual sources of information, individuals can respond as if informed of this referent. But a recipient of a signal should have much less uncertainty about external than behavioral referents. As previously argued, the former should occur whenever the signal does, whereas the latter are probabilistic and conditional: Each kind of behavior occurs in only some of the events in which a signal is used.

The real distinction may thus be less in primacy than in degree of certainty, and even that difference should not always be decisive in the real world. This is because it is reasonable to suppose that animals responding to signals may not use all of the information made available in any one event but may select (or give most weight to) that which appears most pertinent (Smith, 1977:288). Sometimes they may find that information about external referents is more relevant to them than is information about behavior, but they may also find the reverse.

For instance, imagine that a young vervet utters an "eagle alarm" call. Even if the call makes available information about both predators and the probable behavior of the signaller, a recipient with few other sources of information available about the immediate event might give priority to that about predators. Effectively assuming the worst, influenced both by recall of past events and by its inability to see the caller (and thus to be directed toward the alarm-evoking stimulus), it would flee. However, a recipient with others sources of information might treat the signal as if other referents were more salient. If the mother of the young vervet saw that a stork rather than an eagle had elicited the call, she might respond to information predicting that fleeing (to her or into bushes, Seyfarth & Cheney, 1986) is among the probable sequelae. She might then act to accommodate or fend off her child or restrain it before it disappeared unnecessarily into the bushes. These two recipients, differing in the information available to each from sources contextual to the signal, could find different referents the deciding factors in responding to the same event. Whether such flexibility exists to respond selectively to the multiple referents of a signal has yet to be tested.

The chief problem with using responses to signals as indicators of the information (or the salience of the information) made available by signalling is that responses to signals are always context-dependent. More information than that provided just by a signal is used in generating a response. This problem can affect even experiments in which contextual sources of information are minimized as is discussed in the subsequent paragraphs.

What are the Referents of Signals?

It appears that both behavioral and external referents will continue to be found, at least sometimes, both kinds in the same signal. External referents may continue to be found primarily for signals performed when the signallers or the referents are distant from appropriate recipients of the information (Smith, 1986:316), that is, in conditions in which those recipients are least likely to detect the external stimuli themselves. Even then, it is possible that information about external issues may often come not from signals but from sources contextual to them. Behavioral referents may continue to be the more common class revealing private information that can be important to the management of social interactions. Only further research will tell.

Definitive interpretation of the referents of animals' signals may be no more practical than are definitive lexical definitions of the words of our languages. This may not be a serious limitation, however. We need only be sufficiently precise to be able to distinguish among important alternatives. We get by in speech with fuzzy definitions; there are costs, but we can usually make our communication work. That we should need a superior understanding of other species in order to study their cognitive processes seems unlikely.

An admonition I made earlier remains fundamentally important. To the extent that we focus on single classes of correlates of any display (e.g., on an external stimulus or on a single kind of behavior), we will have only a "grossly oversimplified" understanding of that signal's informative potential (Smith, 1977, p. 87). Certainly particular correlates can be studied in isolation, but the limits of what can be concluded from such work must be clearly recognized.

If these limits are underestimated, attempts to understand cognitive mechanisms will founder. This is the point: Until we can learn the full range of information that signals contribute, we can understand neither the cognitive bases of social communicating nor subtopics of current interest such as the extent and nature of deceptive misinforming.

At this stage it appears that we need to reach fuller agreement on necessary and productive research procedures, both observational and experimental, and on the interpretation of observational and experimental evidence. It would also be enormously helpful to come to general agreement on basic terminology. Such key words as meaning, response, context, and others are each employed in more than one way, and this generates confusion.

RESPONDING TO SIGNALS

There remains the second part of the problem of studying cognitive aspects of communicating: to understand how a recipient of a signal devises its responses. In this we must deal with several issues: (a) the sources of information available to recipients, (b) the ways in which recipients may construct mental scenarios, (c) the information that recipients take from each source, and (d) the nature and limits of what we are learning from the study of their observable responses.

Sources of Information

For the last couple of decades, vertebrate ethologists have largely eschewed oversimplified models in which the responses of recipients are "released" by the advent of a signal. The releaser concept implies that a signal acts on responding individuals by evoking particular mental states that set in motion preordained behavior. This may account for some behavior during ontogeny and in other stark highly constrained cases. But most responding is based on more information than that provided just by a signal. As a single source of information, however pertinent, a signal is too limited. In practice, responding animals also attend to information from other sources that are contextual to the signal.

Some of these sources are things that occur when the signal occurs. A vocalizing animal can often be seen as well as heard, for instance, and its visible orientations, movements, and other actions are sources of information contextual to its vocal signalling. One way in which such concurrent sources of information can be experimentally controlled is to eliminate them, as Seyfarth and Cheney (this volume) did by hiding their playback speaker from the sight of the vervet monkeys they were studying. This procedure has its drawbacks (see subsequent paragraphs), but for questions of the sort Seyfarth and Cheney were testing, it is both convenient and useful.

Other crucial sources of information are not concurrent with the signal, however. These are the traces of earlier events (Smith, 1965, 1977). They are part of history and brought to events as memories by responding individuals. Experienced individuals may bring a great deal of information to bear on specific episodes in which a signal is perceived. They may, for instance, know what responses have usually been effective to the signals they most commonly encounter. They also know their companions' idiosyncratic predilections and can bias responding to account for these. They must have considerable knowledge of familiar events and probably organize this cognitively, as humans do, in "generalized event representations" (Nelson, 1981). Any adult ground squirrel, primate, or bird has encountered and responded to the signals of its repertoires many, many times. It would not be surprising if, for any signal, such an individual could predict (in some sense) a number of possible events and rank them by their relative probabilities of occurring and by the potential costs of predicting wrongly. It should do this whether the signal's referents are behavioral, external, or both and should then act on its predictions in ways that have usually been appropriate within its experience.

Information sources of this stored class, "historical" sources, often are not recognized in experiments that seek to control what is loosely called "context". As one result, the sources of the information used by individuals responding to a signal are not fully teased apart, and information from experience is misinterpreted as being supplied by the signal itself. More information thus gets attributed to a signal than the signal may supply. Yet to understand the cognitive bases of responding to signals we must understand just what information animals obtain from each source because they are free to choose which sources they attend to. To estimate incorrectly the information supplied by any source confounds attempts to use the behavior of communicating as a means of studying cognition.

In taking into account that responding to a signal is done in the context of information from various sources, however, we should not overestimate the complexity of information processing in any one event. Although everything in the world is informative, if perceived, no individual can deal with so much information. Animals must be selective both in what sources they attend to and in what information they accept as they assess events. Further, as studies of perception have shown, some stimulus must be selected to be focal amid the attended array of stimuli at any moment. (Signals must often become focal stimuli simply because such formalized acts performed by conspecific individuals are more likely to be pertinent to an individual than are many other sources of information; see Smith 1977:207, 459.) Nonfocal contextual sources must be dealt with in accordance with the relevance of the information they contribute and to the extent to which an individual has the processing capacity to work with them.

Formulating Predictive Scenarios

If information is richly available from both concurrent and historical sources, how might animals use it in responding to signals? How do their minds work? For the most complex functioning, we can follow Griffin's suggestion and formulate a tentative proposal based on our own mental processes.

An individual animal presumably collects information and assesses its circumstances continuously. It must always seek to anticipate the unfolding of whatever events can be significant for it (Smith, 1977:2, 193). To cope, the individual should compare the relevant information it gleans from various sources with expectations that it can base on both its current situation and its store of information. The results of these comparisons should be used in two ways. First, the individual should assess how closely its current circumstances fit the expectations upon which it has just been operating. From this evaluation it can fine-tune or alter its current grasp of the situation and the potential implications. Second, the individual should continue to generate further predictions and should use these both to guide its behavior moment-by-moment and to provide a perspective within which it can organize yet further information as it comes.

There is growing evidence that humans operate this way. We organize and store information about the usual progression of events, using cognitive structures that have been termed "scripts" (Schank & Abelson, 1977) or "memory organization packets" (Schank, 1982). This involves us in constructing "generalized event representations" for classes of events that have recurrent patterns, and we use these representations in particular episodes to predict development and to guide our behavior (Nelson, 1986). What I am calling a "predictive scenario" is simply a specific projection tailored to a particular episode and derived from generalized expectations about events with which that episode can be classed. Even very young children construct almost flawless generalized representations for familiar events suggesting that "such sequencing ability is an innate property of the human cognitive system" (Nelson, 1986, p. 241). If such children have this cognitive capacity, then animals of other species—all sharing the same need to anticipate unfolding events every waking moment of their lives—may have something very similar.

An individual's ability to respond flexibly to uncertain events is enhanced if competing predictions are generated simultaneously, to be chosen among as events develop. That is, whenever possible, an individual should entertain multiple working hypotheses about the nature and future course of its circumstances. As prediction emerges from among competing scenarios, an individual can assess a confidence level: Does available information support primarily one prediction, or is there important ambiguity and risk? Judgments about the significance of missing information must be made. Is it acceptable for certain information to be missing in the circumstances, or is its absence unexpected and troublesome? If prediction cannot be sufficiently confident, a judgment must be made whether to seek further information, go on to some other opportunity, or behave according to some preexisting program based on a class of scenarios. Among possible classes, a responding individual might invoke a "worst case" scenario and behave cautiously or preemptively unable to afford the possibility of dire consequences. Worst case scenarios must be especially likely to be chosen when events may involve predators or other severe dangers. More often, however, an individual might adopt a "typical case" scenario if experience suggests that it is encountering highly predictable kinds of events. Even with sparse information, responding might then be initiated on the basis of the most frequently encountered trend in a class of events (as suggested by Smith, 1985:68). Such responses would usually be appropriate and would be altered as further information warranted.

   The point of this speculation is to suggest a process in which information from numerous sources is actively integrated and compared with expectations that derive from both current and stored information. By following some simple rules that can be elaborated as experience is gained, an individual assesses and predicts events in preparing to respond to a signal. Experimental intervention at just one point in such a process might create problems with subsequent steps. For instance, minimizing the number of immediately available sources of information may violate expectations based on an individual's experience. If unable to obtain information that is usually present, a recipient of an experimentally presented signal may not make confident predictions. It may then search for information, fall back on a worst case scenario, or (if expecting little penalty) disregard the signal. On the other hand, experiments can also elicit responses that reveal stored information and show how animals organize it into a cognitive structure. By playing back screams of juveniles, for instance, Cheney and Seyfarth (1980) found that adult vervets associate different infants with the appropriate mothers and therefore understand at least basic behavioral relations of different mother-infant pairs.

Selecting Information

Among the implications of this process of context-dependent responding is that a recipient might respond to information only insofar as it fits the recipient's currently favored scenario. As in all perception, the responder would be selective in which sources of information it attends to, and it would discard some. Further, even for accepted sources, it might respond to only part of the information made available.

   Each signal with behavioral referents provides information about the conditional performance of not one but several kinds of behavior, including kinds that are incompatible with one another. The several messages of any such signal thus provide recipients with opportunity for considerable flexibility in selecting the information they take.

   Very simple examples include signals providing information about the conditional probabilities that a signaller will attack, vacillate or otherwise behave indecisively, or flee. Early in an encounter a recipient of such a signal may be interested primarily in whether it is about to be attacked or has some opportunity (dependent primarily upon the signaller's indecisive behavior) to negotiate. It might then largely disregard information about the probability of the signaller fleeing. As the encounter develops and the recipient becomes more experienced with its opponent, it might see that it can force at least a standoff. At this point it may become much more interested in information about the probability of the signaller withdrawing. Many other examples are easily imagined. One, with combinations of behavioral and external referents, is suggested in the section titled: The Referents of Animal Signalling. That example has the advantage of more than one individual responding to the same signal in the same event, making it possible to dissect the information underlying their different reactions.

Research on Responses

The responses animals make to signals, especially to playback of vocalizations, are currently one of the main foci of investigations of cognition. Although playback is a powerful procedure for influencing the scenarios animals form, it has some important limitations that are not widely recognized.

First, experimental control of sources of information contextual to the played-back sound is achieved largely by eliminating them (e.g., by hiding speakers). This forces animals to judge how to deal with the absence of information that would often be highly pertinent. Such circumstances may encourage wariness and may sometimes force individuals into extreme or atypical modes of responding.

Second, experimental control of much of the information stored in memory, historical context, is impractical.

Third, any signal that is presented provides several kinds of information, but the subjects respond only to some. Their responses provide few or no clues about what other information was made available. Responses made by recipients of signals often are not the most useful or definitive indicators of the referents of the signals and are too often used as such without adequate observation to determine the full correlates of signalling.

The study of responses to signals does reveal the outcome of the cognitive processes we would like to understand, because how animals respond depends on how they process the available information. Responses to playback of signals have also been used to reveal how animals have organized information they have accumulated through experience, for instance, information about who belongs with whom in the social order of their groups (e.g., Cheney & Seyfarth, 1980). However, the study of responses to signals as yet has revealed little that is readily interpreted about the processes themselves, although there are questions that can be addressed. For instance, Cheney and Seyfarth (in press) have used habituation to playback as an index of the extent to which vervets will classify together pairs of signals that have broadly similar external referents.

SUMMARY

Studying how animals signal and respond to signalling may become an important way to gain insight into the workings of nonhuman minds, but the task will be difficult. It will involve learning (a) the extent to which individuals can alter their signalling to affect other individuals' responses, (b) what information is made available by signalling and by sources contextual to signals, and (c) how recipients of signals devise their responses.

Evidence for selective use of signalling is appearing in work with learned signals for things and abstract concepts and in studies of injury-feigning. Experiments with what are termed audience effects are also promising but limited as yet by the need to consider whether external or behavioral referents better account for effects other individuals are seen to have on a signaller.

To study cognitive processes, it is often necessary to be clear about the full complement of information that an animal makes available with a signal. Behavioral referents, however, have not been adequately dealt with in some of the literature on cognition. They have, for instance, been confounded with (or inappropriately reduced to) motivational or emotional states. This has led to an attempt to distinguish between symbolic and emotive use of animal signals even though having behavioral referents qualifies signals as symbols. Further, demonstrations that different signals do not represent different levels of "arousal" have sometimes been used to imply that the signals may shed little light on behavior. But signals make various kinds of behavior predictable, a contribution that is obscured when behavior is interpreted simply as affect or general arousal. There has been an important loss of perspective here which seriously clouds our understanding of the kinds of information that are made available by animal signals.

Behavioral and external referents correlate differently with signals, and this has been one source of the confusion. External referents such as predators or resources are present when a signal is performed. In contrast, the several behavioral referents of each signal are less obvious to observers because each occurs only conditionally; most are alternatives to one another, and some have relatively low probabilities of being performed.

Using experimentally elicited responses to study signals' referents has also led to some misinterpretation. Because animals respond to signals in context, and because contextual sources of information cannot be fully eliminated, this procedure risks overinterpreting a signal's role. (Even the experimental reduction of contextual sources of information concurrent with a signal creates a special circumstance in which stored sources of information gain proportionately heightened influence over responding.) Alternatively, the various kinds of information that a signal provides may be underestimated if it is not realized that a given response could be due to more than one kind of information. The basic procedure for interpreting the referents of signals should not usually be the study of how animals respond to signals but observation of what correlates signals have in the behavior and physical characteristics of signallers and in the external stimuli that may elicit signalling.

Context-dependent responding probably entails at least capacities to: (a) attend to numerous sources of information and select among them, (b) select among kinds of information and rank them into focal and contextual, (c) develop predictive scenarios based on both current and stored (historical) information, and (d) compare and select among competing scenarios as events develop. Further, animals should in some sense have expectations of what information *should* be present in kinds of events they have experienced, and they should use these expectations in generating typical case and worst case scenarios as the bases for adaptive temporizing when available information does not yet support firm prediction.

Although these cognitive operations may be feasible with a limited set of rules, they also allow for considerable elaboration and flexibility, and for the development of judgmental procedures. This suggests that some complexity of cognitive processing (in the collating and winnowing of information from various sources, in the storing of generalized event representations, and in the sequence of steps used to construct and alter predictive scenarios) is probably a characteristic that is widespread among diverse nonhuman animals.

ACKNOWLEDGMENTS

I thank Don Griffin for being a friend and mentor for many years. For helpful comments on versions of the manuscript, I am indebted to D. Cheney, L. A. Draud, K. Kelley, A. Mostrom, C. Ristau, R. Seyfarth, A. M. Smith, R. Templeton, and especially D. Owings.

REFERENCES

Cheney, D. L., & Seyfarth, R. M. (1980). Vocal recognition in free-ranging vervet monkeys. *Animal Behavior, 28,* 362–367.

Cheney, D. L., & Seyfarth, R. M. (in press). Assessment of meaning and the detection of unreliable signals by vervet monkeys. *Animal Behavior.*

Collias, N. E. (1987). The vocal repertoire of the red junglefowl: A spectrographic classification and the code of communication. *Condor, 89,* 510–524.

Collias, N. E., & Collias, E. C. (1967). A field study of the Red Jungle Fowl in north-central India. *Condor, 69,* 360–386.

Collias, N. E., & Collias, E. C. (1985). Social behavior of unconfined Red Junglefowl. *Zoonooz, 58*(2), 4–10.

Dawkins, R. (1976). *The selfish gene.* New York: Oxford University Press.

Dittus, W. P. (1984). Toque macaque food calls: Semantic communication concerning food distribution in the environment. *Animal Behavior, 32,* 470–477.

Gouzoules, H., Gouzoules, S., & Marler, P. (1985). External reference and affective signaling in mammalian vocal communication. In G. Zivin (Ed.), *The development of expressive behavior: Biology-environment interactions* (pp. 77–101). New York: Academic Press.

Gouzoules, S., Gouzoules, H., & Marler, P. (1984). Rhesus monkey (*Macaca mulatta*) screams: Representational signalling in the recruitment of agonistic aid. *Animal Behavior, 32,* 182–193.

Green, S., & Marler, P. (1979). The analysis of animal communication. In P. Marler & J. G. Vandenbergh (Eds.), *Handbook of behavioral neurobiology: Vol. 3. Social behavior and communication* (pp. 73–158). New York: Plenum Press.

Griffin, D. R. (1976). *The question of animal awareness: Evolutionary continuity of mental experience.* New York: Rockefeller University Press.

Griffin, D. R. (1985). Animal consciousness. *Neuroscience and Biobehavioral Reviews, 9,* 615–622.

Gyger, M., Karakashian, S. J., & Marler, P. (1986). Avian alarm calling: Is there an audience effect? *Animal Behaviour, 34,* 1570–1572.

Hinde, R. A. (1985a). Was 'The Expression of the Emotions' a misleading phrase? *Animal Behaviour, 33,* 985–992.

Hinde, R. A. (1985b). Expression and negotiation. In G. Zivin (Ed.), *The development of expressive behavior: Biology-environment interactions* (pp. 103–116). New York: Academic Press.

Marler, P. (1984). Animal communication: Affect or cognition? In K. R. Scherer & P. Ekman (Eds.), *Approaches to emotion* (pp. 345–365). Hillsdale, NJ: Lawrence Erlbaum Associates.

Marler, P., Dufty, A., & Pickert, R. (1986a). Vocal communication in the domestic chicken: II. Is a sender sensitive to the presence and nature of a receiver? *Animal Behaviour, 34,* 194–198.

Marler, P., Dufty, A., & Pickert, R. (1986b). Vocal communication in the domestic chicken: I. Does a sender communicate information about the quality of a food referent to a receiver? *Animal Behaviour, 34,* 188–193.

Nelson, K. (1986). *Event knowledge: Structure and function in development.* Hillsdale, NJ: Lawrence Erlbaum Associates.

Ogden, C. K., & Richards, I. A. (1946). *The meaning of meaning* (8th ed.). New York: Harcourt, Brace & World.

Owings, D. H., & Leger, D. W. (1980). Chatter vocalizations of California ground squirrels: Predator- and social-role specificity. *Zeitschrift für Tierpsychologie, 54,* 163–184.

Pepperberg, I. (1981). Functional vocalizations by an African grey parrot (*Psittacus erithacus*). *Zeitschrift für Tierpsychologie, 55,* 139–160.

Pepperberg, I. (1987). Evidence for conceptual quantitative abilities in the African grey parrot: Labeling of cardinal sets. *Ethology, 75,* 37–61.

Schank, R. C. (1982). *Dynamic memory: A theory of reminding and learning in computers and people.* New York: Cambridge University Press.

Schank, R. C., & Abelson, R. P. (1977). *Scripts, plans, goals and understanding: An enquiry into human knowledge structures.* Hillsdale, NJ: Lawrence Erlbaum Associates.

Seyfarth, R. (1984). What the vocalizations of monkeys mean to humans, and what they mean to the monkeys themselves. In R. Harré & V. Reynolds (Eds.), *The meaning of primate signals* (pp. 43–56). New York: Cambridge University Press.

Seyfarth, R. M., & Cheney, D. L. (1982). How monkeys see the world: A review of recent research on East African vervet monkeys. In C. Snowdon, C. Brown, & M. Petersen (Eds.), *Primate communication* (pp. 239–252). Cambridge: Cambridge University Press.

Seyfarth, R. M., & Cheney, D. L. (1986). Vocal development in vervet monkeys. *Animal Behaviour, 34,* 1640–1658.

Seyfarth, R. M., Cheney, D. L., & Marler, P. (1980a). Vervet monkey alarm calls: Semantic communication in a free-ranging primate. *Animal Behaviour, 28,* 1070–1094.

Seyfarth, R. M., Cheney, D. L., & Marler, P. (1980b). Monkey responses to three different alarm calls: Evidence of predator classification and semantic communication. *Science, 210,* 801–803.

Smith, W. J. (1965). Message, meaning, and context in ethology. *American Naturalist, 99,* 405–409.

Smith, W. J. (1977). *The behavior of communicating.* Cambridge, MA: Harvard University Press.

Smith, W. J. (1981). Referents of animal communication. *Animal Behaviour, 29,* 1273–1275.

Smith, W. J. (1985). Consistency and change in communication. In G. Zivin (Ed.), *The development of expressive behavior: Biology-environment interactions* (pp. 51–76). New York: Academic Press.

Smith, W. J. (1986). Signaling behavior: Contributions of different repertoires. In R. J. Schusterman, J. A. Thomas, & F. G. Wood (Eds.), *Dolphin cognition and behavior: A comparative approach* (pp. 315–330). Hillsdale, NJ: Lawrence Erlbaum Associates.

Stokes, A. W., & Williams, H. W. (1971). Courtship feeding in gallinaceous birds. *Auk, 88,* 543–559.

10 CONSCIOUS CHIMPANZEES? A REVIEW OF RECENT LITERATURE

Alison Jolly
Princeton University

ABSTRACT

Examples of chimpanzee and pygmy chimpanzee behavior suggest self-recognition, advance planning, symbolic play, social deception, social manipulation, and symbolic communication. Accounts from captivity parallel similar behavior in the wild. We would assume that these observed behaviors indicated conscious purpose if shown by a human being. If we conclude that chimpanzees are conscious, we must then confront the ethics of our treatment of such animals in captivity and in the remaining wild.

INTRODUCTION

When Donald Griffin first wrote *The Question of Animal Awareness* (1976), it seemed heretical to mention animal consciousness in public. Now, after *Animal Thinking* (1984) and the growth of cognitive ethology, the thought of animal thought has become respectable. This volume shows the excitement and controversy that is generated by the cognitive approach.

I shall review here some examples of chimpanzee behavior which may indicate consciousness in chimpanzees and pygmy chimpanzees without disrespect to either gorillas or orangutans (which exhibit some of the same complexities). I shall emphasize recent accounts which have appeared since the work summarized in my textbook (Jolly, 1985). The review begins with behaviors shown by single animals which are often accepted as evidence of consciousness, that is, self-recognition, long term planning, and symbolic

231

play. It then addresses apparent awareness of another animal's desires or state of knowledge, which is often clearest in deception but can also appear in cooperative behavior. I will follow Whiten and Byrne's (1988a) classification of primate deception. The final section deals with three- and four-part interactions in which one animal uses another as a social tool to affect the behavior of others. Within social interactions, as in solitary ones, chimpanzees seem to plan ahead and to be aware of their own and others' likely behavior and knowledge, and they may even use symbolic communication. The social behaviors thus indicate how such subtle intelligence is indeed useful to chimpanzees.

This review is an attempt to build the bridge to animal minds out from the near bank by listing some examples of chimpanzee behavior that, in humans, would appear to be unequivocal demonstrations of consciousness. This at least reaches out across the human-animal frontier. Specifying the characteristics shared by closely related species is the first step in considering any phylogenetic sequence. It would be strange, however, if all animal species had the same kinds of consciousness. Chimpanzees presumably differ from baboons and lemurs in both mentality and in physical form. The ultimate goal for a primatologist is to trace the evolution of our own mental complexity to its first beginnings in creatures very different from ourselves. In the same way we trace the perfection of the vertebrate eye back to the first light-sensitive pigment spot, while showing how each form of eye may have been adaptive for the animal which evolved it.

One of the functions commonly proposed for consciousness is its advantage in deliberating alternate courses of action in pursuit of an imagined goal. Crook (1980, 1988) points out that a fundamental characteristic of human consciousness is a temporal dissonance between the pictured goal or intent and what is perceived as the current situation. It is only in moments of intense physical exhilaration or (says Crook) in disciplined Zen meditation that we approach awareness focussed on the current moment.

A second major function of our own consciousness is in foreseeing the actions of other social companions. Humphrey (1976) and I (Jolly, 1966) independently pointed out that social behavior in primates is far more complicated in its demands on intelligence than most problems posed by the rest of the environment. Since then, both the environment and animal societies have proved to be far more complex than we knew. Social intelligence could have operated by an accelerating ratchet effect such that any advance that allowed an animal to outsmart or out-cooperate its rivals could select for still smarter rivals in succeeding generations. Humphrey (1976, 1983) has developed this argument in terms of consciousness itself. If an animal is trying to reach imagined goals, it would be useful for it to also picture its social companions as having goals — in other words, to deal with others in terms of what they want. As Humphrey says, "A brain might perhaps be designed to be aware of its own neurotransmitters or to register that speech is coded in the left temporal lobe—but a fat lot of good that would be". A useful conscious self-model tells me that, "I love him, but he is annoyed at me," or It's all her fault, so I'm going to get back at her . . ." which is often condensed into a quick flash of annoyance at the sight of his or her silly smile. In other words, our primate minds are sensitive organs of empathy.

This empathy, of course, is what the serious students of behavior have so distrusted in mere pet lovers. When citing examples of chimpanzee behavior, it is a very useful exercise to ask whether we would be ready to call the behavior sequence conscious if shown by a spider, a stick insect, a piping plover, or a hog-nosed snake. It is also relevant to ask what a spider would have to do to convince us it was conscious. Griffin (1984) cogently argues that animals may well be aware of their innate behavior patterns as we are of sneezing, swallowing, or childbirth. To prove that it was conscious, however, a spider would probably have to make innovations in its behavior little short of woven words.

It is easy to doubt many individual sequences of chimpanzee behavior in this way but not, I think, the corpus taken together. Chimpanzees, by their physical and behavioral resemblances to humans, claim the benefit of the doubt. If a chimp or a human child took yarn and wove even the crudest of webs, we would assume the conscious planning we deny to the spider.

In the concluding section, I shall return to empathy not as a problem in the theory of knowledge but as a crisis of ethics—at least for our profession. If our own minds and those of other primates have evolved in large measure to understand other minds, what are our responsibilities toward such conscious animals?

SOLO BEHAVIOR

Self-Recognition

Self-recognition is often considered a behavior that demonstrates awareness of oneself and therefore at least a minimum level of awareness. In a well-known series of experiments, Gallup (1979, 1980) showed that chimpanzees can learn to recognize themselves in mirrors and use the mirrors to remove spots of paint which he had applied to invisible areas like brow-ridge or ear when the chimps were under anaesthetic. Kohler (1927) first described chimpanzees' use of mirrors including the fact that self-recognition seemed to be learned, but once learned, that the chimpanzees used reflecting surfaces such as bits of tin or urine puddles not only to look at themselves but to watch others or scenes outside windows.

Goodall (1986) says that wild chimpanzees do not immediately recognize themselves in mirrors like naive chimpanzees in captivity. "Nevertheless, some individuals spend minutes at a time crouched over still water apparently gazing at their reflection" (p. 589).

Savage-Rumbaugh (1986) has recently explored chimps' use of video to monitor themselves. It would perhaps be more accurate to say that the chimpanzees Sherman and Austin explored the video. "Austin casually glanced over at the television monitor and suddenly appeared to recognize himself. He began staring intently at the screen while bobbing up and down and making funny faces. Next, he approached the TV and positioned himself just inches from the screen and began to scrutinize his lip movements as he ate a muscadine and drank ice water . . . For the next twenty minutes, Austin continued to watch himself on the screen as he experimented with different body postures, facial expressions and methods of eating . . . He could see orange drink in his mouth much better (on the TV monitor) than by looking down over his nose" (p. xx). Sherman did not recognize his image until several months later but then went through a similar performance.

Savage-Rumbaugh (1986) points out that the monitor is rather different from a mirror. The images are smaller than life size, and they are not normally reversed. The camera may show a profile or back view of the animal and may allow scrutiny of otherwise inaccessible body parts. Sherman and Austin, for instance, use flashlights and the video to look down their own throats. Menzel, Savage-Rumbaugh, and Lawson (1985) had the apes reach through a post-box slot to erase a dot on a marked board. They readily coped with reversed or inverted images, and once, apparently Austin looked at an inverted image by turning his bottom to the screen and peering between his legs.

This use of video, like mirrors, extends to other objects. Sherman and Austin clearly distinguished live from recorded scenes. When a children's Halloween party took place in another building, they rushed to watch at the window whenever the screen showed a costumed child about to exit. They do not do this in reruns of the party tape. When watching themselves they check quickly whether the screened image copies their own actions, and then they ignore recordings.

Sherman and Austin watched a teacher play three brief video games using a joystick to guide a cursor onto a small central square. After this much exposure, they demanded to try it themselves. They each copied the teacher's actions, centering the cursor, not just wiggling the joystick at random. At the other extreme of physical gesture, Goodall (1986) recounts how infant Goblin, after watching his mother Melissa wipe her dirty bottom with leaves, picked more leaves and wiped his own clean bottom. I would by no means consider that all examples of animals repeating the gestures of another animal show a concept of self as a causal agent, but for chimpanzees it may be so, particularly in the highly abstract computer system.

Finally, de Waal (1987) describes a game among the pygmy chimpanzees of the San Diego Zoo which he can only explain in terms of self-awareness. They play a form of blind-man's buff not in the social sense but in terms of deliberate self-handicapping. The pygmy chimpanzees put something over their heads, or an arm across their eyes, or simply screw their eyes up tight, and then perform gymnastics on the climbing apparatus. Sometimes the gymnastics are quite daring such as spinning on a rope clear of the apparatus and back, but the rules are taken seriously as shown by the number of times the animals bump into things.

Planning

A second category which is commonly taken as a sign of consciousness is planning a long sequence of behaviors to reach a future goal. Stereotyped sequences, or sequences which can be totally disrupted by the failure of an intermediate step, do not count. The clearest examples are novel behaviors employed to reach a goal which has been previously defined.

The most common daily use of planning for most primates is in the cognitive map of available food and the strategy needed to locate food efficiently. Chimpanzees' route planning has not been analyzed mathematically, but Wrangham (1977) emphasized that chimps arrive at fruit trees from long distances and from many directions. As Goodall (1986) makes clear, travel to food is so entwined with travel for social reasons in chimpanzees' fission-fusion society, that it would be difficult to tease out the purely foraging component.

We have now become so used to the idea that chimpanzees use tools in the wild that one has to cite ever more complex tool use to make an impression. Goodall reports chimpanzees carrying termite-fishing tools from tens or hundreds of meters away to the termite nest. Boesch and Boesch (1984) mapped the transport of hammerstones for cracking coula and panda nuts in the Tai Forest. They found that granite hammers for the harder panda nuts were commonly carried over 50 meters in an area where the maximum visibility is only 20 meters. Chimps carried lighter clubs when about to crack coula nuts, heavier ones for the pandas. Panda trees are commonly out of sight of each other, and the nuts are usually eaten by chimps feeding alone so each animal had to make its own decisions of route and tool size. This is, then, a well-documented case of forward planning in the wild which supports the many laboratory studies (e.g., Jolly, 1985; Rensch, & Dohl, 1967, 1968).

The real sceptic, though, could say that we are still too kind because these are chimps. The weaver ant who takes her larval siblings to sew a nest of leaves is using a tool in the long-term goal of constructing a shelter for her kin, but we are reluctant to call this planning. The best answer comes from Kanzi, Sherman, and Austin, the chimps and pygmy chimp trained by Savage-Rumbaugh. They announce on their computers the destinations they chose to go to in the woods, using symbols for food or toys located at particular spots. In the case of Kanzi the pygmy chimpanzee it is sometimes a toy which he himself has hidden days before and unearths from a pile of leaves to the surprise of the lab staff (Savage-Rumbaugh & MacDonald, 1988).

Symbolic Behavior

True symbolic behavior is widely admitted as conscious. Of course, symbolic behavior is hard to define and largely derives from our own species-specific use of language. This is not the place to embark on the ape language controversy and to what extent chimp or human words are mere conditioned reflexes. Let me cite instead examples of play which their observers believed to be referential. The conservative view would be that some at least are vacuum activities—behaviors Lorenz (1932/1970) described as given to inadequate stimuli or none at all as his caged starling made the motions of seizing nonexistent flies. Lorenz explicitly distinguished such innately driven vacuum activities from true play, but he suggested that in exceptionally intelligent birds such as ravens and cockatoos there might be transitions between the two.

The classic, and still most complex case, is Viki Hayes' imaginary pulltoy. Viki was at the stage when little chimps, like young humans, drag everything possible behind them as a pulltoy. (Goodall, 1986 gives us a picture of infant Flint dragging a palm flower while walking bipedally in the same fashion.) Viki, being an American home chimp, was also being toilet trained and spent long sessions in the bathroom waiting to produce. Cathy Hayes (1951) noted that Viki, while playing in the bathroom, began to trail one arm behind her as though dragging a toy on a string that didn't exist. This went on for days until one day, the "string" apparently caught on the plumbing knobs—at least Viki checked and made the gestures of untangling it. This too became commonplace. Then, after several weeks, Cathy was combing her hair in the bathroom when Viki's "toy" got stuck. Viki sat down with her hands extended as if holding a taut rope. She looked at Cathy Hayes' face in the mirror and called, "Mama, Mama" (one of her four forced breathy "words"). Still half-unbelieving, Cathy got down and went through an elaborate pantomime of untangling the string. Viki stared up into her face, then galloped off again, trailing her toy.

A few days later, the pulltoy disappeared for good, when Cathy decided to test out the situation by inventing a pulltoy of her own, one that went "clackety clackety" on the bare floor and "squush squush" on the rugs. Viki gave a terrified "boo" call and leaped into Cathy's arms and never played that game again.

The language trained apes occasionally use symbolic representation in free situations. They all name pictures from books to themselves in play. Sara, Premack's star pupil, spontaneously added a piece of paper for a "hat" to a pictured face after she had been wearing a hat herself. (Premack, 1986). Washoe at about 2 years old bathed, soaped, and dried her dolls. (Gardner & Gardner, 1971). Lucy also signed to her dolls. As an adult in oestrus, Lucy was given a copy of *Playgirl*. She turned pages and touched or scratched at the male genitalia with her fingernail. Then, on reaching the centerfold, she positioned herself carefully over the pictured genitalia, rubbed her clitoris on them, and dribbled urine accurately on the right spot (Temerlin, 1975).

Wild chimpanzees have infrequent access to *Playgirl*. However, Goodall (1986) describes how adolescent males are sometimes found alone in the woods "practising" male charging displays with nobody around to impress. As a youngster Figan even practised displaying with banging kerosene tins, otherwise the peculiar perogative of Mike, the dominant male. (p. 590) On another occasion, "four-year-old Wunda watched intently from a safe distance as her mother, using a long stick, fished for fierce driver ants from a branch overhanging the nest. Presently Wunda picked a tiny twig, perched herself on a low branch of a sapling in the same attitude as her mother, and poked her little tool down—into an imaginary nest" (p. 591)? We don't, of course, know. Normal termite fishing is learned in play. It may be 2 or 3 years before a young chimp gets much reward for playing round the termite hill with its little twigs. Wunda's performance is more memorable because there is obviously no hope of gain. We cannot dismiss the possibility of chimp imagination.

Hayaki (1985) reported one case of what he calls "imaginary social play" in the wild. An adolescent male, AJ, made a day-nest near some adult males. In a protocol lasting 6 minutes:

> He entwines himself with branches and wrestles with it. He moves a little with the branch and wrestles again, sweeping fallen leaves with his hand. He begins to play-pant. He gets up, slaps the branch, and mounts it with pelvic thrusts. He bites it, rolls over, and fingers it with play-face. He continues play-panting. He gets up again and pushes his way through the bush. He slaps and

slaps branches of shrubs around him. He rolls over and over, elbowing branches. He lies on his back with the branch on top of him, and bites it, moving his legs intensely. He also intensely play-pants. He hears someone pant-hoot nearby and gets up looking around. He moves a little, dragging the branch. The adult males begin to move, and AJ follows them. (p. 356).

Hayaki (1985) adds that he only twice saw AJ play in a similar manner, but that Nishida had once seen an adult female playing as though with her baby who had died. Here is one final example. Hebb and Riesen (1943) wrote long ago about "superstitious" fears in chimpanzees when the Yerkes animals would develop unaccountable terrors of a particular place or object. Field-minded ethologists might point out that in a world of snakes and predators, it is adaptive to be overterrified of anything associated with the chance of real danger. Savage-Rumbaugh and McDonald (1988) tell of Sherman and Austin's piloerection and waa-barks at a traveling cage — just after they first saw the video tape of King Kong who had such a cage. Savage-Rumbaugh and McDonald clearly inclines to the rich interpretation, that their animals were acting as though they feared a terrifying memory not just another piece of iron furniture or even a conditioned stimulus off a video tape. At some point, for our own ancestors, it would be equally difficult for a scientist to decide whether they were barking in conditioned fear of the thicket where the leopard ate Mama last month or of the malevolent thicket where the troop is traditionally afraid of nameless but still imagined evil lurking there.

SOCIAL AWARENESS AND DECEPTION

Dennett (1983) proposed a ranking of orders of complexity of social awareness which would ascend from *I know* to *I know that he knows,* to *He knows that I know that he knows,* and so on ad infinitum. This does not actually ascend ad infinitum. Dennett demonstrates our own limitations by the superbly unmemorable example: "How high can human beings go? In principle forever, no doubt, but in fact I suspect that you wonder whether I realize how hard it is for you to be sure that you understand whether I mean to be saying that you can recognize that I believe you want me to explain that most of us can keep track of only about five or six orders, under the best of circumstances" (p. 343).

Whiten and Byrne (1988a, 1988b) give a more empirically based classification of observed deception in primates, which also allows one to approach Dennett's orders of intentionality. I shall follow Whiten and Byrne's listing, dealing first with concealment, then with distraction, and then with creating an image. I add one more group — indicating or demonstrating—because this paper is concerned with cooperative as well as deceptive uses of awareness.

Concealment

Concealment is hardly a new discovery of chimpanzees; it is practiced by every cryptic animal species. However, few act like the pygmy chimp Kanzi, who frightened a new keeper by disappearing. The trainer thoroughly checked the bedroom, then further and further afield, even on the building's roof. Then, returning to the bedroom, she noticed a very slight movement among the blankets. Kanzi had not only piled bedding over himself, he lay flattened down and fairly still for twenty minutes, emerging with a big play-grin on his face. (Savage-Rumbaugh & McDonald, 1988).

On another occasion, Kanzi secreted the tool which opens the outside gate after he asked to go out and was refused. Savage-Rumbaugh did not see him hide it and thought that they must have dropped it. She asked Kanzi to "help search". He went through motions of looking around his quarters until Savage-Rumbaugh thought that she had checked every possible spot. She never did find out the hiding-place—only that Kanzi unlocked the gate and shot out as soon as her back was turned.

Many animals indicate submission by hunching over and hiding their faces or other provocative parts. Should one consider it self-awareness or something much simpler when a chimpanzee male, like Goliath, turns his back on dominant Mike in a gesture that looks as though he is deliberately not provoking him? The stronger interpretation is supported by de Waal's (1982, 1986) many observations of tactical concealment in chimpanzees at the Arnhem zoo. This included concealment of parts of the body. For example, when young Dandy was courting a female and was surprised by the dominant male, he dropped both hands to cover his erect penis.

Most telling of all was the occasion when Luit, the dominant male, was being challenged by Nikkie, another adult male.

> After Luit and Nikkie had displayed in each others' presence for over ten minutes . . . Nikkie was driven into a tree, but a little later he began to hoot at the leader again. . . . Luit was sitting at the bottom of the tree with his back to the challenger. When he heard the renewed sounds of provocation he bared his teeth but immediately put his hand to his mouth and pressed his lips together. . . . I saw the nervous grin appear on his face again and once more he used his fingers to press his lips together. The third time Luit finally succeeded in wiping the grin off his face; only then did he turn around. A little later he displayed at Nikkie as if nothing had happened. . . . Nikkie watched his opponents walk away. All of a sudden he turned his back and, when the others could not see him, a grin appeared on his face and he began to yelp very

softly. I could hear Nikkie because I was not very far away, but the sound was so suppressed that Luit probably did not notice that his opponent was also having trouble concealing his emotions. (de Waal, p. 133).

Nikkie's act is an example of acoustic hiding or suppression. Wild chimpanzees commonly do this. Females mating with subordinate males suppress their copulation calls. In fact, females who leave to go on consortship with less dominant males have to do so in silence; if they fuss, others take her from that partner. When Figan was about 9 years old, he stayed behind after the group of larger males had left. Goodall gave him some bananas. Greatly excited, he gave loud food barks, and lost his prize when the older chimps raced back. "The following day he again waited and got bananas. This time, although he made faint, choking sounds in his throat, he remained virtually silent and ate his allotment undisturbed. Never again did Figan call out in this kind of situation" (Goodall, 1986, p. 579).

It also happens that chimpanzees suppress others' calls. Goodall has seen mothers shush infants when they might annoy displaying males. On two separate occasions adolescent Goblin vocalized during border patrols when the chimps risked reprisal from males in the next territory. "Once he was hit, the other time embraced. A mother grew agitated and repeatedly embraced her child who had loud hiccoughs on a similar occasion, and noisy human observers may be threatened" (Goodall, 1986, p. 579).

Whiten and Byrne consider inhibition of attention a subcategory of concealment. The classic case was reported by Goodall (1971). Figan spotted a banana in a tree crotch above Goliath's head; the banana went unnoticed by the older male. With no more than a quick glance at the banana and at Goliath, Figan retreated round the house and waited there, where his glance could not give away his intent, until Goliath departed. Then Figan returned and went straight to the banana. Figan also learned to unscrew the handles of the banana boxes but not to actually open them if the big males were in camp; he waited with a hand or foot on the box for as long as 30 minutes until the others left.

A clear example was the occasion when Goodall (1986) was watching four females, and

. . . inadvertently disturbed a francolin which flew up with loud characteristic calls. A moment later the most subordinate of the females, Little Bee, climbed slowly down. . . . I could see from the direction of her gaze and her eye movements that she was visually searching the ground where the bird had been. After thirty-five seconds she suddenly moved rapidly forward and, without hesitation, reached out and picked up two eggs. Almost before she put them in her mouth, the other three females had rushed down and gathered round her, peering at her mouth and feeling about in the area of the nest. If

Little Bee had searched manually instead of standing and using her eyes, it is quite possible that one of the higher-ranking females would have found the eggs before she did. (p. 578)

Again, the reports of captive chimpanzees parallel accounts from the wild. de Waal (1986) describes Dandy walking over the place where grapefruit were buried without breaking stride, so that even the observers assumed he had noticed nothing. Hours later, when the others were taking siesta, he made a beeline for the spot and dug up the fruit. In Premack's (1986) controlled experiments, young chimps learned to suppress indications of which box held food when confronted by a treacherous trainer who would eat the food they showed him. At the age of 1, Panzee (Savage-Rumbaugh & McDonald, 1988) began to inhibit forbidden actions such as drinking out of other's cups, but she could only monitor one trainer at a time at that age. If the person Panzee watched was not paying attention, the little chimp would grab the cup and be caught by another. In the wild, parental rules are more likely to concern not playing with the next new baby. For example, young Gremlin, in this situation, would lie down on her back and inch up to tickle her baby brothers with her toes.

Of course, the pretended disinterest may be reciprocal. Savage-Rumbaugh and McDonald (1988) describe games of "keep-away" between themselves and Kanzi, with each sitting tense, ready to lunge for the ball if the other moves, while both look in any other direction. The forest parallel was old Flo, sitting below her adolescent son Figan who was eating a dead colobus monkey. Flo seemed uncharacteristically disinterested. After 5 minutes she inched nearer, stopped and groomed herself for 7 more minutes, and then ". . . made a lightning grab for the monkeys tail. Figan, however, had clearly been anticipating just such a move, and he leaped even more quickly than she did. . . ." (Goodall, 1986, p. 577) This went on for a whole hour more, but Flo never did get any meat.

Distraction and Lying

Distraction is Whiten and Byrne's next major category of deception. Distraction is more active than concealment, because it involves actively sending false or different cues while keeping the original goal in mind. Chimpanzees distract others by leading them away, by intimate behavior such as grooming, or by a series of behaviors that includes looking away, vocalizing, and symbolism, all of which indicate that something else is important other than the real goal.

Leading away was again invented by Figan, who discovered that he could stride purposefully into the woods, and the bigger males would follow him. When they disappeared, he was free to circle back and eat bananas in peace.

Goodall speculates that he was almost certainly heading toward a real food source, because the adults would not follow an adolescent in an unprofitable direction. The first instance may well have been fortuitous, but later occasions were certainly planned. Once when Figan returned, yet another big male came out of the woods, and Figan lay down in a tantrum. In Menzel's (1971, 1974) experiments, when he showed food to one chimp who would then lead the rest to the cache, the subordinate Belle began attempting to give false information to the more dominant Rock. Goodall summarizes,

> If she sat on the food, Rock learned to search beneath her. When she began sitting halfway toward the food, he learned to follow the direction of her travel until he found the right place. He even learned to go in the opposite direction when she tried to lead him away from the food. . . . sometimes a single piece of food was hidden in a different place from the large pile. Belle would lead Rock to this piece, and, while he ate it, run to the pile. When Rock learned to ignore this decoy and continued to keep an eagle eye on Belle, she threw temper tantrums. (Goodall, 1986, p. 581)

Distracting with intimate behavior is the standard chimpanzee maternal response to obstreperous young. When they fuss over weaning or persist in trying to groom a new baby, instead of slapping, the mother generally plays with or tickles her child. It is also a part of chimp reconciliation and mediation, in that animals who have been threatening or fighting a moment before will seek and give a touch or a groom of contact. This is not true deception, because the grooming animals do not wish to return to aggression, but it serves to deflect and defuse the other's mood. Goodall adds to this distraction-by-tantrum, when a chimp does not get what it wants, usually during weaning.

Finally, there is distraction which involves irrelevant cues, or something close to lying. In Premack and Woodruff's (1978) experiments with the "lying" trainer, Sara eldest of the chimpanzees, learned to indicate false cues for the location of food, not just to inhibit her own attention. Nikkie in a single instance feinted like a soccer player, throwing a stone at a female as she doubled round one side of a tree while turning toward the other side himself, so she predictably recoiled from the stone into his clutches (de Waal 1982).

It seems to be fairly common to get out of situations by giving false alarm calls. Fouts and Fouts (in press) describe Bruno and Booee disputing possession of a hose — one goes outside and gives waa-barks, the other emerges as a result, and the hose becomes available. Kanzi not only gives such alarms when being beaten in a game of chase, he will peer into the woods and then go off and investigate, taking his playmates with him now united, as a group. (Savage-Rumbaugh & McDonald 1988.) (Use of alarm calls to distract has of course been reported for other animals notably by Seyfarth, Cheney, & Marler [1980a&b] for vervets and Munn [1986] for mixed-flock Amazonian birds.) Goodall again gives parallels from the wild, when two 4-year-olds, during the trauma of weaning, gave loud screams as though they saw a snake by the path, and thus conned their reluctant mothers into carrying them. Of course, in the wild it might have been a real snake, but the juxtaposition of all the lab and wild observations gives credence to this behavior as a form of lying.

Sherman, Austin, and Kanzi have engaged in behavior even more like symbolic pretense. Sherman was afraid to go outside in the dark; Austin was not. Austin on occasion went out alone, and strange noises would be heard indoors. Then Austin would return with hair bristling as though he too were aroused and afraid. The more dominant Sherman, instead of asserting himself over Austin as usual, would rush to Austin and embrace him for reassurance. The lab staff could not be sure how Austin made most of the noises, only that they happened when the smaller chimp was outside alone in the dark — but once he was surprised tapping softly on an outside water-pipe (Savage-Rumbaugh & McDonald, 1988).

Kanzi also seems to pretend that he sees, or has, invisible objects. He may hide something and invite the others to look for it, or eat something, or even put a nonexistent something into a trainer's hand. The eating can be elaborate teasing, for he is forbidden to eat mushrooms in the woods. He has a whole series of deceptions, such as pausing behind trees to cram a mushroom into his mouth, but he will also torment his trainers by ostentatiously biting into a mushroom when they are too far to do more than rush over and remove the fragments from his mouth. Once he held a large mushroom at least 10 minutes until Savage Rumbaugh approached and could be teased.

The language-trained apes occasionally use their learned words to lie. Kanzi, when refused a visit to Sherman and Austin, might request melon or some other food which was located beyond Sherman and Austin's quarters. The request is probably a deception, not simply a new idea, because when passing Sherman and Austin he would run off instantly toward them, and when forced to continue toward the melon, showed no interest in eating it (Savage-Rumbaugh & McDonald, 1988).

Creating an Image

Whiten and Byrne's (1988a) final category of one-on-one deception is creating an image. That is, the same behaviors that we have seen when one animal is trying to conceal interest in an object or to deflect another from the object, are used instead to conceal the nature of a social interaction.

Thus, the Arnhem males who seemed blind and deaf to another male displaying a few feet away were presenting a neutral image by suppressing the attention the situation seemed to demand. Similarly, females might apparently ignore the advances of courting subordinates, only to rush to mate through the bars when they were safely locked into their night cages. Yoeren, the most subtle of the males, sustained an injury, and ostentatiously limped in front of the dominant for days — but only when the dominant could see him (de Waal, 1982).

Such social images may also be affiliative. Most primates will cuddle and groom in reconciliation. A few female chimpanzees actively lure humans to their cages by affiliation gestures, only to spit or even bite them. Hebb (1945) described this as individual behavior of certain animals. One of the Arnhem females behaved the same way and so, apparently, has Washoe, at least at some intervals in her career (Linden, 1986). Presumably such feigned friendship is in the repertoire of most or all chimps, but the circumstances of captivity with its succession of new dupes make this behavior profitable and reinforce it.

In the recent discussions of evolved signals, it has become clear that bristling hair and deep voices may give misleading information, though such displays are deceptive only in a formal not a mental sense (Dawkins & Krebs, 1978; Krebs & Dawkins, 1984). Mike, one of the Gombe chimpanzees, apparently deliberately planned such enhanced aggressive displays. Goodall (1986) writes:

> Once, for example, as a group of six adult males groomed about 10 meters away, Mike, after watching them for six minutes got up and moved toward my tent. His hair was sleek and he showed no sign of any visible tension. He picked up two empty (kerosene) cans and, carrying them by their handles, one in each hand, walked (upright) back to his previous place, sat and stared at the other males, who at that time were all higher ranking than himself. They were still grooming quietly and had paid no attention to him. After a moment Mike began to rock almost imperceptibly from side to side, his hair very slightly erect. The other males continued to ignore him. Gradually Mike rocked more vigorously, his hair became fully erect, and uttering pant-hoots he suddenly charged directly toward his superiors, hitting the cans ahead of him. The other males fled. Sometimes Mike repeated this performance as many as four times in succession, waiting until his rivals had started to groom once more before again charging toward them (p. 426).

It is a paradox that deception offers the clearest evidence of such mental calculations. Possibly much of chimpanzees' cooperative behavior also involves a mental picture of others' emotions, but we cannot often be sure because what we see is a straightforward response to the others' communication. Sharing much coveted meat with begging friends could just be a forced or unconscious response to the others' gestures of begging—or it could involve accurate and very human empathy. Menzel's (1971) work on chimps leading others to food is one illustration of what seems deliberate indication by one chimp to others. Premack and Woodruff's (1978) studies of chimpanzees completing a video with the solution desired by a good trainer was an explicit test of empathy, as was the chimps' indication of food to a good trainer. Premack also tested the chimpanzees' reaction to a blindfolded trainer who wore the key to a feed box on a chain around his neck. Even young chimpanzees learned to lead the trainer by the hand; the older, smarter Sarah simply pulled down the blindfold. In the wild, hunting by males may be the best example of cooperation, as the animals move to block the future lines of retreat of their prey.

The signing chimpanzees, of course, indicate all sorts of things by signs, including information which was unknown to their trainers. Washoe actually taught a few signs to her adopted son Loulis (Fouts et al, 1989). Some were rather vague shaping, like *come,* but Washoe molded Loulis hand into the sign for *food* and put it to his mouth in the right context, and demonstrated the sign for *chair* five times after placing a chair in front of him. The Fouts report signing in 54 out of 451 interactions initiated by Loulis (in 1981 when he was about 3 years old) toward other chimps of the colony. The interactions were videotaped without an observer present to influence the proceedings. These signs can function to convey information and coordinate action between chimps, as shown by Savage-Rumbaugh's demonstration that Sherman and Austin could be trained to request and share particular tools and foods.

It may still be objected that the symbols could mean no more to the apes than the buttons labeled *What color?* and *Thank you* pecked by Epstein, Lanza and Skinner's (1980) trained pigeons. Human words instead seem to contain a mutual pretense that these arbitrary sounds have a relation to bits of the real world. The nearest case, outside the controversial symbols, may be de Waal's observation of male chimp reconciliation by looking at a flight of birds in the sky, or even grooming and intently studying something—or an invisible something—in the grass until the two former rivals are sitting side by side in enough peace to begin grooming each other.

Whatever the symbols are to the ape, they can be attached to emotion and intention. Washoe and other apes use the symbol *dirty* as an insult (Gardner & Gardner, 1985). Kanzi, and other apes use *good* to indicate, I'll do what you want or I'll be nice, as in *good* before being given a balloon to indicate that Kanzi will give the popped balloon back instead of eating it. At least, this is Savage-Rumbaugh's gloss. On one occasion, Kanzi, in revolt, popped a balloon in the next room. When Savage-Rumbaugh demanded the pieces, he pointed to his mouth and then his stomach, and signed *bad balloon* (Savage-Rumbaugh & McDonald, 1988).

We have seen, therefore, that in both deception and cooperation all the traits can appear that we cited as evidence of consciousness when they are shown by individuals alone. Forward planning, self–awareness, and even some symbolic pretense are here joined by apparent awareness of others' desires and intentions, at least in the rich interpretation.

SOCIAL TOOLS

We now turn to relations among three or more chimpanzees, where one animal is using another to interact with a third. As in the one-to-one interactions, the relations may be competitive and even deceptive or they may be cooperative. As in the earlier cases, many similar acts are reported for other animals, but the chimpanzees give us some that seem to be planned unequivocally in terms of others' intentions.

The fluid nature of chimpanzee society means that different social groups form and reform. Relevant social partners may be away for days or weeks or may be just out of sight. To quote an example:

> The juvenile female Pooch approaches high-ranking Circe and reaches for one of her bananas. Circe at once hits out at the youngster, whereupon Pooch, screaming very loudly indeed, runs from camp in an easterly direction. Her response to the rather mild threat seems unnecessarily violent. After two minutes the screams give way to waa-barks, which get progressively louder as Pooch retraces her steps. After a few minutes she reappears; stopping about 5 meters from Circe, she gives an arm-raise threat along with another waa-bark. Following behind Pooch, his hair slightly bristling, is the old male Huxley (who had left camp shortly before in an easterly direction). Circe, with a mild threat gesture directed toward Pooch and a glance at Huxley, gets up and moves away. Pooch has used Huxley as a 'social tool.' This little sequence can be understood only because we know of the odd relationship between the juvenile and the old male who served on many occasions as her protector and was seldom far away. In order to behave in an appropriate fashion, it was, of course, necessary that Circe also know the facts of the relationship (Goodall, 1986, p. 567).

In quoting this episode, I hesitated over which bits to cut out to shorten it. In a scientific review is one allowed to say Pooch seemed to scream unnecessarily loud? Yes, because we have had millions of years of common evolution with chimpanzees during which time we were developing our sensitivity to just such cues. And is it fair to end that Circe necessarily knew the facts of this individual relationship? Could it just be any old female retreating from any bristling male? For animals less like us than chimpanzees, we need experiments to be sure that they recognize individuals, as Ristau (this volume) shows for the piping plovers, or that they recognize individual relationships, as Cheney and Seyfarth (1982, this volume) have demonstrated for vervets. But the gist of this paper, as of this book, is that the richer possibility always needs to be considered. Parsimony, and a search for scientific accuracy, does not benefit by throwing out our primate social sensitivity toward closely related animals.

There are a wealth of other accounts of chimpanzees using others or apparently foreseeing other's actions. Both in the wild and in Arnhem Zoo, females take rocks from the hands of males who may throw them. Fifi, after a few bad experiences when her son Freud got into over-boisterous play with Passion's son Prof (which lead to disputes with the dominant Passion) would gather up Freud and leave as soon as their play started to escalate. At Arnhem, old Yeroen sometimes went off to tickle and play with the juveniles as another male started displaying, which would provide both a group distraction and an excuse for Yeroen himself to disregard the threat. Only his tense facial expression and covert glances at the displaying male showed that this was not normal play. At Arnhem as well a female might mediate reconciliation between rival males by grooming first one and then the other, while inviting them to follow and move to either side of her until eventually she slipped away leaving them relaxed and ready to groom each other. Goodall reports that she has not seen this third party mediating behavior at Gombe, and that it may be an invention of the intense social life of captivity (Goodall, 1986; de Waal, 1982).

The sign-using chimps incorporate their learned signs into such social behavior. Fouts and Fouts (1989) describe the distraction of Loulis as a rambunctious juvenile recorded during a remote video-taping session:

Loulis displayed at [females] Moja and Tatu by rushing at them and hitting them both as they sat grooming. Moja and Tatu moved away and started to resume grooming. When Loulis began to charge at them again, [young male] Dar reached out and touched Loulis' arm.

Loulis ignored the touch and continued his charge. As Moja and Tatu moved away from Loulis once more, Washoe reached out and touched Loulis' leg and Dar signed "tickle" on Loulis' arm. Loulis responded to Dar by turning to him and play-wrestling with him. Washoe joined in this game by tickling Loulis with her hand as Dar wrestled with him . . . no further aggression occurred.

Such social tool use occurs often in aggressive contexts. When young Dandy tatttled on a female mating with a subordinate male by running to fetch the dominant, or when he redirected the group's attention by giving waa-barks at something of interest among the zoo public, then hung back with an oestrous female and mated, it is easy to attribute intent (de Waal, 1982). The pygmy chimp Matata would grab something from a trainer, scream loudly, and then use the chimpanzee gestures of enlisting aid from Savage-Rumbaugh, as though the trainer had attacked Matata. Only the trainer's use of language would allow her to tell her side of the story. (It was this behavior in a juvenile baboon which first provoked Whiten & Byrnes [1988] study of deception. The young baboon, seeing an adult with a choice piece of food, screamed loudly as though attacked. The juvenile's mother charged over, attacked the attacker, and the juvenile got the food.) Matata often incited Sherman and Austin to aggressive display by threatening them, by eating in front of their cage, or by presenting and then withdrawing her oestrous bottom. She then incited Savage-Rumbaugh to discipline the two males; in one case she even putt a hose into Savage-Rumbaugh's hands. On her return to the breeding colony, Matata reestablished dominance over another female in an incident where she yanked on an infant's leg. The infant screamed, her still more dominant mother came rushing out of the inner quarters, and Matata threatened the unfortunate scapegoat, who was then thrashed by the infant's mother (Runfeldt, personal communication, 1985).

It is difficult and perhaps impossible to tell how far ahead such strategies are planned, and whether chimps can calculate beyond the immediate interaction. de Waal wisely compares the power shifts among males to the squabbles between human adolescents and their parents. Long term, the fights are clearly about a power shift within the family, but the immediate explosions occur when the other side is being totally unreasonable about some triviality like whether it is necessary to litter the floor with dirty socks. Some long-term strategies may look planned only in retrospect, like Yeroen's shifts of allegiance. When he was too old to hold power alone, he played off the other males against each other, such that the current dominant commonly needed Yeroen's allegiance (de Waal 1982). Nishida (1983) has described similar tactics in the Mahale Mountains. The rising young male Sabongo fought and probably defeated the alpha Kasonta around April 17th, 1976 when both animals appeared with wounds. From April 17th to May 10th, an older male, Kamamemanfu, supported the alpha in his attacks on Sabongo when Kasonta apparently aimed for the same wounds on Sabongo, reopening them at least four times. On May 10th, however, Kamamemanfu changed sides, which led to definitive supremacy for Sabongo. In the succeeding months, when Kamamemanfu met the ostracized Kasonta in the woods, he groomed him thereby raising his own status. Throughout this period, both dominant males let old Kamamemanfu mate — they both needed him.

The old male's tactics Nishida calls "allegiance fickleness" (p. 318). It seems to me there are simpler rules which could explain each episode— "support old friend" in the case of Kasonta or "support new boss" for Sabongo. When these conflict, Kamamemanfu could vacillate in ways that have long been a mainstay of ethological study. I am far from arguing that every case of human-like behavior needs an explanation in terms of human-like foresight, and a dominance strategy pursued over months is where I balk for chimpanzees. I think it is very useful, though, to consider at what point one does balk for the chimps, because it is there that one runs into the same problems of proof which confront people studying simpler species at a much simpler level of behavior.

CONCLUSION

In conclusion, might one speculate that animals are aware of the problems that, for them, demand a decision between almost equally likely courses of action and where the goals which they are able to foresee can be reached by such decidable actions? There is an analogy here to the phenomenon of learning a motor skill. As long as you are conscious of how you ski or how you touch-type, you have not yet mastered the skill. In the same way, other animals (and young humans) may be conscious of actions we have relegated to automatic processes.

We humans make some plans over the scale of years and continents, but our definition of consciousness definitely includes forward planning over the next 10 minutes, awareness of other's intentions over the same time period, self-recognition, and symbols. The accounts cited in this review suggest chimpanzees share these evolved capacities. If we readily concede consciousness to chimps, it is not just because their minds are so like ours, but because their problems are so like ours. It remains for other authors to expound on what may be a problem to a hog-nosed snake or a piping plover—what is decidable and so worth being aware of. The bridge toward animal conscious that goes as far as a chimpanzee does not go a long step out from our own bank of the river.

Our final point, however, is forced upon us. If chimpanzees are conscious animals, and if the content of their minds is recognizably like ours, what are our responsibilities toward these primates that call out to our own primate empathy? We sometimes kill, maim, or starve other humans, but we do have ethics that discourage such acts. Chimps likewise kill and maim other chimps, but they also defend kin and friends. There was even an occasion when Washoe pulled a drowning chimp from a lake shortly after Washoe arrived at Oklahoma when she scarcely knew the other animal. Linden (1986) has written of the fate of several language-trained chimpanzees who had the most intimate of human contacts during their childhood; they were adopted into human families or labored over by trainers who became their social companions. Some of these apes now use learned signs when attempting to make contact with medical personnel who may not even know their names.

If we have even as much humanity as a chimpanzee, we are tempted to rescue baby chimps from solitary isolation and inadequate caging in the worst of laboratories or zoos. Jane Goodall is leading a campaign to revise laboratory caging standards after discovering that in one NIH supported lab pairs of infant chimpanzees are kept in cages 22" × 22" × 24" high, and that 4-year-old juveniles who would be at their most active in the wild, are kept in solitary confinement in cages that seal rather like small refrigerators, these cages are too small for them to stretch out and lie down and provide no auditory and little visual contact with the outside world. (Note that this is not an attempt to stop medical testing for such diseases as AIDS and hepatitis. It is an attempt to stop torturing conscious animals in ways that have no relation or even cast doubt on the medical benefits they may confer on humanity.)

It takes rather more imagination and even more daunting politics to attempt conservation of a species. There are only something under 100,000 chimpanzees in the whole world—the number of humans in a small town. We shall not forgive ourselves if we let the wild populations of our nearest relation dwindle and die.

Not all of students of animal behavior wish to be concerned with the welfare of captive animals, or the conservation of wild ones, and certainly most of us do not want this responsibility at all stages of our careers. However, if we admit the theory of animal consciousness as a theory of knowledge, I submit that our profession must face it also as an inescapable demand for ethics.

REFERENCES

Boesch, C., & Boesch, H. (1984). Mental map in wild chimpanzees: An analysis of hammer transports for nut-cracking. *Primates, 25,* 160–170.

Cheney, D. L., & Seyfarth, R. M. (1982). Recognition of individuals within and between groups of free-ranging vervet monkeys. *Amer. Zool, 22,* 519–529.

Crook, J. H. (1988). The experiential content of intellect. In R. W. Byrne & A. Whiten (Eds.), *Machiavellian intelligence* (pp. 347–397). Oxford: Oxford University Press.

Crook, J. H. (1980). *The evolution of human consciousness.* Oxford: Clarendon Press.

Dawkins, R., & Krebs, J. R. (1978). Animal signals: Information or manipulation? In J. R. Krebs & N. B. Davies (Eds.), *Behavioral Ecology* (pp. 282–312). Oxford: Blackwell.

Dennett, D. C. (1983). Intentional systems in cognitive ethology: The Panglossian Paradigm defended. *Behavior and Brain Sciences, 6,* 343–391.

Epstein, R., Lanza, R. P., & Skinner, B. F. (1980). Symbolic communication between two pigeons *(Columbia livia domestica). Science, 207,* 343–345.

Fouts, R. S., Fouts, D. H & Van Cantfort, T. E. (1989). The infant Loulis learns signs from cross-fostered chimpanzees. In R. A. Gardner, B.T. Gardner, & T. E. Van Cantfort, eds. *Teaching Sign Language to Chimpanzees.* (pp. 280–292). Albany, SUNY Press.

Fouts, R. S., & Fouts, D. H. (1989). Loulis in conversation with the cross-fostered chimpanzees. In B. T. Gardner, R. A. Gardner, & I. van Cantfort (Eds.), *Teaching sign language to chimpanzees.* (pp. 293–307) Albany: SUNY Press.

Gallup, G. G., Jr. (1980). Chimpanzees and self-awareness. In M. S. Roy (Ed.), *Species identity and attachment* (pp. 223–243). New York: Garland STPM Press.

Gallup, G. G., Jr. (1979). Self-awareness in primates. *American Scientist, 67,* 417–421.

Gardner, B. T., & Gardner, R. A. 1971. Two-way communication with an infant chimpanzee, In A. M. Schrier and F. Stollnitz, eds, *Behavior of Nonhuman Primates* vol 4 pp 117–185.

Gardner, B. T., & Gardner R. A. (1985). Signs of intelligence in cross-fostered chimpanzees. *Philosophical Transcripts of the Royal Society, London, 308,* 159–176.

Goodall, J. (1986). *The chimpanzees of Gombe.* Cambridge, MA: Harvard University Press.

Goodall, J. (1971). *In the shadow of man.* London: Collins.

Griffin, D. R. (1984). *Animal thinking.* Cambridge, MA: Harvard University Press.

Griffin, D. R. (1976). *The question of animal awareness* 2nd Ed (1981). New York: The Rockefeller University Press.

Hayaki, H. (1985). Social play of juvenile and adolescent chimpanzees in the Mahale Mountains National Park, Tanzania. *Primates, 26,* 343–360.

Hayes, C. (1951). *The ape in our house.* New York: Harper.

Hebb, W. C. O. (1945). The forms and conditions of chimpanzee anger. *Bulletin of the Canadian Psychological Association, 5,* 32–35.

Hebb, W. C. O., & Riesen, A. H. (1943) The genesis of irrational fears. *Bulletin of the Canadian Psychological Association, 3,* 49–50.

Humphrey, N. K. (1983). *Consciousness regained.* Oxford: Oxford University Press.

Humphrey, N. K. (1976). The social function of intellect. In P. P. G. Bateson & R. A. Hinde (Eds.), *Growing points in ethology* (pp. 303–317). Cambridge: Cambridge University Press.

Jolly, A. (1966). Lemur social behavior and primate intelligence. *Science, 53,* 501–506.

Jolly, A. (1985). *The evolution of primate behavior* (2nd ed). New York: MacMillan.

Kohler, W. (1927). *The mentality of apes* (2nd ed.). London: Routledge & Kegan Paul.

Krebs, J. R., and R. Dawkins (1984). Animal Signals: Mind-reading and manipulation. In J. R. Krebs & N. B. Davies (Eds.), *Behavioral Ecology* (2nd ed.). (pp. 380–402). Oxford: Blackwell.

Linden, E. (1986). *Silent partners.* New York: Times Books.

Lorenz, K. (1970). A consideration of methods of identification of species-specific instinctive behaviour patterns. In K. Lorenz, *Studies in animal and human behavior* (pp. 57–100). London: Butler & Tanner. (Original work published 1932).

Menzel, E. W. (1974). A group of young chimpanzees in a one-acre field. In A. M. Schreier & F. Stollnitz (Eds.), *Behavior of nonhuman primates, 5,* 83–153. New York: Academic Press.

Menzel, E. W. (1971). Communication about the environment in a group of young chimpanzees. *Folia Primatologia 15,* 220–232.

Menzel, E. W., Jr., Savage-Rumbaugh, E. S., & Lawson, J. (1985). Chimpanzee spatial problem-solving with the use of mirrors and televised equivalents of mirrors. *Journal of Comparative Psychology, 99,* 211–217.

Munn, C. A. (1986). Birds that "cry wolf." *Nature, 319,* 143–145).

Nishida, T. (1983). Alpha status and agonistic alliance in wild chimpanzees. *Primates, 24,* 318–336.

Premack, D. (1986). *Gavagai: The future history of ape language research.* Cambridge, MA: M.I.T Press.

Premack, D., & Woodruff, G. (1978). Does the chimpanzee have a theory of mind? *Behavior and Brain Science, 1,* 515–526.

Rensch, B., & Dohl, J. (1967). Spontane Offnen vershiedener Kistenverschlusse durch einen Schimpansen (spontaneous opening of various locked boxes by a chimpanzee.) *Z. Tierpsychol, J. 24,* 476–489.

Rensch, B., & Dohl, J. (1968) Wahlen zwischen zwei ubershaubaren Labyrinthwegen durch einen Schimpanzen. (Choice between two visible maze pathways by a chimpanzee.) *Z. tierpsychol.* 25: 216–231.

Savage-Rumbaugh, E. S. (1986). *Ape language: From conditioned response to symbol.* New York: Columbia University Press.

Savage-Rumbaugh, E. S., & McDonald, K. (1988). Deception and social manipulation in symbol-using apes. In R. W. Bryne & A. Whiten (Eds.), *Machiavellian intelligence* (pp. 224–237). Oxford: Oxford University Press.

Seyfarth, R. M., Cheney, D. L., & Marler P. (1980a). Vervet monkey alarm calls: Semantic communication in a free-ranging primate. *Animal Behavior, 28,* 1070–1094.

Teleki G. (1989). Population status of wild chimpanzees *(Pan troglodytes)* and threats to survival. In P. G. Heltne and L. A. Marquart (Eds.), *Understanding chimpanzees.* (pp. 312–353). Cambridge, MA: Harvard University Press.

Temerlin, M. K. (1975). *Lucy: Growing up human.* London: Souvenir Press.

de Waal, F. B. M. (1982). *Chimpanzee politics.* New York: Harper & Row.

de Waal, F. B. M. (1986). Deception in the natural communication of chimpanzees. In R. W. Mitchell & N. S. Thompson (Eds.), *Deception: Perspectives on human and nonhuman deceit* (pp. 221–244). Albany: SUNY Press.

de Waal, F. B. M. (1987). *Games pygmy chimpanzees play.* San Diego: Zoonooz.

Whiten, A., & Byrne, R. W. (1988a). Tactical deception in primates. *Behavioral and Brain Sciences.* 11:233–244.

Whiten, A., & Bryne, R. W. (1988). The manipulation of attention in primate tactical deception. In R. W. Byrne & A. Whiten (Eds.), *Machiavellian intelligence* (pp. 211–223). Oxford: Oxford University Press.

Wrangham, R. W. (1977). Feeding behavior of chimpanzees in Gombe National Park, Tansania. In T. H. Clutton-Brock (Ed.) *Primate Ecology* (pp 503–538). New York: Academic Press.

11

HUMAN PSYCHOLOGY AND THE MINDS OF OTHER ANIMALS

George F. Michel
DePaul University

ABSTRACT

Unlike other constructs in science that can be described both metaphorically and literally, mind is always metaphoric. Folk psychology allows attribution of mental states and intentions to others by analogy with the common metaphors used in the intuitive understanding of our own mental states and intentions given that there is some perceived similarity between our own behavior and that of others and between the situations within which the behaviors occur. Recent studies of human cognition, category formation, and social skill challenge folk psychology and demonstrate that (a) most human cognitive processes are nonconscious, (b) many conceptual categories are derived from human biological capacities and experience, and (c) the apparent finesse of human social skill rests heavily on error-prone scripts. It is unlikely that folk psychology will form the basis of a science of human psychology. Nevertheless, folk psychological theory pervades human thinking, remembering, and perceiving and creates a very subtle anthropomorphism that can corrupt the formation of a science of cognitive ethology. The challenge in the study of the minds of other animals is to avoid the seductive constructs of folk psychology and find terms in which minds that may be different from our own can be contemplated.

Early in this century, Holmes (1911) proposed that we infer the mental states of others by noting the similarities in the circumstances that evoke such states in ourselves and the similarities in the actions and expressions that accompany such states. Also, because we routinely speak of our reasons for doing things in terms of mental states, we expect that similar reasons motivate the actions of others. Thus, perceived similarity between our actions and those of others and reasoning by analogy with our introspective experience are the major bases for forming inferences about the mental states of others. These inferences may allow fairly accurate prediction and explanation of the actions of others and may play a vital role in the formation of "folk psychological theory" (Stich, 1983, p. 1–10). However, Holmes cautioned that our inferences are apt to be wrong for people of other cultures (cf., Shweder, 1977) and for animals.

Because it is more difficult for animals to correct a mistaken inference, any errors of inference can have graver consequences for the characterization of animals. Therefore, it has been common practice in the study of animal behavior to avoid attributing human mental abilities to animals. During the last 2 decades, this practice has begun to be systematically challenged by those wishing to describe the evolution of human mental abilities and the cognitive abilities of animals (e.g., Griffin, 1978).

According to Humphrey (1976), the cognitive abilities that enable us to draw inferences about mental states in others may have evolved specifically to enable us to function within a social group. Many social primate species appear to use their cognitive abilities to explore, know, understand, and influence other members of their society (Jolly, 1988). It has been argued that in order to contribute to and exploit the organization of their society, social primates must be able to calculate the consequences of their own behavior and the likely behavior of others within a context that is subject to change, even as a consequence of their own actions. The cognitive skills that provide for such social finessse are also thought to be involved in inferring the mental states of others.

Some researchers have thought it reasonable to assume that social primates possess mental abilities similar to those of humans and that these abilities served in the evolution of human abilities. However, similarity among patterns of communication, social structure, roles, and achievement across species cannot be sufficient evidence for similarity of underlying mechanism.[1] Members of each social species, regardless of phyletic level, must exhibit social finesse. That is, members of social species are by definition socially competent, but it is not clear that inferring the mental abilities of others is essential for such competence. Nor is it clear that social

---

[1]This precaution is especially pertinent because perceived similarity and reasoning by analogy to our introspectively derived experience form folk psychological theory and allow for attribution of mental abilities to other humans. A science of the minds of other animals should not begin by adopting the criteria, procedures, and evaluative rules of human folk psychological theory before they have received systematic experimental examination using appropriate disconfirmation techniques. Similarity of mechanism ought to be something that is discovered by careful experimentation. It should not form the initial assumptions of the research.

finesse requires levels of cognitive skill as elaborate as that previously described.

Before attributing human mental abilities to animals, we must understand first the means by which we attribute mental states to ourselves and other humans. By knowing the phenomena and events that induce the attribution of mental states in humans, we can make informed judgments about the phenomena and events that induce the attribution of mental abilities in other animals. That is, we can know on what basis (e.g., similarity of behavioral form, situation, outcome, etc.) we attribute specific mental states to animals. Also, the cognitive skill required for human social finesse must be identified before the skills underlying social finesse in other animals can be determined. Because the science of human psychology examines the cognitive processes underlying both social finesse and the attribution of mental states to others, understanding human psychology becomes essential for studying the minds of other animals.

In the present chapter, the role of conscious processes in human cognition, the processes of category formation in human reasoning, and the contributions of cognitive processes to human social finesse will be briefly discussed. Research on each of these activities has generated information and theories that challenge conventional wisdom about the mind, the logic of our reasoning skills, and the role of mental states in the organization of social relations. This information should be directly relevant to those wishing to assess or comprehend the minds of other animals and/or the evolution of human mental abilities.

CONSCIOUSNESS AND COGNITIVE PROCESSING

Exactly what are the cognitive processes governing the inference of mental states? If Holmes (1911) is correct, then we might suppose that these processes involve a high level of self-awareness, a good deal of self-knowledge, and an extensive capacity for reflecting upon our actions. We commonly label experiences of such processes as consciousness. If social finesse could be manifested in humans without these processes, then we do not have to attribute them to all social species, and we would have to consider how they could be emergent with the evolution of the human species.

Modern cognitive research and theory indicates that the entire domain of cognitive processes, from simplest to most complex, can operate nonconsciously (Kihlstrom, 1987). Indeed, people may not be able to access, consciously, the principles or operations employed in any particular cognitive or social task. Many social judgments, preferences, and inferences are mediated by such nonconscious processes with conscious articulation of the reasons employed being manufactured after the fact (if we are able to articulate them at all) (Margolis, 1987). Thus, consciousness may not be an essential aspect of sociocognitive processes and, consequently, neither complex cognitive skill nor social finesse may be used as evidence of consciousness.

According to Margolis (1987), self–awareness, self–knowledge, and self–reflection are distinctly unique processes that serve to provide another level of correction in the development of sociocognitive skills and which were greatly facilitated in humans initially by the achievement of spoken language and later by written language. Written language, especially as it affects spoken language (i.e., what is discussed and how events and things are described), creates new levels of self–comprehension or consciousness. Because written language appeared rather recently in human history, it is unlikely that reading and writing evolved through specific selective pressures. Therefore, to the extent that reading and writing have formed human mental abilities (especially consciousness), either directly or through their impact on culture and society, there must be qualitative differences between the mental abilities of humans and other primates.

Of course the human processes underlying language are derived, in part, from more fundamental processes that may be shared with other primates. Moreover, reading and writing employ many cognitive abilities only some of which are associated with spoken language. Surely, some of these nonlanguage abilities are shared with other primates. It is the nature of these more fundamental processes and their distribution among other species that should be the basis for further research on the evolution of human mental abilities. However, it is not easy to identify which cognitive abilities may or may not be shared with other species. Moreover, it should not be expected that these more fundamental processes will bear any but the most superficial resemblance to human language–associated processes. The fundamental processes allowed the evolution of human language processes; they must not be confused with those processes.[2]

MINDING CATEGORIES

One fundamental process underlying human mental abilities must involve the formation of categories. By whatever means we choose to characterize the minds of humans and other animals, both the choice and the characterization ultimately depends upon the cognitive capabilities of the humans doing the describing and characterizing. How we choose to describe the

---

[2]It is not necessary to argue that the forelimbs of reptiles are wings or wing precursors in order to examine their role in the evolution of avian wings.

phenomena of mind depends on how we form concepts and categories. Processes of categorization are essential for organizing behavior according to classes of events rather than treating each situation, stimulus, event, and so forth as completely new. To the cognitive scientist, the formation of categories and concepts is fundamental to understanding phenomena of intending, imaging, judging, remembering, reasoning, and awareness.

Both conventional wisdom (folk theory) and philosophy agree that categories are formed by common properties. That is, categories are defined by the necessary and sufficient conditions specifying the properties shared by all and only members of the category. To be sure, we often categorize by shared common properties. However, modern research shows that most categories are not formed in this way (Lakoff, 1987). Obviously, understanding how we categorize events, actions, and abstract relations is fundamental to understanding how we think and function in a social realm. Therefore, changing our notion of how we form categories changes our concept of mind and our understanding of social as well as physical reality.

For most categories, especially those relevant to social relations and mental states, members of the category do not share the same properties that define the category. Rather, there seems to be a family resemblance among members (Rosch, 1983; cf., Wittgenstein, 1953). That is, we can trace connections among members involving shared properties, but there is no single property that is shared by all members. (Similarly, we do not expect all members of the same family to have some trait or set of traits in common.) Indeed, some members seem to be better examples of the category than others. Therefore, even members within a category may be more or less central. Moreover, some categories exhibit degrees of membership so that there are no clear boundaries for determining their membership.

It appears that the properties of certain categories (the family resemblance) derive from human biological, social, and physical capacities and experience (Lakoff, 1987). These categories are used automatically and seem to function as anchor points for the organization of other categories, sometimes in a hierarchical manner but more often in a radiating manner. Therefore, it is likely that other animals, given differences in their biological, social, and physical capacities and experience, form categories of reality that are quite different from our own (cf., Nagel, 1974). In order to understand the ways other animals categorize their words, we will first have to understand exactly how our biological, social, and physical capacities and experience contribute to the formation of human anchor categories and how anchor categories contribute to the formation of other categories. Then we will have some notions of what to examine in the biological, social, and other aspects of experience in other animal species that could contribute to the formation of their anchor categories. By such research we could determine similarities and differences in category formation between humans and other animals just as we identify similarities and differences in sensory processing and motor coordination (Dethier, 1969).

COGNITION AND SOCIAL FINESSE

It is generally recognized that human cognitive skills contribute to the organization and conduct of human social phenomena (Heider, 1958; Jones & Davis, 1965; Kelley, 1967; Nisbett & Ross, 1980). Every social exchange is thought to require a causal judgment (a judgment identifying a reasonable cause for some action or consequence of some action), a social inference (an inference about the dispositions of the participants or the properties of the situation to which the participants responded), and a prediction (an expectation about future actions and outcomes). Thus, we interpret information about our own behavior and that of others by making judgments about the causes and intentions of action and by making predictions about the actions and reactions of others. Those interested in the evolution of these sociocognitive abilities want to know whether other primate species engage in similar cognitive processes for regulating their social actions and whether these processes are continuous with forms that evolved earlier and hence are represented in nonprimate species.

Before these questions can be addressed, it must be noted that most theorists consider that it would be too burdensome a task for humans to engage in these cognitive processes for every social exchange. Therefore, it is not surprising that research shows that we tend to function in social exchanges typically by using a set of intuitive cognitive heuristics (rules of thumb for identifying patterns of relationship) which reduce and simplify information to insure quick processing (e.g., Abelson, 1976; Dawes, 1976; Nisbett & Ross, 1980).

One such social heuristic is the formation of scripts (Abelson, 1976; Schank & Abelson, 1977) which tend to consist of concrete episodes of action and reaction. These concrete episodes serve as prototypical exemplars for the classification of social events and, in turn, govern our participation in them. That is, they frame social action. Thus, a human social behavioral skill consists of the selection of a particular script to represent the situation and the taking of a role in the script. Playing a role reduces the cognitive burden of continual assessment and judgment of the social exchange.

SOCIOCOGNITIVE HEURISITICS

Social scripts are just one form of the cognitive heuristics used to regulate and facilitate daily living. The ordinary discourse and reasoning available for regulating the common social experiences of living in society serve as the foundation and testing ground for these heuristics and allow their formation into a folk psychological theory (Ross, 1978; Stich, 1983). It might be expected that a particular society and its history, language, social values, and so forth ought to produce certain unique heuristics that would lead to cultural differences in folk theories (Shweder, 1977); whereas, common social problems having limited solutions as well as communication across societies ought to yield universals in folk theory.

Although intuitive sociocognitive heuristics play an important role in aiding our adaptation to complex circumstances, they appear to make us subject to several cognitive illusions that lead to faulty reasoning and distinctive errors of judgment and decision making (Dawes, 1976; Johnson-Laird & Wason, 1977; Kahneman, Nisbett & Ross, 1980; Slovic, & Tversky, 1982). For example, in determining causality in a social exchange, we tend to see two unrelated events as related if they are more distinctive than other concurrent events or if we begin with a meaningful association connecting them (Chapman & Chapman, 1967, 1969; Heider, 1944). During social exchanges, we tend to predict the occurrence of low probability events when they happen to resemble what we wish to predict. Indeed, the occasional occurrence of a preferred low probability event enhances our confidence in the validity of our prediction. In other words, one confirmed prediction of a preferred event is worth hundreds of unconfirmed predictions of the preferred event. Thus, our heuristics lead us to ignore base rate information and information about the reliability of the evidence.

When inferring dispositions of social participants or when inferring the properties of the situation to which the participants responded, our intuitive heuristics make us reluctant to deduce the particular from the general but very ready to infer the general from the particular (Nisbett & Borgida, 1975). We tend to ignore statistical and abstract information, which may be logically compelling, and instead rely on vivid, concrete exemplars. That is, we form general conclusions from a few memorable instances.[3] Consequently, we often create poor models of causality but nevertheless twist and

---

[3]It is no wonder that pet owners readily acknowledge the complex mental abilities of their pets. Although long-term observation of and direct experience with the daily activities of animals are essential to the science of Ethology, the simple facts of first-hand experience and lengthy observation (such as occur in our culture with people who have pets) will not yield a science of cognitive ethology. If the evidence provided by the experience and observation of pet owners were sufficient criteria for any science, then folk psychology would be science and there would be no need for a science of cognitive ethology. We have had millenia of direct and long-term experience with observing animals and even more time observing humans. What is so compelling about modern cognitive science is that the accumulated experience and knowledge about human mental abilities can be wrong! Just as folk medicine, physics, politics, and biology can be wrong, so can folk psychology—regarding humans or pets.

distort data to fit the model rather than revise the model. Indeed, we do not have to seek evidence that would disconfirm our hypotheses, models, and theories but rather devise tests of them which can only be confirmatory (Wason, 1977; Wason & Johnson-Laird, 1972).

We prefer to focus on the gist or similarity of diverse events at the expense of attending to the details and nuances distinguishing them. This leads to the exaggeration of similarity into virtual identity and an underestimation of the extent of variability among phenomena. (This may play an important role in the assessment of the mental states of animals based on similarity of behavioral phenomena.) The more complex or complicated the task, the more simple the heuristic that we employ in dealing with it (Slovic & Lichtenstein, 1971). Also, the more complex the event, the more likely that we will believe that our simplest memories of it are valid and the more likely that we will treat more complex memories (that are more valid) with less confidence (Dawes, 1976). That is, confidence in our view of reality is more a function of the simplicity of the view than of its accuracy. Moreover, despite extensive evidence for the limitations of our cognitive abilities, we think we are better processors of information than we actually are (Dawes, 1976).

It is not too difficult to see how the illusions created by our cognitive heuristics might adversely affect the study of animal behavior and animal minds, particularly if we rely on folk psychological notions as criteria for validity. However, knowledge of our cognitive heuristics could be used to promote more sophisticated study of other animals. For example, it might be interesting to search for evidence in other social species of the use of sociocognitive heuristics because these heuristics would identify the biases and mistakes that members of those species make during social encounters. However, it would be important to avoid simple imposition of our own heuristics based on perceived similarity of circumstances.

But if our sociocognitive heuristics are so poor, how then can we function in a society? Of course, the fallibility of the heuristics only appear when compared to a formally rational system. Even folk psychology acknowledges that people act and reason according to a combination of logical rationality and interest and that we readily dispense with logic in order to maximize interest. Hence, in most common situations our heuristics serve quite well. For example, one human social behavioral skill seems to involve the ability to view any situation from the perspective of other roles as well as our own. Asch (1952) calls this the "interpenetration of phenomenal fields;" (p. 11). Humphrey (1976) calls it "sympathy" (p. 310).

Because we develop in a social world, we come to expect to be involved in fluid transactional exchanges with partners who can, with varying degrees of ability, examine the situation from our perspective and recognize that we have some comprehension of the situation as viewed from their perspective (mutual sympathy). We use this expectation to adjust and structure our involvement in the exchange and to solicit adjustment from our partners. This puts a premium on rapid judgment and evaluation of another's performance and the detection of subtle cues revealing the motives behind the previous and concurrent behavior as well as that which could have occurred.

If social exchange is the customary domain for employing sympathy, then we may be expected to behave inappropriately in contexts where sympathy, especially mutual sympathy, cannot in principle occur. Humphrey, along with many cognitive psychologists, notes that we often treat objects and physical events as though they were people with the capacity for sympathy. We entreat and attempt to bargain with nature, chance, and bureaucracies. When the turn of events appears in our favor, we readily believe that our entreaty and bargaining was effective. When things do not go in our favor, we behave as though we were slighted or deceived.

Animals are not objects or physical events, but neither are they humans. However, their behavior can be complex, confusing, and indifferent to our attempts to comprehend it. In the face of such complexity, it is easy to be tempted into dealing with the behavior of animals with the simple heuristics that are so eminently functional in the complex world of human society. Of course this is anthropomorphism. However, it is not the kind of anthropomorphism described in textbooks that can be avoided by focusing on behavioral descriptions, using operational definitions, and employing the scientific method. It is much more subtle, involving all of the biases inherent in our usual modes of cognitive functioning.

Logical rationality is an invention of certain cultures which builds upon, but is different from, patterns of organization inherent in language, social relations, and our cognitive heuristics (Margolis, 1987). It cannot be assumed that some training in the scientific method automatically protects one from cognitive illusions, any more than training prevents perceptual illusions. Even trained physicists can succumb to the seductive illusions of folk physics (Resnick, 1983). Thus, although our heuristics are workable (if not optimal) in most common circumstances, because they are not rational, they can mislead us into ignoring or misusing items of rationally useful information. People must be trained to recognize common cognitive illusions and to employ special strategies to avoid irrational judgments (Margolis, 1987).

CHALLENGING FOLK PSYCHOLOGY

Cognitive illusions can be particularly troublesome when they effect interpretation of and attribution about the mental states of the participants in certain social exchanges. Only when encountering a typical circumstances does it become obvious that our heuristics might be inappropriate and that special strategies must be employed. Consider how each of the following events challenges our sociocognitive heuristics.

A friend introduces you to a man whose face is shaved and whose hair is combed only on the right side, whose left hand is dirty and inactive, and whose left shoe and sock are missing. In conversation the man complains only of arthritis. However, he is a patient in a neurology ward suffering from a stroke that has led to the paralysis of the left side of his body. Not only is the patient's left hand paralyzed, but he does not even recognize that his left hand is his left hand. Indeed, he denies it. Another individual shows distinct signs of not being able to see anything to the left of the focus of his attention. When drawing pictures, the left side is continuously neglected. When questioned about the neglect, the patient is surprised, perplexed, and sometimes defensive. There is no evidence that the patient is aware of the neglect. It is exceedingly difficult for us to employ a social script in which we could assume a role for such patients that would allow us to comprehend their mental states.

Phenomena that challenge our typical heuristics for inferring mental states are quite common among brain damaged people. The number of specific psychological dysfunctions that can be associated with specific types of brain damage is quite large (Filskov & Boll, 1981). Consequently, a number of techniques have been used to identify precisely the functional differences between individuals with and without brain damage. Unfortunately, there is no theory of the mental status of individuals with different forms of brain damage (Marshall, 1980).

What passes for theory is a listing of types of dysfunctions, their relations to one another, and their association with the specific neuroanatomical area that is damaged. The dysfunctions become symptoms of the damage. Because the symptoms usually involve both the loss of some functions as well as an unusual increase in the occurrence of others, some have argued that the brain damage results in a reorganization of functioning. If the dysfunctions of the brain damaged individuals are viewed as the "normal" manifestations of functional reorganization of the brain as a consequence of the damage, then we will have to construct a theory that specifically addresses the mental status of such minds rather than simply note how they apparently differ from explanations derived from folk theory.

The weakness of our current theory of mental functioning as derived from folk theory is most evident in both descriptions and accounts of the disturbances that affect spatial abilities. We lack common linguistic categories for understanding body image, attentional fields, and orientation abilities. Our cognitive heuristics fail to account for, other than to mark as deviant, the mental states of individuals (a) who can observe a part of their body and deny that it is a part of their body or (b) who fail to attend to a part of their visual field even during systematic scanning. The greatest challenge in neuroscience is to construct a theory of mind that would allow incorporation of the manifestations of brain damaged individuals. It is unlikely that that theory will share much with current folk theory because folk theory can only note that the mental states of brain damaged individuals are not normal.

Consider these other challenges to our heuristics. An acquaintance is arrested and taken to a psychiatric clinic. She left her apartment to water the plants (weeds) in the small garden in the courtyard between buildings. Her neighbors called the police because she was not wearing any clothes. She explained to the arresting officers that the plants were not wearing any clothes and that it might offend them to be watered by someone with clothes made from plant fibers. Or a friend tells about a distraught young man who demanded entry into the house at 3:20 a.m. and requested asylum from the KGB and the FBI. He claimed that these organizations were searching for him in order to kill him because he had discovered the secret for world peace. The young man was eventually committed to a psychiatric clinic by his family and placed on lithium therapy. At another time, the news is dominated by reports about a teen-aged boy who murdered an acquaintance in order to find out what it is like to kill another person. The family, neighbors, and friends are surprised and shocked by acts unpredictable from their intuitive understanding of the boy's mental states.

Again, our sociocognitive heuristics are challenged. When attempting to assume the roles of the individuals above in some script, we do not succeed. Because our heuristics fail, we label the person abnormal. Our folk theory simply notes that such behavior is socially unacceptable, and the individual is classified as mentally unstable or ill. However, for much of the actions of individuals labeled as mentally ill our heuristics operate quite well. Indeed, we tend to label the instances when the heuristics fail as psychotic breaks. Even the signs of disturbed mental functioning apparently overlap enough with normal functioning to generate "intern's syndrome" in students. It is often an arduous process for students to keep distinct the symptoms that discriminate those with and without mental illness as well as the various forms of mental illness. This difficulty in discrimination occurs because we have no adequate theory of the structural and functional organization of the mental states of individuals labeled as mentally ill. Neither our heuristics nor folk theory allow prediction or explanation of these mental states. Clearly, the minds of the mentally ill are different from those represented in folk theory.

Consider these other challenging examples. A friend refuses to have the police issue an injunction against her husband to prevent him from entering their home. He has threatened her with bodily harm, and he has attacked her physically several times in the past (events which she tends to forget). She has considered leaving him for many years but has done nothing about it. He is very solicitous and apologetic after each argument (at least one a week) and each time claims that he will change. He always blames their arguments on her and manages to convince her that she is at fault. She seems to have convinced herself that he is changing, and that the fights are just slips. Neither wants to leave the other. Or consider another friend who complains about his bad luck with women. He always manages to get female companions who treat him like dirt no matter how courteous, sensitive, and thoughtful he is to them. Each time his friends have warned him about his newest choice of companion, but he has insisted that she is neither like the others nor like her reputation. His therapist has proposed that his choices for female companionship represent some unconscious desire.

Here, folk theory allows explanation for these phenomena by attributing specific dispositional or character faults to the actors. Rather than seeing these mental faults as a means of coping with certain social problems, they are seen as preventing the individual from behaving rationally in certain situations. Of course, the coping strategies adopted by each of the people above may not be the best. However, because they have worked occasionally, they are difficult to change. Moreover, because they have become frequently used coping strategies, they no longer require conscious control for their utilization. It is instances similar to these two common social patterns that have prompted social psychology theorists to examine the factors contributing to the failure of our sociocognitive heuristics. They are failures when perceived by others, but they may be workable patterns, if not optimal or rational, for the participants in the social exchange.

Each of the challenges examined so far point out the difficulty of trying to build a theory of human mind based on folk psychology. If we have yet to create an adequate account of the human mind, does it seem reasonable to argue that we are creating an adequate account of the minds of other animals? We need a theory or metatheory of mind that can incorporate the similarities and differences among the cognitive functions of normal, brain damaged, psychotic, and neurotic humans as well as other species.

Finally, consider the following example. A 10 year old who is forced to share her juice with her much younger brother pours his into a tall narrow glass and her own into a shorter wider glass. She knows that he will believe that he is getting more than she because he thinks taller is more. She is exploiting a characteristic of young minds demonstrated by Jean Piaget (cf., Gruber & Voneche, 1977, pp. 342–358). He found that young children will lack conservation of physical properties of objects when these objects undergo certain kinds of perceptual transformations. Based on these and many other observations, Piaget devised a theory of mind in which the mind's functioning underwent several distinct changes during development (Gruber & Voneche, 1977, pp 814–832.)

Piaget's theory accounts for much of what constitutes folk theory, but it also reveals several unexpected characteristics. The structure of the mind at early stages of development cannot employ logically rational techniques for judgment, decision-making, and reasoning. However, these early structures allow the employment of heuristics that in many common instances mimic the consequences of logically organized reasoning. By trying to provide a consistent theory that accounted for both the successes and failures of reasoning, Piaget was forced to provide three different descriptions of the organization of the mind during development.

Piaget never claimed that logical reasoning was an intrinsic characteristic of the mature mind, but only that it depended upon the organization achieved by formal operational reasoning and hence could only be mimicked inadequately by the organization of earlier stages of mind. Piaget's theory, because it is well articulated, provides the most distinctive alternative to folk psychology. Perhaps this is why so many researchers have worked quite hard to disprove both the phenomena revealed by Piaget's theory and the theory itself. The question is not so much whether Piaget's theory is correct, but rather will the science of psychology devise theories of mind that challenge folk theory?

Some philosophers have argued that the science of psychology ought to simply codify, systematize, and make internally coherent the phenomena of folk psychology (Fodor, 1975). Others have argued that the science of psychology, like the sciences in general, will generate phenomena and explanations that bear little resemblance to its folk theory equivalent (Stich, 1983). Indeed, the study of sociocognition seems to challenge directly the adequacy of folk psychological theory for understanding human social and cognitive phenomena. Although sentiment may favor Fodor, precedent favors Stich.

FOLK PSYCHOLOGY AND THE STUDY OF ANIMAL MINDS

Because we are members of a society that is comprehended and governed by a tacit folk theory, we have become committed to a set of notions about mental phenomena that derive from that tacit theory. Our vocabulary about mental events and processes gain much of their meaning from the role they play in this folk theory. It is these subtle tacit meanings that will affect our attempts to understand the behavior of animals. Thus, we are inclined to interpret specific animal behavioral events in terms of communicative intentions because of our readiness to interpret and explain so much of their behavior in terms of intentions that are derived from our folk theory about human action. However, it is only the possibility of declaring or expressing our intentions from moment to moment that gives any sense to the notion of intention in folk theory. This poses as much of a problem for interpreting the mental states of nonhumans, who cannot correct misattributions of intention, as it does for humans whose expressed intentions we reject as meaningless, abnormal, or mistaken.

Operationally defining the attribution of intention according to our ability to predict the occurrence of an animal's action can be misleading as well. Consider the following. A researcher notes that infants, within 24 hours after birth, will occasionally show action patterns that consist of hand movements to the mouth region (about 30% of the neonate's action patterns), and that the mouth begins to open before the hand begins to move in about 21% of these hand-to-mouth actions. He reports that neonates have intentions because they open their mouths before the hand moves demonstrating their intention to place their hands in their mouths (Butterworth, 1986).

However, the infant's pattern could represent a "spreading reaction" that has little or nothing to do with intention (Michel, 1986). Because of the incomplete differentiation of sensorimotor systems, early in development the activation of one motor act is likely to inappropriately activate another motor act. Because descending motor control of the hands and arms includes collateral connection to cranial nerves controlling mouth movements, the mouth is likely to move (open) when the hand-arm is moved. Because mouth movements involve very little inertial resistance compared to the arms and hands and because the mechanisms controlling the mouth region involve shorter pathways than those for the hand, the hand will sometimes succeed mouth movements.

Perhaps the studies only differ according to the type of description used. The second study involves description of the neonate's behavior in terms of motor patterns, whereas the first study uses action words which emphasize context, orientation, and goal. According to Taylor (1964), description of behavior with action words entails that we impute intention. Is the attribution of intention to neonates simply a matter of the researcher's personal preference for a description type? Or are there other criteria that may be used to choose between descriptions?

Description according to motor patterns might reveal that the infant's mouth opens when the hand moves, even when the hand moves away from the mouth, or when the hand that cannot reach the mouth moves. If the initial description is made using intention terms, it is unlikely that anyone would raise the question of whether the infant's mouth opens whenever the hands move in any direction, because we cannot fathom any point to such behavior. Calling for more complete descriptions using intention terms will not solve the problem. Description is selective, and instances of temporal conjunction between hand and mouth movements with no plausible intentionality would, in all probability, go unnoticed and not find their way into the data record. Thus, a description in terms of motor patterns may (a) reveal phenomena that were overlooked and (b) account for or predict more phenomena than the other mode of description. It is certain that comprehension of the mental states of humans and other animals will depend crucially upon the mode of description used to describe their behavior.

A similar account was proposed for the nest-building behavior that occurs during a "relief ceremony" (Beer, 1963) during the incubation phase of a black-headed gull reproductive cycle. Although there was no difficulty in characterizing the behavior as nest-building when it occurred during nest construction, continued occurrence of the action after the nest was completed led to the characterization of the behavior as a "displacement activity", with the intention underlying the behavior having nothing to do with building nests. Thus, description in terms of the goals and intentions of the animal resulted in classifying the behavior as anomalous.[4]

By avoiding action terms in his descriptive categories, Beer demonstrated that the behavior was not at all anomalous and that its characterization as a displacement activity was superfluous. His description according to motor acts revealed that the sideways building act was typically associated with the chest-drop act whether chest-drop occurred during the nest-building phase or during the incubation phase (e.g., during nest reliefs). Hence, description according to patterns of motor acts revealed that certain forms of nest-building acts are normal during incubation, given the relation of the act to other motor acts and patterns.

METAPHORS AND MIND

During the last two centuries, it was widely agreed that the study of the phenomena of the mind should occur without the use of metaphoric language (Kearns, 1987). A science of mind should create its own laws and principles according to its own specialized vocabulary and not depend on any forced translation of its phenomena into the vocabulary of an existing natural science. However, according to Kearns (1987), no account of the mind has been able to avoid the use of metaphor. Therefore, the study of mind has been burdened by a tension between the requirement to create a

---

[4]Indeed, in order to retain action description and avoid the problem of anomalous behavior, ethologists expended much theoretical effort to provide an intentional interpretation for displacement activities. These activities were at times interpreted as communicating the ambivalent state of one animal to another, as demonstrating a conflict of motivations, etc. Thus, the displacement activity revealed something about the animal's intention.

nonmetaphoric language of mind and the intrinsically metaphoric character of all such language.

It is difficult, if not impossible, to engage in fluid discourse without resorting to metaphor (Lakoff & Johnson, 1980). Metaphors express complex relations in a compact form that is easy to communicate (Ortony, 1979). All sciences rely on metaphors to articulate existing theory and, perhaps because metaphors are always more vivid expressions than their literal equivalents, they can structure further research. Thus, metaphors are an important component of "normal science" (Kuhn, 1962). Metaphor may also play an essential role in "revolutionary science" (Kuhn, 1962). According to Kearns (1987), the attempt to arrange language by means of metaphor so that it corresponds to theory, has been the process that has led to the discovery of new theory. As new or anomalous phenomena emerge (i.e., phenomena not easily expressed by the accepted metaphor), new metaphors are sought. These new metaphors attract adherents to the anomalous phenomena and help generate the new theory.

The metaphors of most sciences can be replaced by relatively nonmetaphoric literal expressions. However cumbersome nonmetaphoric expressions might be, they can represent the phenomena of most sciences. These literal expressions also serve as the criteria for choosing among different metaphoric representation of phenomena. In contrast, the phenomena of mind are literally inexpressible. It is not possible to represent nonmetaphorically the experiencing of mental phenomena. Therefore, the study of mind relies entirely upon metaphor for the structure and content of its theory. Competing theories of mind must be evaluated according to the character of the metaphors they employ and the phenomena these metaphors express.

Theories of animal minds may be compared with folk theory, but it would be a misleading enterprise if the behavior of other animals was made more comprehensible by metaphoric representation with the folk psychological theory of human behavior and then those metaphors were used as evidence of the evolution of human cognitive abilities and their continuity with other species. It is incumbent upon those who would build a theory of the mind, whether for humans or other animals, that they make their metaphors explicit for comparison with folk and other psychological theory. If the history of other sciences can be a guide, the study of animal behavior will progress only to the extent that we can devise techniques and metaphors that avoid imputation of human mental phenomena to animals which result from metaphoric extensions of our folk psychology.

SCIENCE AND THE STUDY OF ANIMAL MINDS

Scientific progress is often associated with increased ability to predict the causal effects of certain events. Such increased predictability is presumed to depend on better descriptions of reality. However, the ability to make predictions is not proof of a true description of reality. Predictability only means that the current perspective is not divorced from reality and that it provides enough understanding to allow relatively successful functioning. Science is not distinguished from other modes of inquiry by its progress toward the correct descriptions of reality. Rather, it is distinguished by its logical rigor and empirical context. Scientific rationality is not reducible to any form of logic but is distinguished by the critical character of its historically evolving pattern of investigation.

The science of psychology must be distinguished similarly. Our intuitive folk psychology promotes in us attribution processes about the mental states of others that enable us to get on in a social world. However, these attributions often work poorly for understanding cognitive processes, especially if they involve (a) humans in situations that are out of the ordinary or (b) the behavior of other animals. A science of mind may have to extend beyond the limited power of folk psychology.

Examination of the science of medicine may be instructive for determining how best to deal with folk psychology in the science of psychology. By adopting the logical rigor and empirical context of the other sciences, medicine became quite different from the folk theories that enabled people to live reasonably healthy lives. However, the complexity of the institutional structure for the deployment of medical services has often resulted in the increase in medical problems inadvertently induced by the physician or the treatment. These iatrogenic problems, in combination with a nostalgic interest in the successes associated with folk medicine, have fostered a distrust of the science aspect of medicine. Because medicine lacks a systematic, coherent, unifying theory, its practitioners are sometimes vulnerable themselves to the conventional wisdom associated with folk medicine. However, interest in the successes of folk medicine can only arise to the extent that the success of scientific medicine compensates for the failures of folk medicine. Scientific medicine allows achievement of a level of health unattainable through folk medicine. Modern medicine provides us with the luxury of exploring folk theoretical alternatives, but it would be inappropriate to structure modern medical theory on folk medicine.

The science of "mind" must be no less critical and no less rigorous in its empirical investigations than any other scientific discipline. Because mental phenomena are only comprehensible through metaphor, there is no set of literal expressions against which one could compare the folk psychological and cognitive science theories. However, it should be possible to empirically compare the alternative theories according to the phenomena revealed using the metaphors they each employ. Those interested in the study of the minds of other animals would do well to devise their own metaphors and to look for guidance more from those aspects of cognitive science that have challenged folk theory than from those aspects that have sought to structure theories of mind on folk psychological notions.

CONCLUDING REMARKS

Cognitive science is no longer dominated by the behaviorism prevalent during the first half of this century, but neither has it embraced the intuitive notions about mental states inherent in folk psychology. Although it is far from a coherent discipline, cognitive science provides a body of knowledge that can be of direct use for those interested in studying the minds of other animals. Knowledge of the conditions that affect how we attribute mental states to ourselves and others would help the researcher avoid the cognitive illusions and subtle anthropomorphism that can occur when examining the minds of other animals.

Cognitive illusions and subtle anthropomorphism are doubly dangerous. First, because they are hidden, few researchers realize just how pervaded are their thinking, perceiving, describing, and conceptualizing skills with sociocognitive heuristics and biases. Second, because they are derivative of folk psychology, they prevent us from contemplating minds whose structure and functioning may bear little resemblance to our own.

ACKNOWLEDGMENT

I would like to thank Celia L. Moore, Linda Camras, and Debra A. Harkins for comments on earlier versions of this chapter.

REFERENCES

Abelson, R. P. (1976). Script processing in attitude formation and decision making. In J. S. Carroll & J. W. Payne (Eds.), *Cognition and social behavior* (pp. 33–46). Hillsdale, NJ: Lawrence Erlbaum Associates.

Asch, S. E. (1952). *Social psychology.* New York: Prentice-Hall.

Beer, C. G. (1963). Incubation and nest-building behaviour of black-headed gulls IV: Nest-building in the laying and incubation periods. *Behaviour, 21,* 155–176.

Butterworth, G. W. (1986). Some problems in explaining the origins of movement control. In M. G. Wade & H. T. A. Whiting (Eds.), *Motor development in children: Aspects of coordination and control* (pp. 23–32). Boston: Martinus Nijhoff.

Chapman, L. J., & Chapman, J. P. (1967). Genesis of popular but erroneous diagnostic observations. *Journal of Abnormal Psychology, 72,* 193–204.

Chapman, L. J., & Chapman, J. P. (1969). Illusory correlation as an obstacle to the use of valid psychodiagnostic signs. *Journal of Abnormal Psychology, 74,* 271–280.

Dawes, R. M. (1976). Shallow psychology. In J. S. Carroll & J. W. Payne (Eds.), *Cognition and social behavior* (pp. 3–12). Hillsdale, NJ: Lawrence Erlbaum Associates.

Dethier, V. G. (1969). Whose real world? *American Zoologist, 9,* 241–249.

Filskov, S. B., & Boll, T. J. (Eds.). (1981). *Handbook of clinical neuropsychology.* New York: Wiley.

Fodor, J. (1975). *The language of thought.* New York: Thomas Crowell.

Griffin, D. R. (1978). Prospects for a cognitive ethology. *The Behaviorial and Brain Sciences, 1,* 527–538.

Gruber, H. E., & Voneche, J. J. (Eds.). (1977). *The essential Piaget.* New York: Basic books.

Heider, F. (1944). Social perception and phenomenal causality. *Psychological Review, 51,* 358–373.

Heider, F. (1958). *The psychology of interpersonal relations.* New York: Wiley.

Holmes, S. J. (1911). *The evolution of animal intelligence.* New York: Holt.

Humphrey, N. K. (1976). The social function of intellect. In P. P. G. Bateson & R. A. Hinde (Eds.), *Growing points in ethology* (pp. 303–317). New York: Cambridge University Press.

Johnson-Laird, P. N., & Wason, P. C. (1977). *Thinking: Readings in cognitive science.* New York: Cambridge University Press.

Jolly, A. (1988). The evolution of purpose. In R. W. Byrne & A. Whiten (Eds.), *Social expertise and the evolution of intellect.* New York: Oxford University Press.

Jones, E. E., & Davis, K. E. (1965). From acts to dispositions: The attribution process in person perception. In L. Berkowitz (Ed.), *Advances in experimental social psychology* (vol. 2). New York: Academic Press.

Kahneman, D., Slovic, P., & Tversky, A. (1982). *Judgments under uncertainty: Heuristics and biases.* New York: Cambridge Univ. Press

Kearns, M. S. (1987). *Metaphors of mind in fiction and psychology.* Lexington, KT.: University of Kentucky press.

Kelley, H. H. (1967). Attribution theory in social psychology. In D. Levine (Ed.), *Nebraska Symposium on Motivation* (Vol. 15). Lincoln: University of Nebraska Press.

Kihlstrom, J. F. (1987). The cognitive unconscious. *Science, 237,* 1445–1452.

Kuhn, T. S. (1962). *The structure of scientific revolutions.* Chicago: University of Chicago Press.

Lakoff, G. (1987). *Women, fire, and dangerous things: What categories reveal about the mind.* Chicago: University of Chicago Press.

Lakoff, G., & Johnson, M. (1980). *Metaphors we live by.* Chicago: University of Chicago Press.

Margolis, H. (1987). *Patterns, thinking, and cognition.* Chicago: University of Chicago Press.

Marshall, J. C. (1980). On the biology of language acquisition. In D. Caplan (Ed.), *Biological studies of mental processes* (pp. 106–148). Cambridge, MA: The M.I.T. Press.

Michel, G. F. (1986). Unpublished raw data.

Nagel, T. (1974). What is it like to be a bat? *Philosophical Review, 83,* 435–450.

Nisbett, R. E., & Borgida, E. (1975). Attribution and the psychology of prediction. *Journal of Personality and Social Psychology, 32,* 932–943.

Nisbett, R. E., & Ross, L. (1980). *Human inference: Strategies and shortcomings of social judgment.* Englewood Cliffs, NJ: Prentice-Hall.

Ortony, A. (1979). Metaphor: A multidimensional problem. In A. Ortony (Ed.), *Metaphor and thought* (pp. 1–6). New York: Cambridge University Press.

Resnick, L. B. (1983). Mathematics and science learning: A new conception. *Science, 220,* 477–478.

Ross, L. (1978). Some afterthoughts on the intuitive psychologist. In L. Berkowitz (Ed.), *Cognitive theories in social psychology* (pp. 385–400). New York: Academic Press.

Rosch, E. (1983). Prototype classification and logical classification: The two systems. In E. Scholnick (Ed.), *New trends in cognitive representation: Challenges to Piaget's theory* (pp. 73–86). Hillsdale, NJ: Lawrence Erlbaum Associates.

Schank, R., & Abelson, R. (1977). *Scripts, plans, goals and understanding.* Hillsdale, NJ:

Lawrence Erlbaum Associates.

Shweder, R. A. (1977). Likeness and likelihood in everyday thought: Magical thinking and everyday judgments about personality. In P. N. Johnson-Laird & P. C. Wason (Eds.), *Thinking* (pp. 446–467). New York: Cambridge University Press.

Slovic, P., & Lichtenstein, S. (1971). Comparison of Bayesian and regression approaches to the study of information processing in judgment. *Organizational Behavior and Human Performance, 6,* 649–744.

Stich, S. (1983). *From folk psychology to cognitive science.* Cambridge, Ma: The M.I.T. press.

Taylor, C. (1964). *The explanation of behavior.* New York: Humanities Press.

Wason, P. C. (1977). Self-contradiction. In P. N. Johnson-Laird & P. C. Wason (Eds.), *Thinking* (pp. 114–128). New York: Cambridge University Press.

Wason, P. C., & Johnson-Laird, P. N. (1972). *Psychology of reasoning.* Cambridge, MA: Harvard University Press.

Wittgenstein, L. (1953). *Philosophical investigations.* New York: MacMillan.

12 INTEGRATING COGNITIVE ETHOLOGY WITH COGNITIVE PSYCHOLOGY

Sonja I. Yoerg
Alan C. Kamil
University of Massachusetts

ABSTRACT

Cognitive ethology has been defined by Griffin (1978, 1981, 1984) as the study of mental experiences in animals, restricting the domain of the field to phenomena thought to reveal intentionality, awareness, and conscious thinking. We argue that attempts to study these processes, while revealing impressive behavioral complexity, have proven unsuccessful in establishing the importance of mental experiences in determining animal behavior primarily because of the intractability of the problem. We suggest a different approach that draws upon the rich theory and sophisticated methodology of human and animal cognitive psychology while retaining an ecological and evolutionary perspective. Brief accounts of the conceptual underpinnings of cognitive psychology are presented as well as examples of empirical work, including the analysis of imagery in human and nonhuman animals. We hope our broad redefinition of cognitive ethology provides a rigorous framework within which to examine the role of cognition in ecologically relevant behavior.

The term cognitive ethology could have many meanings given the variety of meanings attached to the word cognitive and to the word ethology. Griffin (1978, 1981, 1984) defined cognitive ethology as the "study of the mental experiences of animals". In this paper, we will argue that this definition of cognitive ethology is impractical and unproductive, because nonobservable conscious mental events constitute the very heart of the field. In overemphasizing conscious events and largely ignoring the efforts of cognitive scientists, this definition is unduly restrictive. There is a more suitable definition possible for cognitive ethology, one that involves true integration of the cognitive and ethological approaches and offers hope of eventually understanding the structure, evolution, and function of mind.

When defined in terms of mental events, cognitive ethology has two major flaws. First, it suffers from the absence of theories that make testable predictions. This problem stems partly from the nature of the subject matter that the field has defined as its domain as well as from a reluctance to convert vague and unparsimonious mentalistic accounts of cognitive phenomena into viable hypotheses amenable to empirical test. Second, because of the narrow scope of cognitive ethology, it remains virtually untouched by the theories, data, and methodological developments of human and animal cognitive psychology. This is not healthy. We contend that cognitive ethology can and should be more broadly defined.

In the next section of this paper, we outline the defining characteristics of current cognitive ethology, give its interpretation of the domain of cognitive analyses, and identify some of the problems caused by this definition and interpretation. The field of cognitive psychology is then defined, emphasizing the centrality of the information processing metaphor to both the initial development of the discipline and its current status as a powerful agent in the study of cognitive events. We describe how cognitive processing and organization are examined in nonhuman animals, provide examples, and outline the new trend toward ecologically motivated studies of animal cognition. We argue that cognitive ethology should be this ecological comparative approach to the study of animal cognition.

COGNITIVE ETHOLOGY

According to Griffin (1978, 1981, 1984), the subject matter of cognitive ethology is consciousness, awareness, emotion, intentionality, and conscious thinking in animals; in short, mental experiences. For example, Griffin (1984) states that the challenge of cognitive ethology "is to venture across the species boundary and try to gather satisfactory information about what other species may think or feel" (p. 12). This is a restricted use of the word cognition, which is usually defined as the process or faculty of knowing. Cognitive psychology operates within this broader definition as the study of how knowledge is acquired, processed, and used. Throughout cognitive psychology, the category of cognitive processes includes not only those involved in mental experience but those involved in all mental events regardless of whether the animal itself experiences those events. (An elaboration of the goals of cognitive psychology is given in a subsequent section.)

Certain characteristics of cognitive ethology are consequences of this definition. First, there is an emphasis on continuity with human mental experiences (e.g., Griffin, 1978). This occurs because the best (and perhaps only) source of evidence of consciousness comes from ourselves. The second best source of evidence results from our willingness to generalize from our own experience to those of other humans. And if we are willing to make that generalization among humans, it can be argued that the generalization should be extended to include nonhuman animals as well. For example, most humans would agree that they have had mental images, picture-like experiences in the absence of a concurrent visual stimulus, and assume that this holds for humans in general. Why not, then, grant the likelihood of imagery in other animals? Arguments based on evolutionary continuity are used to support the parsimony of this generalization (e.g., Griffin, 1978).

Second, defining cognitive ethology as the study of mental experiences promotes an emphasis on communicative behavior. The reasoning is that because human thought is largely language mediated, then ". . . insofar as animal communication shares basic properties of human language, the employment of versatile communication systems by animals becomes evidence that they have mental experiences and communicate with conscious intent" (Griffin, 1978, p. 528). First, formal and functional similarities between human and nonhuman communication do not demand the operation of conscious processes in both instances. Second, because it is assumed that mental experiences are particularly visible through the window of communication, the relation between communicative behavior and thought, intent, and awareness may be exaggerated. Do words necessarily speak louder than actions?

Collecting Evidence

If we accept for the moment that cognitive ethology is the study of mental experiences, we can then ask how this enterprise is and ought to be conducted. Griffin (1984) has suggested some criteria for inferring conscious thought: (a) "plastic" behavior, (b) modifiable aspects to a complex behavior pattern, and (c) anticipation or intentional planning. The plausibility of these criteria are not at issue. Rather, we need some way to progress from criteria that are suggestive of conscious thought, imagery, or awareness to criteria that are indicative of them. General arguments based on continuity with human mental experiences (given that we have adequate methods for assessing them) can only imply the possibility of the existence of similar attributes in nonhuman species. They cannot establish the continuity. There are certainly enough examples of complex behavior in animals to allow inferences about almost any sort of mental experience to be drawn if the only criteria were the possibility of the existence of such experiences. But if cognitive ethology is to be a science, it must do more than point to interesting cases in which one interpretation of the observed behavior involves conscious thought or intent.

Current cognitive ethology is virtually atheoretical. Without theory, there are no meaningful predictions. Without meaningful predictions (ideally from competing theories) data are difficult, if not impossible, to evaluate. If cognitive ethology is defined as the study of mental events in animals, its theories should consist of possible answers to the question: What should behavior look like if it is influenced by mental experiences? Of course the question asks about behavior and not about mental experiences themselves because we cannot observe mental events directly. It is critical both that the theories make specific predictions and that the postulated mental experiences be distinguishable in their effects from other mental experiences and from internal (and external) events in general. For example, a theory of the effect of visual imagery on orientation to remote food sources would have to do more than predict the use of visual information in finding food. It would have to propose a working definition of what it means to use a visual image and then predict behavioral outcomes that follow from that definition and do not follow from the use of visual information in a form other than an image.

Consider Ristau's (this volume) work on injury feigning in plovers. When an intruder approaches the nest, parent plovers may exhibit a broken-wing display, fluttering along on the ground in a position that gives the appearance of an injured bird. Among other goals, Ristau is interested in determining the extent to which the plover is intentionally leading the intruder away from the nest. That is, does the plover know that feigning injury will lure the intruder away? Does the plover know that it is deceiving the intruder in doing so? The data collected demonstrate that the form of the display is sensitive to the behavior of the intruder; the bird adjusts the direction of the display or its intensity depending on the intruder's response. How do these data bear on the question of intentionality? Although the data do indicate that the function of the behavior is to direct intruders away from the nest, there is nothing that necessitates the invocation of conscious intent as an explanation. Ristau (this volume) has more recently shown that an intruder that threatened a nest earlier evoked a more intense display on subsequent intrusions. This result is also silent on the question of intentionality. It does suggest that the plover remembers individual intruders and can use that memory in determining the strength of subsequent displays — an interesting finding.

In order to assess the role of intentionality in the plover's behavior, a theory must be formulated that specifies behavioral outcomes that would not occur if the plover did not intend to lure the intruder away from the nest. To justify the use of the concept of intentionality, a behavioral equivalence class must be defined, and a prediction about behavior must be made that depends uniquely on the awareness of the plover of its own behavior. We cannot think of a theory that would make that prediction. That does not mean that we cannot bring ourselves to believe that plovers or any other animal may be capable of intention. It means that we cannot conceive of an experiment that would prove it.

One aspect of cognitive ethology that tends to obscure the absence of theory is the tendency to confuse the thought and words that experimenters use to formulate research questions with the explanations assigned to the resulting data. It is a common if not ubiquitous practice for students of animal behavior to place themselves in the position of an animal confronted with a situation, problem, or task and ask, "What would I do?" Our own phenomenology is clearly a rich source of ideas about what animals might do or how they might do it. Indeed, Tolman, perhaps the first cognitive psychologist, said: "I, in my future work intend to go ahead imagining how, *if I were a rat,* I would behave" (1938, p. 24). There is nothing wrong with asking oneself: "If I were a plover and I were trying to get an intruder away from my nest, how would I behave?" It is, however, wrong to assume that the subjective experience that stimulated an experiment is isomorphic with the experience of the animals in that experiment. The interpretation of data should follow from a careful analysis of the consonance of those data with the predictions of a theory and not with one's own introspections. We may talk or think loosely under some conditions about what our animals might be doing or thinking, but we should be circumspect in our evaluation of the level or complexity of explanation the evidence demands.

It is informative to consider an analogous problem in behavioral ecology. Optimal foraging models assume that foraging animals have been selected to maximize some quantity related to fitness, usually intake rate. These models, therefore, describe a method of calculating rate of intake as a function of various environmental and behavioral parameters such as prey value and handling time. The calculations often entail high-level mathematics, and some computer simulations require significant processing time on powerful machines. But one cannot contend, when the predictions of an optimal foraging model are confirmed, that the forager calculates optima the way the model does; evidence for how information is processed necessitates a different sort of theory. Cognitive ethologists must maintain the distinction between the tactics of the theoretician and those of the animal.

AN ALTERNATIVE APPROACH TO COGNITIVE ETHOLOGY

We have been very critical of cognitive ethology as defined in terms of mental experience. One aspect of cognitive ethology, however, has had a positive impact. Animal behaviorists—ethologists, behavioral ecologists, and comparative psychologists—all face a substantial challenge illuminated by Griffin (1978, 1981) and others: the complexity of animal behavior. The development of cognitive ethology has helped emphasize that animals routinely engage in behavior more complex than most ethologists or psychologists would have thought plausible as is amply demonstrated in other chapters of this volume. The discovery of this complexity suggests that there ought to be a field called cognitive ethology, but it should not be loosely slung in a net of mentalistic verbiage. Rather, it should be defined as the rigorous, wholly scientific study of cognition in an ethological and ecological context.

Many phenomena show that cognitive processes such as learning, attention, categorization, recognition, and memory can play important roles in the lives of animals in the field (Kamil, 1988; Yoerg, in prep). As we have discussed extensively elsewhere (Kamil, 1988; Kamil & Yoerg, 1982; Yoerg, in prep), evidence for the importance of behavioral complexity has come from psychology, ethology, and behavioral ecology. How do we integrate these different approaches to the study of behavior? In the remainder of this paper, we develop the idea of a cognitive ethology that combines the best of cognitive science with the best of ethology.

COGNITION

The history of the study of cognition is not a simple one. Its initial development cannot be attributed to the work of one, two, or even a few people. Furthermore, the study of cognition was, and continues to be, influenced by many fields. (For historical accounts see Gardner, 1985; Knapp, 1986). Most scholars agree, however, that Neisser's (1967) book *Cognitive psychology* was a seminal work, the first to establish the use of the term that serves as its title. Neisser (1967) states that:

> Cognition refers to all the processes by which the sensory input is transformed, reduced, elaborated, stored, recovered, and used. It is concerned with these processes even when they operate in the absence of relevant stimulation, as in images and hallucinations. Such terms as sensation, perception, imagery, retention, recall, problem-solving and thinking, among many others, refer to the hypothetical stages or aspects of cognition. (p. 4)

More recent definitions are essentially similar to this.

The development of cognitive psychology was tremendously influenced by, if not wholly dependent on, the advent of the communication and information sciences (Lachman, Lachman, & Butterfield, 1979). Abstraction about the nature of man-made physical systems was borrowed from communications engineering and information theory and applied to the study of human mental states and processes: Environmental stimuli became inputs of information, responses (behavior) became the system's output. Conceptualizations about what might intervene between input and output were formulated in the same language using terms such as channel capacity, serial and parallel processing, and coding to refer to how information travelled through and was transformed by the human mind.

Palmer and Kimchi (1986) identify and discuss at length the fundamental assumptions of this information processing approach to the study of cognition. We will outline only the essential points here. First, mental events are functionally analogous to informational events, which consist of an input, an operation performed on that input, and a resulting output. The temporal order among components of informational events specifies the characteristics of information flow through the system. Information in this system is embodied in states called representations; the operations that are performed on that information are embodied in changes of state called processes. The task of the cognitive psychologist from an information processing perspective is to determine the nature and organization of the processes which transform, encode, represent, and use information from the external (or internal) world to produce behavior.

The domain of cognitive psychology can be divided into two interrelated areas: (a) the nature of the representation of information (cognitive content) and (b) the nature of the processing (cognitive structure and function). One question about representation concerns coding: What are the rules that relate the features of the stimulus input to the features of the representation of the information in that input? For example, in remembering someone's face, what is the relation between the contents of memory and the real face? When we form a concept do we represent distinct features, an ideal standard, or an array of exemplars from our experience (Smith & Medin, 1986)?

Issues of representation and coding are linked with those of processing and organization. Early views of cognitive processing (e.g., Broadbent, 1958) accepted a linear view of information flow in which information was transformed in a series of discrete stages beginning with sensation and ending with long-term memory and/or output to effectors. Emphasis was given to the temporal dimensions of the system with little attention to content or the kinds of processing involved. More recent models attempt to accomodate the wealth of empirical data that suggest less linear, more complex flow dynamics. For example, cognitive psychologists now distinguish between bottom-up (sensory-driven) and top-down (concept-driven) processes. In bottom-up processing, the form of the input determines the nature and extent of the processing—the animal is a relatively passive receiver of information. In top-down processing, the evaluation of sensory input depends on previous experience, expectations, and the current context. Most cognitive activity seems to involve the simultaneous interaction of both top-down and bottom-up processing (e.g., Neisser, 1976). For example, perception is usually conceived of as a bottom-up process in that we appear to perceive directly what exists in the world. But expectations can affect perception drastically: Many apparent road kills are really paperbags or pieces of tire. Similarly, remembering would appear to be a top-down process because it requires and depends on past experience. However, the features of the cues used to guide recall are critical to its efficiency. Other questions about the functional organization of cognition include whether component operations of processes are carried out serially or in parallel (e.g., Sternberg, 1966), and whether processing is modular and content-specific (e.g., Fodor, 1983), or more global and content-independent (Anderson, 1983).

The Role of Computer Science

The information processing approach to the study of cognition is, of course, allied with computer science which represents the most advanced information science. However, the influence of concepts and methodology from computer science is not uniform throughout cognitive psychology. Two major positions can be identified: (a) adherence to "weak artificial intelligence (AI)" and (b) adherence to "strong AI" (Searle, 1980). Believers in weak AI consider the computer only a powerful ally in attempts to understand cognitive processing, especially when modelling cognitive functions. Believers in strong AI contend that a computer with the right programs has a mind and cognitive states; hence, the programs are explanations of the cognitive phenomena. Not even a belief in weak AI is demanded by the information processing approach (Palmer & Kimchi, 1986).

The point of drawing these distinctions in attempting to characterize cognitive psychology is to ensure that information processing is not falsely rejected as a plausible way to address questions of import to cognitive ethologists. Griffin (1984) states that an information processing approach leads to viewing the human mind "as nothing more than a computer system" (p. iv). As a consequence, according to Griffin, the possibility of consciousness in animals is rejected, and a major portion of psychological function is disregarded. This rejection of the information processing approach is an error for several reasons.

First, many cognitive psychologists hold that the computer is limited in its ability to mimic human cognitive processing—conscious or unconscious. Second, a belief in strong AI does not deny the reality of consciousness;

consciousness is one cognitive phenomenon of many that might be an emergent property of a properly programmed computer. A human mind, in the strong AI view, would be nothing less (or more) than a computer program. Third, not all information processing models are computer-based. In new parallel distributed processing (PDP) models (e.g., Rumel-hart & McClelland, 1986), neural networks are the conceptual analogue. Information is represented as the state of activation of a large network of simple units. PDP models can account for many perceptual phenomena and are now being applied to the domains of memory and language learning.

Nonconscious Cognitive Processing

Perhaps one result of cognitive ethology's distance from cognitive psychology has been the concentration on conscious processes. Cognitive psychology has clearly demonstrated that many crucial aspects of human cognition are not conscious. This is hardly a new development. Freud's most lasting contribution to psychology was probably his discovery of the importance of nonconscious influences on behavior.

There are many examples of important nonconscious phenomena in human cognitive processing. Consider the process of skill learning. Early on, conscious attention to the components of a skill such as driving a car is possible and may even necessary to the acquisition of the skill. After extended practice, however, the process becomes inaccessible to conscious-ness and attempts to attend to the process may interfere with its execution, as with skilled musicians and typists (Kihlstrom, 1987). The changes in the accessibility of the processes underlying skilled behavior are thought to be concomitant with changes in the representation of the knowledge acquired. Highly skilled abilities may require little or no attention and therefore do not necessarily compete with other processes for limited attentional re-sources—hence our ability to drive a car and carry on a conversation simultaneously. Such processes are called automatic and operate with little monitoring. Automatic processes sacrifice modifiability for speed and reduced attentional demands.

Many different kinds of studies have shown that information from the external environment can be processed, and thereby affect other concurrent processing, without awareness. For example, in the shadowing task, subjects are required to repeat words that are presented only in one ear (the target ear), while other words are presented in the other ear. Lewis (1970) showed that the presentation in the nontarget ear of synonyms of the words being repeated caused a delay in the repetition. The subjects could not, however, report any of the words presented in the nontarget ear though these words had apparently been processed sufficiently to allow semantic comparison. Similarly, MacKay (1973) presented ambiguous sentences in one ear (e.g., Three men sat on the board) and a single word (e.g., executives or workers) in the other ear. Again, even though the subjects could not remember the words that were presented in the nontarget ear, they interpreted the ambiguous sentences as if they did.

Because of the interaction between unconscious and conscious processes and the importance of each in the performance of many behaviors (simple and complex), it is imprudent to restrict the domain of cognitive ethology to conscious processes alone. If we are to develop a truly comprehensive account of the minds of animals, we cannot turn our attention (pun intended) away from any classes of cognitive events.

AN EXAMPLE OF STUDIES OF ANIMAL COGNITION

One consequence of the broad and intense development of human cognitive psychology was a revival of interest in animal cognition during the 1970s (e.g., Hulse, Fowler, & Honig, 1978). For the 30 years prior to this, the field of animal learning within psychology was almost completely dominated by the radical behaviorist tradition. The strength of that tradition is now much reduced, with most students of animal learning and behavior adopting the cognitive approach that has its historical roots in Tolman's brand of cognitive psychology (Riley, Brown, & Yoerg, 1986). The goals of the study of animal cognition are similar to those of human cognitive psychology: to understand what occurs in the temporal gap between environmental events and behavior. Because a review of the field is beyond the scope of this chapter, we will only provide one example of animal cognitive psychology. Our primary goal is to illustrate how methods borrowed directly from cognitive psychology are powerful tools for examining mental events in nonhuman animals. Two symposium volumes provide other examples (Hulse, Fowler, & Honig, 1978; Roitblat, Bever, & Terrace, 1984).

Sternberg (1966, 1969) developed a procedure for studying memory retrieval processes in humans which has proved invaluable. The essence of this procedure is that the human subjects are shown word lists of various lengths and then asked whether or not a particular word appeared on the list. Sands and Wright (1980, 1982) adopted this procedure for use with rhesus monkeys. The monkey sat before a screen on which it was shown a series of distinct color slides; this was the list of items to be remembered. The length of the list varied from one to six items. A single probe slide was then presented. By moving a lever to the left or right, the monkey indicated whether the probe slide matched a slide in the original list or was different from all the slides in that list. The primary dependent measure was reaction time—the latency to make the same/different choice.

When the probe item matched an item on the original list, reaction times increased with list length. Specifically, the addition of one more list item increased the latency to make the same response by about 13 msec. This finding supports the notion of memory scanning: The probe item was compared to each list item held in memory sequentially. Consequently, longer lists yielded longer reaction times. When the probe item did not match any of the list items, reaction times were slower than on same trials, though the slope of the function relating reaction time to list length was similar. This result constitutes additional support for the hypothesis of a serial memory scan because, on the average, it should take longer to find that no item on the list matches the probe than to find a match.

Furthermore, Sands and Wright (1980, 1982) found evidence for an effect of the serial position of the probe item in the original list; probe items that matched list items presented first (the primacy effect) or last (the recency effect) in the sequence were remembered better than those presented in the middle. All the results described have also been obtained with humans (Sternberg, 1966).

The data generated by this simple task have illuminated one aspect of cognitive processing in rhesus monkeys and humans: that the retrieval of an item in memory, in this situation, is a systematic serial process. The processes responsible for the serial position effects are not completely understood, but any model of this type of memory must account for them.

THE ANALYSIS OF IMAGERY IN HUMANS AND ANIMALS

Cognitive ethology has not yet had a strong impact on the study of animal behavior. This is not because questions of animal cognition are not relevant to attempts to understand the role of behavior in adaptation; the analysis of the relations among behavior, cognition, ecology, and evolution is not only a legitimate area of study but a necessary one (Yoerg, in prep). Rather, cognitive ethology, when defined as the study of mental experience, has suffered from confining itself to the most intractable issues of cognition — consciousness, intentionality, and emotion. The difficulty of studying these concepts is, of course, not sufficient reason to abandon them, but the standards of what constitutes convincing evidence still apply. The purpose of this section is to explore how one phenomenon of interest — imagery — to current cognitive ethology has been studied within human and animal cognitive psychology. Whether other concepts such as conscious intent or awareness can be similarly analyzed is not at all clear and awaits future attempts.

Human Imagery

Images are perception-like experiences. The study of imagery is the elucidation of the processes that underly their formation, transformation, and use. Although introspective evidence for imagery is abundant, its status as a theoretical construct is uncertain. The source of this uncertainty is the difficulty in specifying the nature of the image: What is the relation between the part of the physical world being imagined and the image? What sort of representation is an image? Some argue that images are epiphenomenal or nonfunctional, but as Pylyshyn (1981) correctly indicates, only when we have ascertained what images are will we be in a position to determine if they are epiphenomenal.

Two major approaches to the conceptualization of images can be identified: the analogue and the propositional. According to the analogue view, the way in which images can be transformed can be attributed to the medium in which images are represented or to the processes that transform images (e.g., Kosslyn, 1981). That is, the medium of visual image representation is analogous to coordinate space and mimics its properties. According to the propositional view, images are transformed in certain ways because people use their interpretation of the task and tacit knowledge about the physical properties of the world and apply them to images (Pylyshyn, 1981). The phenomena, then, that appear to support a correspondence between imaging and the act of seeing are really only evidence for what subjects believe about physical space and what they perceive is the goal of the task.

Consider the following experiment. Imagine a baseball diamond and focus on homeplate. Now shift your focus to first base. Suppose the latency to make this shift was recorded, for instance, by pushing a button when the instruction to shift was given and pushing it again when you successfully focussed on first base. Now return your focus to homebase and then shift it to left center field. The common finding in this type of experiment is that the latency to make the second shift is greater than the first; indeed, the difference corresponds to the actual difference in physical distance in the scene, assuming it has been accurately imagined. In the mental rotation task (e.g., Shepard & Metzler, 1971), subjects are asked to judge whether a rotated object was the same as a standard form or the mirror image of the form. The latency to make this response depends on the angular disparity between the rotated and standard forms suggesting that the subjects were mentally rotating an image of the form.

Proponents of the analogue account of imagery use such data to identify properties of images, for example, "images have spatial extent" and preserve "relative metric space" (Kosslyn, Pinker, Smith, & Schwartz, 1979, p. 536) and to develop elaborate models of image representation and processing. The correspondence between the time to scan an image and the actual physical distances represented in that image are taken as evidence that images have properties in common with the external world. Proponents of the propositional account dispute this claim; they argue that the empirical evidence suggests only that images represent distances not that images have distances (e.g., Pylyshyn, 1981). The difference is that the laws of the physical world that govern events in the actual scene are not necessarily the laws that govern representations of those events. A model that accounts for the scanning data must indicate why it takes longer to scan representations of greater physical distances. "There is no law of nature that demands that it must take longer to go from *representation* A to *representation* B when A and B merely *represent* locations that are further apart in the world" (Pylyshyn, 1979, p. 562).

Nonhuman Animal Imagery

Our aim in presenting these accounts is some detail (and we have omitted the lion's share of it) is to demonstrate the difficulties inherent in the study of mental experiences. Scores of well-designed experiments have been aimed at clarifying the nature of mental imagery in humans — a phenomenon that (in humans) is generally not disputed, and there is little agreement among researchers about the meaning of the results. We can expect that the study of imagery in nonhuman animals will be fraught with additional difficulties.

Neisworth and Rilling (1987) have developed a procedure that they believe is a first step in the study of imagery in animals. The task requires pigeons to respond appropriately to a moving clock hand that disappears and then reappears. The authors are circumspect in interpreting their findings, claiming only that the pigeon's ability to accurately represent movement may have required imagery. They suggest that additional experiments using a variety of procedures are needed to establish imagery in pigeons.

But their definition of imagery is imprecise: A representation is an image if it contains perceptual information (e.g., size and color) and if it can be transformed similarly to the represented object. They assert that "transformations of a mental representation *require* memory in picturelike form" (Neisworth & Rilling, 1987, p. 203). They do not specify what picturelike means. This is, of course, exactly the focus of the Kosslyn-Pylyshyn debate, and would seem to be less of a logical necessity than a plausible hypothesis. Neisworth and Rilling's (1987) results are intriguing, but whether they constitute even preliminary evidence for imagery in pigeons is unclear and will remain unclear until theories of image representation gain precision.

We do not advocate abandoning such research but, like Neisworth and Rilling (1987), suggest that we proceed extremely cautiously.

It should be noted that the phenomenon of imagery may be more amenable to rigorous analysis than that of consciousness or awareness. Most cognitive psychologists would agree that images are a type of representation, but images and/or representations need not be conscious. However, there is little consensus on what constitutes consciousness or awareness. This is not to say that an information processing approach precludes an analysis of consciousness with the appropriate scientific procedures; indeed, such attempts have been recently made (e.g., Johnson-Laird, 1983; Marcel, 1983a, 1983b).

Finally, these two case histories — serial scanning and imagery — occasion an important methodological cautionary note. In each case, very careful detailed laboratory work was required to establish what we now know about these topics, and we do not know much about the role of consciousness, awareness, or intentions in either case. It seems unlikely that we will make much progress on the complex issues raised by the cognitive approach without some of the research being carried out under highly controlled conditions.

The Ethological Approach to Animal Cognition

The four questions about behavior distinguished by Tinbergen (1963) — mechanism, ontogeny, function, and phylogeny — define the central core of the study of animal behavior. If ethology is the study of animal behavior, then obviously these four questions are the issues ethologists must address. In these terms, cognitive ethology should be the attempt to study the mechanisms, development, functions, and evolutionary history of cognitive processes. This attempt will have to cut across the traditional boundaries between several academic disciplines, primarily psychology and ethology, but also the other cognitive sciences (computer science, linguistics, and anthropology).

The boundaries between experimental animal psychology and ethology are crumbling. Meaningful integrative theoretical and empirical work has been taking place. For example:

1. Psychological models of timing, particularly the scalar expectancy model (Gibbon, 1977) has been successfully applied to foraging problems (Lucas, 1987), and integration of this mechanistic theory and optimality theory may prove extremely useful;
2. Psychological techniques and theories have been applied to the ecological and ethological concept of the search image resulting in

new insights into the mechanisms underlying the detection of cryptic prey (Getty, Kamil, & Real, 1987);

3. The mechanisms responsible for the recovery of cached food by parids (Shettleworth & Krebs, 1982) and Clark's nutcrackers (Kamil & Balda, 1985) have been studied by biologists and psychologists working collaboratively, and this research is increasing our understanding both of spatial memory and of the ecology of scatter-hoarding (Balda, Bunch, Kamil, Sherry, & Tomback, 1987).

In view of these and other developments, a comprehensive integration of psychological information processing approaches with those of ethology and behavioral ecology is at hand. Explicit detailed knowledge of the history of the advances made and problems encountered by each approach will expedite this integration. The history of the psychological study of animal cognition contains much that is useful to the modern ethologist interested in cognition. A study of this history can lead to the avoidance of errors committed and the acceptance of valuable procedures and concepts (Kamil, 1983).

The core of the matter is as follows: Cognitive organization and processing has an evolutionary history and, it is reasonable to assume, serve adaptive functions. Because behavior is determined by the interaction of environmental (ecological) and cognitive events, an interdisciplinary approach to the study of behavior is demanded, whether the behavior of interest is the result of processing that is simple or complex, conscious or unconscious. This interdisciplinary approach will follow logically from the broad definition of cognitive ethology that we suggest.

ACKNOWLEDGMENTS

Preparation of this chapter was supported by NSF grant BNS-8418721.

REFERENCES

Anderson, J. R. (1983). *The architecture of cognition.* Cambridge, MA: Harvard University Press.

Balda, R. P., Bunch, K. G., Kamil, A. C., Sherry, D. W., & Tomback, D. F. (1987). Cache site memory in birds. In A. C. Kamil, J. R. Krebs, & H. R. Pulliam (Eds.), *Foraging behavior* (pp. 645–666). New York: Plenum.

Broadbent, D. E. (1958). *Perception and communication.* London: Pergamon Press.

Fodor, J. A. (1983). *The Modularity of Mind.* Cambridge, MA: M.I.T/Bradford Press.

Gardner, H. (1985). *The mind's new science: A history of the cognitive revolution.* New York: Basic Books.

Getty, T., Kamil, A. C., & Real, P. G. (1987). Signal detection theory and foraging for cryptic or mimetic prey. In A. C. Kamil, J. R. Krebs, & H. R. Pulliam (Eds.), *Foraging behavior* (pp. 525–548). New York: Plenum.

Gibbon, J. (1977). Scalar expectancy theory and Weber's law in animal timing. *Psychological Review, 84,* 279–325.

Griffin, D. R. (1978). Prospects for a cognitive ethology. *Behavioral and Brain Sciences, 4,* 527–538.

Griffin, D. R. (1981). *The question of animal awareness.* New York: Rockefeller University Press.

Griffin, D. R. (1984). *Animal thinking.* Cambridge, MA: Harvard University Press.

Hulse, S. H., Fowler, H., & Honig, W. K. (1978). *Cognitive processes in animal behavior.* Hillsdale, NJ: Lawrence Erlbaum Associates.

Johnson-Laird, P. N. (1983). *Mental models.* Cambridge: Cambridge University Press.

Kamil, A. C. (1983). Optimal foraging theory and the pscyhology of learning. *American Zoologist, 23,* 291–302.

Kamil, A. C. (1988). A synthetic approach to the study of animal intelligence. *Nebraska Symposium on Motivation.* Vol., 35, 357–308. Linclon: Univ. of Nebraska.

Kamil, A. C., & Balda, R. P. (1985). Cache recovery and spatial memory in Clark's nutcrackers *(Nucifraga columbiana). Journal of Experimental Psychology: Animal Behavior Processes, 11,* 95–111.

Kamil, A. C., & Yoerg, S. I. (1982). Learning and foraging behavior. In P. P. G. Bateson & P. H. Klopfer (Eds.), Perspectives on ethology, vol. 5 (pp. 325–364). New York: Plenum Press.

Kihlstrom, J. F. (1987). The cognitive unconscious. *Science, 237,* 1445–1452.

Knapp, T. C. (1986). The emergence of cognitive psychology in the latter half of the twentieth century. In T. J. Knapp & L. C. Robertson (Eds.), *Approaches to cognition: Contrasts and controversies* (pp. 13–35). Hillsdale, NJ: Lawrence Erlbaum Associates.

Kosslyn, S. M. (1981). The medium and the message in mental imagery: A theory. *Psychological Review, 88,* 46–66.

Kosslyn, S. M., Pinker, S., Smith, G. E., & Schwartz, S. P. (1979). On the demystification of mental imagery. *Behavioral and Brain Sciences, 2,* 535–581.

Lachman, R., Lachman, J. L., & Butterfield, E. C. 1979. *Cognitive Psychology and Information Processing: An Introduction.* Hillsdale, NJ: Lawrence Associates.

Lewis, J. L. (1970). Semantic processing of unattended messages using dichotic listening. *Journal Experimental Psychology, 85,* 225–228.

Lucas, J. R. (1987). Foraging time constraints and diet choice. In A. C. Kamil, J. R. Krebs, & H. R. Pulliam (Eds.), *Foraging behavior* (pp. 239–269). New York: Plenum.

MacKay, D. G. (1973). Aspects of the theory of comprehension, memory and attention. *Quarterly Journal of Experimental Psychology, 25,* 22–40.

Marcel, A. J. (1983a). Conscious and unconscious perception: Experiments on visual masking and word recognition. *Cognitive Psychology, 15,* 197–237.

Marcel, A. J. (1983b). Conscious and unconscious perception: An approach to the relation between phenomenal experience and perceptual processes. *Cognitive Psychology, 15,* 238–300.

Neisser, U. (1967). *Cognitive psychology.* New York: Appleton–Century–Crofts.

Neisser, U. (1976). *Cognition and reality.* San Francisco: W. H. Freeman.

Neisworth, J. J., & Rilling, M. E. (1987). A method for studying imagery in animals. *Journal Experimental Psychology: Animal Behavior Processes, 13,* 203–214.

Palmer, S. E., & Kimchi, R. (1986). The information processing approach to cognition. In T. J. Knapp & L. C. Robertson (Eds.), *Approaches to cognition: Contrasts and controversies* (pp. 37–77). Hillsdale, NJ: Lawrence Erlbaum Associates.

Pylyshyn, Z. W. (1979). Imagery theory: Not mysterious — just wrong. *Behavioral and Brain*

Sciences, 2, 561–563.

Pylyshyn, Z. W. (1981). The imagery debate: Analogue media versus tacit knowledge. *Psychological Review, 88,* 16–45.

Riley, D. A., Brown, M. F. & Yoerg, S. I. (1986). Understanding animal cognition. In T. J. Knapp & L. C., Robertson (Eds.), *Approaches to cognition: Contrasts and controversies* (pp. 111–136). Hillsdale, NJ: Lawrence Erlbaum Associates.

Roitblat, H. R., Bever, T. G., & Terrace, H. S. (1984). *Animal cognition.* Hillsdale, NJ: Lawrence Erlbaum Associates.

Rummelhart, D. E., & McClelland, J. L. (1986). *Parallel distributed processing: Explorations in the microstructure of cognition.* Cambridge, MA: M.I.T Press.

Sands, S. F., & Wright, A. A. (1980). Serial probe recognition performance by a rhesus monkey and a human with 10- and 20-item lists. *Journal of Experimental Psychology: Animal Behavior Processes, 6,* 386–396.

Sands, S. F., & Wright, A. A. (1982). Monkey and human pictorial memory scanning. *Science, 216,* 1333–1334.

Searle, J. R. (1980). Minds, brains and programs. *Behavioral and Brain Sciences, 3,* 417–457.

Shepard, R. N., & Metzler, J. (1971). Mental rotation of three-dimensional objects. *Science, 171,* 701–703.

Shettleworth, S. J., & Krebs, J. R. 1982. How marsh tits find their hoards: The roles of site preference and spatial memory. *Journal of Experimental Psychology: Animal Behavior Processes. 8,* 354–375.

Smith, E. E., & Medin, D. L. (1986). *Categories and concepts.* Cambridge, MA: Harvard University Press.

Sternberg, S. (1966). High-speed scanning in human memory. *Science, 153,* 652–654.

Sternberg, S. (1969). Memory scanning: Mental processes revealed by reaction-time experiments. *American Scientist, 57,* 421–457.

Tinbergen, N. (1963). On aims and methods of ethology. *Zeitschrift für Tierpsychologie, 20,* 410–433.

Tolman, E. C. (1938). The determiners of behavior at a choice point. *Psychological Review, 45,* 1–41.

Yoerg, S. I. (in prep). Ecological frames of mind: The role of cognition in behavioral ecology. *Quarterly Review of Biology.*

13 COGNITIVE ETHOLOGY: AN OVERVIEW

Carolyn A. Ristau
The Rockefeller University

ABSTRACT

The contributions to this volume are compared and integrated. Donald R. Griffin outlines the main concerns of cognitive ethology. He suggests that animals might have simple thoughts about matters of consequence to them, and he explores some lines of evidence for the presence of consciousness and possible functions consciousness might serve. Colin Beer provides a summary of contemporary ideas in folk psychology and other views in the philosophy of mind as they bear upon the study of animal minds. The philosophical foundation of belief/desire concepts, one of various possible folk psychological approaches that can be applied to cognitive ethology, are examined by the philosopher Jonathan Bennett.

Misgivings about attempts to study consciousness are voiced by Yoerg and Kamil, who suggest that cognitive ethology look to cognitive psychology for useful concepts. Likewise, the developmental psychologist George Michel is concerned about using folk psychological concepts and cites difficulties from the field of developmental psychology with the use of such terms.

Other contributions note the rich research findings that have been developed through entertaining possibilities of consciousness or at least complex thinking by animals. Such approaches have led to the design of experiments not otherwise likely to have been undertaken. Alison Jolly reviews primate laboratory and field behavior that suggests consciousness, and Dorothy Cheney and Robert Seyfarth discuss possibly deceptive behavior of vervet monkeys and other animal species. I study, by means of field experiments, the injury-feigning behavior of plovers as well as other antipredator acts which suggest considerable cognitive ability. Gordon Burghardt examines the death feigning of hognose snakes in the laboratory. Both Ristau and Burghardt explore the advantages and disadvantages in applying an intentional stance (and belief/desire statements) in research on animal behavior.

Detailed aspects of animal cognition are discussed by several contributors. Irene Pepperberg cites the usefulness of a parrot's artificial communication system (the use of spoken English words) in revealing the parrot's cognitive abilities. Peter Marler, Marcel Gyger, and Stephen Karakashian describe their experiments which examine the effects of different audiences on the communication of chickens. This is a question of particular interest if one considers the possibility that animals may be intending to communicate as opposed merely to emitting vocalizations in the presence of certain classes of eliciting stimuli. Finally, W. J. Smith discusses the experiments by Marler and colleagues and examines, in more general terms, the messages and meanings of animal signals, the nature and limitation of playback experiments, and the conclusions to be drawn from such experiments.

The foremost conclusion to be drawn from the diversity of opinions is that the field of cognitive ethology, broadly construed, is a most exciting and important one. The present time is an era of pioneering studies and a time to encourage a diversity of approaches and integration with fields such as philosophy, child development, experimental and comparative psychology, and linguistics. Donald R. Griffin had a pioneering role and continues to have a most productive role in stimulating and provoking important scientific experimentation, analysis, and discussion.

The central conceptual issue in most of the papers in this book is how we should approach and study the mental states of animals or, in some cases, *if* we ought to engage in studies of their mental states (e.g., Burghardt, this volume; Yoerg, this volume; & Kamil, this volume).

COGNITIVE ETHOLOGY: DEFINITIONS, EVIDENCE, AND THE SOLIPSIST'S POSITION (GRIFFIN)

Donald Griffin begins the volume by outlining the main concerns of cognitive ethology. He takes issue with the preceding behavioristic tradition which was accompanied by the explicit avoidance of topics relating to animal mentality and consciousness.

He urges us not to become bogged down in quibbles of definition and thereby continue to neglect these subjects. Effective scientific analysis of the phenomena of learning, metabolism, and so forth has occurred despite the lack of wholly satisfactory rigorous definition. His advice is to start with the simple cases, the least complicated ones. Might animals ". . . experience relatively simple thoughts about things that are important to them?" For example, ". . . does a hungry animal think about what a particular food will taste like" (Griffin, this volume)? This approach suggests the following preliminary working definition of elementary animal consciousness: "An animal may be considered to experience a simple level of consciousness if it subjectively thinks about objects and events" (Griffin, this volume). Such a definition assumes the presence of ". . . internal representations or mental images about which the animal thinks and also of simple beliefs and desires about what it likes and dislikes" (Griffin, this volume). The simple definition does not include self–awareness or thinking about the process of thinking, though more complex levels of consciousness may well include these. A first task of cognitive ethologists is to learn how to determine the presence or absence of the simpler consciousness. This is a difficult task, but Griffin warns scientists not to decide a priori that it is not a worthwhile endeavor.

He notes that a solipsist will argue eloquently ". . . that no one can ever prove, with logical rigor, that another person is conscious," and he will further claim ". . . that he is the only conscious organism in the universe" (Griffin, this volume). Yet as we go through life assuming other people do have conscious thoughts and intentions, ". . . it is difficult to imagine how human societies could function effectively if their members acted as consistent solipsists" (Griffin, this volume). Likewise, species solipsism looms as a deterent to our scientific endeavors. Assuming we can know only our own species' conscious thoughts and plans, we may not bother to attempt to infer what another species might be thinking and thereby prevent effective research into their abilities. (See also Ristau [this volume] & Burghardt [this volume] for arguments against the solipsist position.)

What functions might consciousness serve in animals? "Cognitive creativity," for one, suggests Griffin (this volume)—the ability to think about probable results of alternative actions so as to choose one most likely to achieve the desired result. It is, in fact, "enterprising versatility of behavior" which Griffin (this volume) notes serves as a criterion we tend to employ for conscious awareness. Here Griffin cites, among other examples, the use of bait by a few, but only a few, greenbacked herons to attract fish. Individual herons differ in their bait-fishing techniques. Some use pieces of bread, others bits of inedible vegetation; some even modify the bait, for example, by breaking the twig to an appropriate size (Higuchi, 1986, 1987). These differences argue against a fixed genetic basis for the behavior. "Is it reasonable to suppose that a heron develops this kind of behavior, and uses it successfully, without thinking about what it is doing and looking ahead for at least a short time to what it hopes to achieve" (Griffin, this volume)? Griffin suggests each of us can probably think of other cases in which simple short-range planning by animals could be useful and cites several sources of examples (Byrne & Whiten, 1985; deWaal, 1986; Mitchell & Thompson, 1986; Munn, 1986; Whiten & Byrne, 1988).

Another line of evidence about animal thinking, suggests Griffin (this volume), is to look to communication as a "window into the minds of animals." Various views of this possibility are discussed further in this overview chapter.

PHILOSOPHICAL OVERVIEW: THE INTENTIONAL STANCE AND FOLK PSYCHOLOGY (BEER)

Many contributors specifically note that "cognitive ethology assumes a kind of common sense theory of mind which has been described as folk psychology" (Beer, this volume). The ethologist who is probably most well-versed in the philosophical literature, Colin Beer, provides what he terms a "tour" through the philosophical versions of the theory of folk psychology and other recent views in the philosophy of mind from which we, ethologists and nonethologists alike, approach animal minds. Behaviorism, viewed for many years as the best approach from which to study animal behavior, is now falling into disfavor. But what is there to take its place? Folk psychology, translated into the philosophical terms of intentionality, is one widespread offering as propounded by Bennett (1976, this volume) Dennett (1983, 1987) and Searle (1983). (At the same time, some philosophers such as Dennett are generally critical of folk psychology, considering that the only worthwhile concepts therein are belief, desire, and intentionality, essentials of the intentional stance.) There is an important caveat however. The philosopher's use of *intentional* has a much broader meaning than simply "on purpose" or "acting with intent", although intentional terms such as "believing that", "wanting it to be the case that", and "knowing that", are included among intentional terms. Intentionality in the philosophical sense concerns "aboutness" and makes reference to the content of statements or beliefs. As Beer aptly phrases it "Thus believing is always believing that something is the case. You cannot just believe in the way that you can just sleep" (Beer, this volume).

Several of the papers discuss the likelihood that organisms display gradations of intentionality, and such gradations must necessarily be explored in any empirical account of intentionality, if it is to have any biological validity (Beer, this volume; Bennett, this volume; Burghardt, this volume; Ristau, this volume). One important criterion for intentionality is rationality, the extent of which needs to be explored by experiments with different organisms. Another criterion is termed *referential opacity,* a simple example of which (as used by Dennett) is the change in truth or falsity of a proposition when another term referring to the same person or object is substituted. (See discussion in Dennett, 1983, 1987.) Note, for example, how the meaning of the following statement about the referentiality of a belief is changed by a few substitutions: "George IV wondered whether Scott was the author of Waverly" and "George IV wondered whether Scott was Scott" (Russell, 1905/1956), as discussed by Dennett (1983). A future challenge facing cognitive ethologists who wish to apply an intentional stance to the behavior of animals is to translate such language-based criteria as these into nonlinguistic terms if this is, indeed, feasible. Alternatively, ethologists may choose to turn away from anthropocentric conceptions of intentionality and instead attempt to create their own biologically oriented approach to the same underlying issues. It would also be profitable for ethologists to explore the biological applicability of machine-oriented theories deriving from systems theory and artificial intelligence.

Beer notes that the intentional stance is not universally accepted by all philosophers, but no other theory yet exists to fill the gap. Beer thus ends on a note of cautious optimism, with an inclination to view the application of intentionality in scientific investigations in cognitive ethology as potentially fruitful. He finds himself receptive to the philosopher Ruth Millikan's concept of the "proper functions" of animal and human behavior (Millikan, 1984, 1986). Although she is critical of folk psychology, she deals with the terms believe and desire in a new manner to which ethologists are more likely to be sympathetic.

DEVELOPING BELIEF-DESIRE CONCEPTS: THE SIGNIFICANCE OF UNIQUE EVENTS (BENNETT)

The philosopher Jonathan Bennett, who served as a commentator on various papers at the Animal Cognitive Symposium, has since developed new ideas about the application of intentional analysis to animal behavior. Because these ideas were not presented at the symposium, other participants have not had the opportunity to incorporate them into their thinking or the submitted papers.

Bennett worries about the need for clarity in the most basic underlying concepts of cognitive ethology, pointing out the lack of concordance about methods and approaches within the discipline. "What is at stake is the integrity of cognitive ethology as a field of intellectual endeavor; and since I do believe in it and think it important, I want to see it equipped with solid enough foundations to support a respectable, coherent, disciplined practice" (Bennett, this volume). In one of many constructive suggestions, Bennett considers belief/desire concepts to be explanatory of animal mind but noncausal explanations. He assumes, correctly I think, that cognitive ethologists are ultimately materialists and as such are not likely to invoke nonmaterial entities such as spirits or the soul into their scientific explanations of the workings of the mind/brain — animal or human. Yet, one does not want to submit totally to a neurophysiological approach because "Mentalistic explanations involve groupings that would be missed altogether by neurophysiological explanations" (Bennett, this volume). For example, the various behaviors exhibited by an animal because it thinks such behavior would lead to food may have no significant neural common factors.

With every other contributor to the volume, Bennett notes that one always strives for explanations expressed in terms of the simplest mechanisms. Only when the immediate triggering of responses by stimuli fails as an interpretation of an organism's behavior does one look to a description framed in terms of the organism's goal. But, notes Bennett, there is a need to escape from the notorious triangle of belief/desire/behavior explanation which can be too libertine in its lack of constraints on the possible number of belief/desire pairs postulated for an animal. Some such belief/desire pairs might be: "The male bird believes this is a safe area for a nest site and wants to establish his territory here." Or . . . "he thinks there are larvae here which will provide good food for nestlings and wants to establish his territory here" . . . "he was nearby last season and wants to have that territory now occupied by another male he thinks he can displace" Bennett emphasizes that belief/desire explanations must be grounded in the sensory inputs to the animal.

But the sensory input/belief/desire/behavior quadrangle must not be based on a one-time event. The issue of the status of a unique or few time occurrence repeatedly arises in the contributed papers (e.g., Jolly, this volume; Burghardt, this volume; Ristau, this volume) and is discussed by Dennett (1987) as well. It is likely, when observing spontaneous naturally occurring behaviors, especially intelligent adaptive responses to novel challenges, that some behaviors may happen only once or a few times. An oft repeated behavior is a learned behavior—interesting perhaps, but not necessarily revealing of intelligence. As a way out of this dilemma Dennett (1983) suggests a "Sherlock Holmes" method of experimentally creating a unique circumstance that "captures the crook." One example is not sufficient; converging lines of evidence are needed. Dennett (1983) goes so far as to say that "by themselves, unique occurrences are uninterpretable;" but they can provide the grist for experiments which must be done to provide an adequate interpretation. Rather than a single event, Bennett states one must find the class of events which constitute the range of sensory inputs in the described quadrangle. To make the strongest case that explanation in terms of beliefs and desires are required (rather than a stimulus trigger for the observed behavior), one would try to determine a wide range of events/ conditions preferably quite different from each other, which are marked off, made sense of, or characterized by the animal's beliefs. The belief might be that doing any of a variety of behaviors in these contexts will lead to the same goal, such as access to food.

Bennett, like Dennett (1987), carefully notes that "There could be some indeterminacy: Given two somewhat different accounts of what an animal thinks and believes, there may not always be any fact of the matter as to which is correct. The question of how much determinacy there can be is an empirical one . . ." (Bennett, this volume). The possibility of such indeterminacy is to some a significant deterrent to scientific investigation (e.g., Burghardt, this volume). Until more empirical work is done, it remains to be seen how serious a limitation this will prove to be.

CAUTIONARY NOTES ABOUT MENTAL STATES (YOERG AND KAMIL)

Yoerg and Kamil, basing their arguments on Griffin's definition of cognitive ethology as the study of animals' mental experiences, ask that criteria be indicative of mental experience rather than merely suggestive of such experiences. What they are wishing is that the philosophical problem of other minds be solved. Of course, it hasn't been; that is, one can have direct evidence for only one's own consciousness. One cannot, in that direct sense, know another's mental perception of red, feeling of pain, and so on. The researchers who discuss consciousness (for instance Griffin, this volume; Jolly, this volume; Ristau, this volume) — cognizant of the fact that the problem of other minds has not been solved — are careful to offer only suggestive criteria for consciousness. Yoerg and Kamil do not mean to claim that animals don't have mental experiences, only that they have not identified an experiment to prove such. Of course.

Griffin has argued, as did Darwin (1872), for the likelihood of mental continuity given the evolutionary continuity of so many other processes and structures between man and other animals. Griffin concludes it is highly plausible that creatures besides ourselves do have at least some kinds of consciousness. Given the importance of consciousness to humans, he notes it is also likely that animals' mental experiences and their probable impact on behavior are important to animals. But how to investigate this scientifically? As a reasonable strategy I suggest that for animals experiencing certain kinds of consciousness, differences in other abilities may occur. Conversely, animals with certain kinds of abilities, for example, intricate social relations, (as proposed by Chance & Mead [1953], Humphrey [1976] and Jolly [1966] are also likely to have fairly highly evolved forms of consciousness. Griffin suggests that consciousness and simple thoughts (want food) might be useful simplifying devices for an organism with a little brain, in contrast to the complicated circuitry presumably required for a large number of prewired motor responses. These issues are discussed further in *Consciousness: Some possible examples* section of this chapter.

Despite the likelihood of mental continuity, others besides Yoerg and Kamil are concerned about attempts to study consciousness. Though they do not make this point, the intentional stance does not necessarily require an attribution of consciousness. The philosopher Dennett, for instance, applies the stance to such possibly intentional systems as thermostats and computers as well as animals and people. Determining the levels of intentionality of systems is of particular interest. Other philosophers such as Searle (1983) distinguish between intrinsic and derived intentionality, claiming that people and possibly other animals have real beliefs and wants in a way that computers and thermostats do not; the intentionality of the latter derives from the designer.

Certainly the approach of considering that creatures other than humans are conscious has been useful; even Yoerg and Kamil attest to that. A most important contribution of their paper seems to me to be describing existent research and potential in which approaches used in the study of human mental processes can profitably be applied to the study of those processes in animals. For example, they note the work of Wright, Santiago, Sands, and Urcioli (1982) studying serial learning in rhesus monkeys and pigeons as such an example. This aspect of their approach is indeed useful, certainly falls within the domain of problems to be investigated in cognitive ethology, and deserves careful attention.

ANIMAL COMMUNICATION: WHAT SORT OF "WINDOW" ON ANIMAL MINDS? THE REFERENTS OF SIGNALS (SMITH, AND MARLER, ET AL.)

Donald Griffin suggested in *The question of animal awareness* (1974), that animal communication provides a potential window on the minds of animals. Several contributions to the volume are either accounts of species-specific communication or commentaries on the nature of communication in animals. W. J. Smith notes that "The behavior of both signallers and individuals responding to signals can indeed provide clues about how individuals represent to themselves the information they process during communication" (Smith, this volume). In Smith's view, the signals of animals can provide information about the probable behavior of the signaller both currently and in the immediate future, as well as the signaller's identity, and information about external stimuli to which it is currently responding. The signal recipient is typically confronted with a wealth of information including the context which is defined by Smith as every source of information other than the signal itself. Thus, context includes such aspects as the social relationship of signaller to recipient, other signals it may be emitting at the same time in other modalities, the presence of predators or other members of its own species, the stage of the reproductive cycle, information stored in memory, and so forth. The signal recipient must select, attend to, focus upon, and rank order the importance of all of these aspects of the communicative situation, making use of pertinent stored information as it does so. Due to the complexity of this range of possible information in an animal's signals which influences the recipient's responsiveness to the signals, it is extremely difficult to design and interpret experiments concerning the meaning of animal's signals to individuals that respond to them.

Smith is particularly concerned with the proper interpretation of signal referents. Note that Marler and colleagues typically study referents which they construe to be objects (eg. food and predators), while Smith includes objects and acts as referents. Such a referential interpretation of animal signalling is typically pitted against that which is derived from a more classical ethological approach — what Griffin (1985) has termed the groan of pain (GOP) interpretation. This classical approach assumes that what animal communication is about is indicating, by means of signals, the internal, emotional and motivational state of the signalling organism. Smith (1965, 1977), like Griffin and Marler, Karakashian, and Gyger (this volume), holds that animal communication is much more complex than a GOP interpretation. However, he suggests that the referents of animals' signals are usually current and future behavior of the signaller rather than (or in addition to) external objects.

The specific experiments Smith examines closely are those about the food calls of chickens (Marler *et al.,* this vol.). Rather than referring to the presence and quality of food, Smith suggests the calls have behavioral referents, namely the reactions that can be expected of the signaller, if the recipient approaches or changes its behavior in some other way. Specifically he suggests that the signaller will probably interact in some positive way with an individual who joins it, although it will not, at least while signalling, itself move towards the recipient. The interpretation is based upon previous research with avian behavior (Collias and Joos, 1953; Collias, 1987).

Playback experiments, a common tool of those studying animal communication, entail a vocalization tape recorded from one animal and played over loud speakers to another individual. The technique is viewed by Smith as a useful means to elicit responses that provide clues to the meanings of animal signals to the individuals who receive them. The method, however, suffers from some drawbacks including the loss of some contextual information. How does that loss affect the observed responses of recipients? In particular, how does the recipient deal with the fact that the vocalizing animal is not there to provide contextual cues? Smith suggests that, especially for calls made by signallers responding to predators, the recipient may invoke a worst case scenario to avoid possible dire consequences which lead it to "behave cautiously or preemptively" (this volume). In more naturalistic situations, it may be more likely to opt for a typical case scenario, responding on the basis of the most frequently encountered trend in this class of events, either as experienced overall or when that particular signal has been heard.

Considering Smith's point in general, alterations and loss of contextual information may be of greater or lesser significance depending on the species, the type of vocalization, and also the recent history of recipients. When long distance signals are used by animals such as rain forest monkeys, which spend most of their time in the canopy, the monkeys are often obscured from each other's view. They frequently have only a vocalization as a signal, and thus do not experience an unusual state of affairs during a playback. Vervets, though not canopy dwellers, are not infrequently behind a bush, out of sight of other conspecifics. Thus, playbacks of calls of visually absent monkeys resemble a fairly common state of affairs for these monkeys. With signals used at closer range by a group-living species, Smith's point is well taken. In either class of situations Smith's concern is that an overly simple interpretation has been made of the communication without sufficient attention to the whole range of usage and the role of information from remaining contextual sources. Notwithstanding the merits of Smith's points, the reductionist spirit may favor the use of playbacks in an experimental analysis of signal meaning as a first step in building up a complete analysis of the communicative nexus in a rigorous fashion.

Marler et al. are concerned with the general issue of determining an animal's intent to communicate. From a philosophical perspective, that problem becomes bound up with the more general problem of intentionality as previously discussed in this chapter. Criteria for intentionality are currently embedded in linguistic phrasing, which are difficult to translate into terms readily applicable to nonlinguistic animals. Therefore, for purposes of simplicity, Marler et al. choose to restrict their studies and interpretations. Using the everyday meaning of the term *intent* as purpose, rather than the philosophical term intentionality, they investigate one aspect of the intent to communicate in animals, namely the effects of the social context on communication and whether animals have the option to emit signals or withhold them depending on that context.

Specifically, the experimenters measured, in a laboratory setting, the rate of calling as influenced by the presence of an audience and the characteristics of that audience with respect to gender, species, familiarity, and so on.

Characteristics of the signaller were also considered, in particular, the reproductive status (e.g., hens in broody condition vs. non-egg laying and males that were castrated vs. implanted with testosterone). Two different call systems were investigated in males—alarm and food calls—and found to differ in the audience characteristics which influenced the rate of calling.

The experimenters also suggested that some usage of food calling appears to be deceptive, for in the presence of an inedible object, the male would rarely call to its mate, but would call at an appreciable rate to a strange female. In other observations in more naturalistic settings, it was found that females tended to approach a male uttering food calls, particularly when the rate of calling was high, as most often occurs when a preferred food item is present. Thus a likely effect of a male food calling is that a female approaches, hence the apparent motivation for the deception. (Smith's view is that the food is not obviously a referent for the food call, but rather the call may be an indication that the signaller will interact positively with the recipient who approaches the signaller; hence, in his view, no deception is involved.)

One could argue that the experiments on referential signalling in animals conducted over the past few years alluded to by Smith and Marler et al. have revealed many more complexities in the information contained in animal signals than had previously been suspected. Yet this may be only the first step in exploring the even greater complexity of at least some animal signalling. Whether future experimentation will reveal additional information, or require a revision of the current referential interpretations of signal content, researchers are converging on a consensus of the need for sensitive, detailed and indeed subtle data collection and analysis. Smith, Marler, and colleagues, and most other scientists concerned with animal communication would acknowledge that the first steps have been taken. Science is a collective enterprise that evolves and will continue to do so in this area as well.

Again, it should be noted that Donald Griffin's ideas inspired many of the endeavors leading to the otherwise unexpected degree of richness in the findings. His early seminars in cognitive ethology at The Rockefeller University helped formulate the research conducted by Seyfarth, Cheney, and Marler to explore the possibility of semantic communication by vervet monkeys.

ANIMAL COMMUNICATION: THE POSSIBILITY FOR DECEPTION (CHENEY AND SEYFARTH)

The possibility for deception in animal communication is investigated further by Cheney and Seyfarth. They note that much animal communication provides accurate and reliable information to recipients, but some signals provide others with false information (their functional definition of deception). The authors consider that "Whether any animal is conscious of its own attempt to deceive remains an open question" (Cheney & Seyfarth, this volume). However, the authors do speak in terms of monkeys manipulating others, bluffing, and falsely limping, which would seem to imply a knowing (i.e., conscious) use of the behavior. Alternatively, one would have to invoke unconscious learning in which the deceiver's behavior was unknowingly being shaped by the interactant's responses and reinforcement outcomes, becoming what finally appeared as effective deception, bluffing, and so forth.

Numerous examples of simple and complex deceptive signalling are given from scorpion flies to birds, monkeys, and apes. The authors examine factors which place limits on the ability of animals to deceive each other. Among such constraints are (a) social history and structure, (b) the need to invent new signals, and (c) the receiver's skill in assessing signal meaning.

Social History and Structure

Due to social constraints, such as remembered and frequent interactions between recognized individuals, deceptive signalling would have to be subtle. One could argue that as long as the deception is not detected, there is no requirement for rarity (Marler, personal communication, 1989). Group living dependent on cooperation also stresses the need for reliable communication. However, some "cheating" could occur as an evolutionarily stable strategy, a situation which has been analyzed by numerous scientists as a type of prisoner's dilemma (e.g., Axelrod & Hamilton, 1981).

Inventing New Signals

New signals are often needed for deceptive purposes for many existent ones cannot be faked such as those dependent on size or physiological conditions.

Assessing Signal Meaning

A recipient's ability to assess signal meaning, a likely skill of intelligent species, can result in interactants learning to be skeptical of certain signals or signallers as they evaluate communicative episodes in light of past history of the signaller's veracity or deception.

Cheney and Seyfarth investigate this last matter in considerable detail, emphasizing their own experimental field research into the vervet monkeys' signalling. In these experiments, Cheney and Seyfarth played tape recorded vocalizations of specific individuals; some vocal classes were rigged to convey false information for the context in which they were played (i.e., "crying wolf"). Did recipients learn to be wary of communications by such individuals? They did learn to be wary of some communications. The vervet listeners generalized across vocalizations of similar meaning but different acoustic structure and responded skeptically to those. The vervets did not generalize skepticism over similarity in acoustic structure if meaning domains were very different. In short, yes, vervets at least can learn to be skeptical recipients of communication and their skepticism is expressed in interesting and specifiable ways.

Cheney and Seyfarth cite other research indicating that various species can vary signal rate, particularly inhibiting or concealing information, and can signal false information. For example, a sentinel bird in a flock gives alarm calls in the absence of predators, very often resulting in that bird's access to a prey insect likely to have otherwise been captured by another flock member (Munn, 1986). There is, however, no evidence that any non-human species systematically varies the rate and context of false signals, which would permit the most effective use of false signalling. As yet there are few experimental analyses of animal deception and these are for primates. No satisfactory theoretical analysis of levels of complexity of animal deception yet exist, though several authors, including Cheney and Seyfarth, have described several functional classes. Of these, inhibiting communication and otherwise varying the rate of signalling may be among the simplest (see also Ristau, 1988).

CONSCIOUS BEHAVIORS: SOME POSSIBLE EXAMPLES (JOLLY)

In her chapter, Jolly cites recent examples ". . . of chimpanzee behavior that seem to be unequivocal demonstrations of consciousness" (this volume). Both the common species (*Pan troglodytes*) and the bonobo or pygmy chimpanzee (*Pan paniscus*) are discussed; observations derive from researchers in the laboratory and the field. Jolly notes that the behaviors suggest self–recognition, advance planning, symbolic play, social deception, social manipulation, and symbolic communication.

The most compelling examples involve fairly complicated, apparently pre–planned behaviors which seem to require making predictions of another's intentions or at least their behaviors. These examples incorporate what Jolly has described as two of the commonly proposed possible functions of consciousness: (a) deliberating between alternate courses of action, a function also suggested by Griffin (this volume) and (b) complex social interactions which seem to require interactants being able to imagine not only their own goals but the goals and intentions of others.

Jolly's approach is to consider, in species closest to humans, complex behaviors which require considerable intelligence. Her rationale for an attribution of consciousness is that if observed in a human, the behaviors would be assumed to indicate conscious purpose. Although it can be frustrating not to have more explicit criteria from Jolly for consciousness, the fact of the matter is that even the most hard-nosed of us will find it difficult not to accept at least some of the instances as indicative of consciousness, given that we are willing to make that attribution to any nonhuman or any human other than ourselves.

The examples Jolly discusses involve, for the most part, both intelligence and likely consciousness. It is important to note, though, that not all conscious behavior need be particularly intelligent, a point Griffin makes in his chapter (this volume). "Simple conscious thinking may be an efficient and economical mode of operation . . . it may be most advantageous for animals with small brains" (Griffin this volume). It is difficult to find (in humans) examples of intelligence which are not conscious, though clearly, unconscious cognitive processes are involved in intelligent behaviors such as our use of language.

Bootstrapping downwards (a top-down method) as Jolly has done is a reasonable approach when attempting to determine likely conscious activities in another species. Yet a danger, as noted by other contributors (e.g., Michel and Yoerg & Kamil), is that a particular behavioral sequence — even a complicated one — does not by itself reveal the process by which it arose, nor does a single example always indicate that intelligence or consciousness is involved. Amassing many diverse examples as Jolly has done is more persuasive. Even so, because neither she nor anyone else has been able to specify criteria for consciousness, many of the examples will not be persuasive to all. Understand, as discussed previously, stipulating criteria for consciousness is probably an impossible task, though proposing suggestive criteria is not impossible. And, as previously noted, it may be possible to find in different species, groupings of abilities which may involve different kinds of consciousness and levels of intelligence. Certain of the many examples noted by Jolly in chimpanzees are unlikely to be found in many other species; however, elephants and members of the canine family, cetaceans such as porpoises and whales, and corvids such as ravens and crows may be particularly interesting, complex, intelligent other species in which to look. Parallel research examining similar phenomena in quite diverse species may be another fruitful approach. For example, the research by Ristau on injury-feigning birds and Burghardt's research on death-feigning snakes may come to reveal both interesting similarities as well as different limits on the abilities of those species.

COMMUNICATION: ANIMAL ARTIFICIAL "LANGUAGE" AND COGNITION RESEARCH (PEPPERBERG)

In addition to studies of the natural communication systems of animals, researchers have investigated the abilities of various species to learn simple artificial "languages"; subjects are usually apes, but dolphins, sea lions, and a parrot have also served as subjects (reviewed in Herman, 1987; Ristau, in press; Ristau & Robbins, 1982).

It is work with her African gray parrot that Pepperberg describes. Avoiding the controversy of whether the parrot's vocal productions are linguistic, Pepperberg emphasizes the usefulness of the arbitrary communication code in revealing both communication capacities and cognitive abilities. Pepperberg notes that the parrot can identify, request, and categorize more than 80 different objects, some of which are novel. The parrot can use the labels "two" through "six" to identify groups of objects. Likewise, he can answer questions concerning an object's color or shape. Even more interestingly, he can correctly respond "color", "shape", or "matter" (i.e., wood, plastic, etc.) to "What same?" or "What different?" when presented with two objects. He was approximately 70% (familiar exemplars) to 82% correct (novel exemplars) on first trial tests. Pepperberg incorporates test procedures which invalidate any criticisms that her results can be explained by a "clever Hans" effect, that is, subtle cuing of correct answers to the animal subject.

In her chapter Pepperberg does not deal with issues of intentionality, deception, or audience effect, though in other reports she notes evidence that the parrot's communications reflect the parrot's wants. For example, Alex has been observed to say "want banana" and then choose a banana or "want out" and fly to the door. These are not experimental studies, but they are interesting nevertheless.

The relevance of the parrot's skills to the nature of animal communication would seem to be that he can in the least be trained to label external referents and some of their characteristics; his vocalizations need not reflect a particular physiological state or his probable forthcoming behavior. These abilities do not, however, necessarily imply that the parrot's natural communication system is used in a similar way. Extremely little is known about its vocal system or even the use to which the parrot's exceptional imitative abilities are put. Since the parrot has been tested almost entirely in the productive mode, his receptive skills remain unknown, that is, when so instructed can he correctly choose a red three-corner plastic from an array of objects? More interestingly, can he use the labels in diverse ways? His present usage of labels for external referents is consistent with labels being used merely to request items, a rudimentary linguistic skill and the most easily trained in the various animal language projects. Pepperberg, however, explicitly opts to avoid the controversy of whether the parrot's vocal productions are linguistic.

THE PITFALLS OF FOLK PSYCHOLOGY: THE VIEWS OF A DEVELOPMENTAL PSYCHOLOGIST (MICHEL)

As a developmental psychologist, Michel is deeply concerned with the pitfalls of using a folk psychology in cognitive ethology because of its failings in understanding our own species. He points out that there are important differences in cognitive processing between individuals who are normal, mentally ill, and brain damaged, and that children pass through different developmental stages in thinking as described, for example, by Piaget. The ideas of folk psychology account for none of these differences. Nonconscious thinking is likewise an important part of human thinking, again not accounted for by folk psychology. He reminds us that humans are not purely rational beings. We are biased in our everyday predicting of patterns, (e.g., when we predict that a low probability event will occur when this would comply with our wishes). Likewise, our predictions rely on vivid concrete examples instead of the actual statistical probabilities. The categories we form to think with are derived from distinctively human cultural and biological bases. How can we expect animals to share them?

As do many of the other commentators about cognitive ethology, Michel expresses concerns about when to emphasize the differences between humans and animals and when to emphasize the similarities. Often, important differences and the most illuminating aspects of an organism's abilities and limitations can be revealed in the errors that human or animal subjects subjects commit (or similarly their gaps in intentionality). These limits must be understood within the framework of some model or theory, however. Perhaps, as Michel may be interpreted as saying, the proposed framework (folk psychology) is both overly idealized and unduly vague. What should we then do? Should we improve the folk psychology theory by striving to ". . . codify, systematize and make internally coherent the phenomenon of folk psychology" (Michel, this volume, p. 265) (Fodor, 1975) or abandon it altogether (Stich, 1983)?

Some of the mental states postulated in human folk psychology are, of course, too complex and too different from those of other organisms to be applicable to animals. Yet basic constructs such as wanting, believing, and ascribing intentions to others may well be usefully applied across species.

Michel opts for describing behavior in terms of motor patterns rather than actions. But it does seem that without an action description, we have an animal "lost in its motoric activity;" will we (or it) ever know if it was locomoting to water or to a mate? In the examples used by Michel, he objects to the use of the term "intending" as applied to infants as in "an infant intending to move its hand into its mouth." In his view, a description in terms of motor patterns would include much more relevant data such as the base rate of mouth opening with and without hand movement and the direction of movement of the hand. The problem seems to me to lie not in the choice of action words or motor patterns to describe the behavior, but that to do decent science, one needs to collect relevant data. Folk psychology, intentional analysis, and action words are not adequate substitutes for the collection of data. Quantitative observations provide the basis against which the validity of such models and interpretations may be judged. Likewise, models guide the selection of data to be collected.

No anthropomorphisms, states Michel. Perhaps, we may add, at least be wary of them. We should be constantly mindful of the uniqueness of each species. The ecological niche, the sensory capacities of an organism, must all be understood before we can hope to achieve a full interpretation of its behavior. In the hands of an able investigator, the problem may be more tractable than Michel fears. Consider, for example, the findings of Gould (1988) concerning the discriminative abilities of honeybees. They can distinguish between a pattern when it is placed vertically up or down but not when the same pattern is placed flat on the ground. Even to contemplate conducting such an experiment requires knowing bees intimately and attempting to imagine in our limited way what it would be like to be a bee (with apologies to Thomas Nagel [1974]). A bee may fly in almost any direction. A flower may be approached from any angle and must still be perceived as a flower. But bees do not fly upside down, and the vertical remains a stable frame of reference for them. One wonders whether different principles might pertain in the discrimination of very large horizontal objects such as bodies of water. Perhaps tests of the ability of honeybees to discriminate between flower-sized patterns and lake-sized patterns would reveal quite different principles of organization.

To summarize Michel's views, then, he is concerned both with the overrichness of folk psychological terminology and with the failing of folk psychologists to deal with certain aspects of human mental activity and therefore probably of animals as well. His cautionaries notwithstanding, it seems inadvisable either to give it up altogether or to let folk psychology be the only approach.

APPLYING THE INTENTIONAL STANCE (A FOLK PSYCHOLOGICAL TERM) TO ETHOLOGICAL RESEARCH (BURGHARDT AND RISTAU)

Two researchers who have applied folk psychological terms — in particular, the intentional stance — to interpretations of their research are Burghardt who conducted laboratory experiments with death-feigning hognose snakes and Ristau who did field experiments with injury-feigning shorebirds. Both chapters deal with specific research results and with more general issues of how a scientist attempts to study mental states of animals given direct access only to their behavior.

Part of Burghardt's chapter concerns the adaptive behavior of a two-headed snake. This discussion will concentrate, however, on parallels between the research of Burghardt and Ristau.

The term hognose snake's death feigning refers to a series of responses, terminating in quiescence, which are made in the presence of a predator/intruder. Burghardt and his colleagues observed monitoring by the snakes and responsiveness to the environment as measured by prolonged recovery times when a snake was confronted with a human standing a meter away and looking directly at the snake. The recovery times were longer than those to a person in the same position with eyes averted and also longer than those in a control condition in which the person moved out of the snake's sight as soon as the snake became quiescent. Snakes also show considerable individual differences in their responsiveness, recovery time, habituation rate, and reliance on particular behavioral elements of the display. Because, in Burghardt's view, some of the variability is likely to be genetic and/or historic in origin, it behooves scientists interested in demonstrating versatile adaptability to observe and experiment broadly with their species. Isolated observations of rare natural behaviors or detailed study of one or two individuals are thus suspect including, in his opinion, the parrot cognition studies and the ape language studies.

This issue has arisen repeatedly in the emerging information about spontaneous and naturally occurring behavior of animals and has been discussed earlier in this chapter. It suffices to say once more that although experimentation is necessary to establish many facts, the existence of just one "talking horse" (or talking parrot or ape) is not to be ignored. In the least, it demonstrates an ability of the species — possibly of a particularly capable species member — but an ability nevertheless. Elucidating the prerequisite experiences and underlying mechanisms of the ability, however, requires experimentation with more than one individual.

As a general method, Burghardt (this volume) espouses what he terms "critical anthropomorphism" — basically the freedom to put one's self in the animal's place to generate ideas and to help predict outcomes of naturally occurring and planned experiments. The intentional stance, he states, ". . . can at best be a component of critical anthropomorphism. We need to know the details of the snake's behavior repertoire, possible predators . . ." (this volume).

Ristau deals with many of the same issues as Burghardt in her chapter about cognitive and communicative aspects of the antipredator behavior of injury-feigning birds, in particular, the piping plover. The impetus for her research and initial guidance in her research design arose from taking seriously the intentional stance and the possibility that organisms may be aware, that a piping plover may want to lead an intruder away from its nest or young. Burghardt's research arose from other factors. Perhaps without explicitly adopting an intentional stance, he was, even at the time of his studies, implicitly taking an anthropomorphic approach. He does, in his chapter, "try on" the intentional stance and suggests further research he might do with the hognose snake. It is extremely useful to do parallel comparative work. In doing so one can assess the limits and extent of abilities and the nature of mental terms which might or might not be applicable to the species' behavior or at least their behavior in certain contexts. The two research endeavors were not planned in parallel and indeed are not exactly so, but it could be useful for various researchers to plan collaborative efforts.

Applying the intentional stance and the possibility of awareness by the organism, Ristau considered the kinds of evidence that would be needed to evaluate the following hypothesis: The plover wants to lead the intruder away from nest/young. From (a) background reading in artificial intelligence; (b) the writings of such psychologists as Tolman, who many decades ago applied mentalistic terms such as purpose to the behavior of rats; (c) work of various philosophers; and (d) serious consideration of Griffin's views, Ristau made the following predictions about the plovers' behavior. (Data that was gathered did support a hypothesis of purposeful action).

She predicted that (a) The direction in which a plover moves while making broken-wing displays (i.e., injury feigning) should be adequate to lead an intruder away from nest and young, though not necessarily always correct; (b) the plover should monitor the behavior of the intruder during the course of its displaying; and (c) the plover should modify its behavior as needed to keep the intruder away from the nest and young.

Ristau noted the importance of behavioral details not previously investigated which further substantiated the attribution of purposive behavior. Such details included the precise location of plover displays with respect to the intruder's gaze and/or direction of walk and the location to which a plover flew before displaying.

The experiment most similar to Burghardt's was her study of the effect of intruder attention—defined by Ristau as direction of eye gaze—upon the plover's behavior. There are considerable differences between the two experiments. In Ristau's work, the intruder is between 12 and 20 meters away from the plover's nest, whereas Burghardt's human is approximately 1 meter from the death-feigning snake. Ristau's observers walked parallel to the dunes, gazing either towards the dunes where the plovers' nests were located or in the opposite direction. The human did not specifically look towards the bird. In contrast, Burghardt's human observer either looked directly at the snake, averted his/her eyes, or left the area as soon as the snake became quiescent. Nevertheless, both experiments showed an effect of intruder eye gaze on the recipient's behavior.

Ristau also investigated whether piping plovers could learn to react differentially to two human intruders one of which behaved dangerously, that is, approached the nest while the other did not. After experiencing only two close approaches by the dangerous intruder, the plover reacted in a more aroused fashion to that intruder when each intruder walked by the nest at a distance of approximately 20 meters away. In short, the plovers were not bound merely by innate constraints to determine which were dangerous intruders, but they could learn rapidly.

Although her research is indeed guided by the possibility that organisms may be consciously aware, Ristau well recognizes the philosophical conundrum arising from attempts to attribute consciousness to any but one's self. (See her discussion about consciousness and solipsism.) At the very least, the intentional stance provides a useful heuristic device to study many behaviors of organisms. In a spirit of continuing a dialogue with other researchers who are wary of discussions of animal consciousness, Ristau emphasizes the positive heuristic benefits of the approach. Likewise, when discussing purposiveness in animals, Ristau indicates the need to look for gradation in any belief/desire system such as might exist in a snake or plover in contrast to humans' occasional preplanned, conscious, and intelligent behavior. She notes Bennett's (1976) reflections about the transitions from registrations and goals, for example, those of a blowfly sensing sugar and then feeding upon it, to the more full-fledged beliefs and desires of higher organisms and/or humans.

In Ristau's view, purposeful behavior is particularly interesting because it may well reflect a general organizational principle for animal behavior. Purposeful behavior is functional. In the blowfly, reflex-like actions seem to best describe the behavior. Only gradually do goals and registrations become more and more voluntary. This transition may occur both over the course of evolution and, in higher animals, ontogenetically during that organism's transition from infancy to adulthood.

As a strategy for future research, Ristau suggests examining the gaps in intentional systems that indicate limits to abilities. Although Michel warns us of the pitfalls of folk psychology, these same warnings can provide a structure through which to examine animal capacities. In other words, as previously suggested, by assuming a rational creature and adopting an intentional stance, one can make predictions about an animal's behavior and then note specific failures. This sometimes occurs in human's natural reasoning, as contrasted with the reasoning of a completely logical, rational creature; the experiments of Tversky and Kahneman (1983) provide relevant evidence. It is extremely likely to happen in animals as well. Yet humans are sometimes rational; likewise, there are indications that animals may be as well.

Most striking is the basic similarity in view of any researcher who admits the possibility of mental states in animals. So I do not conceive of Burghardt's method as new, though the label is novel. It is useful in generating ideas to put oneself in the animal's place. Yet to be a good scientist one needs to know the species, design experiments well, be sensitive to the impact of contextual and/or environmental stimuli on a behavior, and possess a host of other attributes which constitute the art of science. Even for those who would deny the usefulness of this folk psychological approach, (e.g., Michel), there is almost without exception an implicit assumption of folk psychology. For example, for a strict analysis of behavior in terms of stimulus effects, a scientist must choose which stimuli to study, that is, which stimuli matter to the animal in a given circumstance or physiological state. The implicit folk psychological assumptions lie in the making of such choices. Heated differences arise between scientists as to the nature of mental states, whether conscious or unconscious, and whether it is scientifically proper to presume to investigate such issues as purpose and belief in animals.

But the tide has turned. Animal cognition, cognitive ethology, the minds of other animals, particularly as these minds deal with real world problems of their species, have gained a stronghold on the minds of an ever increasing number of scientists. We honor Donald Griffin for his contribution and leadership in this endeavor.

ACKNOWLEDGMENTS

I am grateful to Peter Marler for his constructive scientific comments and editorial suggestions and Esther Arruza for her manuscript preparation.

REFERENCES

Axelrod, R., & Hamilton, W. D. (1981). The evolution of cooperation. *Science, 211,* 1390–1396.

Bennett, J. (1976). *Linguistic behavior.* Cambridge: Cambridge University Press.

Byrne, R. W., & Whiten, A. (1985). Tactical deception of familiar individuals in baboons (*Papio ursinus*). *Animal Behaviour, 33,* 669–673.

Chance, M. R. A., & Mead, A. P. (1953). Social behavior and primate evolution. *Symposium of the Society of Experimental Biology VII,* (Evolution), 395–439.

Collias, N. E. (1987). The vocal repertoire of the red jungle fowl: A spectrographic classification and the code of communication. *Condor 89,* 510–524.

Collias, N. E. and Joos, M. (1953). The spectrographic analysis of the sound signals of the domestic fowl. *Behaviour 5,* 176–188.

Darwin, C. R. (1872). *The expression of the emotions in man and animals.* London: Appleton.

Dennett, D. C. (1983). Intentional systems in cognitive ethology: The "Panglossian paradigm" defended. *Behavioral and Brain Sciences 6,* 343–390.

Dennett, D. C. (1987). *The intentional stance.* Cambridge, MA: M.I.T. Press.

deWaal, F. (1986). Deception in the natural communication of chimpanzees. In R. W. Mitchell & N. S. Thompson (Eds.), *Deception, perspectives on human and nonhuman deceit* (pp. 221–244). Albany: State University of New York Press.

Fodor, J. (1975). *The language of thought.* New York: Thomas Crowell.

Gould, J. (1988). A mirror-image ambiguity in honey bee visual memory. *Animal Behaviour 36,* 487–492.

Griffin, D. R. (1974). *The question of animal awareness* (2nd ed.) New York: Rockefeller University Press.

Griffin, D. R. (1985). Animal consciousness. *Neuroscience and Biobehavioral Reviews, 9,* 615–622.

Herman, L. M. (1987). Receptive competencies of language-trained animals. In J. S. Rosenblatt, C. Beer, & M. C. Busnel (Eds.), *Advances in the Study of Behavior* (pp. 1–60). New York: Academic Press.

Higuchi, H. (1986). Bait-fishing by the green-backed heron *Ardeola striata* in Japan. *Ibis, 128,* 285–290.

Higuchi, H. (1987). Cast master. *Natural History, 96*(8), 40–43.

Humphrey, N. K. (1976). The social function of intellect. In P. P. G. Bateson & R. A. Hinde (Eds.), *Growing points in ethology* (pp. 303–317). Cambridge: Cambridge University Press.

Jolly, A. (1966). Lemur social behavior and primate intelligence. *Science, 53,* 501–506.

Millikan, R. G. (1984). Language, thought, and other biological categories: New foundations for realism. Cambridge, MA: M.I.T. Press.

Millikan, R. G. (1986). *Thoughts without laws: Cognitive science without content. Philosophical Review, 95,* 47–80.

Mitchell, R. W., & Thompson, N. S. (Eds.). (1986). *Deception: Perspectives on human and nonhuman deceit.* Albany: State University of New York Press.

Munn, C. A. (1986). The deceptive use of alarm calls by sentinel species in mixed-species flocks of neotropical birds. In *Deception, perspectives on human and nonhuman deceit* (pp. 169–175). Albany: State University of New York Press.

Nagel, T. (1974). What is it like to be a bat? *Philosophical Review, 83,* 435–450.

Ristau, C. A. (1988). Thinking, communicating and deceiving: Means to master the social environment. In G. Greenberg and E. Tobach (Eds.), *Evolution of social behavior and integrative levels* (pp. 213–240) Hillsdale, NJ: Lawrence Erlbaum Associates.

Ristau, C. A. (in press). Animal language and cognition research. In A. Lock & C. R. Peters (Eds.), *The handbook of human symbolic evolution.* London: Oxford University Press.

Ristau, C. A., & Robbins, D. (1982). Cognitive aspects of ape language experiments. In D. R. Griffin (Ed.), *Animal mind–human mind* (pp. 299–331). New York: Springer–Verlag.

Russell, B. (1956). On denoting. *Logic and knowledge* (pp. 41–56). London: Allen and Unwin. (Reprinted from *Mind, 1905, 5,* 79–93).

Searle, J. (1983). *Intentionality: An essay in the philosophy of mind.* Cambridge: Cambridge University Press.

Smith, W. J. (1965). Message, meaning and context in ethology. *American Naturalist 99,* 405–409.

Smith, W. J. (1977). *The behavior of communicating.* Cambridge, MA: Harvard University Press.

Stich, S. (1983). From folk psychology to cognitive science. Cambridge, MA: M.I.T. Press.

Tversky, A., & Kahneman, D. (1983). Extensional versus intuitive reasoning: The conjunction fallacy in probability judgement. *Psychological Review, 90,* 293–315.

Whiten, A., & Byrne, R. W. (1988). Tactical deception in primates. *Behavioral and Brain Sciences, 11,* 233–273.

Wright, A. A., Santiago, H. C., Sands, S. F., & Urcioli, P. J. (1982). Pigeon and monkey serial probe recognition: Acquisition, strategies, and serial position effects. In H. L. Roitblat, T. G. Bever, & H. S. Terrace (Eds.), *Animal cognition* (pp. 353–373). Hillsdale, NJ: Lawrence Erlbaum Associates.

Author Index

Subject Index

A

"Abstract aptitude," 167
Adaptiveness, 3, 67, 120
  of behavior, 15
  of conscious thinking, 5
  evolutionary, 7
Aerial predators, *see* Predator-prey interactions
Affective states, 56
African grey parrot
  categorization abilities, distinguishing shape and color, 165–167
  concepts of same and different, 167–176
  conceptual abilities, 153–177
  mimicry, 160
  training, 161–177
Agnosia, 84
Alarm calls, 12, 14, 29, 48, 128, 132, 134–135, 138, 141–144, 145–148, 155, 189, 190–191, 192, 193–198, 200, 205, 211, 213, 301
  eagle, 132, 142, 143, 146, 220
  false, 132, 137, 139, 148, 149
  leopard, 132, 142, 143, 146
  predator-specific, 132, 142, 143, 146, 157
  production, 190–192
  social context, 195–196
  see also Predator-prey interactions
Altruistic behavior, 61
American Sign Language, 155

Androgen therapy, 197
Anecdotes, 54–55, 56, 58, 77, 133–134, 137, 156
  see also One-time occurences
Animal Behavior Society, *xii,* 3
Anthropomorphism, 53–87, 253, 261, 270, 307, 209
  critical, 53–87, 308
  limited, 118, 119, 122, 308
  projective, 73
Antipredator display, 53, 62–73, 93–102, 308–310
Aphasia, 84
Arousal, 219, 227
  audience effects, 200–201
  olfactory, 58
  relative levels of plovers, 110
Artificial intelligence, *see* Computers
Attention, 102, 278
  intruders, 100, 123
  by plovers, prey, 101
  selective attention to signals, 223, 225
Attracting fish, in herons, 11–12, 293
Audience effects, 14, 135, 187–206, 211, 213, 292, 300–301
  calls with food as a referent, 196–200
  hormonal effects on, 195–196
  mediation, by arousal, 200–201
  other species, 194–195
  see also Communication, Behavior
Awareness, *see* Cognition, Consciousness

Species Index